The Huey slick carrying Taylor's team was about fifteen feet off the ground when it was shattered by enemy fire. Taylor said, "The chopper split in two. The head end went down with all of us still in it. Our team was just behind the cockpit, which was pulverized by fire. I can remember hitting the ground and the front end was skidding around with the rotors still spinning.

"Then the team jumped out and set up quick positions under fire. The NVA were hitting us hard. The Huey gunner was blasting away with his M-60, and the shell casings were landing on my back. Normally I carried a shotgun but this time I had an M-16, and the damn thing jammed. The gunner handed me his 16, and I started using it. I know I hit six of the NVA.

"We couldn't lob grenades because the rotors were still spinning directly over our heads. The NVA started coming in waves at us. I got hold of the radio and asked for Spooky to get out there and blast the area. . . ."

By Lawrence C. Vetter, Jr.
Published by Ivy Books:

BLOOD ON THE LOTUS
 A Novel of Vietnam
NEVER WITHOUT HEROES
 Marine Third Reconnaissance Battalion in Vietnam, 1965–70

Books published by The Ballantine Publishing
Group are available at quantity discounts on
bulk purchases for premium, educational, fund-
raising, and special sales use. For details, please
call 1-800-733-8000.

NEVER WITHOUT HEROES

Marine Third Reconnaissance Battalion in Vietnam, 1965–70

Lawrence C. Vetter, Jr.

IVY BOOKS • NEW YORK

Copyright © 1996 by Lawrence C. Vetter, Jr.

http://www.randomhouse.com

Library of Congress Catalog Card Number: 95-95314

ISBN: 0-8041-0807-2

Manufactured in the United States of America

First Edition: August 1996

10   9   8   7   6

Acknowledgments

I know it is a cliché to say that I cannot express my appreciation enough, but this book simply could not have been written without the help of so many. If those who put together the 3rd Reconnaissance Battalion Association had not done so, this story would have been very limited in scope. If all those to whom I talked had not agreed to share their emotions and memories, this story would be empty. Those individuals are mentioned throughout this book, and to them, from my heart, I say "Thank you."

Some are not mentioned in these pages, and I would like to say "Thank you" to them also—my wife, Deborah (I love you), for the patience, editing, and help with typing; and my friends John and Nancy Rowe, for putting me up and transporting me around D.C. And to the many women supporting the men of the battalion, like Sandy, Dianne, JoAnn, Kathy, and Karen, God bless you.

I am also grateful for the helping hand and just tremendous public service and assistance that I received from the personnel at the Marine Corps History and Museums Division in Washington, D.C., particularly Joyce Bonnett and Danny Crawford. The same is true for those true public servants at the Lyndon Baines Johnson Library in Austin, Texas—particularly Jon Wilson and Linda Hansen. Most of the statistics and data regarding 3rd Recon Battalion patrol reports and North Vietnamese and Vietcong order of battle information were derived from the documents contained in the files of these two offices.

I would also like to thank Bill McBride for his help with preparing the maps of Vietnam.

I would like to repeat here my sincere gratitude to Floyd Nagler. And there is one individual who must be mentioned again and his name underscored, for without him in particular there would be no present book: <u>George Neville</u>.

3rd Recon Battalion Association
15642 Heywood Way
Apple Valley, Minnesota 55124

Author's Note

At any one time, the strength of the 3rd Recon Battalion ranged from 500 to 900 Marines and Navy Corpsmen, and approximately 2,800 served with the battalion between March 1965 and November 1969. I was one, and the seven months I served with the battalion in 1966 were the zenith of Marine camaraderie and gung ho team spirit that I experienced during my six-year Marine Corps tour of duty.

However, that teamwork was not without its price. Between 1965 and 1969, Recon teams suffered an estimated 40 percent casualties: 1,133 Reconners killed, wounded, or missing in action.

Of the men I knew and have since met who shared the 3rd Recon privilege with me, not one would define himself as a hero. Yet, operating mostly in small teams, those Marines confronted the enemy on his own turf, miles from friendly units. Wherever they went, they were the eyes and ears of the body of Marine infantry units behind them. In less than five years, those teams counted over 37,000 enemy soldiers or workers, enough to constitute five enemy divisions.

The men of those teams faced challenges and responded to them by daily placing their lives in jeopardy in service to their fellow Marines and to Duty, Honor, Corps, and Country. Their pay was peanuts, pain, and pride; their bed was often a poncho over muddy clay or hard rock, often a tree served as a brace to keep the Recon Marine from sliding down a hillside in the dark of night; their food came from unappetizing little green cans and sometimes their water came from ponds they shared with animals. But they never retreated from the demands placed on them.

In the Editor's Note of the December 12, 1969, issue of *Life* magazine, reporter Jan Mason is quoted as saying that while she was on a tour of American college campuses she was repeatedly and emphatically told, "Heroes? Man, we haven't any heroes left!"

My heart cries out to those college students. They were never without heroes! I wish they could have seen what I saw: young Americans risking their lives for one another—and often giving the greatest gift they had. I saw them suffering for others and for what they had been taught was a worthwhile cause.

Never Without Heroes is the story of the 3rd Reconnaissance Battalion, 3rd Marine Division, during its time in Vietnam from 1965 until 1969. But it is more than that; it is a reflection of the best of American heroism.

CONTENTS

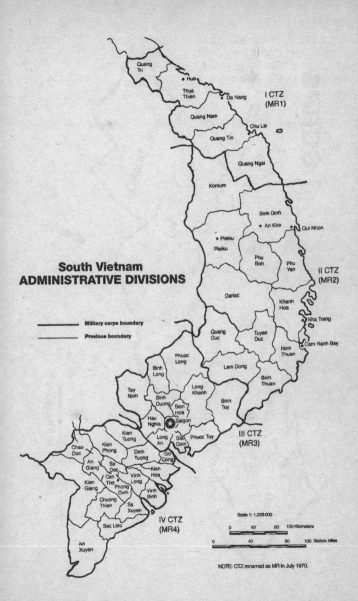

**South Vietnam
ADMINISTRATIVE DIVISIONS**

Quang Tri

Hue

Thua Thien

Da Nang

I CTZ (MR1)

Quang Nam

Chu Lai

Quang Tin

Quang Ngai

Kontum

Binh Dinh

An Khe

Qui Nhon

Pleiku

Pleiku

Phu Bon

Phu Yen

II CTZ (MR2)

Darlac

Khanh Hoa

Nha Trang

Quang Duc

Tuyen Duc

Cam Ranh Bay

Ninh Thuan

Phuoc Long

Lam Dong

Binh Long

Long Khanh

Binh Thuan

Tay Ninh

Binh Duong

Bien Hoa

Binh Tuy

Hau Nghia

Saigon

Kien Tuong

Long An

Gia Dinh

Phuoc Tuy

III CTZ (MR3)

Chau Doc

Kien Phong

Dinh Tuong

Go Cong

An Giang

Sa Dec

Kien Hoa

Kien Giang

Can Tho

Vinh Long

Phong Dinh

Chuong Thien

Vinh Binh

Sa Xuyen

Sac Lieu

IV CTZ (MR4)

An Xuyen

Military corps boundary

Province boundary

Scale 1: 1,250,000

0   40   80   100 Kilometers

0   40   60   100 Statute Miles

NOTE: CTZ renamed as MR in July 1970.

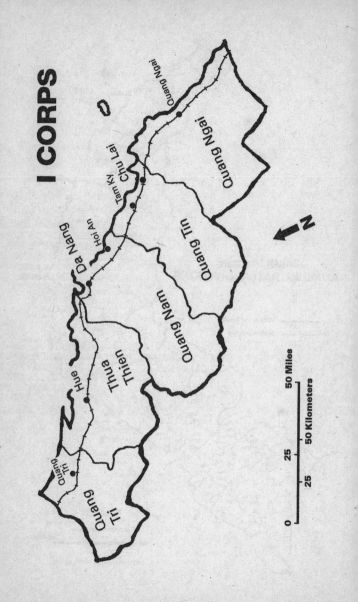

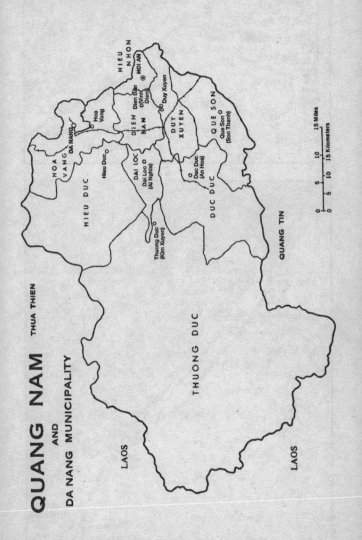

QUANG NAM
AND
DA NANG MUNICIPALITY

THUA THIEN

LAOS

HIEU NHON

HOI AN

Dien Ban
(Vinh Dien)

Duy Xuyen

Hoa Vang

DIEN BAN

DA NANG

DUY XUYEN

QUE SON

Que Son
(Son Thanh)

HOA VANG

Hieu Duc

HIEU DUC

DAI LOC

Dai Loc
(Ai Nghia)

Duc Duc
(An Hoa)

DUC DUC

Thuong Duc
(Kim Xuyen)

THUONG DUC

QUANG TIN

LAOS

| 0 | 5 | 10 | 15 Miles |
| 0 | 5 | 10 | 15 Kilometers |

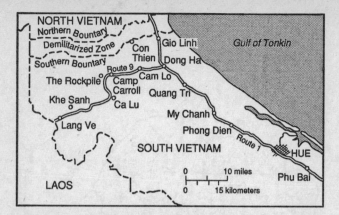

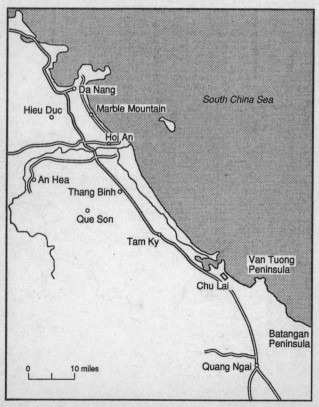

NEVER WITHOUT HEROES

The Beginning

On May 7, 1965, the Headquarters of the 3rd Reconnaissance Battalion landed in Vietnam. Several platoons from the battalion had preceded it as attachments to the 9th Marine Expeditionary Brigade, which had landed on March 8. During the next four and one-half years, Marines of the 3rd Recon Battalion conducted reconnaissance operations in Vietnam; the battalion was withdrawn in November 1969. In that time period, approximately 2,800 Marines served as part of the battalion. Colonel Patrick G. Collins (Ret.), who was one of the first Recon Marines in Vietnam, has researched the records and found that, while on duty with the 3rd Recon Battalion, four of those Marines received the Medal of Honor, thirteen received the Navy Cross, and seventy-three the Silver Star. Because of those men, the countless others who received awards, and the even greater number who were better honored by the respect of their peers, the battalion itself was awarded one Presidential Unit Citation, two Navy Unit Citations, one Meritorious Unit Citation, and eleven battle stars for Vietnamese service. Not noted in that list are the unit awards that elements of the battalion received when attached to other commands. But statistics are devoid of life. Behind each award were human emotions, and quite often blood.

The anxiety that did not show on the faces of Recon Marines but stirred their stomachs as they sat waiting for the "birds" to come can be understood a little better by examining the substantial odds they faced while in action against enemy units. During their time in Vietnam, 1,121 Marines and 12 Navy Corpsmen from the battalion were killed, wounded, or missing in action. Encountering enemy forces far superior in number, confronting them in jungles, mountains, valleys, and villages miles distant from friendly faces, resulted in

1

countless moments of personal crisis. In spite of swearing never to be taken alive, a few Marines were captured, usually after being wounded.* During those four and one-half years, seven Recon Marines and one corpsman were missing in action although two of the MIAs escaped back to the battalion and the bodies of two others were recovered.

The casualty figures show that approximately 40 percent of the Marines and U.S. Navy Corpsmen who served in the 3rd Recon Battalion during the Vietnam conflict were wounded or killed in action. Unmentioned is the fact that all the others from time to time had excellent reason to fear death. The acts of courage that are the foundation for those facts and figures are, for the most part, an as yet untold story, remaining in the memories of men who served. Recon Marine or Navy Corpsman, all were united by a unique and extraordinary psyche that fused allegiance, vitality, and resolve into a fighting spirit that enabled individuals to overcome personal fears and unexpected odds. Floyd Nagler, a veteran of the battalion in 1969, states:

> Those of us who left 'Nam and the experience of being a Recon team member also left a piece of our souls somewhat disconnected. While none of us can ever regain the adrenaline high or unbelievably close social bond we experienced, an understanding of the slight pain we all feel from that vacuum in our souls, resulting from the team separation, is a need we all equally share.

The unit command chronologies held in the U.S. Marine Corps Historical Center at the Washington Navy Yard indicate that battalion recon teams sighted a total of 37,049 enemy and accounted for 2,534 enemy killed in action (KIA), 2,712 either wounded or suspected KIA, and 76 individuals captured who were either known enemy or suspected to be so.

Not accounted for in this data is the additional effect of responses by infantry or air units in support of a recon patrol but not observed by the patrol. Neither do the patrol reports include numbers that were not recorded in the battalion records because they were submitted to infantry units by Recon teams attached to them.

In spite of the battalion's accomplishments, the Recon Marine's worth in Vietnam has not yet truly been acknowledged. But the words

---

*There is a near-legendary case in 1st Force Recon of a Marine who was wounded and captured but who succeeded in capturing two of his captors and forcing them, at knifepoint, to carry him back to his base. See *Sergeant Major, U.S. Marines*, by Maurice Jacques and Bruce H. Norton, Ivy Books, 1995, for more detail.

of Bill Buhl, a respected "mustang"* lieutenant in the battalion in 1965–66, are perhaps most appropriate: "Those fine young Recon Marines who performed so well, before, during, and after our respective tours, need look only to their peers for the recognition they genuinely deserve."

The 3rd Reconnaissance Battalion did not simply appear for the first time in Vietnam. The lineage of the battalion begins with Company E (Scouts) 3rd Tank Battalion, 3rd Marine Division, which was created in 1942. In April 1944, it was redesignated the Amphibious Reconnaissance Company, Headquarters Battalion, 3rd Marine Division. During World War II, the unit participated in the Bougainville, Solomon Islands, Guam, and Iwo Jima campaigns. Then it was deactivated until the Korean War. In 1956, it was again deactivated, but on April 15, 1958, it was reactivated as the 3rd Reconnaissance Battalion, 3rd Marine Division. It remained an active unit in the Fleet Marine Force, headquartered in Okinawa, until recently, when it was deactivated and its mission assumed by Scout companies assigned to infantry units.

Most of the publicity surrounding the special elite units of the Marine Corps during World War II has been devoted to the Raider battalions, but a little bit of history will tell us something about the forerunner of the Recon Battalion, the Scout companies. In August 1942, the United States took the offensive against the Japanese war machine, and Guadalcanal in the Solomon Islands was first on the hit list. Just twenty miles across Iron Bottom Sound from "The Canal" was the smaller island of Tulagi, and that's where the Raiders hit the beach. However, the unsung heroes that were the Scout companies received orders for the main battle on the ninety-mile-long island of Guadalcanal. They were the units that evolved into the reconnaissance battalions that served in Vietnam.

George Neville, Sr., was a Marine Scout in the early days of World War II. Neville states that his unit had been conducting cold weather exercises in Iceland when Pearl Harbor was attacked. He describes how they trained using motorcycles and lightly armored vehicles sporting .50-caliber and .30-caliber machine guns. Before long the units were aboard a ship and sailing into the "Slot," shown on the maps as Sea Lark Channel, a charming name for a body of water later to be known as Iron Bottom Sound. The channel was given this nickname in grim tribute to the work of the skilled and deadly Rear Admiral Gunichi Mikawa and his 25th Air Flotilla. In the early morning of August 10, 1942, Mikawa's eight-ship task force sank four

*An officer commissioned from the enlisted ranks.

American cruisers and one destroyer, and severely damaged a fifth cruiser, in the channel—thus, Iron Bottom Sound. This battle occurred within sight of Mr. Neville and his Marines, fighting on Guadalcanal with Japanese to their front, and now with a good portion of the American navy sunk in the waters behind them.

The Scouts had landed on August 7, 1942, but had gone ashore without their vehicles. They returned to the ship on August 9, intending to bring the armored vehicles off the next day. But that night they were rushed over the side because the enemy navy had been sighted entering the Slot. The Marines got to the shore safely but their scout cars were made into fish houses by the Japanese. The real battle lasted only forty-six minutes and sent 1,024 Allied seamen to their deaths. With 5,000 Japanese troops on the island ready to do battle, the Marines couldn't spend too much time worrying about who controlled the seas behind them.

Mr. Neville relates:

During the battle for Guadalcanal the recon scouts were used basically according to the dictates of the infantry commander we were attached to. Our patrol size varied from small groups (three to four) to platoon size, depending on the mission. We scouted ahead of the infantry, but we were not able to go too far in front of our lines because the enemy was hiding in the jungles not far away. In fact, those front lines got mixed up quite often—with us in the middle of it.

The platoon was constantly moved around and separated into small groups. Our mission was never very clear, nor was it uniform. It all depended on the infantry officer who was using us. We carried '03 Springfields, Thompsons, and light, air-cooled machine guns. Those, however, didn't do a hell of a lot of good when we were being shelled by the enemy cruisers from the Slot.

One particular mission we were given was to counter the Japanese who were sneaking through our lines at night. They would hide in trees inside our lines and snipe at us during the day. We were told to lay in knee-high grass inside our lines, at night, and wait for them to try to get through. Our orders were to engage them with bayonets and hand-to-hand combat for fear of shooting our own men. Remember, this was in the dark. Doesn't that sound like John Wayne for you. Hell, I was scared to death. My platoon left the "Canal" in December, and I was proud of my time in the Corps, but I was glad to survive.

Recon Marines have been on foot ever since those scout cars reached the bottom of Sea Lark Channel. However, after the war, two basic types of Marine reconnaissance units evolved.

Assigned to conduct preassault and distant postassault reconnaissance in support of the landing force are the Force Reconnaissance companies. There were four active duty Force Recon companies in the Marine Corps during the Vietnam War, although the 3rd and the 5th were later deactivated. In the 1980s Force Recon companies began the highly specialized training designed to prepare them for such missions as the capture or rescue of oil rigs, aircraft, and other point targets. In theory, Force Recon units are to be attached to the Amphibious or Expeditionary Force, which is a superior command to the division; therefore, they are designed to operate over a wider and deeper battlefield than the Recon battalions and should not be attached to the division or infantry regiment or battalion. Each of those companies had six platoons. Scuba and jump schools were mandatory.

On the other hand, the Recon Battalion is attached in general support of the division within or near the division's tactical area of responsibility (TAOR). Quite often this means that reconnaissance units are attached to subordinate division units—that is, regiments and battalions. Recon companies or platoons attached in direct support report to the infantry regimental or battalion commander and operate for him, rather like the Recon Battalion's operating for the division but on a smaller scale. During the Vietnam War, there were four active duty Recon battalions: 1st, 2nd (in Camp LeJeune, North Carolina), 3rd, and 5th; however, the 5th Recon Battalion, which was created during the war, was deactivated in 1969. Today the active duty Recon battalions have been deactivated and once again Scout companies are attached to the infantry regiment. The 4th Recon Battalion is the Reserve Battalion.

The basic operational unit of the Recon Battalion was the platoon, which, until 1968, consisted of one officer and twenty-three enlisted (a Force Recon platoon consisted of one officer and fourteen men each). A platoon in the Recon Battalion was divided into two squads and one headquarters section. In 1968, a third squad was added to the platoon's Task Organization, and at the same time, a Company E was added to each battalion. The platoon was normally attached to the basic seaborne maneuver element of Marine infantry, the Battalion Landing Team (BLT), and the Recon platoon commander responded to orders given him by the infantry Battalion Commander, selecting patrols to accomplish the assigned objective. Patrols varied in size from the four-man team to an entire platoon, as necessary.

However, in Vietnam, for most of the war, the entire Marine Amphibious Force—a division or more with all attached and supporting units established in their own camps—was ashore. So the Recon Battalion operated primarily in general support of the division, and the

Recon platoons received their patrol orders from their own Battalion Operations Section (S-3).

As well, for all but the first few months of the war, the 3rd Reconnaissance Battalion in Vietnam had a Force Recon Company attached to it. Sub-unit 1 of 1st Force Reconnaissance Company was operating in Vietnam or off its coast in 1964, as were elements of the 3rd Recon Battalion. However, 1st Force Recon was attached to the battalion from October 3, 1965, until November 18, 1966, then served with the 1st Recon Battalion, and returned to the United States in 1971. Three platoons of 3rd Force Recon Company arrived in Vietnam in May 1966, and over a period of several months the platoons were attached to the 3rd Recon Battalion. A fourth platoon from 3rd Force Recon joined the battalion in October 1966, and all remained attached until October 1969. In early 1970, 3rd Force was deactivated. In addition, one platoon from the newly activated 5th Recon Battalion, coming from the United States, joined the battalion at the same time the 3rd Force platoons did.

In Vietnam, both Force and Battalion reconnaissance units participated in the same type of mission in the same recon area of responsiblility (RAOR). Much of the story of Force Recon Marines is told in *Inside Force Recon* by Michael Lee Lanning and Ray William Stubbe.*

It is the intent of this account to outline the history of the 3rd Reconnaissance Battalion and to include many individual stories to show how "history" impacted the individual Recon Marine.

One special note should be mentioned. There are times when the Marines described the land into which they were being flown or through which they patrolled as "Indian Country" or referred to the VC or NVA as "Apaches." Such reference was made with two thoughts in mind: (1) Recon patrolled land that belonged not to us but to the foe; (2) the VC and the NVA who fought against us were warriors of the highest quality, and we ranked them alongside the fiercest warriors of the American Indian tribes.

Both these feelings wove themselves together to create in the minds of the Marines a great respect for most of the Vietcong and North Vietnamese. Hollis Stabler is a Native American veteran of the 3rd Recon Battalion. He states:

> Omaha Indians and Indians of other tribes have served honorably in all branches of the service since the Civil War. My father lost his younger brother in Sicily. He was awarded a Purple Heart and Bronze Star

*Ivy Books, 1989.

while serving with Darby's Rangers. The Navajo Marine Corps Talkers exemplified the highest standards of the Corps. Indian warriors serving with the U.S. Forces have a record to be proud of. Indians were heavily represented in 3rd Recon. ... The Vietnamese soldiers who fought against us deserve our greatest respect. They were a tough and worthy enemy.

I would like to add that all Americans who served in 3rd Recon were, as Tom Renard said, "brothers." They were Anglo, Hispanic, Afro-American, American Indian, Oriental, but above all, they were Marines.

"The Charge of the Light Brigade" by Alfred, Lord Tennyson is a favorite poem of many Americans, and in many ways its description of the heroism of the British troopers in the Crimean War in their charge through the "valley of death" also describes the heroism of the 3rd Recon Battalion in Vietnam. Both units had approximately the same number of troops, and both suffered similar casualties. Thirty-seven percent of that famous brigade lay dead or wounded after its immortalized battle; 40 percent of the 3rd Recon Battalion fell into the same categories. Listen to this part of the story:

The Charge of the Light Brigade

... Forward the Light Brigade!
Was there a man dismayed?
Not though the soldier knew
Someone had blundered.

Theirs not to make reply,
Theirs not to reason why,
Theirs but to do and die.
Into the Valley of Death
Rode the six hundred. ...

When can their glory fade?
O the wild charge they made!
All the world wondered.
Honor the charge they made!
Honor the Light Brigade,
Noble six hundred!

God bless 'em. Honor the charge they made!

CHAPTER ONE

"Land the Landing Force"

An image is permanently etched into my mind. In the gray light of early dawn, a Marine dressed in shadow-green, standard-issue utilities is sitting on the last small hump of earth in front of a helicopter landing zone named LZ Finch. Greasepaint crossing his face at an angle deepens his threatening appearance as he sucks up the last smoke in the cigarette pinched between his thumb and forefinger. A Marine Corps–issue soft cover is pushed back on the top of his head, and he leans against the huge pack he carries, takes a deep breath, slowly releasing a smoke ring perfected by many hours of practice. Almost methodically, he bends over and fieldstrips the remains of that tiny bit of tobacco and paper and buries them forever in the soil of Vietnam. The seventy-pound pack is carried without complaint. A rifle rests in his right hand. Then the early-dawn silence is suddenly broken by the thunder of helicopters as they jump from around the corner of the hill behind him and settle down onto the landing pad. I often wonder what was going through that Marine's mind in those final moments. I knew what was rushing through my own. I knew the crosscurrents of anxiety, challenge, and responsibilities that spun around my own consciousness. I'm not sure whether I felt threatening or threatened. Fear or excitement, one didn't show those emotions. We were going to meet enemy soldiers, but another kind of warfare was going on: the conflict that pits courage, duty, and responsibility against fear.

On March 8, 1965, 3,500 Marines of the 9th Marine Expeditionary Brigade (MEB) landed by sea and air at Da Nang, South Vietnam. Marines had been in and out of the country on a lesser and more inconspicuous scale since 1962, and beach reconnaissance missions by units of the 3rd Reconnaissance Battalion and Sub-unit 1, 1st Force Reconnaissance Company, had been under way since November 1964. Then, when the 9th MEB landed, a platoon from Company D of the 3rd Reconnaissance Battalion hit the beach attached to Battalion Landing Team (BLT) 3/9. Three other platoons from the Recon Battalion attached to other infantry battalions, which were also part of the MEB, then landed in quick order. These latter were the two other platoons of Company D and one from Company B. On April 13, all the recon platoons were regrouped as Company D, 3rd Reconnaissance Battalion, under the command of Capt. Patrick G. Collins. In those first weeks of the war, this unit acted as the Reconnaissance Company for the brigade.

Captain Collins held a unique position from which to analyze and critique reconnaissance tactics in Vietnam. These accounts would not be complete without drawing on the experience of this outspoken Marine, who retired as a colonel after serving the Corps in the enlisted ranks as well as in the officer corps. He commanded Company D, 3rd Reconnaissance Battalion, in 1964 and into 1965. The year 1964 found his company scattered on various ships floating off the coast of Vietnam. He was with the Reconnaissance Group aboard the U.S.S. *Cook*. The group consisted of his company, units of Force Recon, and the Navy's Underwater Demolition Team 12. Beginning in about October, the Reconnaissance Group began performing beach surveys, and some of its personnel were assigned to temporary additional duty (TAD) as advisers to Vietnamese Marine units ashore.

However, it was a frustrating situation for Captain Collins as the Recon commanding officer. He was not able to establish a training syllabus that would provide the type of reconnaissance work that he felt was needed while "we were strung all over hell's half acre . . . The company was deployed as individuals, as teams, and as platoons." It was six months before Captain Collins could get his company under one roof. However, while there were individuals who knew what they were doing, Collins did not like the system that limited the ability of the company commander to carry out the training he felt was necessary. During this time period, he stated, training was "sketchy."

Complicating Collins's dilemma was a near-universal lack of understanding of the reconnaissance mission. The 1958 Marine Corps Table of Organization stated, "The (Division) Reconnaissance Battalion may be employed as a unit to screen the advance of the Division or execute reconnaissance missions." The "screening" task placed the battalion patrols directly in the role of a combat unit. This was reflected in the 1958 Battalion Table of Organization, which called for a recon platoon to have one officer and thirty-four enlisted. This included two rifle squads of nine men each, and one machine gun section of nine men. The platoon was equipped with twenty-four M3A1 (.45-caliber) submachine guns, two .30-caliber Browning light machine guns, and four .30-caliber Browning automatic rifles. In 1961 the Table of Organization was changed to read, "The Reconnaissance Battalion . . . will be employed to gain intelligence . . . It is not equipped for decisive or sustained combat . . . It is not capable of screening or counterreconnaissance missions." However, the 1961 change added that when a Recon patrol was in danger of being overrun by enemy forces, the division could "reinforce the reconnaissance force, directing that force to destroy the enemy." Prior to the landing of the Marines in Vietnam, a final revision of this statement eliminated the "destroy the enemy" portion of the mission. The Table of Organization was changed to reflect a Recon platoon consisting of one officer and twenty-three enlisted. It still had two squads, but no machine gun section, and the equipment changed. Only in unusual conditions was an M-60 machine gun to be taken on patrol, and the submachine guns were replaced by the M-14 rifle.

There is no doubt that these repeated changes led to a misunderstanding of the mission, equipment, and method of employment of the Recon units on the part of the commanders from the Recon Battalion commanding officer to the commanding generals of the brigade, division, and force. Collins described the situation just prior to Vietnam as being totally dependent upon the philosophy of the commanding officer. Some units felt that Recon teams were not at all to be in combat situations, but their ideas went to extremes. Collins stated that

in parts of the reconnaissance community there was a policy that Recon would never be seen, never be heard, never be contacted and so on. I remember vividly on one occasion going into the Dominican Republic and not being allowed to take weapons. And at another time we were to go into a hotbed of insurgent activity along the Thailand-Malaysian border and were told not to take our weapons. I said screw it, and we tore our weapons down and buried them in our packs. And I knew one commander in Force Reconnaissance who had the philosophy that the PFC would operate some fifty miles behind enemy lines, then after layers of supervisors, the goddamn officer would be 350 miles in the rear overseeing the whole show. They had some strange ideas, and we had to reteach them the hard lessons we learned in the Korean War.

However, in spite of the system, Collins had nothing but praise for the Marine:

> Jesus Christ, those young Marines broke their asses! They were courageous, brave, worked hard, and did everything that was demanded of them. But it was the goddamned system. I've had a hard-on for the system since Christ was a corporal in Korea. Some units were good, but it was because of the personalities of those unit commanders and not the system.

Collins led the first Recon company ashore in Vietnam in March 1965. It was a composite organization composed of his Delta Company platoons and one platoon from Bravo Company. Then, on April 21, his group consolidated into Delta Company, 9th Marine Expeditionary Brigade, and operated as such until May 24, when it was reattached to the newly arrived 3rd Recon Battalion. Delta Company was involved with short- and long-range patrols in front of the infantry.

Bill Vankat, then a lieutenant platoon commander, stated that they learned lessons quickly, including how useless the "grease gun" (M3A1) was. After an April 25 firefight near Da Nang, his radio operator, Tony Molina, was wounded in the head, and their submachine guns, in Vankat's words, "only kicked up dirt in front of us . . . M-14s became our weapon of choice after that."

The battalion landed, on May 7, 1965, approximately fifty-five miles south of Da Nang, at Red Beach One, Chu Lai, Republic of Vietnam. It was commanded by Lt. Col. D. H. "Doc" Blanchard and landed in support of Regimental Landing Team 4 (RLT-4). It immediately moved into a command post (CP) to the left of the RLT. Its mission was to screen the regiment's left flank. Platoons from the battalion conducted screening patrols and established listening and observation posts in front of the infantry lines for two weeks.

While the battalion worked out of the Chu Lai enclave, Delta Company continued patrolling around Da Nang. At times its patrols were unique efforts, in part due to the lack of infantry. Captain Collins led one such mission near Elephant Valley, northwest of Da Nang and well beyond any infantry support, on May 14–15. The operation consisted of four ten-man teams, with Captain Collins in command and Lieutenant Vankat the patrol leader of the westernmost team. The Reconners worked along a ridge overlooking the main valley, but then tangled with a Vietcong patrol that proved to be only a small element of a much larger unit. Vankat said, "I think we picked on a VC regiment. After sixteen hours of fighting, my team had suffered one killed and all the rest of us were wounded. I was hit twice. Two Army chopper pilots pulled us out of that battle and saved our butts."

Then at 0030 on May 23, the battalion displaced from Chu Lai to Da Nang aboard the LST *Westchester County*. The new mission of the battalion was to support the MEB headquartered at Da Nang and to "establish a reconnaissance net between the Phu Bai, Da Nang, and Chu Lai enclaves."

After Company D rejoined the battalion, Company C, commanded by Capt. B. S. Colassard, was moved by motor convoy on May 26 from the new battalion CP to the Hue–Phu Bai area to conduct reconnaissance operations in that tactical area of responsibility (TAOR). Lt. Frank Reasoner's third platoon of Company B, which had earlier been assigned to that sector, was relocated back to the main CP at Da Nang the next day by the same vehicles. The balance of Company B, which had been stationed in Hawaii, was to land shortly at Chu Lai, and the third platoon would then rejoin its parent company in reconnaissance of the Chu Lai TAOR. However, Lieutenant Reasoner had asked for and received command of Alpha Company: a fateful decision for the young lieutenant.

Maj. Gen. Lewis Walt commanded the brigade that later developed into the III Marine Amphibious Force (MAF). He and his three regimental commanders had all been World War II Raider Battalion officers. The gung ho attitude of the Recon Battalion Marines blended with that same Raider train of thought, and in 1964, Company C was trained as a raid company, conflicting with the statements of the Table of Organization that specified that Recon units were not designed for combat missions. Therefore, the Recon atmosphere was influenced significantly by the raid-and-combat-mission attitude of the brigade's 1965 commanders.

However, Captain Collins's composite Delta Company, and then the battalion a few weeks later, established a training program that focused on basic recon skills. Patrolling techniques were emphasized, and instruction included map reading, communications, immediate action drills, weapons, movement, observation, photography, stream crossings, and the use of supporting arms. A little work was done with demolitions and rubber boat training, particularly as confidence builders, but the emphasis was on how to move, communicate, and call for supporting arms.

The battalion program attempted to give each Marine ten "training" patrols that ran from the base, at the foot of Hill 327, to the Hai Van Pass. Many patrols were designed to feel out the situation. There were different types of missions, some probing from the infantry lines. Colonel Collins reported:

In fact, they first wanted us to run two-man teams, and they weren't worth a damn. Then we went to four-man patrols, and they weren't worth two hoots. Initially, we trucked up to a point, and then from there the team moved by foot. Then we used helicopters. Sometimes the teams were sent beyond artillery range, and the infantry was too few and far away to be of much help. But the small teams weren't worth a damn because you couldn't carry the goddamn gear for the radios, and you couldn't carry casualties and fight. The radio batteries were unreliable; they might last one hour or four days. After a lot of experience we found that the best size patrol was from nine to ten men.

However, in the first year of the war, Recon found itself quite often on its own out in the boondocks. Therefore, the company-size patrol was not unusual. Each company had three platoons of two squads each (later in the war, a third squad was added). Given lame, wounded, and men on R & R, each squad would have eight to ten men. The company would be inserted by truck and walk out, or be flown out by helicopter, but in either case it would operate out of a company patrol base. The company headquarters operated as the base team, and the six squads patrolled from there in different directions. Platoon commanders and platoon sergeants served as team leaders. In this type of mission, all teams relied on each other in case of contact with enemy units.

Sometimes patrol time in the field might be as long as two weeks, but experience proved that, generally, the three- to four-day patrol was best, given the amount of water and food that had to be taken along. During the dark of the moon, more teams were sent into the boondocks than at other times. Colonel Collins indicated that teams often spent three out of four weeks in the bush in 1965.

Although habits developed—for example, the same teams with the same weapons being sent out repeatedly—the philosophy behind a Recon patrol, as was emphasized by Colonel Collins, was that each patrol should be organized for the assigned task; the mission varied according to the situation, the terrain, and the nature of enemy forces. Patrols were to be organized with a reconnaissance team, a security team, a patrol leader, and an assistant patrol leader. If the patrol included a combat mission, an assault team was added. However, Collins emphasized that the organization should be based "upon a reconnaissance patrol function and not an infantry function."

Initially, the number of Marines in Vietnam limited them to the environs of the main base areas within limited TAORs, primarily the heavily populated agricultural lands near the main communities, and not the more distant rice paddies or the mountains. Therefore, prior to the Reconnaissance Battalion's receiving an expanded recon area of responsibility (RAOR) that extended into jungled mountains, the battalion's patrols primarily operated close to infantry lines and in the middle of the more populated countryside—the numerous villages, hamlets, and rice fields. In many cases, these missions could be defined as screening patrols that put the patrols in combat, not reconnaissance, situations. Lt. Frank Reasoner's first patrol as Alpha Company's commander is an example of the results of such a mission.

After the RAORs were extended, Recon patrols began to go deep and had to use radio relay sites high in the mountains. However, radio communications equipment also proved to be a hindrance to patrolling. The PRC-47 had the range but was too big and heavy for light patrolling. The most used radio until November 1965 was the PRC-10, which was small and lightweight but had a limited range that often restricted the depth of the patrols. Moreover, patrols had to take a stockpile of extra batteries if they wanted to be safe, but it wasn't unusual for many of these batteries to be dead when the patrol needed them.

The combination of the recon-raid attitude and operating in the relatively open agricultural areas occupied by rice fields and villages created initial difficulties for the battalion. Some of those problems appear in the statement of Sgt. Richard A. Van Deusen of Company D, 3rd Recon:

> It's very hard in an alien country to hide yourself—I mean, you're going along, and people are all over the place, and they know you're out there, so this compromises any chance of "recon." It all depends on the area you're in. Now if you're in the mountains, you can live there for days before they realize you're up there. Sometimes, they never know you're up there. But if you're south—and each tree line has a village on it—the only good chance you have is moving at night.*

In addition, intelligence about the local populace and the enemy forces was virtually nonexistent during the first months of operations. Marine Recon patrols were sent into areas that taught them lessons, many of which were learned in very tough and deadly situations. For example, only after patrols had been sent into the area south and southwest of Da Nang for months did Marine intelligence learn that

---

* Jack Shulimson and Maj. Charles M. Johnson, USMC. *U.S. Marines in Vietnam: The Landing and Buildup.* Washington, D.C.: Headquarters, U.S. Marine Corps, History and Museum Division, 1978, page 175.

one battalion and two separate companies of Vietcong basically controlled much of that countryside. A III MAF intelligence report compiled some months after the initial landing identified the R-20 Battalion and the independent Hoa Hieu and Dai Loc companies, which totaled 780 enemy soldiers. Their weapons included five 81-mm mortars, ten 60-mm mortars, two heavy machine guns, seven light machine guns, two 57-mm recoilless rifles, forty-eight submachine guns, eighty-one automatic rifles, and numerous other semiautomatic rifles and other small arms. The only weapon in that group that might have come as a surprise was the American-made M-18 recoilless rifle. This rifle was relatively light, weighing twenty-two kilograms (or about forty-eight pounds), and could be carried by one man, although it normally was a two-man weapon. Its maximum effective range was 450 meters, although it could fire out to 4,000 meters.

Operating throughout the provinces around Da Nang was the regional and more mobile 1st Vietcong Regiment. Then, very early in the war, the 2nd North Vietnamese (NVA) Division was found to be operating in the Da Nang–Chu Lai area, and it absorbed the 1st Vietcong Regiment. This division also contained the 3rd and the 21st NVA regiments and totaled some 5,500 infantry. It was determined that the division and its attached units operated primarily in the northern Chu Lai and southern Da Nang enclaves. This included the area south of Da Nang.

Therefore, enemy forces in the immediate sector south and southwest of Da Nang included 780 soldiers in organized local units and at least portions of the 5,500 infantry in the 2nd NVA Division somewhere within a twenty-mile radius. Making the situation extremely deadly for the spread-out Marine command was the significant degree of support the VC and NVA received from the rural populace. Patrols from the battalion were sent into these outlying rice-growing flatlands ahead of the Marine infantry, but they came face-to-face with numerically superior, well-armed, and people-supported VC units. But, since intelligence estimates of the enemy situation were not accurate, the Marine teams were generally unaware of the true nature of the enemy forces.

As the situation unfolded in the Recon Battalion RAOR, it was obvious that the Marines in Quang Nam Province around Da Nang walked into enemy country without a good estimate of either the friendly or the enemy situation. The battalion, after several bad experiences of sending out two-to-four-man listening or observation posts, began to send platoon-size patrols. A good example of this type of patrol and the difficulties it faced can be seen in an account of the

Alpha Company Reasoner patrol on July 12, 1965. Its mission was south of Da Nang in and near the village of Dai Loc. Lt. Frank Reasoner, the company commander, led the patrol.

South of Da Nang was an area of near-sea-level rice paddies with countless villages and hamlets spread over them for mile after mile. The government of South Vietnam (GVN) had lost control over most of the population, and the Vietcong ruled the night, if not the day. Many areas that were claimed by the GVN to be secure were not. However, in the beginning, that was not known to the Marines. Marine units were advised that the Regional Force (RF) and Popular Force (PF) militia units were the local defense units battling the Vietcong.

The PF units were made up of villagers who reported to the district chief. However, he was often difficult to find. The RFs were organized over a larger area and reported to the regional chief. Then there was the regular ARVN, which was the Vietnamese national army and had its own regular chain of command. However, as was reported in *U.S. Marines in Vietnam, 1966,** the chain of command did not function well. Paul Hare, an American civilian official, commented (in another situation): "Basic to the problem is the relationship of Major Nhat (pacification leader) and Captain Hoa (District Chief of Hoa Vang). Cadre generally speak to Major Nhat; village and hamlet chiefs to both; ARVN to Colonel Lap; RF to nobody; and the PF . . . to anyone who happens to talk to them. The situation is confusing to the extreme." With that situation, the PFs could easily be infiltrated and controlled by the Vietcong. It is estimated that 20 percent of the villagers had direct family involvement with the VC, and that added to the problem facing the Reasoner patrol.

---

* Jack Shulimson. Washington D.C.: Headquarters, U.S. Marine Corps, History and Museum Division, 1982, pages 80–81.

CHAPTER TWO

The Reasoner Patrol—July 12, 1965

In mid-1965, the battalion's command post at Da Nang was renamed in honor of Lieutenant Frank Reasoner, who was killed while attempting to help a wounded Marine. One Medal of Honor, one Navy Cross, and three Silver Stars would be awarded to members of the Reasoner patrol.

At about noon on July 12, 1965, the first platoon, Company A, 3rd Recon Battalion, was helilifted from the battalion's headquarters at Da Nang to the large district town of Dai Loc, approximately ten air miles south. It is hard to describe the type of mission given to this patrol. It was not a reconnaissance mission or a screening mission, and although it could possibly be considered a combat mission, the patrol was not equipped with the proper weapons to face main force enemy units.

In the days leading up to July 12, Captain Collins had been preparing a mission in which his Delta Company would go high into the mountains to establish a radio relay on Ba Na, the highest mountain near Da Nang. With an elevation of over 4,000 feet, it rises directly out of the sea-level valley below. However, on July 10, the captain was directed to send a platoon across the Cau Do River into the flatlands and villages just south of Da Nang to patrol ahead of a 9th Marine infantry unit. Lt. Bill Vankat led that team on what Collins called a basic route reconnaissance. On July 11, Vankat led his platoon into what was supposed to be a secure area. The Delta Company commander then described what happened on that Sunday:

> Christ, he no more than got across the river in that area that was supposedly secure, than they got into a world of shit—just across the

17

bridge on Highway One. I took the rest of the company down there to help extract them, and the 9th Marines sent in their 2nd Battalion to help, and they got into a big goddamn row. In a relatively short period of time the entire 9th Marine Regiment was committed to the fight. On the second day of that battle was when Frank Reasoner was sent with his patrol several miles to the south of us.

Reasoner's mission took him to Dai Loc, where the platoon landed to begin its patrol. Dai Loc might have been about ten air miles from the headquarters at the foot of Hill 327, but it was about three times that in road miles—and ten light-years in reality.

Lasting ten to fifteen minutes, the patrol's flight in UH-34 helicopters flew down the eastern edge of the Annamite Mountains, which roughly parallel the coast at a distance of ten to twelve miles. A near-mile-high barrier, the mountains walled off the coastal port of Da Nang and the fertile coastal rice fields from the interior of the country. Looking out the wide hatch of each chopper, the teams could see Ba Na, where Captain Collins was shortly to establish a radio relay site. Below it, to the south, was Happy Valley. Opposite the valley from Ba Na was Charlie Ridge, which stretched for almost ten miles toward Laos and towered over valleys and great fields of rice from not-quite-Ba Na heights. From about 2,000 to 2,500 feet, and for about 1,000 more feet, the ridge was covered with triple-canopy jungle. This jungle was dark and ominous, and the Marines did not yet know the dangers that would await future patrols along the ridge. However, the attention of this patrol was on the vast fields of rice and the villages below them.

In this part of Vietnam, it was the dry season—hot, dusty, and humid, the way only the devil could have planned it. Although at this time of year an occasional rainstorm would sweep across the land, the rice paddies were rock hard. Tiny hamlets, villages, and a few larger towns passed beneath the birds. The team flew over the battle involving the 9th Marines, and Delta Company, and kept heading south.

The villages below were scattered without apparent rhyme or reason. Thatched huts and tree groves clustered among the paddies. Quite often hedgerows and "fences" of bamboo and cactus served as barriers around and within these villages. It was a very sizable sea of alien faces into which a small unit of Marines was descending.

The patrol consisted of a Recon-size platoon, and present were both the platoon commander, 2nd Lt. Bill Henderson, and the company commander, 1st Lt. Frank Reasoner. Although it was not normal procedure for a Recon Company commander to accompany his patrols, it was often the case that the officers did so to stay in touch with what was happening in the field. Lieutenant Reasoner had significant experience as a platoon commander in Company B and then had been attached to Captain Collins in Delta Company, but he had only within the last two weeks been given the command of Alpha Company. One other platoon from the company was also in the foothills, a few miles away.

In addition to the two officers, there were sixteen enlisted Marines, one Navy Corpsman, and one Vietnamese dog handler, with his German shepherd, from the Army of the Republic of Vietnam (ARVN). Two of the Marines were to stay in a small ARVN outpost in Dai Loc as a radio relay team. The outpost maintained two 105-mm howitzers. A unit of Popular Force (PF) soldiers was also assigned to the area. It was the understanding of the Marines on this team that the PFs were friendly militia from the local villages.

Shortly after noon on July 12, the helicopters dropped the patrol in Dai Loc and left. The Marines quickly reassembled, established their radio relay at the little ARVN fort, and moved through the town toward the open road. The men of the patrol noted that the villagers, including the little children, stood off from them and didn't act friendly. Team members felt exposed and vulnerable.

Dai Loc sits on the Vu Gia River about three miles southeast of Charlie Ridge. Routes 4 and 540 (hardly more than large dirt pathways) intersect just outside the town, and the patrol's route took it to Route 4, an open dirtway through the villages and dry rice fields that was to take them about eight kilometers, bending and weaving through the rice paddies, villages, and hamlets in a northerly direction. However, before the platoon cleared the town, it passed a unit of about fifty uniformed and armed Vietnamese. It was the platoon's understanding that this was the PF unit. Their ARVN dog handler, however, nervously and repeatedly stated that the armed men were not PFs but Vietcong.

As the patrol continued along its assigned route toward the outskirts of the town, the PF unit was seen leaving the town to their right flank, also in a northerly direction.

Except for the radio relay left at Dai Loc, the patrol used PRC-10 radios, the walkie-talkie–type predecessors of the PRC-25 and PRC-77. The "Prick-10" had limited range and value when the operator was burrowing into the dirt or mud to escape incoming fire. The patrol order had specified the minimum amount of ammunition, meals, and water to carry, but some individuals carried more ammo or water, cutting back on the chow. All carried the M-14 rifle, but some carried a hundred rounds and others carried double that and then some. Some took only two canteens of water, knowing there were water sources along the route, while others carried four. Each Marine carried several grenades, including illumination and smoke. One M-79 grenade launcher was taken, and it was to prove a lifesaver. The M-79 looked like a very heavy gauge, short-barreled shotgun. It weighed 6.4 pounds and could accurately fire a specially designed grenade up to 400 meters.

The mission took them to the west and then back to the north. The experienced Recon Marines on the patrol had been trained to patrol in smaller units and much more clandestinely, and were uneasy walking in the open in daylight. They immediately realized that they were not in friendly villages.

Approximately three hours along its route, the patrol received inconsequential sniper fire as it approached the small hamlet of An My (3). Lieutenant Henderson took half the platoon in search of the sniper and entered the village from the left flank. The rest, with Lieutenant Reasoner, continued down the road and entered the village along the main route. All the Marines were alert and ready.

The village appeared empty, but some villagers were noted hiding in protective shelters below ground; none seemed to pose a direct menace to the teams.

However, Sgt. Maj. Fred Murray (Ret.), then a lance corporal, remembers telling Lieutenant Reasoner that the situation didn't look good: too many people were missing or hiding. But the hamlet was small, and it didn't take long to work through it. The intimidating feel of the situation was only heightened by one of the infrequent summer rainstorms that quickly blew up; this one drenched the divided patrol.

Lieutenant Reasoner's team was the first to push through the storm, pass a barrier fence of bamboo and cactus, and cross a ditch that circled the hamlet. In front of them was an open field. To their left front was a small graveyard with low, rounded grave mounds. On the other side of the graves, 200 meters away, was a grove of trees, and to the left of that the ground rose slightly toward a low knoll.

Then Cpl. B. C. Collins and Lance Corporal Murray, in the lead, saw three men in ponchos wearing helmets. The Vietnamese, Vietcong, were near the trees. The three simultaneously noticed the Marines and ran toward the slight rise in the landscape. Collins and Murray saw their weapons, immediately dropped into firing positions, and took them under fire. As quickly as the two Marines fired on the VC, they were taken under fire by a machine gun from a position on the rise. That gun was joined by a fusillade of small arms fire from the same area. The only protection the Marines had was the circular graves, which varied from four to six feet in diameter—although their two-foot height was not much in the way of protection. Murray and Collins were caught in the low ground and under heavy fire.

From their vantage point, the enemy soldiers kept the Marines pinned down and attempted to envelop the teams from two flanks. Lieutenant Henderson's team was still pushing through the village but began to receive fire from the left flank. Staff Sergeant Knee, the platoon sergeant, was with Henderson and was the first wounded.

At the front of the unit, Murray and Collins exposed themselves to enemy fire in order to find better positions and to cut off another enemy unit, which was maneuvering to outflank them to the right front. All the while the enemy was continuously pouring rounds into the patrol. Collins and Murray sighted their weapons on the enemy soldiers moving through the trees and put several of them down, effectively stopping that envelopment for a time. Murray said that Collins was yelling to keep their rifles on semiautomatic fire. However, behind them, Lance Corporal Hall had been wounded. He carried the M-79, which was desperately needed. The machine gun, almost 400 meters away, had to be taken out, and the patrol had neither artillery nor air support.

The use of the machine gun by the VC was of note. Local guerrilla units did not normally carry the weapon because of its large size and the need for extra ammunition. That type of unit would want to hit quickly and move away just as fast. However, when a main force unit wanted to stand toe-to-toe and fight in earnest, then you saw it. In this case the machine gun was probably a Soviet RPK, a light machine gun (LMG). It looked very much like the AK-47 rifle but had a longer and heavier barrel, a bipod, and a greater-capacity magazine. It could use the standard 30-round AK-47 magazine, a 40-round magazine, or a 75-round drum. It weighed about eleven pounds without the ammo. Its cyclic rate of fire was 660 rounds per minute, but it was limited to less because the barrel would overheat. The RPK required a well-trained gunner who used fire discipline, firing only in short bursts. That would reduce his practical rate of fire to about 80 rounds per minute.

Now, under fire from the RPK, Murray had to run back across the graveyard to get to Hall while Collins remained by himself and put down covering fire. Then, at a fast low crawl, Collins made it back. The sun was edging ominously close to the horizon by the time Henderson's team reached Reasoner's. Both teams were together again, some in the ditch and others nearby, but enemy fire was coming in from three directions. The patrol later estimated that the enemy unit was a company of 75 to 125 soldiers. The Marines, alone and outnumbered six or seven to one, continued to fight back.

It was typical at this time in the war that the ARVN interpreters, dog handlers, scouts, and others did not participate well with the Marines in combat. Murray stated about their ARVN dog handler: "We had to carry extra water for the fucking dog . . . but as soon as the first shot was fired that VN and the dog went in the ditch and stayed there." (The dog handler and dog did come out with them aboard the rescue choppers.)

Jim Shockley retired as a major, but on that day he was a lance corporal radio operator. He relates:

We lost comm. Then the shooting started, and I said to myself, Shit, I better get to the lieutenant [Reasoner]. He's gonna want to call somebody. . . . So I ran to where I thought I'd find him. I ran through the bushes, and you know those big ditches that go around the village, I saw a bunch of guys in the ditch, including Pipes [the other radio operator], and he had his radio antenna shot off. And he had been with or close to Reasoner. Lieutenant Reasoner was out in the field and so was Lindy [Hall], and Lindy was already shot. . . . So I figured he [Reasoner] needed a radio. So I ran out there and plopped down next to him. They [enemy fire] missed me going out. The machine gunner couldn't swing around fast enough to come around on me, so I made it. The guy was really dinging. He took nice short bursts like he knew what he was doing. I happened to have my arm exposed, and he got me in the left elbow. But we never could get comm. Pipes's radio was shot up, and with PRC-10s the comm was bad with them anyway. But, see, I was lying flat on the ground. You had to either sit up or stand up with a PRC-10 to make it work very well. . . . I saw some 34s [helicopters] circling, and I tried to come up with them, and I couldn't get them either.

Fred Murray added:

By the time I got a bandage on Hall, and I was sending him back toward the ditch to some safety, we got the word that Shockley had been hit, and Reasoner was gonna go try to help Shockley. And the next thing I know, Shockley is saying that Reasoner's been hit. Because it was just an open field out there with just a few mounds to get behind. And they [the Vietcong] are up on that damn little hill and putting heavy machine gun fire down on us along with small arms fire. Jimmy [Shockley] is hollering to stay away and don't come to get him. By that time some of the guys with Lieutenant Henderson had made it to us. They had been taking fire from another unit of VC in the village. What had happened, as best as we could figure out, was that while they [the VC] were trying to pull an envelopment around us [Reasoner's team], they were also pulling an envelopment around the other side of the village. And that's when Henderson's group ran into them.

Lieutenant Henderson's team, still within the village, had been hit by fire from two sides, and Henderson had received word from Reasoner to withdraw toward the landing zone, on the south side of the village. Then Pfc. Hahn, with fire direction from Corporal Collins, knocked out the machine gun with the M-79. With covering fire from the remainder of the unit, Collins, Hahn, Pfc. Thomas Gatlin, Pfc. Thorace L. Pannell, and Murray then moved forward to bring back Shockley and Reasoner. However, Lieutenant Reasoner, who had exposed himself to machine gun fire to help Shockley, had died. By then the fight had been going on for over three hours, and darkness, as well as the Vietcong, was surrounding the patrol.

The five moved forward to Reasoner and Shockley and managed, with night swiftly coming on and them at a low crawl, to pull the lieutenant's body out of the open. They then got Shockley back. The Marines had to cover about thirty yards under fire to retrieve them.

At that time, the entire unit had to move out of the ditch toward the road and the landing zone. They had established communication by then, and helicopters were on the way to extract them from their untenable position. In the dark, as they moved toward the landing zone, helping the wounded and carrying the lieutenant, they were repeatedly hit by enemy fire.

While some gathered up what loose gear they could, others returned the fire and protected the wounded. An illumination grenade was used to signal the birds coming in out of the blackness overhead. It was now past 2100 hours. The first chopper took the dead and wounded; the second took the main part of the unit. Then, in the dark and with the surrounding enemy units maneuvering closer, the third bird extracted Lieutenant Henderson and Doc Lewis.

The 34s brought the patrol back to the battalion headquarters, with the wounded and Lieutenant Reasoner's body being taken to Charlie Med, a medical company just down the clay-dirt road from the headquarters. One person (Reasoner) had been killed, and three were wounded: Staff Sergeant Knee, Lance Corporal Shockley, and Lance Corporal Hall (on a second tour of duty, Lindy Hall was killed in action on Hill 881 in the battle for Khe Sanh). For this action on July 12, 1965, Lt. Frank Reasoner received the Medal of Honor. Cpl. B. C. Collins received the Navy Cross, our nation's second-highest award; and 2nd Lt. Bill Henderson, L.Cpl. Fred Murray, and Pfc. Thomas Gatlin each received the Silver Star.

Although the facts were never positively known, it was estimated that the first platoon, Company A, 3rd Recon Battalion, had encountered an enemy company that had intended to join at least one sister company in an attack on the ARVN outpost at Dai Loc. (An attack did commence on that fort at about the same time as the attack on the patrol at An My.) In addition, the Marines felt that the PF unit in Dai Loc had really been VC, as the ARVN dog handler had stated.

In the country south of Da Nang, including the Dai Loc area, enemy troops had severed all roads leading to Da Nang and other parts of the coast, with the questionable exception of Highway One. Concerning this area from Dai Loc to the south (regarding the period from late 1965 to early 1966), Col. Edwin Simmons, then the III MAF G-3, stated: "My own feelings . . . were that an accommodation had been reached between the VC and local ARVN commander . . ."* Later, as 9th Marines commanding officer, he stated: "We can march from Dien Ban (nine miles east of Dai Loc) to Dai Loc any time of day we want to. This didn't mean anything. You had to take apart each one of these hamlets bit by bit and see what was in there and put it together again."

Concerning this same area and time period, Col. George W. Carrington, Jr., stated: "There were tremendous anachronisms and inequities that stick in my memory. . . . I seem to recall that there were French resident engineers in An Hoa (south of Dai Loc) who continued to live in very comfortable homes and enjoyed speed boating and water skiing on the lake there."** Yet the area was deadly for Marines. Too much of the population was sympathetic to the cause of the Vietcong.

A few months after the Reasoner patrol, the Ngu Hanh Son Campaign was initiated five to seven miles north of Dai Loc, just across the Câu Do River, south of Da Nang and near where Delta Company had been engaged on July 11. This campaign was designed as a pacification program with the 9th Marines providing security for a sixty-man South Vietnamese elite rural reconstruction ("Can Bo") platoon. The VC, operating with ease in the villages and hamlets, avoided the Marines and continually harassed the Can Bo platoon and other PF and RF units. Within weeks, 15 percent of that "elite" platoon had quit. During the Ngu Hanh Son Campaign, the American airbase at Da Nang was hit by enemy 120-mm heavy mortars fired from somewhere in the operational area of the campaign.

The Marines, with Lieutenants Reasoner and Henderson, were outnumbered by an estimated 100-man company, and it is a credit to

*U.S. Marines in Vietnam, 1966. page 76.
**U.S. Marines in Vietnam, 1966, page 41.

each Marine that they were able to hold off the enemy without artillery support until the helicopters were able to extract them. Basic Marine Corps discipline and training held the teams together, and their marksmanship held back the enemy forces for about four hours. Then, in the dark and under fire, the helicopter crews established what was to be a long and close working relationship with Recon. Flying into a hot LZ, they were able to bring all the Reconners back even though the birds themselves were being hit. In tribute to Lieutenant Reasoner's concern for the Marines of the unit, the battalion headquarters' main camp was renamed Camp Reasoner.

Those Marines, although assigned an objective that was poorly conceived and impossible to achieve, stuck together and fought their way through the contact, carrying their wounded and the body of their commanding officer.

A few months after this patrol, an enemy document was captured near the patrol route. In part, it stated:

To: Local authorities and units. In compliance with the policy of higher headquarters, effective immediately, U.S. and ROK soldiers captured in action by guerrilla or local units will be treated according to this regulation. They must be properly detained and timely evacuated to higher headquarters. Unreasonable shooting, killing, or torturing because of difficulty met in the process of evacuation or because of the enemy situation, are inconsistent with the principles of the regulation and absolutely forbidden. Violator(s) of this directive will answer to higher headquarters for their action(s).

On the other hand, effort should be made to obtain bodies of U.S. soldiers killed in action, and all papers, pictures, insignia will be removed before burying them secretly. The case will then be (timely) reported to higher headquarters. Thus the enemy KIAs will then be listed by the enemy (U.S./ROK) forces as missing or captured.

(Party) Committee echelons of local and main force units should disseminate this urgent and important directive to cadre and soldiers of the military and paramilitary forces for proper implementation. The matter should be kept absolutely secret.*

The area south of Da Nang proved fatal for many Marines as the infantry attempted to maneuver within and establish bases near the villages. It was particularly difficult for a reconnaissance unit to operate in such situations: it was not possible for such units to be so

---

*Copy of document is held in the History and Museum Division, Headquarters, U.S. Marine Corps, Washington, D.C.

well-manned as to be the superior force in a battle, and they could never be clandestine enough to remain unseen.

Bill Vankat summed up the situation that had come to pass when he said:

> Before Frank Reasoner's death, I remember that when we had a chance, Frank, Bill Henderson, and myself would go into Da Nang, have some drinks downtown, and felt exhilarated like you were living the life of a Marine that you had long wanted. After Frank was killed and the other events around that time, the attitudes changed. It had quickly become deadly serious. Still, I want to say that the people that I served with made it a memorable experience: Blanchard, Oliver, Collins, Henderson, Reasoner, Miller, Lagle, Ducloix, Wynn, Molina, and so many others.

CHAPTER THREE

Recon Marines . . . Black, White, Brown . . . Brothers

There were three brothers in Tom Renard's family, and although all joined the Marines, Tom was the only one to serve in Vietnam with the 3rd Recon Battalion (1965–66). He came from the 1st Recon Battalion in California and was trained by some who later served in the 3rd Recon Battalion in Vietnam. However, before he would talk about the events that happened on patrols, he told of the bonding that occurred among Marines of the Recon Battalion:

> *I have to go to the very beginning. It goes back to 1st Recon Battalion at Camp Pendleton, California, where you might say that it all began. I say that because there were so many men who were so important in how the bonding began between those of us in Recon. Bill Buhl, a gunnery sergeant then, and Fred Wilson, now a retired sergeant major, were in charge of RIP (Recon Indoctrination Program) at Camp Pendleton. I look up to those men. I can't explain how much I look up to those Marines and value the knowledge that they taught us. We were so fortunate to be one of the first platoons to have that knowledge, and we handed that down to those who came after us. And during my time in Recon, there was no color—no black, no white, no brown—we were brothers and proud to be Marines.*

When 3rd Recon Battalion left Okinawa for Vietnam in 1965, it was joined by its own Bravo Company, which had to sail across the Pacific from Hawaii. In that first year a platoon from 1st Recon Battalion sailed from California to Vietnam. Later, in 1966, four platoons of the 3rd Force Recon and one platoon from the 5th Recon Battalion transplaced from the States to Vietnam and were attached to the 3rd Recon Battalion.

27

Bravo Company had been separated from the main headquarters by half the Pacific; it was a part of the 1st Marine Brigade, stationed in Hawaii. The 4th Marine Regiment was the nucleus of the brigade, and Bravo Company was its Recon element. Lieutenant Reasoner was then one of its platoon commanders, and Dan Hill was the company first sergeant.

First Sergeant Hill joined the Kaneohe Marines on the Mokapu Peninsula in 1964, and he very quickly established a new screening and selection process in order to insure that top-quality Marines would be assigned to the company. In Hill's own words:

> For basic Recon philosophy, I believed that we could take almost any Marine and build a body, but we couldn't build a mind, and that's what I went out to find—Marines with the IQ to be good Recon. I accepted no one without a high school diploma, and by the time we shipped out for Vietnam a year later, we had created an entire company that had at the minimum completed high school.

First Sergeant Hill talked his friend, the sergeant major of the brigade, into allowing him to go in on Sundays to screen service record books (SRBs) to select those Marines for further review in person. Part of that "review" was handled by Lieutenant Reasoner, who ran and swam the potential recruits on the sandy shores and just off the beaches of the island. Only when both were satisfied that they had Marines with sharp minds and enough physical endurance and strength to be trained further did they give the final approval. In the background, quietly smoking his pipe and approving the work of his subordinates, was Captain Philon, the company commander.

However, the first sergeant not only had to intercept his future Marines' service record books before they were assigned to a unit, he also had to "encourage" some Marines whom he considered "hot dogs" to request transfers out of the company. He quite often succeeded, but his methods were not always kosher. One method used to promote within them the desire to leave the company was to take them out on night dives in the waters off the island while "Animal," the NCO in charge of the dive shop, threw shark bait into the Pacific and "called" sharks.

Although the company did some training with submarines, using rubber boats to hit the beach during darkness, basic patrolling techniques were emphasized, including land navigation, communication skills, and the use of supporting arms—that is, artillery, naval gunfire, and air support. Bravo Company did not agree with one philosophy that existed in parts of the recon community, which was: when in contact with enemy forces, break contact, split into two-man teams, and escape and evade back to friendly lines. In many parts of the reconnaissance community, there was a growing belief that it was better for the team to stay together. While the team generally was not manned or equipped to fight battles with enemy forces, and therefore had to break contact, its members also needed to stay together.

By the spring of 1965, Bravo Company had lost both its commanding and executive officers. First Sergeant Hill stated that within the company, the officers and staff NCOs reviewed the applicants for the job, encouraging the selection of Capt. James L. Compton. They got their wish, but Compton did not check into the company until it had already received orders to join the battalion for the assault into Vietnam. Actually, the company gear was stacked on the parade deck, and the first sergeant's wife was using their VW camper to help haul it to the dock.

Dan Hill said that his battles began in Okinawa, not Vietnam, because the battalion command "could not believe the quality of troops that the company had, and the battalion commanding officer wanted to redistribute the wealth to other companies." He said that he and Lieutenant Colonel Blanchard never got along, and he fought as hard as he could to keep the company intact.

Bravo Company was assigned to land at Chu Lai, and remained there after the battalion headquarters and other units sailed for Da Nang a short time later. It was not until March 1966 that the company left Chu Lai and relocated closer to the battalion. Even then, the company was not assigned to Camp Reasoner but was sent farther north to be responsible for the Phu Bai TAOR. Hill stated that his greatest sense of pride came from the fact that of those Marines they had trained in Hawaii, not one had been killed in Vietnam by the time he left in March 1966.

That summer, units of the 1st Recon Battalion, in 1965 headquartered in Camp Pendleton, California, shipped out for Vietnam. The 1st Recon Battalion was attached to the 1st Marine Division, as the 3rd was to the 3rd Marine Division. The 1st Recon Battalion established its headquarters at Chu Lai and remained there until the latter part of 1966. However, one of 1st Recon's platoons ended up a part of the 3rd Battalion once it got to Vietnam. One of the platoon's Marines, Tom Renard, said: "I don't recall anyone who had less than two years in the Corps. I was a lance corporal with three. Gunnery Sergeants Bill Buhl and Fred Wilson trained us in the Recon Indoctrination Program. I still look up to those men."

The platoon landed at Chu Lai, then was sent to Okinawa for additional training and did not return to Vietnam for three months. "I remember our disappointment when we were told that we wouldn't stay in Vietnam," Tom said. "We had trained hard to go to war if necessary for our country, and we didn't feel like we were carrying our share of the load sailing around the Pacific and being in Okinawa, while others were in the middle of danger."

By the first of November 1965, the platoon had landed again in Vietnam, but this time it was in Da Nang, attached to the 3rd Recon Battalion. Renard stated:

> We heard stories of the Reasoner patrol, and we got a lot of inspiration handed to us by members of the battalion. But the first patrols had a lot of confusing moments. First, we didn't like the "walk out" patrols. We didn't like them because we walked through friendly lines, and at night you were always afraid that you would get shot by another Marine in the infantry units nearby. And, second, the teams were small and in the middle of the villages south of Da Nang. The village areas didn't seem that friendly, and you felt exposed.

Tom described one of the small patrols into that heavily populated rice-growing region south of the city of Da Nang:

> The first time I ever had a VC in my sights, there were six of them and three of us. It was right off Highway One, just south of Da Nang, and we were poorly set up—lying against the embankment with the VC walking down a trail on the other side, and we couldn't tell how many were coming. I knew all they had to do was to pop grenades over that small hump of earth and we would be dead. In that area there just weren't any good places to remain unseen and undetected. Anyway, we just lay there and let those VC go by. Recon teams, particularly small teams, were very vulnerable in those populated flatlands. They did not speak the language, they stood out almost like an alien race, and when working in four- or three-man teams, they could not afford to take a casualty.

The platoon and the battalion underwent numerous changes as the patrols of 1965 blooded them. Hardest for the young Marines to adjust to was the splitting up of their platoons and companies. In Renard's platoon, Sergeants Johnson, Ward, and Young, and Gunnery Sergeant Buhl, made grade and were reassigned to other platoons as theirs was becoming top heavy with the higher ranks. Buhl was commissioned a lieutenant and became a valued officer for Capt. George Best in Alpha Company. Renard and others made corporal, and new Marines showed up. Many of the new men were assigned to Recon after a simple show of hands at the Marine Corps air freight terminal at the Da Nang airstrip. Tom Renard, who had looked up to others as his leaders for months and through many patrols, found himself in the role of counselor-leader to the new guys. Renard said:

> I remember the names of some of those new people: Green, Taylor, Burrato, Hopkins, Lothian, Meidel, Olsen, Powless, Stringer, Richards, and the list goes on. I'll never forget how they tried to talk us into extending our tours, worrying that they wouldn't make it without people like Thompson, Boyda, and me. But they did, and they became the old experienced "salts" for the new Marines who came later. The tradition and experience kept being passed down, and that's a good part of what the Marine Corps is all about.

However, the battalion was also changing direction. Gradually, it was beginning to have more helicopter support, and its recon area of responsibility (RAOR) was extended farther into the mountains. Teams of Marines probed those jungled hills and valleys searching for signs of enemy units from Charlie Ridge to Elephant Valley. They found more than signs as the 2nd NVA Division absorbed the 1st Vietcong Regiment and began to make its muscle felt in the Da Nang–Chu Lai sector of Vietnam.

As 1965 progressed into 1966, it wasn't just the Marines who were beginning to experience a new war. Even the Department of Defense noted the degeneration of the political and military situation. A memorandum from Secretary of Defense Robert McNamara to President Lyndon Johnson described the situation as follows:

> The situation in South Vietnam is worse than a year ago (when it was worse than a year before that) . . . the government is able to provide security to fewer and fewer people in less and less territory as terrorism increases. Cities and towns are being isolated as fewer and fewer roads and railroads are usable and power and communications lines are cut. . . .
>
> Rural reconstruction (pacification) . . . has lost ground . . . (300,000 people have been lost to the VC, and tens of thousands of refugees have poured out of these areas). . . .

One population base on which the Vietcong relied was that of the mountain-dwelling ethnic minorities. The dominant ethnic group in Vietnam is the Viet, or Kinh, which constituted 88 percent of the Vietnamese population during the war. The Viet people primarily inhabited the agricultural lowlands and urban centers. The balance was made up of minority groups that descended from the Chinese or the ancient kingdom of Champa and the Khmer Empire.

The Rhade tribe descended from the ancient Champa Kingdom, and many of its customs are derived from the mixed Hindu/Muslim heritage of its past. The Rhade are believed to be racially linked to the Polynesian people of the Pacific Islands. They preceded the Vietnamese to Vietnam and generally lived in the highlands, separating themselves from their lowland countrymen, whom they did not trust. Although small in numbers, such minorities were viewed as critically important by both the VC/NVA and the United States. But many South Vietnamese officials disregarded the minorities' heritages and attempted to force them to change their ways. When trying to ferret out the Vietcong, South Vietnamese officials often viewed the minorities in the same way they viewed the Vietcong. Efforts of the United States to obtain the assistance of these mountain people were limited primarily to the work of units such as the Special Forces, but Marine Recon teams had encounters with them in the highlands.

The difference between the Vietcong/NVA policy and that of the government of South Vietnam can be seen in a document captured in 1966:*

In South Vietnam, there are over ten Montagnard (people of the mountains) groups of 2 million population over two-thirds of the south; they constitute the strategic base of the South Vietnamese and Indo-Chinese revolution. The South Montagnard races are guided by indomitable and valiant tradition, have a high spirit, and are filled with resentments of the enemy. To properly implement the civilian proselytizing activity, we should have three togethers (eat together, sleep together, and work together), respect the customs and habits of each race of Vietnamese people to develop good morale and customs of each race. The concept of the people's equality and the mutual origin of the people in the highlands and in the plains should be spread far and wide. . . .

Seven points to remember in the ethnic policy:
1. Properly comply with the basic principles of our party toward the ethnic minority policy, union, equality, and solidarity.
2. When located in their area, we should respect the customs and habits of the people.
3. Do not touch the people's property hidden in forests, in rice fields, or in their own cemetery.
4. Do not ask the relatives of the family in local areas if we need

*Copy is held in the History and Museums Division, Headquarters, U.S. Marine Corps, Washington, D.C.

to borrow or beg something or if we should want to barter or deal with them.

5. Do not tease the women.
6. Do not defecate in rice fields, near the roads, beside graves or streams.
7. If we are careless and do anything contrary to the habits and customs of the local people, we should tell cadre to ask pardon from the people and not pretend to forget them.

—Political Office of the 324th Division

In the contest of winning the "hearts and minds" of the people, the Vietcong and the North Vietnamese were able more successfully to implement their policies, gaining the allegiance of the ethnic minorities who lived in the mountainous regions farther from the cities. One large mountain area southwest of Da Nang was inhabited by elements of the Rhade tribe, and it became a large base area for the NVA. The 3rd Recon Battalion pushed its patrols into those regions.

CHAPTER FOUR

Charlie Ridge—1966

"The recon platoon that I joined upon entering country was the closest-knit bunch of individuals that I have ever encountered in my life. They had been performing gallantly since the first half of 1965 without incurring a single Marine killed and had run patrols for Operation Double Eagle and Starlight. When we lost Sergeant Kirchoff on Operation Taut Bow on Charlie Ridge, we were all devastated."
—Dale Sare

The ridge began about twelve air miles southwest of Da Nang, and it extended that same distance west, toward Laos. Jungle-covered mountain peaks rose irregularly over the ridgetop, which ranged from one and one half to two miles wide. To men afoot, this vast expanse of mountainous ridge appeared even larger and more ominous as it rose out of the sea-level rice paddies to a height of about 1,200 meters (approximately 4,000 feet). From the 800-to-900-meter elevation, the ridge was covered with triple-canopy jungle that rose 100 to 150 feet. Under the canopy, the ground was covered with underbrush, and military maps did not reveal the numerous chasms and draws. One enemy-held route from the north toward Charlie Ridge passed through the A Shau Valley, which, in March 1966, became a scene for tragedy as the 95th NVA Regiment (of their 325th Division), overran a 434-man Special Forces CIDG base. While attempting rescues of the Americans and South Vietnamese, twenty-one of Marine Corps helicopter squadron HMM-163's twenty-four helicopters were shot down or so damaged they had to be replaced.

Charlie Ridge was another strategic location for enemy forces located between Da Nang and Chu Lai and within rocket range of the vital Da Nang airstrip. One month prior to the NVA attack in the

A Shau, the 3rd Recon Battalion began one of the most unusual operations in the history of the unit—a battalion-size patrol into the high ground of Charlie Ridge.

Maj. Dwain Colby, who planned and participated in the operation, dubbed Taut Bow, described it as being worthy of note because of "its daring nature and the odd command relationships . . . the attachment of an infantry unit to a reconnaissance unit. It was contrary to doctrine, but it was done and should be so reported." The unit consisted of elements of Headquarters and Service Company from the battalion, including the commanding officer, Lieutenant Colonel Van Cleve, and Colby, his S-3. The line units were Alpha Company and Charlie Company. Attached in support were Company A, 1st Battalion, 1st Marines (infantry), artillery liaison and forward observer teams, a forward air-control team, and a detachment from the 3rd Engineer Battalion. Artillery on call included one platoon of 155 howitzers, one platoon of 8-inch guns, and one 155 gun. The mission statement read as follows:

> Mission. Commencing G-Day, 3rd Reconnaissance Battalion conducts reconnaissance of the east end of Happy Valley from previously established patrol base(s) to determine location, identity, strength, movement and armament of VC/PAVN unit; capture prisoners; and locate assembly areas, training and logistics base and infiltration routes.

The concept of operations was that the unit would move from its Camp Reasoner base, at the foot of Hill 327, just below the division command post, to Hill 41, just northeast of the ridge and about four miles north of where Lieutenant Reasoner had been killed. The eastern end of Charlie Ridge rose slowly and was covered primarily by elephant grass, scattered clumps of trees, and occasional boulders. Happy Valley lay just to the north of the ridge. On the map, the east end of the ridge looked like an open boxing glove, the thumb a low ridge extending north into Happy Valley and its smaller companion, Leech Valley. The route of march for the battalion with all attachments approached the ridge from the northeast, passed the valleys, and went up the thumb toward the high ground.

The Reconners were not used to "patrolling" in force, particularly with infantry attached. They received sniper fire between Hill 41 and Charlie Ridge, and the Marine grunts from 1/1 carried heavy gear, made noise, and did not understand the "swift, silent, and deadly" attitude of the teams of Recon who alternated running point for the mixed unit. Tom Renard took part in the operation as a member of Alpha Company. He noted: "At night when we set up, some infantry guys would be yelling or cranking off a few rounds at some shadows. I had no idea if Charlie was around, but the grunts were not helping my nerves at all."

The east end of the ridge that ascended only gradually and was covered primarily by brushlands ended at about the 300-meter level. At that point there was an abrupt 500-meter climb to approximately 2,625 feet above sea level and the rice paddies below. That was a grade of about 36 percent. The jungle began at about the 800-meter elevation, staring down at the Marines like a 100-foot-high green wall. Although the Reconners did not yet realize it, a bamboo wall built by human hands began at the same line. Occasionally the Marines would pass punji stakes and wonder about their usefulness, as the stakes could be easily kicked away. Corporal Thompson ran point up a steep finger that jutted down out of the jungle on the mountains above.

As they moved closer to the wall, Thompson spotted a Vietcong behind a rock ahead of him. The Marine opened fire on the lone enemy, and those behind him dove for cover. In his dive for cover, Lieutenant Wyatt, of Alpha Company, got two punji stakes imbedded in his body and had to be medevacked. The Marines gained new respect for those devices that they had previously questioned.

As quickly as Thompson had taken the VC under fire, a line of enemy soldiers began firing down on the Marines from behind the bamboo wall. In front of the wall an open space had been cleared for the length of the firing positions held by the Vietcong. The wall rose ten to twelve feet, and there appeared to be no place for the Marines to go but straight up the finger into the face of the enemy small arms fire peppering them.

Dale Sare, who had recently joined Charlie Company, described the initial fighting:

> I had scrambled behind a tree, and grenades were detonating nearby. I thought at first that the grenades had stirred up a hornets' nest, and I swatted at the buzzing insects while I tried to return fire. Then a grenade rolled near me and I dove down to a boulder. The blast threw me against the rock and knocked me out temporarily. When I regained consciousness I found that my canteen had been sliced by a piece of shrapnel and the water had poured down my trousers. Then I looked at the tree I had been hiding behind, and it was shattered and almost cut in two by enemy fire. Those insects, I realized, were of 7.62-mm, gas-propelled variety.

Despite the enemy's strong tactical advantage, Pfc. Green charged the wall through Vietcong small arms fire, threw grenades over the barrier, then ran back down for more. He grabbed white phosphorus grenades, then ran back while his buddies laid down covering fire. The WP grenades succeeded in establishing enough smoke to screen the Marines from 3rd Recon as they charged the wall, with Green leading the way again—this time with a machete in his hands to chop down the enemy barricade.

According to Dale Sare, First Lieutenant Carter had taken half the platoon and circled around near Hill 886 to outflank the enemy. Sergeant Kirchoff, from Charlie Company, was killed in the fight, and a corpsman and radio operator were wounded.

Corporal Thompson led a team of Reconners to a position on some boulders and began to deliver small arms fire on the VC, driving them back into the jungle. Tom Renard stated, "We were able to overrun the enemy positions, but it wasn't without its costs. There were five wounded in my platoon."

During Operation Taut Bow, the battalion stayed in the field for about ten days. They contacted enemy forces fourteen times, but after that initial battle at the wall, the contacts were more sporadic and less well organized. In all, two villages; six campsites; seventy-five caves, tunnels, and fighting holes; and eight thousand pounds of rice and grain were located and destroyed.

One typical campsite was located near a stream under tall jungle canopy. The ten thatched huts were large enough to hold about thirty men each, so a total of 300 soldiers could have been accommodated in the one village. One hut contained a barber chair, and it had been recently used. The camp also had two animal pens. A tunnel network shored with timbers connected the huts and led into the surrounding ridges. The huts that appeared to be officers' quarters overlooked the rest of the camp.

The battalion could not accurately determine the number of enemy soldiers located in those mountains as the Vietcong withdrew higher and to the west. However, of interest to the Reconners was a sign fixed over one of the trails leading to the higher ground. In poor Vietnamese (possibly written by members of the Rhade Montagnard tribe) it said, ABSOLUTELY NO VISITORS OR STRANGERS ALLOWED IN THIS AREA. On each side of the sign were what appeared to be guard booths.

Lieutenant Colonel Van Cleve noted in his analysis of the operation: "The people in this area are hostile to non-communist forces. They apparently will not present an opportunity for civic action in any operation. Ethnically they are of the Rhade tribe and apparently do not speak or read much Vietnamese." The operation revealed that the area was being used as a military and political training area and supplied the Da Nang sector with personnel and equipment. The Recon commander also warned that from the eastern side of the area the enemy could launch mortar or rocket attacks on Marine positions, and he recommended that extensive infantry operations be conducted there. His conclusions also were highly critical of the radio communication equipment, stating that use of the PRC-47, -10, -9, and -6 should be discontinued for such operations, but that the PRC-41 and PRC-25 were reliable.

The new M-16 rifle was tested on the operation, and proved to be worthless. Unknown to the Marines, who were to use the rifle and experience its often-fatal results in the early years of the war, the Stoner's AR-15 had been previously tested in Vietnam by Army Special Forces and Air Force Special Operations, both of which approved it. However, before approving its use in the field, the Army Ordnance Corps required changes to the original design because of its deduction that a bullet fired from the rifle in extreme subzero temperatures would wobble. Therefore, it required a change in the degree of barrel twist and also changed the combat-tested IMR powder to a slower burning powder that produced a faster muzzle velocity. However, that also resulted in a significantly increased cyclic rate of fire. The modified rifle was named the M-16. With its altered ammunition, the rifle was sent to Vietnam despite a 1965 Colt Manufacturing Company report that said that no rifles were likely to fail using the original IMR powder, but that half could be expected to fail with the Ordnance Corps–mandated ball powder.*

It is not known what the Marine Corps Command thought of the battalion's report; no infantry operations were conducted into the area. Thereafter, only Recon teams probed the eastern half of Charlie Ridge, but even they did not venture again onto the high ground. It seemed to be accepted at the battalion that Recon had located a large concentration of enemy, and it should now be the job of the infantry to go after them. Reconnaissance teams settled into a pattern of running primarily nine-man teams to check portions of the east end of Happy Valley and the lower section of the ridge.

Except for the month of August 1966, that was the standard patrol

*1. Edgar C. Doleman, Jr. *Tools of War: The Vietnam Experience*. Boston: Boston Publishing Company, 1985, pages 38-40.
2. Maj. Gary Telfer (USMC), Lt. Col. Lane Rogers (USMC), and V. Keith Fleming, Jr. *U.S. Marines in Vietnam: Fighting the North Vietnamese, 1967*. Washington, D.C.: Headquarters, U.S. Marine Corps, History and Museum Division, 1984, pages 229-231.
3. Terry Gander. *Guerrilla Warfare Weapons*. New York: Sterling Publishing Co., Inc., 1990, pages 60-73.

mission for Charlie Ridge—and it continued to be until the 3rd Recon Battalion relocated with the division to more northerly sectors of the country in late 1966. Then the 1st Recon Battalion moved to Camp Reasoner to assume responsibility for the Da Nang TAOR. However, seventeen months after Lieutenant Colonel Van Cleve's warning that the eastern end of the ridge could easily be used for mortar or rocket attacks on the main Marine bases, one such attack in fact occurred. On July 14, 1967, from the mouth of Happy Valley, the enemy launched a 122-mm rocket attack on the main Da Nang air base, setting up the rockets at six different locations with six rocket launchers at each site. Fifty rockets pounded the air base, destroying ten aircraft and damaging forty more. In addition, thirteen barracks and a bomb dump were destroyed.

CHAPTER FIVE

Charlie Ridge and the Last 3rd Recon Patrols

"During my six years in the Corps, I never experienced any unit with more esprit de corps and camaraderie than the 3rd Recon Battalion. I was and still am proud to be Recon. But I will say that one of the most dangerous situations we faced was in mid-1966 when we had a new division commanding general, a new battalion commander, a new battalion executive officer, and a new battalion operations officer at about the same time. I don't care how good they might have been, that was too many critical decision makers not knowing the situation and terrain, and decisions were made that did not take into account past experiences and lessons learned."

—Larry Vetter

By this time, a little more than a year since landing in Vietnam, patrolling had taken on some definite characteristics. As Colonel Collins had stated, for the good majority of situations, the nine-man team proved to be the most workable. The patrol was divided into three teams of three men each. The point team had the best point man and the assistant patrol leader in charge and operated as a threesome. Because this group was most likely to first encounter either evidence of the enemy or the unfriendly unit itself, those three Marines were the key elements of the patrol.

Next came the command-and-communication team, also composed of three men: the patrol leader, the primary radio operator, and the corpsman. The patrol leader was either the platoon commander or the platoon sergeant. From the two-squad platoon (until December 1967, platoons had two squads—after that, three), the platoon commander was always in command of one patrol, while the platoon sergeant commanded the other. This was one difference between Marine Recon battalions and other special units in other services: as long as they were on the rolls and healthy, the officer platoon commander and staff NCO platoon sergeant normally led patrols.

Finally, the rear team acted as the security in case one or both of the first two teams moved forward into dangerous or attack positions, and as rear guard in all situations. It was not unusual for the rear team to be the first to contact the enemy, whether by accident or by intentional pursuit.

In the nighttime defensive positions called harbor sites, each of the three teams would set up separately, but within each team the men would be within touching distance. One man in each team would be awake while the other two slept. One hour out of three each man would be awake, which meant that three members of the patrol would be awake at all times.

After Operation Taut Bow, the battalion's Charlie Company was given a company recon area of responsibility (RAOR) that focused on the eastern sides of Happy Valley and Charlie Ridge. Teams patrolled in sparse terrain and, when on the higher ground, sat in observation posts. On occasion, the teams served as eyes for infantry units conducting sweeps of the Vu Gia River valley south of the ridge. As necessary, the teams were in direct radio communication with the infantry units down to the platoon level, at times being able to direct Marine infantry units toward small teams of Vietcong who were escaping ahead of the infantry or hiding in streams. That was an ideal use of Recon teams, but it was largely dependent on the terrain. However, there was no longer any attempt to patrol into the mountainous end of the ridge where the battalion had probed earlier that year on Taut Bow. In fact, no Marine infantry had ever gone up there except for the one company that had been the 3rd Recon reserve-and-reaction force on the same operation. And none had ventured into Happy Valley.

There had been only occasional contacts with small enemy teams, and the Marines had now established a significant system of fire support by means of artillery and aircraft. Via their radios, the small teams of Marines packed an extraordinary amount of firepower. However, as the months went by attention was diverted north, to the DMZ. Then, in a short span of time in mid-1966, the 3rd Marine Division received a new commanding general, and the Recon Battalion got a new battalion commander, a new executive officer, and a new operations officer.

It was inevitable that the new men would point their fingers at a map and ask, "What's out there?" All the old data found by previous patrols were dated material by then. The first of these new missions of discovery was a Charlie Company patrol to fly into the deep western sector of Happy Valley to an LZ sited in the middle of the open valley.

Lt. Larry Vetter (the author of the present work) had just returned from another mission and so was given the assignment. An overflight of the area confirmed to the lieutenant what he already knew: any LZ in the middle of that valley would be fatal. The terrain was too open, and just to the west was a free bomb zone where the U.S. and South Vietnamese airplanes could unload their ordnance without clearance. There were no friendly villagers, and there were no local South Vietnamese Army outposts. To Vetter, Happy Valley was almost as bad as the A Shau. He returned to the S-3's office and told the new operations officer that the new LZ should be located among the foothills of the Ba Da Mountains, on the northerly side of the valley.

The LZ site was agreed to, and the Reconners were in the air within two days. The LZ turned out to be covered in a ten-foot-high carpet of elephant grass through which the Recon team had to drop—hard—to the ground underneath. For the next four hours the team sweated through the miserable heat and humidity within a sea of dense, razor-sharp grass that extended above their heads. There was no communication with anyone except the birds above. Finally, the team reached a small hill overlooking the valley and set up a harbor site.

As the hilltop was the only place from which they could communicate with supporting units, Vetter chose to violate the standing policy of always being on the move. Over the next two days small Recon teams probed from the hill into the surrounding terrain, but because of the vegetation, the Marines had to climb trees when attempting to watch the valley below them. However, the hill had to remain as their communication base camp. Lieutenant Vetter suspected a problem with artillery because of the distance from the nearest artillery and the intervening hills, so he tried to spot some H&I rounds but could not get them to drop where he wanted. He concluded that the only supporting arms the team had available were from the air wing.

However, the days went by without event until the choppers were on their way to retrieve the patrol. Then, with the birds in the air, the silence of the jungle surrounding the patrol base was shattered by an exchange of automatic weapons fire. Vetter was adjusting the pack he had just saddled on his back when incoming small arms fire began impacting around him. Simultaneously, the radio operator beside him started firing his M-14 from where he stood. As the patrol leader rolled into a firing position he looked up at the radio operator, still standing next to him. The young Marine's eyes were wide in disbelief as he stared into the jungle surrounding the base. Then he quickly told the lieutenant that a VC had been just outside their perimeter. The VC had been uniformed so like the Marines that he had thought it was one of the Recon team until the enemy soldier had opened up with his AK from about thirty feet away. How he had missed everybody with that burst of automatic fire no one understood, but unfortunately for him, his body was now lying over a log where the Marine's bullets had blown him.

The team had to carefully move down the hill for the LZ, but that was the direction from which the enemy had come. Two hundred meters down from the team's base was a saddle between their smaller hill and the steep incline that started the ascent to the heights of Ba Na, the better part of a mile above them. The saddle was covered with elephant grass, but unless they descended to the lower ground, it was the only place where they could clamber aboard helicopters.

As the nine Marines set up on line in the last jungle bush at the edge of the saddle, they watched a squad of enemy soldiers disappear into the jungle opposite them and about 100 meters away. By then, the CH-46s were on station overhead and asking for a smoke grenade to guide them to the team. Vetter advised them that enemy troops were in the area and to pass over at about 1,000 feet to see what happened. They did, and all hell broke loose as automatic fire burst from around the Reconners. The firing came from the lower areas to the west and to the east of the team and from across the saddle in front of them. The choppers were not hit, but when they were advised by Vetter that the birds had attracted heavy fire and that the Recon team had enemy troops close by on three sides, the pilot radioed back that they were low on fuel and needed to return to get more. Vetter advised that the team did not have radio comm with anyone but them and firmly requested that the pilot not leave the area until additional comm was available in the air over the team. The pilot complied, and shortly a light fixed-wing observation aircraft, which the team thought might be one of the new Cessna Birddogs, was in the air above and the choppers were gone.

With the new pilot on station, the team was able to call in fixed-wing fighter-bombers for an aerial show. In all, six fighters dived out of the sky at the direction of the aerial observer (AO) and dropped napalm and fired their cannons into the area surrounding the team. Within thirty minutes, the CH-46s were back and the Recon team leader requested that they try to put the entire team aboard one chopper. He feared that the second bird, coming in for the second half of the Reconners, would get hit by enemy fire, but felt that the first might be able to make it free and clear if the enemy troops were still recovering from the fixed-wing attacks. That was the strategy, and it worked; the Recon team scrambled aboard the chopper and got out of the area as quickly as possible.

The day following the team's return to Camp Reasoner, the S-3 called Lieutenant Vetter again and gave him his team's new mission. It was to land by helicopter on Charlie Ridge between Hills 722 and 886, where the bamboo wall had been encountered on Taut Bow. The two hills had become known to Recon teams as enemy OPs (observation posts). The mission called for the squad-size patrol to move unnoticed to the west and straight into the heart of Apache Country.

Lieutenant Vetter was immediately concerned, and discussed the situation with the new S-3, explaining that patrolling between two known enemy observation points was like setting a grasshopper down in a henhouse. He requested that his patrol route be altered—at least that he be given a chance to find an alternative. Later that day, after a helo overflight of the ridge, he proposed a different route that might give the patrol a chance to get into jungle cover without being detected. It was new terrain to the west that not even the battalion had covered earlier that year.

Vetter suggested that the team be flown down the south side of the ridge to the maximum extent of the protective 8-inch gun artillery fan and land on the edge of the jungle at about the 800-meter (2,625-foot) level. This was a little farther to the west and on the opposite side of the ridge from where the battalion had ended Operation Taut Bow.

To his credit, the new operations officer accepted this suggestion. Vetter then went about preparing the team for the mission. The assistant patrol leader (APL) was normally the squad leader, and he served as the man who really got the team ready; the patrol leader set up coordination with supporting units and determined the best patrol routes. However, they collaborated on all points. In the first year of the war, the company commander was also very involved in the preparation of patrols and in the assignment of patrol missions.

The day of the patrol, Lt. Tim Huff checked into the battalion. He had served in Vietnam in 1964 for a short time with an air delivery platoon, and his jump wings had got him assigned to the Recon Battalion. Upon checking in at battalion, he was told that in five hours he would accompany Lieutenant Vetter's patrol to get some "on-the-job experience." With only a short time until the birds were to come in for the pickup, and with battalion supply out of the necessary "782" gear (packs, canteens, etc.), Vetter grabbed Huff and prepared a hastily drawn alternative plan. Within an hour Huff and Vetter were in "Dog Patch," the roadside collection of huts that was a part of Da Nang's black market. They bought what gear was not available in the battalion supply. Huff did manage to borrow a rifle and pistol from others, and Vetter assigned him to the rear team.

At 1700 hours, August 9, 1966, the patrol was in the air, retracing the flight of the Reasoner patrol, with the exception that near Dai Loc

NEVER WITHOUT HEROES 45

the choppers turned to the starboard and followed the Vu Gia River west toward Laos. Approximately eight miles west of the town, the birds banked again to the starboard and suddenly aimed for a landing zone on the edge of the jungle and about fifty to a hundred meters off a large trail previously noted by Vetter. The Marines didn't like the idea of a trail and refused to use any unless there was no other choice, but in this case, the terrain dictated the LZ.

The mission order for the patrol stated: "Conduct reconnaissance patrols and establish OP sites in the area outlined on the patrol overlay to determine the extent of enemy activity in assigned area and maintain surveillance of the Song [river] Vu Gia Valley in support of the 2nd Battalion, 3rd Marines." Vetter knew that there could be no observing the valley below once the team moved into the jungle toward the higher ground. He preferred to land close to dusk and move into difficult terrain for the night because unless the team landed in the middle of enemy troops, it would be difficult for the VC to locate in the ravines with only an hour or so of light left. However, the actual time of the flight was dictated more by the availability of helicopters, and the Marine Corps was always short of that vital means of transport.

With the sun slowly lowering toward Laos, the patrol anxiously watched the approaching ridge, and the choppers, like ponderous slow-moving prehistoric monsters, flew the last few thousand meters and dropped down on a flat, grassy shelf near the jungle. The Marines jumped and ran quickly away from the trail and into terrain that was very rough, characterized by interwoven "just-a-minute" vines, steep ravines, streambeds not shown on the map, and a jungle canopy a hundred feet in height. Before dusk, and just inside the jungle, the unit found a harbor site and planned on-call artillery strikes around their position. Map reading after dark was done using a red-lensed flashlight with the patrol leader completely covered by a poncho.

The first night they were close to the edge of the jungle, and their position did offer limited views of the lower hillsides. "Right below us we could see, not flashlights, but some kind of lights, and we could hear people walking and talking," said Pfc. Benny Duron, the point man. "They were walking right below us, and we didn't know what we were going to do. We just laid there and didn't move. We called in artillery, and they put out their lights."

"I remember that Vetter went under his poncho with his flashlight and plotted and called the artillery mission," Tim Huff added.

"The VC passed by us in the bush no more than fifty meters below us, and the lights were unusual—more like fluorescent lamps," Duron said.

Throughout the night, the patrol noted noises different from their past experience. It was hard to tell what they all were; most were un-doubtedly the calls of animals that the Marines had not encountered before, but Huff added, "Some of the sounds were like machines working in the distance. The noises floated down through the draws and hills above us." No one slept well, and Huff said, "This was my first patrol, and I don't think I slept all night. I was scared to death—there were noises like people building things."

The next day the patrol continued to the north, but the team couldn't go a hundred meters without finding campgrounds cleared out of little areas of jungle—just old fire beds and training areas. Duron said, "Everywhere we turned there was evidence that others had been in that spot not long ago." The team was very careful not to make noise, since the trail that the VC had used the previous night roughly paralleled their position not too far away. However, the patrol leader noted that even though they were not using the trail, it seemed that they were in well-traveled terrain. In fact, he noted that the jungle reminded him of the officer training grounds around Quantico, Virginia. Although he had previously felt that there was a battalion of enemy forces in the mountains of the ridge, he now altered his estimate to two battalions—one of permanent personnel, and another that was training, on R & R, or just in transit.

Late in the morning, the Marines had to cross a ravine by carefully walking on a log that spanned the deep chasm, and shortly thereafter the point signaled back to Vetter that they were at a trail. Everybody crouched low as the patrol leader crawled forward to the point and saw a ten-foot-wide hard-packed earthen path, obviously well used. He brought the patrol up on line about ten feet off the trail, hiding and watching from the bush.

Only a few minutes went by before two women carrying hundred-pound sacks of rice passed by, casually talking. Vetter decided to fol-low them up the trail. He positioned the rear team with Huff to cover the trail behind them before he had the point team move onto the pathway about 30 meters behind the women, who had now disap-peared into the jungle ahead. He then moved his command team be-hind the point. Benny Duron, at point, remembers, "We followed, uphill, for about thirty to fifty meters when the trail turned sharply to the right. Then I saw about five VC with rifles in an open area. They were just around the bend in the trail and hadn't seen us. I turned around and signaled back to the lieutenant."

"Benny signaled me that there were VC ahead of us in a static po-sition on or near the trail," Vetter continued. "He had seen five, but it sounded like more were nearby. They had weapons. I crawled up be-side the point and then a little more. When I was ready to carefully part the jungle brush to look at these enemy soldiers not more than fifteen or so meters away, somebody grabbed my leg and shook it."

Focusing on the enemy just above him, the lieutenant almost jumped out of his combat utilities when his leg was grabbed. It was Huff, who had quietly scrambled up from the rear to advise Vetter that they could hear Vietnamese coming up the trail from down below the team.

Before even God got that piece of news, the lieutenant looked up and saw one of the VC from above walking along the trail across his front. In three steps the VC would be turning the corner and would be immediately facing the Marines. Vetter signaled his team into the jungle undergrowth, and cringed as he said, "We sounded like a herd of elephants, and I figured that we were going to be dead meat."

The noise must not have bothered the Vietcong soldier, for with his weapon slung casually over his shoulder, he turned the corner and walked right into Benny Duron, Corporal Morrow, who was the point team leader, and the two lieutenants.

Duron said, "I got behind a tree and Morrow was standing behind me. When that VC got almost on top of me, I was gonna grab him. But when I was face-to-face with him Morrow shot him. I remember that he had a backpack on. Then I opened up on the area where the other VC had been. It was through the bush, and I couldn't see them, but I knew about where they were."

"Everybody up at the front spent a magazine of twenty rounds each," Vetter added, "blasting the hell out of that place, and then my concern was to get us back down to the rear team and out of the area. I don't know if we hit any of the other VC ahead of us, and we didn't hang around to take a head count because I was worried what was coming up the trail behind us."

Before the shooting started, Benny Duron had said that he also heard the Vietnamese down below the team. However, the point and command teams quickly covered the short distance to the rear team, and together they began to move to the south and away from the two groups of enemy. About a quarter of a mile through the jungle, the patrol leader set the team in boulders and had his radio operator call the battalion to let them know what was up and to call for the artillery again. When the tape antenna proved useless, the longer whip antenna was screwed onto the PRC-25 and did the job. A fire mission was given, and after a ten-minute wait a forty-seven-round barrage was under way. Under the cover of the artillery and a rainstorm that quickly deluged the jungle, the team continued the mission, but very carefully now. Their direction was back toward the original landing zone.

Vetter felt that with the enemy alerted to their presence, the opportunity for the team to reach the higher levels of the ridge from its location had changed from difficult to impossible. He continued to move his Marines away from what he expected were teams of enemy soldiers searching for them.

At one point along their route, Duron noted Ho Chi Minh sandal prints crossing the patrol's direction of travel, but they were going east, and the patrol continued through the jungle, watchfully, to the south. Vetter decided to call for an extraction and try to return on another day from a different direction. However, no LZ could be reached that evening, so the team harbored in the jungle one more night.

The next morning, at 0730, the birds were out to get them, and the team of Reconners was safely brought back to Camp Reasoner.

After debriefing, they were informed that in a few days they would be inserted at a location about 1,500 meters east of the first patrol route. The debriefer, S.Sgt. Doug Phelps, the battalion S-2, commented about the new mission: "[It's an] area long suspected to be a sanctuary for enemy forces. Possibly used as storage, production, training, and base camp for VC forces operating throughout this area." Staff Sergeant Phelps was one of the old hands in the command operations center of the battalion and knew what was likely the situation in those mountains from having debriefed many patrols.

On August 13, at 1700 hours, the patrol was retracing its flight of a few days earlier. The landing zone this time was in a protected little three-sided bowl. The mountains were to the north, and a small rise with a tree line covered their east and south. Again they were at about the 800-meter level when they jumped off the choppers into that bit of open, short-grass, bottom-of-the-bowl landing zone. Vetter had given instructions that they were to move out quickly and head for the jungle about 50 meters to the north, then hide on the slope of a steep ravine throughout the night. Whereas the previous patrol had been farther away from the enemy OPs on Hills 886 and 722, this one would be only one klick—1,000 meters—west of the two hills and about 1,200 meters south of Hill 1078, also an area of concern, directly to the north of the patrol.

That night the Marines tried to rest on the side of a ravine that was so steep the men had to use trees as braces to keep themselves from sliding to the bottom. Vetter again went under his poncho to plot on-call artillery fires around their harbor site in case they were needed during the night. Their strategy, however, had been to place themselves in the most difficult terrain possible to keep the enemy from finding them during the night, when they were the most vulnerable.

Just above them, the smaller hilltop was inside the edge of the jungle. The map indicated that the other side of the hill was a 100-meter decline on about a 30 percent grade to a creek. From there it was a sharp rise of 378 meters to the top of Hill 1078. Once atop 1078, the patrol would be near Hill 1025 and two klicks from the western extent of Operation Taut Bow.

After a short bit of early-morning tin can ration, which Vetter felt might be the last food they had that day, the patrol slowly climbed the 50 meters to the top of the knob. They were less than that distance inside the edge of the jungle. At the top, their path and a trail coincided. There was no choice but to follow it. To stay off the trail would mean dropping down into the thickets of the ravine, where they'd be making enough noise to wake the comatose. So Benny Duron carefully led the column of eight Marines and one corpsman up and then down the hill. About 20 meters down the other side, they encountered a hootch on the left side of the trail. After quietly watching for a few minutes, the team checked it and found that it apparently had been used for rice storage, but not much was left.

The trail then brought them down to near the bottom, overlooking the creek. They peered out from the jungle bush into the south side of an enemy training camp. Beside the trail where Benny crouched was a fighting hole. In front was a flat shelf, and on the right of it was a large hut. To the left in the small jungle clearing was an almost life-size mock-up of a 105-mm howitzer. Trying to be certain that no one was around, the team moved into the complex, and Vetter began to report back by radio what they were finding.

The large hut had bamboo bunks and rifle racks with nameplates. On both ends of the hut were underground shelters. To the left side, near the "105," were a latrine and a chicken coop. There were benches and other fighting holes and one punji pit. Beside a large boulder on the northern end of the flat piece of ground, about 20 meters away, was another and larger underground shelter. From the boulder, the path split into two branches, one on either side of the rock, and continued on down to the creek. The trail down had steps made from ammo boxes and whitewashed posts with interconnecting ropes for handholds. Below, a trail complex paralleled the stream, where six more huts were located. Each of the huts was about fifteen by thirty feet and could sleep twenty to thirty men. The camp was very similar to the one found during Taut Bow.

The barrel of the 105-mm howitzer mock-up was a piece of large-diameter bamboo about five feet long. It was mounted on rubber tires and was built with workable elevating and traversing mechanisms. There was a three- to four-foot-long train behind the "gun" for towing.

While Vetter and the rest of the patrol were checking the area where the first hut and the "105" training aid were located, Pfc. Duron, L.Cpl. "Greg" Gregorich, and the point team leader, Corporal Morrow, were stationed forward near the boulder to watch the creek, which was only about 20 meters downhill.

Within minutes, the Marines heard sounds of a large engine about 1,000 meters to the west, and then Duron saw VC coming along the stream from the east. He stated:

> What happened was that they were coming down the trail—we heard them—they were talking. Then we saw 'em, but they hadn't seen us yet. They didn't look like any rookies. Some were in black PJs and others were in green uniforms, and all had weapons. There were ten to fifteen, maybe more were coming—it was hard to tell for sure. Then suddenly the man in the front stopped and motioned for those behind to stop, and they stood there for a moment. It was like they were listening and smelling for us.

Huff went to the boulder, but on the west side of it discovered a number of uniformed enemy coming at the team from that direction. "I saw a column of enemy soldiers coming from the west on the trail with their weapons at the ready," Huff said. "It was like they already knew we were there."

Then Duron said that the enemy to the east scattered and went for cover. Corporal Morrow had gone to tell Vetter, and as he got to him, the lieutenant told him he already knew what was up and that the corporal should get his team and move out—back up to the top of the hill and into a better position.

Duron, still not aware of the enemy unit to the west, saw the VC begin to circle the team up the ravine to their east. Then Gregorich looked around and saw that the patrol had started moving back up the hill. Corporal Morrow had started back for his men, but had been mistakenly given the word that Duron and Gregorich had already gone up. Thinking that they had left their positions by the boulder and gone with the rest of the team, he turned to go up the hill himself.

Vetter now thought that he was the last to leave and was quickly moving around the corner of the hut to follow his team. He could hear the VC moving up the ravines on both sides, from the east and west.

At that point, Duron said to Gregorich, "Let's go." As they jumped to run, they were hit by machine gun fire. "I remember that Greg was hit, and I jumped into a foxhole," Duron said. "Several rounds had hit me in the back, but my pack stopped all of them. Then Greg said, 'I'm hit.' Then they must have started to throw grenades because there were explosions around us. Then we jumped to run again, and that's when I saw that Greg had his bicep blown out by that first round."

Tim Huff said:

When the firing started, I was almost across that open shelf near the 105 mock-up not far from Vetter, and I hit the dirt with bullets flying all around me. I looked back to the west and saw this enemy in uniform with a light machine gun with a bipod. Then he disappeared and I heard him changing magazines. I jumped up to run again. That guy was only about thirty feet from me and had come up around one side of that boulder. I don't know what happened with him after that because I was up and trying to catch up with the rest of the team. He must have rejoined his main unit.

The VC soldier was on the other side of the boulder from Vetter and out of his sight. The patrol leader then shoved off after Huff to bring up what he thought was the rear of the team. What he didn't know was that Gregorich and Duron had not yet gotten out. Another burst of machine gun fire shattered the jungle just behind Vetter, and he leaped across the clearing at the foot of the incline and for a brief few seconds watched the rear from behind the jungle undergrowth before he jumped up again to make an uphill sprint. About four strides uphill, he pulled himself behind a tree and aimed his M-14 to cover the rear of the team. It was then that he saw the two Marines running past the hut toward him. Duron was helping the wounded Gregorich. As Vetter listened to the enemy units shouting in Vietnamese and crashing along the nearby slopes to get around them on both sides, he called the corpsman, Doc Pat (Kirkpatrick), back down to wrap Gregorich's arm. He then sent Duron on to the point and called in an artillery fire mission on the map coordinates where he stood. He said, "I don't remember who the radio operator was, but we are all alive today in part because, knowing that I would need to call in artillery, that Marine found me and he then stayed tight with me throughout the next two hours, regardless of the danger."

Vetter knew that the supporting artillery was 8-inch guns, and this situation was totally different from the patrol into Happy Valley. The 8-inch guns were the most accurate the Marine Corps had for lobbing rounds high and bringing them down literally on a pinpoint, and the team was within range. But the point the patrol leader was aiming for was where he, Doc, Gregorich, and the radioman were standing.

Doc stuffed gauze into the hole in Gregorich's arm and wrapped it. As Doc finished, Vetter completed calling for the artillery fire mission, but he worried that they were falling too far behind the rest of the patrol. He also knew they were in a footrace with the VC for the top of the hill. The enemy was now farther uphill on either side in the ravines. They were very close on both sides and could still be heard crashing through the thickets and shouting commands. But the VC had the rougher go of it.

As he was calling for artillery, Vetter planned in his mind to get across the top of the hill, out into the elephant grass, and to the military crest* of the hill, where he had noticed clumps of boulders when they were landing the previous evening. Those rocks would be protection against both the enemy and the 8-inch guns, which would be "on the way" in barely minutes. He felt that if there were to be a last stand, that would have to be the place. But he prayed that the big guns would be able to hold off the enemy until some choppers reached them in the bowl below the boulders, because a recon team's staying in contact with superior enemy forces was, as one of his Marines was fond of saying, like being dealt aces and eights, the dead man's hand.

Above them, Huff and Duron had reached the lead and were alternating smashing through the six-foot-tall, razor-sharp grass. The point man carried his rifle in both hands, swinging it to crush a pathway through the thicket. Vetter and the other three had outraced the VC and rejoined the patrol as the point drove his rifle into a large bees' nest hidden in the tall grass. In a second, Duron was covered with huge, hairy, brown bees, the likes of which the Marines had never seen before. Huff screamed at Duron to dive and roll downhill, but Benny was already doing exactly that. They were quickly followed by the rest of the patrol. Fortunately, a downhill tumble of about 30 meters got them away from the bees and just below the boulders Vetter had wanted to reach. Huff said that just after they hit the bees, he also saw the lead element of the VC unit coming out of the jungle to their front. Duron confirmed that.

Knowing that the artillery was going to be landing somewhere near them at any second, Vetter—the radio operator managing to stay right with him—yelled at everyone to get into the boulders. Just as they scrambled among rocks four to eight feet in girth, a sound like semi trucks thundered overhead. Then the air rolled with explosions, the ground heaved, and the Marines hung on to the boulders as the 8-inch shells crashed and tore through the top of the ridgeline above them, not 100 feet away. The patrol leader called for repeated fire missions as the men stayed tucked under the rocks and shell fragments landed

---

*The highest defensible point on an elevation from which all territory below it may be observed, but just below the topographical crest.

in the three-foot-tall grass around them. Only the 8-inchers could do that with the accuracy the Marines desperately needed.

Below them about 50 meters was the landing zone they'd used the day before, and Vetter had already called for an emergency extraction. The helicopters were warming up their engines about fifteen miles away at the Marble Mountain airstrip, near China Beach.

However, adjacent to the LZ, immediately on its lower side, a low, fifteen-foot ridge covered by a tree line partially circled the proposed landing zone, and there Huff and Duron now spotted fifteen more enemy soldiers. They yelled up to Vetter and his radio operator, who were above the others, separated by about twenty feet.

Vetter said:

At this point something very strange happened. We were way the hell out of range of our mortars, being about twelve thousand meters west of Dai Loc. Normally, they were no closer than somewhere around there, or even farther toward the east, but not to the west where we were. But the call sign for Marine 4.2-inch mortars came up on the radio net and they asked if they could fire for us. I said, "Hell, yes!" and gave them the coordinates of those VC in the tree line just below. White phosphorus was shot out for adjustment first. I couldn't believe they landed exactly on target, and I called for a fire for effect. Now we had 8-inch shells landing around our topside and 4.2-inch mortars within a hundred meters below us. It was one hell of a show, but I don't know whether the team was more afraid of the VC or of me calling artillery. Shell fragments continued to land around us. We stayed tight with those boulders. Later, I tried to find those Marines with the mortars to find out where the hell they had been. I was never able to find out who it was or where they were. No one knew of any friendly mortars that had been out that far. But I took the gift, whoever they were.

It took about two hours from the time when the patrol initially sighted the VC until the helicopters arrived to attempt the rescue. Huff remembers:

We were laying down below Vetter and his radio operator in a different set of boulders, and Benny was with us there. There was an incline down about fifty or so meters, covered by short grass maybe two to three feet tall, and then there was this three-sided cup where the choppers were to come to try to get us. But on the south side of the cup was a piece of higher ground with a tree line, and that's where the new bunch of VC had appeared. In spite of the mortar fire on those trees, we were worried about going into the open for the choppers. Enemy soldiers had been noted in the tree line that would be overlooking our birds when they landed. I remembered asking Greg if he needed some morphine for the pain. He was bleeding like a stuck pig but he said he didn't want anything that would make him less able to do things on his own to get out of there.

When the choppers were on station above the patrol, just out of the path of the incoming artillery, Vetter decided to call off the supporting fire, call in the birds, and scoot downhill in the low grass to the landing zone. The team, some sliding on their butts, quickly covered the downhill and popped smoke grenades. The first two were duds, and Huff went off to the right as they faced west and threw a third. It exploded, and as the CH-46 came in using that smoke as a guide, Huey gunships were strafing the enemy in the tree lines around them.

Vetter had positioned himself on one knee to wave the team into the rear entry of the 46, and was expecting that they would be shot at on the way in, but with all the chopper noise and gunship fire, he couldn't hear any enemy fire. Finally, thinking that the last Marine had come aboard, Vetter ran in. However, Huff wasn't with them.

Tim said:

> I was still off to the right and started to run to the rear of the chopper. But falling in potholes slowed me up. I realized that the damn bird might take off without me. So I ran across the nose of the chopper, waving at the pilot to make sure he knew that I was still coming. Then I continued running down the side and into the back hatch. I thought that I was going to be shot into a piece of Swiss cheese while running alongside of the chopper. But I couldn't hear any rounds being fired by the VC. Maybe between the artillery, the Hueys, and the bees they had given up.

The choppers took off and safely got out of the area. On the way back, they dropped Gregorich off at Charlie Med, about a quarter of a mile down the road from Camp Reasoner. He was later medevacked out of country. The patrol then was taken to LZ Finch, at the battalion headquarters. Unfortunately, it was a somewhat hostile reception—hostile because the new battalion executive officer felt that the team should have stayed and fought.

Throughout the debriefing, it was repeatedly noted that the enemy had established major training, storage, and bivouac areas throughout those high jungles. The debriefer, Staff Sergeant Phelps, wrote, "Concur with the patrol leader; area long suspected of harboring enemy force." The conclusion was: "area is being utilized by enemy forces of undetermined size as a training, storage, and bivouac site."

Phelps recommended that "this area be exploited by infantry units immediately."

As happened after Taut Bow, no action was taken on that recommendation. However, orders quickly came to send in a smaller, four-man team. It was thought that the smaller team could evade detection. That team's assigned landing zone was between the previously mentioned Hills 886 and 722. It was then to patrol in the direction of the hostile contacts that the two previous patrols had made 1,000 to 3,000 meters to their west.

Vetter remembers:

> I was still ticked off about the encounter with ExO, and the insinuations he made about us not standing and shooting it out with the enemy hurt. Maybe because of my emotions at the time, I didn't pay close attention to what was happening with the next patrol. But with the first report of them sighting VC shortly after they landed, I checked in to the COC and found out that they had been landed between 722 and 886, exactly where I hadn't wanted to go initially. It is to the credit of those Marines that they managed to avoid the enemy for two more days.

The patrol did not go far before noting signs of enemy activity, primarily between Hills 886 and 1078. The patrol report stated: "Patrol found huts, sniper positions, (1) large trail and numerous small trails . . . marks carved into trees and found one possible animal snare. Voices were heard several times. . . . "

On August 18, at 1345 hours, the patrol was attacked by Vietcong dressed in "striped, camouflage utilities and camouflage soft covers . . . armed with automatic weapons . . . " The patrol returned fire, and the VC broke contact. However, the Marine radio operator, Edward Rykosky, was dead, his radio was destroyed, and the corpsman was shot through the back.

G.Sgt. E. L. Myers and Sgt. Peter "Ski" Gorczewski, the two remaining healthy members of the team, fought off the enemy attack and then tried to get their wounded corpsman and the body of their dead radio operator out of the jungle. But the body had to be left; the M-14s belonging to the radioman and corpsman were dismantled and effectively destroyed. The two Marines continued to keep ahead of enemy soldiers, who were searching the bush for them, and carried the corpsman to the east back toward the LZ, hoping that the battalion had sent helicopters to the rescue when radio contact was lost. This was the established procedure, and they followed it.

In fact, the choppers were sent, but without radio contact the pilots were not willing to set down. The three members of the team had reached the LZ and popped smoke grenades, but the pilots spotted what they felt were Vietcong, thought the situation was an ambush-in-waiting, and didn't land. In fact, enemy soldiers might have been in the area and spotted by the pilots, but the three Reconners were also in the bush.

Myers and "Ski" then made the long journey out of the mountains carrying with them their corpsman, who lived and was medevacked from the country later. Meantime, the battalion had changed its tactics and sent Capt. Don Gardner, Charlie Company's commander, with a twenty-man reaction force from the company, to land at the LZ and find the missing team.

The time it took for the reaction force to land in the mountains also gave Myers and "Ski" the time to reach friendly forces in the Vu Gia River valley, below. At this point, however, the 2nd Battalion, 3rd Marines ("2/3"), was ordered to send up a two-company reaction force to assist the recon unit under Captain Gardner's command. Thus began Operation Allegheny. The two Recon Marines, Myers and "Ski," immediately volunteered to return to the mountains to help their friends and find the body of the radioman they had left behind, and they were sent. They weren't the only ones to return. Benny Duron and others from the previous patrols went back as well.

Operation Allegheny was not a great experience for Recon. The method of operation used by 2/3 was for the two companies of infantry each to use a five-man Recon team as point and guide in its attempt to penetrate the jungle. But the terrain was so difficult that the companies had to stay in long columns, which meant that the Recon team in the lead was exposed, without infantry support to either flank. They were in mountainous terrain with draws and steep climbs, covered by 100-foot-tall triple-canopy jungle. One infantry platoon and the other ten-man Recon group were left to provide protection for the LZ.

Benny Duron, together with four Recon Marines, including Captain Gardner, was running point for one company, and L.Cpl. David Burkhardt, with another four Reconners, ran point for the other. Burkhardt said: "The sniper fire was so continuous that we had to call up the grunts. They actually used machine gun fire to tear up the trees. The VC snipers had hollowed out positions inside the trees and sometimes survived the firing at them because the trees were so big." Captain Gardner, who years later retired as a Major General, was out front with the Reconnors checking tunnels and enemy positions.

Duron said:

Sometimes they [the snipers] let us go by, and then they'd hit the grunts. The area that we went into on Allegheny was different from the one on the patrol with Lieutenant Vetter. The first VC complex we went into on the earlier patrol was more of a training base. This one now was more like a regular village. There were pots and pans with food still in them and chickens running around, and no fighting positions. But when we reported what was ahead to the grunts, they refused to go in and told us to move into the village. I looked at Captain Gardner, and he said to go on, and he was with us. There was like a ravine where this place was, and a stream went through the village. When we were down there is when we got hit. All the Recon with me were wounded, but Lance Corporal Knight, regardless of his wound, took some grunts around to the side to try to outflank the VC.

After Duron was wounded, he was medevacked. In total, nine of the first ten from Recon who went forward running point for the grunts were wounded in those first three days. That lucky tenth man was David Burkhardt. The body of the radioman was never found, and Burkhardt said, "We heard that a VC was later captured at the foot of Charlie Ridge, and he said that they had found the body of the radioman and had taken it away."

However, after the first three days, Lieutenant Vetter, who had stayed back with the balance of the company at Camp Reasoner, could no longer sit still. He requested permission of the battalion commander to go back into the mountains and help. He stated:

I found Lieutenant Colonel Wilder,* the battalion commander, and told him that Charlie Company was running ninety percent casualties out there, and I had to go back up there to send the wounded back, including Captain Gardner. Then I had to try to rework things because at this rate there wouldn't be a Charlie Company left. He let me go. I took one corporal, Chuck Rudd, with me. We got a hop down to Hill 55, which was the battalion headquarters for 2/3, and went up into the mountains with another company of infantry that they were sending.

Once back on the ridge, Vetter went about finding the rest of the Recon wounded and sent them back. The first stop was the base at the LZ. There he found Corporal Sare, who was back up in the high ground of Charlie Ridge for the first time since Operation Taut Bow.

---

*Gary Wilder was promoted to Lieutenant Colonel shortly after taking command of the battalion.

Dale took point, and the last of the Reconners pushed into the jungle to find their buddies who had been wounded. Dale found Gunnery Sergeant Myers lying in the trail with five bullet holes in one arm. He was grinning with a big cigar in his mouth. Captain Gardner was also wounded, and in addition had a fly-infested leech bite on one leg. Later, he had to go through frostbite therapy to kill the worms crawling around under the skin. For his actions during Operation Allegheny, Captain Gardner was awarded the Silver Star, but first he had to be helped out of the jungle on Sare's shoulders.

For the balance of that fourth day of the operation, Vetter found out firsthand how the Recon team was being used. He had taken forward the ten Recon Marines who had been at the LZ and continued the same operational maneuvers: Reconners leading each infantry company. Vetter said:

> I spent most of that day eating dirt with bullets snapping bush around me. It wasn't S.O.P [standard operating procedure] to see Recon trying to run point for a long column of infantry. That was just not what we were made to do. That evening I found the infantry battalion commander and explained that it was my recommendation that Recon be regrouped in its entirety to his CP; that the way things were operating was not good, and that he alone should assign missions for us out of his CP—not the company commanders using us as point. I know that Doc Kirkpatrick, who was back up there with us, just about got himself in trouble telling a company commander that he didn't know what he was doing.

Sare added, "I remember Lieutenant Vetter arguing with the grunts that running point for them was not the way for Recon to be used." To his surprise, Vetter found the battalion commander finally agreeing. Then, for the next week, the Recon team ran special patrols for the battalion commander. When they were asked to lead a grunt unit through the bush, across creeks, and up hills—off the trails—they did it. But as soon as the infantry commander said he wanted to use a trail, Vetter said, "I called the first platoon of infantry forward. If they wanted to follow a trail, there was no need for us to be used as the guides."

On one occasion, Vetter remembered:

> We led an infantry platoon through the jungle to the west, across a creek, and then back in a circle toward the battalion command post. Recon was in the lead and spotted two VC between us and the command post, setting up to snipe at the battalion. Immediately, we took

them under fire, killing one, with the other escaping. When we got back and reported, I remember the battalion CO talking with his ops officer and deciding to report that thirteen VC were confirmed KIA by that patrol, not just the one that there had been. I'll never forget how surprised I was when that one VC KIA turned into thirteen in the official report. That was my first experience with the "body count" mentality.

On the eighth day of the operation, the battalion CO called the Recon team leader to his position and asked his opinion of the situation. Vetter said, "Sir, there is a battalion or two of enemy soldiers in these hills above us. They outnumber us. The terrain is so damn difficult that we can't get up there except in a long column. If you aren't going to have any more Marines up here than you've got, I'd recommend that you step back down the hill and blow the hell out of this place with B-52s." Lieutenant Vetter went back to his team and waited. The next orders were that the battalion would leave the mountains and sweep back down the Vu Gia River valley from the west toward Dai Loc and Hill 55, eight to ten miles off in the distance. While the infantry was sweeping down the valley, Recon would be used to screen the battalion's flank by staying in the lower foothills between them and the mountains. The three infantry companies and twelve Reconners were going to leave Charlie Ridge to the Charlie.

Operation Allegheny's last two days saw Recon moving through the elephant grass in the foothills about 1,000 to 2,000 meters to the left of the three infantry companies as they marched east. Worried that the VC would be coming down out of the mountains above them, and worried that their own infantry would sight their team and mistake them for VC, the Recon patrol moved, hid, and moved again with an eye cocked in both directions. They did their jobs, and no more casualties were taken.

The debriefer for Gunny Myers's patrol was again Doug Phelps, but Second Lieutenant Phelps. A long 3rd Recon Battalion history on Charlie Ridge was coming to a close with Phelps's comments: "[Because of] the observations made by this patrol in association with the patrol report of 14 August noting the VC training camp, and the patrol report of 16 August of the enemy [observation post near Hill 722], it is felt that the entire area of hill complexes 886, 1025, 1078, 722, and 819 contain VC/NVA concentrations of undetermined size. Possibly the major base camp for this [the Da Nang] area."

Because of the casualties suffered on Allegheny, a completely new platoon was created, commanded by a new "mustang" lieutenant, Jerry Siler. Sgt. Conrad Giacalone was the platoon sergeant, and

Corporals Morrow and Sare were the squad leaders. They were to be shipped to Okinawa to train for sixty days. Unfortunately, the need in Vietnam was so great that they would spend only twenty days on Okinawa before boarding the LPH *Iwo Jima* and steaming back to Vietnam.

The 3rd Recon Battalion had already begun to phase out of the Da Nang area to the north, where the North Vietnamese were steadily coming across the DMZ. Lieutenant Huff had left for Dong Ha and the battle zone there following his ojt patrols on Charlie Ridge with Vetter. He was medevacked home in March 1967, after trying to fulfill a mission that was personally assigned by Gen. Lewis Walt. Benny Duron was also to go north after Operation Allegheny, and would stay until he rotated home in February 1967. Lieutenant Vetter stayed with the last of the 3rd Recon Battalion in the Da Nang–An Hoa area, although he did not again patrol on Charlie Ridge. He stayed until the first of December, and then he also went north to Dong Ha for a short time before he returned home for Christmas. Chuck Rudd extended twice and didn't get his orders for home until December 1967.

The 1st Recon Battalion relocated from Chu Lai to Da Nang in stages. So for a while Camp Reasoner was home to both the rear elements of 3rd Recon and the advance portion of 1st Recon.

For a long time the Marines from 3rd Recon wanted to know just what really was on the top of Charlie Ridge. On Lieutenant Vetter's second tour of duty to Vietnam, in 1969, he was a captain and commanded Alpha Company, 1st Battalion, 26th Marines. Although 1/26 was not sent to Charlie Ridge, the 3rd Battalion, 26th Marines, and two battalions of the 7th Marines did attack into the depths of Charlie Ridge's high ground during Operation Oklahoma Hills, after four years of war the first major infantry operation to attempt to root out the enemy.

Vetter watched with interest. The battles for the high ground identified base camps for two North Vietnamese regiments, the 141st and the 31st, and a medical complex. Hill 1025, specifically noted by Recon in 1966 as some type of training/base complex, was found by the 2nd Battalion, 7th Marines, to be the base camp for the 31st NVA Regiment. The camp contained over two hundred buildings.

The body count mentality that Vetter had noted on Operation Allegheny resulted from the American high command's need to establish a quantifiable method of determining the progress of the war. However, measuring the war's progress was not only compounded by misreporting, but also made more difficult by the fact that the enemy better maximized the number of people that could be placed in infantry units.

The VC/NVA had a ratio of close to one support soldier to one combat soldier, far better than our ratio. In January 1963, throughout South Vietnam, the guerrilla army had an estimated 23,000 men in regular and regional units in twenty-five battalions; unit strengths ranged from 150 to 300 men. Two years later, the total enemy manpower had more than doubled. In all of South Vietnam, the Vietcong had been trained by January 1965 into seventy-three battalions—uniformed and consisting of up to 600 to 700 men in each. Sixty-six of these battalions were infantry, and the balance were in heavy weapons and antiaircraft units, in all 56,000 men. They were backed by an estimated 40,000 in base area units that provided training, supply, medical, and other support services.

At the end of 1966, two years later, there was almost the exact same number of Marines stationed in I Corps (considering all units, infantry and supporting personnel); however, there were only twenty-two Marine infantry battalions. Even though they were lighter and smaller units, the VC had organized and trained sixty-six infantry battalions from approximately the same total personnel; this is indicative of how the enemy units were able to field three ground combat units to each American using the same total number of troops.

However, within I Corps, the twenty-two Marine infantry battalions were required to guard bases, provide support to the villages, and hunt down main force enemy units in the hills and outlying areas. The straight-line length of I Corps was approximately 340 miles. In this one region, it is estimated that by the end of 1966 there were eleven battalions and seven independent companies of Vietcong, and twenty battalions of the People's Army of Vietnam (PAVN or NVA). The enemy's combat battalions and independent companies in this one zone totaled approximately 24,000 soldiers, not including the support units and local forces/village workers. In addition, two NVA divisions were crossing the borders into South Vietnam. The 325th was near the A Shau, and the 324B was near the DMZ. Each added nine battalions and about 8,000 troops.

Even though it could be said that there were superior numbers of Marines in I Corps, when one counts only the maneuver battalions, the Marines were outnumbered by approximately thirty-three battalions to twenty-two, and that excludes the NVA division across the border. Regardless of the Marine Corps' superior firepower, when those Marine battalions that were used to guard the main base areas are eliminated from the count, the disparity between the two forces is weighted further in favor of the combined VC/NVA. Then note the ability of the enemy to concentrate his forces when and where he wanted, moving clandestinely through rural areas that were primarily friendly to him, and one can quickly determine the difficulties facing the Marines in Vietnam in 1966.

However, unknown to the Marines in Vietnam, a serious dispute was raging between the Army and Marine high commands. The Army command felt that the primary focus of American power should be directed at the increasing numbers of main force units appearing within South Vietnam, and that the job of winning the "hearts and minds" of the people should primarily belong to the South Vietnamese themselves. On the opposite side of the argument, Marine Corps Generals Walt, Krulak, and Green argued that if the American units could provide the necessary security for the villages, they could sever the enemy command from what had been its main source of strength: population centers in the lowlands. In addition, the Marine command did not believe that the NVA were coming across the border in the numbers necessary to cause very great concern, and if they did, the command believed American power could quickly take care of the intrusions. Both theories were right in part—but in other concerns, each was wrong.

Regardless, in an attempt to determine enemy strength, the 3rd Recon Battalion was sent to find the NVA 324B division near the border with North Vietnam in 1966.

CHAPTER SIX

Born in the North
to Die in the South

Tattooed on their arms and incorporated into the songs of a genera-
tion of North Vietnamese army-age young men were the words "Born
in the North to die in the South." Beginning in 1959–60, the North
Vietnamese government provided assistance to its southern brothers.
Sau Thuong, a political officer in the NVA B38 Division, describes a
situation in 1959*:

> *But Ho [Ho Chi Minh] surprised us again a few days later, just before*
> *our departure, when he and other leaders came back to wish us*
> *farewell. When he appeared, everyone was so surprised that we*
> *couldn't speak for a moment or move. Then we went to him and em-*
> *braced him. He hugged each of us as if he were a father hugging his*
> *sons. His final words brought tears to our eyes: "All the brothers going*
> *South should give the Southern people my best wishes and greetings.*
> *There is no doubt that one day I will come to see our Southern blood*
> *brothers." We answered that we would give our best, including our*
> *lives, so that the sacred mission would succeed, so that we would see*
> *him in the South.*

When the U.S. Marines went north to the DMZ in 1966, they were
sent to find out if information about the arrival of units of the North
Vietnamese Army was accurate. However, elements of that army had
been within South Vietnam for some time preparing for this new
phase of the war. The escalation in the fighting had already begun. In
March 1966, on the Laotian border thirty miles west-southwest
of the city of Hue, a reinforced, almost 500-man, garrison of Special

*David Chanoff. Portrait of the Enemy. New York: A. E. Knopf, 1986.

63

Forces–Civilian Irregular Defense Group (CIDG) in the A Shau Valley was overrun by the 95th Regiment, 325th NVA Division. Over a harrowing, nerve-shattering two days, the fort was destroyed by the enemy, with some survivors being rescued because of the unbelievable heroics of Marine helicopter pilots. The costs of the rescue included twenty-one Marine helicopters lost or damaged beyond repair, and two fixed-wing aircraft were shot down in the action. The DMZ was farther north by about sixty miles, and there was very little Marine infantry activity near there; Recon did not patrol along that demilitarized zone.

At this time in the war the 3rd Recon Battalion was still head-quartered at Camp Reasoner, Da Nang, with a detachment to the north at Phu Bai. That detachment included Bravo Company of the battalion and the 1st Force Recon Company. Major Colby, who had engineered Operation Taut Bow as the battalion's S-3, had been given command of the 1st Force unit. According to Col. Pat Collins:

> 1st Force was attached to the 3rd Recon Battalion in October 1965 for the purpose of retraining. They had gone into Vietnam as a sub-unit of the company, but could not perform their missions. It wasn't the Marines in the company who were the problem, it was the goddamn captain. Force Recon is very dependent on the personalities of the officers who run it. Some of the outfits were very, very good, while others were nothing more than jump clubs. Unfortunately, the jump club was the first to hit Vietnam. After four or five months in the war zone, General Walt transferred them into the 3rd Recon Battalion for retraining. Later on, they became a hell of a good outfit.

In March 1966, Maj. Dwain Colby was given command of 1st Force and was shortly to command Task Unit Charlie, the first Marine operation of the war with the mission to probe the hills and valleys below the demilitarized zone to determine if the North Vietnamese were crossing into South Vietnam. In April 1966, one battalion of Marine infantry had been sent into the small town of Khe Sanh, in the northwestern part of Quang Tri Province—only four miles from Laos and seventeen from North Vietnam—but no enemy units had been located. The infantry battalion then marched the thirty road miles along Highway 9 to Dong Ha without firing a shot. However, they had not conducted Recon-type, small-unit missions into the areas well off the main roadways. These areas were beautiful, wild, and untouched by civilization. The mountain tribes there had been living a changeless existence for centuries, untouched and untroubled by outsiders—except for a few Frenchmen who had found ways to assimilate their pioneer farms into the Vietnamese countryside.

However, in Saigon, General Westmoreland wasn't satisfied. In *U.S. Marines in Vietnam: An Expanding War, 1966* (p. 157), he is quoted as saying: "I was operating on a shoestring, maneuvering battalions all over the place. I had to have more intelligence on what was going on up north, and there was no better way to get it than by sending in reconnaissance elements in force." Thus began one of the unique Recon missions of the war—and arguably one of the most dangerous.

It was simply called Task Unit Charlie, and it was composed of units from the 3rd Reconnaissance Battalion and the 1st and 12th Marines. From 3rd Recon, the first platoon of Company A (commanded by 1st Lt. Terry Terrebonne) and the second platoon, 1st Force Recon Company (commanded by 2nd Lt. John Freitas), were assembled. In support were Company E of the 2nd Battalion, 1st Marines (infantry); and Battery H, 3rd Battalion, 12th Marines (artillery). Maj. Dwain Colby, the new company commander of 1st Force Recon, was assigned by Colonel Van Cleve, the 3rd Recon Battalion CO, as the commanding officer of the Task Unit.

Major Colby commented on the situation that the Marines of 1st Force had been faced with before their attachment to the battalion:

In March of '66, I took over 1st Force Recon Company. Although they were now attached to the battalion by General Walt, their headquarters was still at Camp Merrell at Marble Mountain. Their platoons were out and about in various parts of I Corps. I pulled them back to Marble Mountain. We went through a pretty good retraining. I wanted them to focus on other things than jumping out of airplanes. It was unusual to have a CO of Force Recon who was not jump-qualified, but maybe that was what they needed at that particular moment. The thing that General Walt wanted was Reconners out there getting done what he wanted, and he didn't feel like he was getting it. I believe he felt like he had a bunch of prima donnas on his hands, and they weren't doing what he wanted them to do.

But these were awfully good men—just absolutely terrific. It was not difficult to make them see that we had a particular type of war out there to fight, and we had to screw our heads on differently to fight it. You could probably say that they had previously directed their attention on how to get in and get out of the target area, but not how to perform the mission while they were there. Therefore, we worked on controlling artillery and aircraft, and patrol tactics, including staying on the move and radio communications. But like I said, I was working with the cream of the crop. They were terrific people. It certainly wasn't their fault that they weren't operating correctly, and it didn't take them long to get reorientated.

On June 24, 1966, orders were issued that created this unique Recon, infantry, artillery, and helicopter unit to find the enemy along the DMZ. A major difficulty was that the Army command in Saigon believed that the NVA were crossing the border in significant numbers while the closer Marine command did not.

Colby stated:

> I'm really not sure of the military terminology for that operation, because there just wasn't a word in the military lexicon to describe a situation where the Recon commander was given control over infantry and artillery, and in addition six helicopters were almost attached directly under my command. As it turned out, they were stationed near us to support us, but not directly attached.

The major did not create different types of missions for the two units—one for 1st Force and a different one for the Alpha Company platoon. They were assigned missions simply as Recon. The only exception was a planned jump insert, which had to be assigned to the force platoon (however, that mission was scrubbed by General Walt).

Major Colby established the headquarters for Task Unit Charlie adjacent to the airstrip located next to and south of the town of Dong Ha. The infantry company was to maintain one platoon on a thirty-minute alert to reinforce or extract reconnaissance elements in contact. Another platoon, reinforced with one section of 106-mm recoilless rifles, was to provide defense for the artillery battery but was also to be on two-hour alert to assist recon patrols that made contact with enemy forces. The other platoon was to be engaged in patrols and ambushes within 3,000 meters of the base.

The Operation Order, dated 1800H 23 June 1966, gives the following summary of the enemy situation:

a. There have been many reports of enemy units moving South through the Cam Lo district of Quang Tri Province.
b. Reports indicate that units move from the Ben Tat area south along the southern edge of the DMZ to grid square YD 0868 at which point movement is made South or Southwest along the rivers into the Cam Lo area.
c. Units have been observed passing through the Cam Lo area on

    Highway 9 between YD 04 and 09 and grid squares XD 9556, 9656, 9756, 9856, and 9956.

d. Small guerrilla units of squad and platoon size have been reported operating along the Cam Lo River between grid squares YD 1359 and YD 2160. These units have engaged in harassment activities through this area.

e. A Regional Force Company has been observed in the Cam Lo area acting in support of the local guerrilla units. This unit was last seen on 23 June 1966 in the vicinity of YD 1262 moving south.

f. On 13 June 1966, a Main Force Battalion was sighted in grid square YD 1050 moving to the south.

g. On 2 June 1966 one VC Company was seen moving South at grid square 9956. This unit was equipped with (2) 60-mm mortars.

h. On 22 June 1966 the 808th Battalion attacked an ARVN outpost at YD 267585 suffering heavy casualties.

i. *Local Population.* The local population in the areas west of Cam Lo are not to be considered as trustworthy or cooperative. The people in this area are Montagnard and lowland Vietnamese.

Of all the enemy units listed above, only the 808th was a North Vietnamese force; the rest were local Vietcong. But the summary of the enemy situation that was given to the Marines of Task Unit Charlie was inadequate on two additional points. First, MACV had decided not to count local enemy militia in the enemy order of battle, and second, an entire division, not just one battalion of NVA, awaited the small Recon teams.

The North Vietnamese division that was on the prowl in the rolling hills, mountains, and jungles was the 324B. That entire division had crossed the border, and the Cam Lo area, not far west from Dong Ha on Route 9, was its infiltration route. Its total strength was listed at 3,600 infantry, 4,140 headquarters and support unit personnel, another 1,100 soldiers in an antitank battalion, a 120-mm mortar battalion, an antiaircraft battalion, and engineer, signal, and transportation battalions.

Confronting this shadowy but extensive enemy force, consisting of both NVA and Vietcong, the two platoons of Recon Marines from the 3rd Recon Battalion had orders to accomplish the following mission:

a. Determine the exact locations of enemy infiltration routes, harbor sites, supply caches, weapons, and ammunition storage areas.

b. Determine the direction and techniques of movement of VC forces.

c. Determine the VC communications and signal systems, location of sites, types of equipment, antenna systems, and telephone equipment.

d. Determine the VC defenses and countermeasures against reconnaissance, surveillance, and detection techniques and devices.

e. Determine the trafficability of roads, trails, and waterways encountered. Include bridge type, location, construction, and condition.

f. Determine the location and size of possible helicopter landing zones (HLZs). Record all trails located.

g. Determine location, types, and number of crew served weapons.

Two platoons of Americans, not more than forty men in all, were to go into an area where as many as 10,000 hostile and well-trained enemy soldiers waited, building their support base.

One other interesting point about the operation order that sent the Recon Marines to the DMZ was the instruction regarding captured enemy personnel. It stated: "The term 'prisoner of war' will not be used in connection with captured personnel taken in counterguerrilla operations against Viet Cong since the Viet Cong are not foreign nationals, and this is not a declared war. For operations in Vietnam, the term 'captive' will be used in reference to all prisoners taken by Task Unit C elements."

Patrols led by Lieutenant Freitas and Lieutenant Terrebonne were dropped into the hills and jungles north, west, and south of Cam Lo. Between July 1 and July 19, 1966, seven patrols, or patrol attempts, were made by 1st Platoon, Company A, of Task Unit Charlie and quickly gained the attention of everyone involved.

The Reconners going north had their concerns. If, in fact, there were significant units of NVA coming across the border, the Recon teams could be facing very dangerous missions, more so than the ones they had faced in the past. Their concern was highlighted by the stories from U.S. Air Force personnel stationed at Dong Ha. While there was no American infantry in the area, there were other units such as the Air Force helping at the small airstrip. They reported that it wasn't unusual to observe Vietcong patrols within Dong Ha and to see them walking across the landing strip. Why enemy units with that much confidence had not made a bigger bang around the area was not known, but the Reconners felt that something of major consequence could be on the make, regardless of what the Marine command believed.

The Recon experience from early in the war, when teams had to protect themselves without adequate infantry support, led the teams of Task Unit Charlie to pack more weapons and ammo than food. In addition, the Recon teams operated with platoon-size patrols that ranged from thirteen to sixteen men.

1st Lt. Terry Terrebonne, of 1st Platoon, Company A, a former football player at Tulane University, and S.Sgt. Juan Trinidad, of San Antonio, Texas, were, respectively, platoon commander and platoon sergeant. L.Cpl. Alan Gordon ran point, and Cpl. Ray Strohl coordinated the point team and was second in the column. Strohl said, "I remember all the patrols, but that first one is near and dear to Al and myself."

Their method of insertion was for two CH-46s to carry the platoon—one squad in each—to the LZ. However, the birds would stop at three potential LZs, hoping to confuse those enemy who might be watching. The patrol would jump and run at one of them. The site for this first patrol was about nine miles west of Dong Ha and two and a quarter miles northwest of Cam Lo, exactly where many of the reports had placed enemy troops. The area was characterized by low rolling hills, not more than 100 meters tall. Head-high elephant grass, areas of thick brush, and scattered clumps of trees interspersed with well-used trails covered the patrol's zone. It was about four miles below the "Provisional Military Demarcation Line" that had separated the Vietnams since 1954. The Ben Hai River was actually the "provisional" boundary, and it was in approximately the middle of the four-to-five-mile-wide DMZ, which was supposed to be a neutral area. This patrol was to land about 2.4 miles south of the DMZ.

Al Gordon said:

We jumped out of the chopper and immediately began to make our way through a thicket of head-tall elephant grass that was better called "razor grass." It was about 1800 hours and there was still light. Our intent was to work our way some distance from the LZ and find a harbor site for the night. We had been told to wear the Ho Chi Minh sandals over our boots as we were the first Americans in the area, and the brass thought this would be a good way of not giving ourselves away! But that didn't last long.

We had to use a trail to avoid making too much noise. We were only moving from the LZ for a short time before I came to a clearing of low bush and started out into it. Ten meters out, I came to a trail that was well packed down. After I moved across it, I heard the signal that enemy had been sighted nearby. I dropped into the bush and hid. It wasn't very long before I heard 'em coming up the trail. They passed by me a few feet away, but I couldn't really tell how many there were—maybe five or six.

Gordon found himself alone when he tried to reach the other team members and couldn't. The others were still in the thickets and had pulled back on hearing the NVA. Ray Strohl had just stepped into the clearing before he ducked back at the signal of the patrol leader. However, he couldn't reach Al and was very concerned about his buddy. Strohl had disappeared into the brush to hide from the approaching NVA, but was now in a quandary: not knowing that Al Gordon was caught in the clearing, the main body of his team had pulled back out of his sight, but they were also getting farther from Strohl. The corporal decided to circle alone through the bush to look for his point man. In the meantime, Al had let the NVA pass by and was now moving toward a clump of trees to hide and watch for the team.

Strohl said:

When I got back to the edge of the thicket, I saw five khaki-uniformed enemy soldiers with weapons where I thought Al should be. I knelt down and flipped the selector switch on my M-14 to the automatic position. Al had a shotgun, and I figured if they saw him, I'd open up on them from this side, but I sure didn't want to start anything.

Then I heard a gunship flying over. I think both the NVA and I hid, 'cuz I didn't see them anymore, and I pushed myself into a big bush. I knew the pilot would probably think that I was an enemy in the grass if he saw me, and I hid.

After it was gone, I waited a bit and then moved up to the trees, hoping to get another look for Al. By this time, I was really concerned for both of us. When I found a good place behind a tree where I could get a good view of the clearing, I whistled. It scared the hell out of me when I got a return signal, not from out in the open bush but from the trees just to my right.

It was Al Gordon, and the two had a quick reunion before they retraced their steps. Finally they found the team, only to learn that the gunship overhead had reported that NVA were now in position on several sides of the Marines and advancing toward them.

The Huey gunships began laying down a base of fire on the surrounding NVA, and 46s were called in to extract the team. The Marines were picked up a little more than an hour after they had been dropped in, but they got out of a potentially serious problem before anyone was killed.

The patrol was debriefed after it returned to Dong Ha, and that report states:

Upon insertion the patrol moved in a Southeast direction. Approximately thirty minutes later, the 3rd member of the patrol observed an estimated fifty (50) VC [later these soldiers were reclassified as NVA]. The VC were moving in a Northeast direction, along a trail, in a column, well dispersed [Comment: The VC did not fire on the patrol when visual contact was established. It is the opinion of the patrol leader that the reason the VC did not fire was because of the possibility of an additional friendly (VC or NVA) force in the area]. Upon the commencing of withdrawal of Recon, the VC split into two (2) groups, one moving to the Northeast and behind Recon's position, while the second group moved on line from the East toward Recon's position. . . . The VC were wearing a mix of khaki and green uniforms; all were wearing banana leaves or brush. One automatic weapon was observed; all VC were armed. Enemy unit was well disciplined and appeared to be hard core. The only firing was by the VC at the gunship on its second run.

The next day, July 2, the platoon tried again—this time about 3,000 meters south of the first try. This second patrol was scheduled to land almost on the bank of the small Khe Chua River, near rice paddies with the same rolling hills across their entire northern front. The Cam Lo, a major river that flowed east and later merged into the Cua Viet between Dong Ha and the Gulf of Tonkin, lay only 1.2 miles to their south; 2.5 miles to the southeast was the large village complex of Cam Lo. The valley all along the Khe Chua River to the Cam Lo River was filled with rice paddies, although most were now dry in the hot summer.

The choppers made their feints before dropping down toward what was to be the real LZ. Ray Strohl said that he first realized there was a problem when Sgt. Dan Stransky, standing at the back hatch of the 46, began firing into the LZ, only 100 feet below. He unloaded a magazine at two enemy soldiers in the LZ, killing one. In the next moments, Lieutenant Terrebonne and the pilots decided to abort the mission as they saw enemy emplacements adjacent to the LZ. The patrol report stated:

The terrain in the LZ was a dry rice paddy with four-foot bushes around the edge. Behind the bushes was a tree line with trees approximately 30 feet in height. . . . To the south of the LZ approximately 100 meters was a bunker with three or four huts nearby. . . . Air support consisted of (1) UH 1-E gunship and (3) A-4 Skyhawks. The UH 1-E gunship fired rockets and M-60 machine gun. The A-4s dropped 12 Napalm bombs and fired 600 rounds of 20mm. Thirty 105mm howitzer rounds were fired in support.

The first two attempts by the platoon to get onto the ground had resulted in less than an hour and a half of patrolling, and uniformed enemy soldiers were seen in both locations. The command immediately planned a third mission for insertion the following day. The LZ for the third attempt was farther to the west, about 4.5 miles southwest of the second and 1,000 to 2,000 meters southeast of the Rockpile, at the time an unnoted hill still without nickname. To the patrol's immediate north lay Highway 9 and the Trinh Hin River. Both ran past the Rockpile in the valley below the patrol route. However, the patrol's immediate concern was a mile-long ridge and its dominant feature, Hill 254. This time the patrol managed to stay in longer.

As was normal, the patrol inserted in the early-evening hours. Al Gordon, at point, felt uneasy during the entire patrol: "I hadn't seen anything, but I kept telling Terrebonne, 'I feel funny. We're being watched.' "

Strohl said, "That night on the ridgeline, we harbored in elephant grass. By now we all knew that the NVA had come across the border in force and had emplacements and base camps throughout the countryside. We all felt exposed, and all of us were wired. I don't think anyone got any sleep. Our ears were acute to any sounds."

The next morning the patrol moved through the tall grass until they found a vantage point from which to watch the valley below. At about 1115 hours, they sighted twelve enemy soldiers on the opposite bank of the river about two klicks (2,000 meters) to their north. Terrebonne called for the supporting 155-mm howitzers and saw their target covered by the resulting arty mission, reporting a probable twelve enemy killed. However, later in the afternoon, the patrol heard carbine rounds being fired along the ridge on both sides of them. The Marines knew that these were signals and that they were the object of a VC counterrecon mission. Then they heard movement from unidentified sources on both sides. The patrol attempted to slip undetected from the area through the high razor grass and called for helicopter support.

Upon arriving overhead, the choppers reported sighting previously unseen gun positions and bunkers near the Recon team and enemy soldiers converging on the Marines. The 46s swiftly came in to extract the Reconners. The birds received hostile fire from crew-served weapons, and one bird flying gun support dropped thermite grenades around an enemy position, starting fires in the dry grass. M-79 rounds were fired from the choppers into the enemy trapped by the flames.

After the patrol was safely extracted, fixed-wing craft were brought in to strafe enemy positions on the ridge. By then the platoon was very concerned about its ability to get into an LZ undetected or to accomplish any kind of mission. It was obvious that the woods and hills were full of unfriendly soldiers, and patrolling was going to be very dangerous and difficult.

The next patrol, three days later, confirmed these fears. It really was a combination of two attempts. The first patrol zone was to be about 4.5 miles southwest of Cam Lo in a pocket with ridgelines on all sides. The only openings were made by the Rao Vinh River where it flowed into and then out of the bowl. The method of operation was the same.

Al Gordon was on the first chopper to land and remembers:

> The back hatch dropped, and I ran down the ramp into the grass followed by Ray. The whole squad was out and heading for the tree line when we suddenly realized that the second chopper had come under heavy fire and couldn't get in. There seemed to be a couple of automatic weapons, and I don't know how many other small arms firing away at the birds from a nearby hill not more than two to three hundred meters away. We took cover in the trees and watched our helicopters in the air trying to stay out of range, and we wondered what the hell was going to happen next.
>
> Then we got the word that jets were coming in to rip the area, and we should mark our positions. So I took a colored panel out in front of us and then just sat back and was fascinated by the air show that came in. Our squad hadn't yet come under fire, and now it was an air-to-ground battle with us as spectators.

"The Huey gunships came in first," Ray Strohl added. "We always had two of them nearby during these DMZ patrols. They were the first to hit that hillside. When the jets came in, I swear they were so close I believe I saw the pilot of one of those jets wink at me."

Sitting in the trees and wondering about its fate, the first squad didn't have long to wait before the 46 returned under fire to extract the Reconners.

The platoon was flown back the nine miles to Dong Ha. The men were starting to unpack when the word came that they were going back immediately. Within the hour, the platoon was back in the air. Ray Strohl stated that they had just about made up their minds that there was no need to take any chow, just stock up on ammo. In fact, at that point they started taking an M-60 machine gun with them. This time the patrol insertion point was going farther south, about two miles southeast of the last attempt and at a higher elevation, a three-hill complex about 300 meters tall. They were to land in the middle and just to the side of the center knoll.

The first chopper, with Gordon, Strohl, and Lieutenant Terrebonne,

dropped down to the planned LZ and immediately was hit by enemy
fire. Before the team was able to jump out, the chopper pulled away,
under fire all the while, and miraculously made it out. The second
chopper wasn't so lucky. The first tried to warn the second away but,
hit by ground fire, the second helicopter lost power, tried to jettison
fuel, but instead came in for a crash landing. The pilot did manage to
fly a short distance to the west before bouncing down and rolling over.

A fire burst out within the chopper as the Marines on board fought
to get out of the bird in both directions. The lead chopper had turned
and followed its crashing wingman. It quickly set down not far from
the first, and the first squad scrambled out the back hatch to set a security perimeter for the Reconners trying to get out of the crashed
chopper. Al Gordon and Lieutenant Terrebonne, however, both ran
for the helicopter, which was lying in heavy brush on its side.

Al Gordon said:

> We landed below the other 46 before those guys had been able to get
> out. I ran for them, and Terrebonne was right behind me. It was lying
> on its side, and I climbed up on the topside and looked in the window.
> And to this day I can still see Longenecker sitting there, on his
> back now as the chopper was on its side. He was dead, but his eyes
> were staring straight ahead. Then a little voice told me to get the
> hell out of there. The fire was starting to burn more, and everybody had
> gotten out. Some had to stumble and run through the fire. I ran,
> and when I was about fifty meters away, the chopper blew sky-high
> behind me.

Strohl couldn't tell what exactly was happening at the helicopter
because he was a part of a defensive position in the bush farther
out. But one Marine had been killed and seven wounded in the crash.

The Reconners were angry by this time. Everywhere they went,
their teams were up to their necks in uniformed enemy soldiers. Teams couldn't stay in the bush, and they were lucky that more
Marines weren't being killed. From the perspective of the Reconner
on patrol, those in command positions did not understand the
dangers.

However, III MAF Headquarters, back in Da Nang, was beginning
to think that it should check out the reconnaissance reports a little
more seriously, and a battalion of infantry now was sent to Dong Ha.
Task Unit Charlie was terminated, but Recon remained as Detachment A, Recon Group Bravo, now attached to the infantry.

The MAF headquarters had developed intelligence that the 90th
NVA Regiment, estimated at 1,500 men, was using the Ngan River

valley, five to six miles northwest of Cam Lo, and that its parent division (the 324B) had its command post on Hill 208 overlooking the southwest side of the valley. It was located a mile or two south of the DMZ.

Brig. Gen. Lowell English, the commander of the new Task Force Delta, prepared his plans to "take the enemy by surprise on his key trails and behind his own lines and to smash and destroy him before he had a chance to regain his balance and momentum."*

Thus, Operation Hastings was planned to commence on July 15, 1966, but amazingly, Recon Group Bravo was excluded from the intelligence and operational briefings, and Recon missions were now being planned without the Marine command's advising Major Colby of its estimate of the enemy situation. Colby stated:

> Just a few days prior to the time of the D-Day for Hastings, we had a bunch of high-ranking people up there, and an intelligence briefing had been set up. I assumed I was to go as the Recon commander on the scene. When I got there, General Walt met me and asked if I had a security clearance that I had never heard of. It was called an "Omega" clearance. When I told him I'd never heard of it, he told me that I obviously didn't have it and, therefore, could not attend the briefing.

While Recon Group Bravo was aware that the friendly force situation had changed, it had to compile its own information about the size and location of enemy forces. Therefore, on July 12, Lieutenant Terrebonne's platoon was to be inserted just to the western flank of the coming operation, although the patrol order made no mention of the newly designated Operation Hastings, nor did the team members know about it. Additionally, unknown to Recon, the patrol's insertion LZ was within 800 meters of the suspected location of the 324B Division Headquarters!

Al Gordon was again ready to run point as the patrol boarded the choppers. "Morale was not very good," he said. "The whole province, wherever the hell we went, seemed to be alive and busting with North Vietnamese troops. Then, on top of that, we felt that these guys who were assigning us missions knew we were going to be up to our eyeballs in shit, and it seemed like a game to them. No, I would say morale was not good."

Ray Strohl added: "On this fifth patrol, I think everybody thought this was crazy. It seemed like no one would believe us about how many enemy were out there, and we felt like these patrols were

*U.S. Marines in Vietnam, 1966, page 163.

suicide. At this point the main interest of patrol members was simple survival."

As the Recon team approached the LZ, and the first helicopter was within a hundred feet of the ground, enemy gun emplacements opened up. Automatic weapons and small arms were fired at the choppers from several different locations. The bird was hit, but pulled back to a higher elevation and out of range. This time the second chopper was not so quick coming behind the first, and it too pulled up. Gun emplacements were noted in several locations, and the Americans were close enough to observe that three uniformed NVA were handling one gun. In addition, fire was taken from the jungle around, but no enemy locations were noted because they were protected from observation by the canopy.

A week later, and only a short 400 meters from the proposed Recon landing zone, Marine infantry on Operation Hastings found an underground, 200-bed NVA hospital. They also found the headquarters for the 8,000- to 9,000-man enemy division at the top of a hill directly overlooking the proposed LZ.

The helicopters safely returned with the Marines to Dong Ha. In the patrol report, Lieutenant Terrebonne noted that artillery and air strikes should saturate an area immediately when enemy units are seen. He also recommended trying early-morning insertions, as the late-afternoon/early-evening times were getting them nowhere. Additional debriefer comments noted that the helicopter pilots reported that Vietnamese-speaking people were on their radio frequency, but that when the insertion was canceled, the radio interference stopped. Three days later, July 15, Operation Hastings commenced in the valley of the Ngan River with four battalions of Marine infantry plus supporting arms. LZ Crow was their landing zone; it was only 1,000 meters from the Recon platoon LZ of a few days earlier. Four Marine CH-46 helicopters were destroyed that first day of the operation, and the area became known as Helicopter Valley.

Less than twenty-four hours before Operation Hastings was to begin, the first platoon of Company A was on its way out for its sixth mission attempt. Al Gordon was gone on R & R, and he was to miss the next two patrols. Corporal Strohl was assigned to the point position. This time the platoon was sent about three miles south of the last mission, between Cam Lo and the Rockpile. The hills were taller, rising to over 500 meters, and the canopy was taller.

Ray Strohl said:

We landed in the late afternoon again. Moving as silently as we could through the jungle, we again found a lot of trails. They were three to four feet wide and well used. We went far enough from the LZ to feel safer and made a harbor site. We were close to a trail and set up in three-man teams with strings pulled between each of the teams. We would use the strings for signals if necessary. The terrain was covered by large trees and low grass and bushes. During the night, three groups of enemy soldiers passed by us on that trail, all heading northwest. They didn't have a clue we were around and didn't use noise discipline. The first group came by at 2230; the next at 0100; and the last at 0130 hours.

About ten minutes after the first group passed them, the patrol observed yellow lights at about 1,500 meters north by northeast. They also heard what sounded like a generator starting. The lights remained on for about ten minutes; the motor ran for about an hour.

The next morning, the patrol moved to a new position, and at 0930 called in sixteen rounds of 155-mm artillery on a VC position about 1,000 meters to their west. An hour later, they called in another artillery mission on an enemy position about 1,500 meters north of them. Then, on July 14, the patrol was extracted without making further contact with enemy units. Lieutenant Terrebonne again recommended heavy air strikes to saturate the area.

The next morning, at 0730 hours, Operation Hastings kicked off in Helicopter Valley. Marine Recon teams screened the western approaches to the area of operation. One of those screening locations was to be atop the Rockpile. On a helicopter reconnaissance of the area, Major Colby had previously noted and named the clifflike hill that abruptly rose 700 feet skyward from the valley floor about fourteen miles west of Dong Ha. To its north was a ridge that looked like the back of a dinosaur jutting out of the same valley floor; it later became known as the Razorback.

The final of the seven patrols Terrebonne led was on July 18–19. Operation Hastings was by then three days old, but the Marines on the Recon teams were not aware of the internal battle taking place behind them. Colby sent patrol reports and messages back through the division to MACV describing how the Recon teams repeatedly encountered uniformed enemy and could not stay out for the planned duration of the patrol, in some cases could not even land in the LZ. As far as Colby and the Reconners were concerned, NVA were wherever Recon went. In one ten-day period in early July, fourteen of eighteen Recon patrols from both the Terrebonne and Freitas platoons had to be withdrawn because of contact with the enemy. A serious problem had developed, however, that almost cost Colby his position. It was, simply, this: the Marine command had not believed him or his team reports.

Major Colby explained:

I sent reports back on a daily basis. They questioned me from that level: Why couldn't I keep my patrols in the field longer? Particularly since it had been General Walt's conviction that there were no NVA coming across the border, I have to suspect that his various staff people interpreted our information so as not to conflict with Walt's preconceived ideas. Therefore, my reports were called into question.

General Kyle, 3rd Division CG, got ahold of me and asked what in the world was going on. I explained as best as I could, and it wasn't long before General Walt was paying me a personal visit. I met him at the Dong Ha airport, and it was pretty obvious what his disposition was like. The look on the man's face told me this guy was mad enough to chew nails. It was certainly my impression from the various messages that had gone back and forth that my job was in jeopardy. I had to figure out how to convince him what was happening along the DMZ.

I knew that this former football player, and a bulldog of a Marine, was an infantry trooper's Marine and would often listen to the troops in the field before others, so I took him to our camp to meet my Reconners.

The troops were all lined up, including one patrol that had just gotten back from the bush. Walt went down the line, starting with these Marines who still had their bush paint on their faces. The stories he heard, one after another, would make your hair stand on end. He talked to just about every Marine I had.

By the time he was finished, he put his arm over my shoulder and said, "Colby, by golly, it really looks like we got a war going on up here." He started instantly to change the nature of operations at Dong Ha.

However, the U.S. military command continued to underestimate the morale and purpose of the Vietnamese who fought against the combined forces of the United States and South Vietnam. Huong Van Ba, who had been a colonel in the People's Army of Vietnam (the PAVN or NVA), described their indoctrination:

When the Americans came to Vietnam, they didn't bring with them a hatred for the Vietnamese people. But we had it for them! . . . We had seen pictures of the South Vietnamese people being beaten, arrested and tortured. We had seen pictures of Ngo Dinh Diem's [Diem was the first president of the newly created country of South Vietnam] cruel suppression of the Buddhists, of people being shocked with electricity and women being raped. These pictures had built up our rage and our determination to liberate the South. . . . We had such hatred for the enemy and such devotion to the noble cause of liberating our suppressed people that we felt we could overcome any difficulty and make any sacrifice. . . . To save fifteen million South Vietnamese . . . was the highest moral obligation . . ."*

These professionals from the NVA were causing the tactics of the war to change. The Marine Corps was being drawn farther away from the population centers as it was forced into the mountains and rolling hills of the borders to seek out and attempt to destroy the divisions of Vietnamese regulars from the North who were on their way south. The year 1966 would see more battles near the DMZ with Recon teams ahead of the infantry.

*Portrait of the Enemy.

CHAPTER SEVEN

"Two Days and I'll Bring Back Your F——— Bodies"

Interviews with General Westmoreland during the war recorded the following: "[Westmoreland speaking] The Navy and Marines based their troops . . . along the coast whereas I thought they should move out against the enemy. General Green [Commandant, Marine Corps] argued against this. . . ."

The interview went on to state that General Westmoreland objected to the Marine strategy of holding the coast, an "enclave strategy." Westmoreland is also quoted as saying that the Marines did not have enough helicopters and in any case "did not know how to use them." The interview comments continued: "He [Westmoreland] was determined to get the Marines off the South Vietnamese's backs, to strike at the enemy's main forces and let the South Vietnamese deal with the guerrillas. . . . In response to my question as to why he did not simply order the Marines out, General Westmoreland replied, 'You don't order but engage in a professional dialogue.' "

Other comments recorded from the discussion include: "Concerned about I Corps. The Marines have tied up too many troops in the areas they will have a difficulty moving out of without abandoning the population. . . . Marines seem complacent about enemy possibilities. Walt dedicated and sincere but found it hard to grasp the big picture and project into the future. . . . Marines had no interest in armed helicopters. Their old dual-rotor chopper was slow. . . ."

However, Westmoreland had high regard for the Marine Recon teams and urged the Marine Corps to create more such units: "I thought [the Marines] might organize a new . . . Recon Battalion without increasing numbers of Marines in Vietnam." *

*These statements are taken from interviews on file at the LBJ Library in Austin, Texas.

* * *

Marine Recon teams had started their experience in Vietnam with "walk-out" patrols, then had begun to use the old UH-34 helicopters, and later the CH-46s, but as General Walt was persuaded through "professional dialogue" into moving more forces away from the populated lowlands and closer to the DMZ, Marine resources were stretched thin. Some situations became very difficult for the helicopter, and Recon teams began to use more walk-out patrols again. Often the teams would be trucked to areas along the roadways from which they would quickly move into the bush and the hills. On other occasions, the teams would be flown to small U.S. or ARVN outposts from which they would walk out.

While Lieutenant Terrebonne's patrols were providing information and influencing a change in the course of the war, other patrols, both from 1st Force Recon and Company A, were probing the jungles and hills, attempting to identify the elements of the NVA that had slipped into South Vietnam. It seemed that wherever the command suspected a large concentration of enemy forces, that's where they set down a small Recon patrol. The commander of Alpha Company, Capt. George Best, was given orders to join Detachment A, Recon Group Bravo, at the Dong Ha CP with two additional platoons from Camp Reasoner. It was an attempt to use new blood with a different approach to try to penetrate enemy territory.

Best brought with him one platoon from Company A and one from Delta Company. 2nd Lt. Bill Buhl, recently promoted from gunnery sergeant in Alpha Company and reassigned to Delta, was the commander of the Delta platoon. He brought with him a wealth of experience in Recon. He had taught Recon indoctrination at Camp Pendleton, California, in 1st Recon Battalion, and had worked with Captain Best in Alpha Company; he and Best had a long and good working relationship.

Best arrived in Dong Ha early on July 12, and spoke at length with his platoon commander, Terry Terrebonne, about the nature of the operations and the enemy forces. At 1825 on that same day, Best rode aboard one of the gunships in support of the next Terrebonne patrol. This was the patrol that attempted to land at the foot of Hill 208, adjacent to Helicopter Valley on the Ngan River. Best said, "Hell, they didn't get closer than a hundred feet off the deck when the NVA opened up from all different directions, and the helicopter was lucky to pull up and get out of there without going down."

Operation Hastings was scheduled to kick off on July 15 in the valley of the Ngan, while Lieutenant Terrebonne was to reinsert south of that area of operation, between Cam Lo and the Rockpile, on the day before, July 14. On the fourteenth, Captain Best was to take another patrol south of Cam Lo. At the same time a patrol from 1st Force was to insert on top of the Rockpile to establish the first Stingray observation post from that location. The Marine infantry was using Recon to screen areas to its west and south.

Captain Best was to attempt a company operation on a walk-out and stay-behind patrol. That meant that Best and his two platoons were going to walk out with an ARVN company from their camp, D-5, then drop off at an agreed location while the ARVNs patrolled back to D-5. Captain Best would then conduct operations from that point farther out into the hills.

When they reached D-5, the Marines found a nervous bunch of Americans and South Vietnamese. Best said:

There was a U.S. Army adviser named Captain Culpepper there who met us. He told me, "You're looking at the happiest person in the world, 'cuz I've got my orders back to the world. And I'm on my way outa here. The NVA have been probing our position nightly, and they're about ready to overrun us. If I live through this one last night, I'll be so damn happy."

Then the ARVN commander told me, "You come down here with thirty-four Marines, and I've got two thousand soldiers here. When I probe outside my perimeter twelve hundred meters, I get so pinned down by enemy gunfire that I can't do anything. You come down here with these few Marines to bring back big VC trophy, and in two days I'll go out and bring back your fucking bodies."

Best said that the ARVN commander spoke very fluent English.

However, the Marines did get out and back, bringing with them one of the biggest "VC trophies" of the war. They moved south out of the camp, and the Marine captain expressed his respect for the way the ARVN patrolled. He said they were professionals, and when they didn't feel good about an area they had to move into, they called in artillery to prep the place before entering. Two years later, the map sheet that covered the area used for the patrol identified sixteen hamlets surrounding the D-5 camp, the name for each hamlet followed by the parenthetical notation "destroyed."

When the combined ARVN and Marine patrol reached a point about three klicks south of D-5, the ARVN company commander told Best that he had to return in order to get back before dusk. So the Marines quietly dropped out of the unit and set up in the jungle of the lower hills, watching as their escort swung around and started to patrol back the way they had come. The Marines hoped that any-one watching wouldn't notice that the unit returning was short thirty-four men.

The thirty-four Marines silently moved through the jungle to the south, their painted faces blending with the vines, trees, and bush. They worked their way toward a Y in the stream that ran down from the hills where, only a short distance away, Terrebonne's patrol had lost one helicopter and was shot out of two landing zones on July 8.

Opposite the main stream from the company was a larger hilly ridge that ran from the northwest to the southeast, blocking the patrol's southerly route. On either side of the Marines were lower hills and fingers that reached out toward them. The smaller branch of the stream flowed to the northeast and was paralleled by paths that ran out of the jungles toward D-5.

With darkness descending, Captain Best set his people into nighttime positions. He felt that the next day he would move into a good position from which he could establish a base and send smaller patrols on deeper probes into the hills. This was a reversion to earlier days of Recon in Vietnam, when a company-size patrol would establish a patrol base from which to conduct smaller unit missions out some distance from the base.

The hours went by, one man out of each team of three Marines always on the alert. Then, in the early-morning gray, the sudden and unexpected pounding, shaking, and shrieking screams of 500-pound bombs rocked the Marines around their side of the little valley. Across the basin and up into the foothills within a klick of them, the slopes were being pulverized by a B-52 strike. Best and his Marines lay still as the ground rocked and rolled under them. A short time later, at daybreak, Best said he received an emergency radio call advising him that helicopters would be out to pick them up in two hours because a B-52 strike was coming through the area. The captain informed the caller that the strike had already happened, but, nevertheless, the command wanted to extract them.

With two hours to go until extraction, Best didn't want to waste time dangerously by waiting near the landing zone, so he sent Lieutenant Buhl with his platoon to the southwest, toward the main stream, while he took the other platoon a few hundred meters to the east. Both were to try to establish short-term ambushes as they waited for the helicopters.

Bill Buhl maneuvered his platoon toward a stream. They were in jungle amid low hills. After thirty minutes Buhl halted the platoon to check the area. He positioned two Marines farther up the stream to provide security on their west side. The hilly jungle on the opposite bank anchored its roots at the edge of the stream. Not more than thirty feet wide, the ribbon of water flowed around a bend not far away and disappeared into the early-morning jungle gray. The two Marines were about fifty meters from the main body, and Buhl had just gotten back to the platoon, when all hell broke loose behind him.

The lieutenant went charging back through the jungle to find the two Marines reloading their rifles and three dead enemy soldiers lying in the stream. "I had told 'em if anybody steps into that stream, waste 'em, and they did," Buhl said. The men reported to Buhl that one other enemy had been wounded but had escaped into the jungle on the other side. Buhl set out security and checked the bodies. Documents and other evidence indicated that the dead men were North Vietnamese VIPs.

The ambush had killed a North Vietnamese battalion commander, his adjutant, and a company commander. The documents were the first ones captured by any Americans that proved the existence of the 324B NVA Division in South Vietnam. The papers included overlays with unit positions, unit rosters, and other maps. While the headquarters and most of the 324B Division might have been located adjacent to Helicopter Valley, other battalions of the division were located south of the Cam Lo River about ten miles away, where Buhl and Best were located.

An April 1966 CIA memorandum had stated: "Two unidentified units (regiments of the PAVN) have been reported infiltrating western Quang Tri Province in I Corps in the past two weeks. . . . Because of the scarcity of information on these reported units they have not yet been accepted in the order of battle. The weight of evidence and past experience, however, suggest that the presence of some of these units will eventually be confirmed." Three months later Captain Best's unit gave that confirmation in writing.

Best stated that later it was determined that these NVA commanders were reconnoitering for a final assault on D-5, as feared by Captain Culpepper. However, the Marines were extracted at 0945 hours as planned. That same morning Operation Hastings kicked off about six miles northwest of Cam Lo. Commanded by Brigadier General English, Task Force Delta had been created to assault the suspected position of a regiment of the 324B Division in the valley of the Ngan River and the adjacent hills just south of the DMZ. The task force consisted of four infantry battalions plus supporting units. In the end, the operation saw the deployment of 8,000 Marines and 3,000 ARVN. Recon played a vital role, being used to screen the south and west flanks of the infantry.

However, enemy resistance stiffened, and after being debriefed,

Captain Best was told to wait for new orders. They came in the early-evening hours of the same day, catching up to Best as he stood in the chow line. He and his men were to walk out from Cam Lo that night and patrol up a ridgeline north of the Cam Lo River and south of the infantry, who were embroiled in vicious fighting a few miles to the north.

The captain said:

I sent Lieutenant Buhl and Gunny Lovingood to get the troops and supplies rounded up—we didn't have much time. In fact, I was not happy with the way we had to operate. There wasn't the time to coordinate with supporting units like I had always worked before.

They told me that I was to take two South Vietnamese Popular Force (PF) troops with me as guides. They told me not to worry since these two knew the area and would be a big help. We were told that we would start our walk-out a little past midnight and cross the river west of the Cam Lo village heading generally to the north. I tried to find someone who could tell me where our front lines were. If I was going to have to walk through them in the dark, I damn sure wanted to know where they were. But no one could tell me. The only way I found out was to walk out myself and find the last squad leader and check out Marine positions with him. When I was about to leave him and go back to the CP, he warned me about two PF patrols that had passed by a little earlier with the stated intent to establish ambushes out near the river.

This really ticked me off. I went back and tried to find someone to tell me where the hell those PF ambushes were. Nobody knew! I was getting more pissed and damn sure didn't want to walk my Marines into a friendly ambush. I had never seen anything so uncoordinated.

Lieutenant Buhl added: "I was mad and probably getting a little mouthy. We weren't even given time to coordinate with our supporting units. It was dangerously put together."

Captain Best said that the ridiculous got worse when the two PFs showed up and couldn't speak English. They were ready to move out, and Best was running around trying to find somebody who could speak some Vietnamese. Finally, they were able to get a little communication going, and Best found out that the two Vietnamese thought that this was just a one-night-out and back-the-next-day patrol and weren't ready to go out as the Marines had planned. When the PFs found out where they were to go they responded by saying, "Beaucoup VC. Bad, bad place." But go they did, with Best's size-ten boot and Buhl's anger giving them certain encouragement.

Captain Best continued:

Well, we had to walk out through the villages at 0030 in the night to the river. It was one of the worst experiences of my life. People were all around in the shadows. You could even hear bolts snapping home out there in the dark. I had no idea whether they were owned by PFs or unfriendly folks. Shit! There was even people walking behind us signaling with flashlights. There wasn't a fucking thing we could do but to keep on the move and get through the area.

Continuing to the west, they reached the Cam Lo River, which they had to ford. While they never ran into any friendly PF ambushes, it was at this point that the two PFs refused to go farther, and Lieutenant Buhl took the point. The team forded the river and, in the early dawn, found itself facing the lower end of the Dong Kio ridgeline. As the skies lightened, Lieutenant Buhl called to the captain to come forward. Best said:

There was all this freshly cut brush that had been used as camouflage on helmets and uniforms. It was lying around and hadn't even begun to wilt yet. We passed on and kept moving into the higher ground, starting up the ridge. The place was fairly open until we reached the tree line about a klick away. It was very much like a logging area in Oregon. A lot of the trees had been cut, but the undergrowth was real bad. The treetops had been cut off and left, while the main body of the tree was gone. It was so thick that you had no choice but to use the trails. I didn't like it. It was nut-tightening. You couldn't see but a few feet ahead in the brush, but it looked like the place had been traveled considerably. There could have been bunkers just meters from us, and we would not have seen them.

We made it through that area and breathed easier. About two hours on farther, I get a radio call saying that the S-3 wanted me to go back into that thicket because they had picked up an enemy radio transmit from in there somewhere. I told 'em that the place was really bad to try to move through or see anything. We hadn't seen anything the first time, and I doubted that we would the second. Fortunately, they didn't argue and let us go on. The place reminded me of parts of Charlie Ridge, except that it was not nearly as tall.

Captain Best stated that they could hear the air strikes across the valley in the hills south of the Ngan River. The Recon team knew that the 4th Marines involved in Operation Hastings were hammering and getting back the same from the NVA, only about three miles away. Then Best received orders to get closer to the battle by dropping off the ridge they had been patrolling and crossing a narrow valley where the small Khe Mai River flowed and then patrolling up to the top of Hill 100. From there, they would have a better view of the back side of the Operation Hastings battle, going on just beyond that.

Their trip to Hill 100 caused them to wade the Khe Mai River about two klicks from where a Terrebonne patrol had been shot out near the NVA hospital and division headquarters. Crossing the river put the Marines into chest-deep water, and Best felt very vulnerable. For the entire patrol, he had unsettling feelings about the nearby presence of the enemy.

As they made their way across the 300-meter-wide valley floor and the river, they found themselves facing a steep cliff about 100 meters tall—Hill 100. The climb was tough, and the Reconners could smell the presence of enemy soldiers. They came upon concealed fighting holes and prepared defensive positions in that cliff that they had not been able to see until they literally put their hands or feet into them. It was as if the NVA had left only minutes before them and the Marines had been in their rifle sights.

Captain Best stated: "I could feel it. We were very close to making major contact. Then, when we got to the top of this hill, I could see that our direction of patrolling meant crossing a narrow saddle which led to another, higher, jungled ridge. The signs and our instincts indicated we were walking very close on the heels of large groups of NVA."

Cpl. George Neville was on this patrol, and he described the scene on Hill 100: "I was really taken aback by the bunkers, fighting holes, and trenches. Maybe the one thing that impressed me the most was the stone-and-mortar building that was used for a latrine. I knew we were no longer fighting a guerrilla war. These guys were prepared, and they were there for the duration."

Best added: "I was glad that the S-3 radioed that they were sending out the choppers to pick us up. Ahead was some real bad news, and it was fine that we get out of there." It was never the Recon mission to be a combat team looking for a fight, and Best knew that there ought to be a lot more infantry out there to go after the numbers of NVA that were obviously nearby.

Corporal Neville stated:

I remember being extracted from that patrol and being dropped back at the Dong Ha airstrip. It was really a small, metal-planked runway with not much else but a few old French masonry buildings and the tents we had set up. There was this infantry battalion that had just off-loaded and were to join the battle at Hastings. I recall walking down the airstrip past hundreds of Marines who were lying all over the place taking it easy. They looked at us, still wearing our painted faces and bush hats, and I can remember telling one Marine lying there on the ground, "Marine, those aren't guerrillas out there you're going to fight. Keep your eyes open and your ass down."

At about the same time, Major Colby had landed a 1st Force patrol on top of the Rockpile. It was to be the pioneer of what Colby termed the Stingray mission. Sgt. Orest Bishko was the patrol leader, and Capt. Francis J. West, from Marine Corps Headquarters, accompanied the team on special assignment. That made a total of four Reconners and one officer. Colby agreed to the presence of West on the mission as long as West understood that Bishko was in command.

Two howitzers were placed in direct support of the team. Bishko established several observation points atop the pinnacle, and it wasn't long before the team had spotted approximately 200 NVA troops about 3.5 miles southwest. The enemy was not in the valley but on grass-covered hills close to the same elevation as the Recon team. Bishko called for artillery, adjusted it on target, and noted that about fifty of the enemy stayed behind as the balance disappeared into the draws and hills, out of sight.

Captain West was impressed with the Stingray concept, and later he reported to General Walt his positive impressions of coupling a Recon team OP and artillery in direct support. The philosophy was accepted officially at the III MAF headquarters, and a special element of the reporting section was created and code-named Stingray.

The concept of the Stingray patrol had developed over the years and was used by various Reconners, but Colby had practiced it in the early 1960s in Hawaii, where he was the commanding officer of Bravo Company, 3rd Recon. However, working against main force NVA units near the DMZ called for an adjustment in the Recon operating procedures, although the basics were much the same. According to Colby, factors that influenced a change in the methods included (1) the need to send out more patrols to cover larger areas with the same number of people, (2) the arrival of the UH-1D helicopter (the Huey "slick"), and (3) particular situations where it was felt that a large team simply could not be adequately inserted undetected and avoid the enemy who were present in overwhelming numbers.

However, the Rockpile remained a special situation. Colby sent in a larger team to develop the site as an observation post. Lt. J. G. Hart led a fifteen-man team to the Rockpile in July. There were two special communicators, two engineers, and two snipers. Two starlight scopes, eighteen claymore mines, and ten M-72s were taken. The patrol was very successful, and the Rockpile became a fixture for Recon teams.

Based upon their experiences as Task Unit Charlie and then as Recon Group Bravo, Major Colby established four general, but basic, rules:

1. Stay together no matter what happens; under no circumstances should the patrol break up and attempt to escape and evade the enemy.
2. Upon reaching an observation post, call artillery fire upon a set of known coordinates so later fire missions can be called by shifting from a reference point.
3. Maintain constant radio communications with headquarters; report the situation hourly; do not put a patrol into an area that is masked from the base and relay stations; establish a set procedure if communication is lost; ensure that people are fully familiar with the characteristics of the radio and with the need to maintain constant communications.
4. Never stay in one spot more than twelve hours; if the area is hot, move more often.

Regarding the last point, Colby noted that on one occasion, a young patrol leader stayed in one spot over several days, even though he was calling changes in location. The reasons for that are not known, but it proved fatal for the team leader, because the NVA found them. Colby stated: "That was a lesson I wish we didn't have to go through, but the rest learned."

The patrol with Captain Best in mid-July was Lieutenant Buhl's last patrol before he shipped back to the United States. Having been a Recon instructor in California, and with the experiences of a year of actual Vietnam combat, Buhl also left behind advice on the best methods of operation:

Recon teams would often have more supporting arms available than an infantry battalion. This support is critical to the team's mission and survival. Therefore, each member's abilities to navigate and communicate are critical. Strict discipline in the preparation for and conduct of the patrol, cross training, and keen utilization of all the senses will produce the best results. Salty attitudes and bad habits beget casualties. Everybody on the patrol has to know how to use the compass and map, how to organize a patrol, and how to move quietly on the alert through the bush. Everybody has to know radio procedures and the equipment. You never know when you are going to have to be the one calling in supporting arms or information about the enemy. And everybody has to know the capabilities of the supporting arms and aircraft. On a given day, any PFC might be the one having to call in artillery and adjust the rounds on target. Scuba, rubber boats, jump school are great for confidence, and that is important in the bush. But the key words are navigate, communicate, and eradicate.

Proper attitudes and professionalism were absolutely key to the accomplishment of the mission and to personal survival. The forces that the young Marines were pitting their skills against were good. Nguyen Van Mo, a master sergeant in the 40th Mine Sapper Battalion, described his reconnaissance and raid teams:

The training was elaborate. We learned how to crouch while walking, how to crawl, how to move silently through mud and water, how to walk through dry leaves. We practiced different ways of stooping while we walked. In teams of seven men, we practiced moving in rhythm to avoid being spotted under searchlights, synchronizing our motions, stepping with toes first, then gradually lowering our heels to the ground, very slowly, step by step.

Wading through mud, we were taught to walk by lowering our toes first, and then the rest of the foot. Picking our feet up, we would move them gently (to break any suction), then slowly pull up the heels to avoid making any noises. If you just pulled them up, without first moving them around gently, you'd make sounds. The same things happen if you don't put your toes down first. We used the same method for walking through water. On dry leaves, we'd sling our weapons over our backs and move in a bent-over position using hands as well as feet. We were taught to move the dried leaves away with our hands, then pull our feet up underneath our palms so that we wouldn't step on the leaves. We kept moving that way until we reached the objective. Time made no difference. In training, it might take two or three hours to crawl like this through five fences of barbed wire.*

The men from the sapper units refined their skills, including patience, for hours. Camouflage techniques varied according to the terrain and vegetation, and it would take two hours or so to camouflage the body. Tracks simply were not left behind, and often these sappers were in and out of U.S. or South Vietnamese installations without ever being detected. It seems impossible that those small teams went through minefields, under razor wire and searchlights, into U.S. positions, and then out again with no one knowing. The first hint that they

Portrait of the Enemy.

had been there was when the main attack came later, after their command had studied the models of the U.S. positions made by the sappers on their return. Casualties suffered by the sappers did not occur during the reconnaissance missions but primarily when they led the main attack—often a suicide attack—from within U.S. positions as their own infantry attacked from outside.

However, the mission and skills of Marine Recon were different from those of the sappers. For the most part, the Vietnamese had the cooperation of the local villagers and could live in the locale without being noticed by the Americans. Marines faced the opposite situation at every turn.

CHAPTER EIGHT

Hoover's Hunters and
the DMZ War Continues

After his reassignment from Vietnam, in an interview by Paige Mulhollan, General Walt was asked his thoughts about the war. In part they are as follows:

Some of the Army commanders, I guess, probably didn't see the value of working with and winning over the people like we did in I Corps. . . . I believe very strongly in the pacification effort. . . . I think there are two enemies in Vietnam [the guerrilla and the main force units]. I think the guerrilla—the one down among the people, the one that has got the stranglehold on the people—he is the one that had to be destroyed and eliminated. . . . The North Vietnamese Army . . . [had] two missions assigned them. I know this from papers we captured. . . . One was to go down and fight the U.S. and South Vietnamese Army forces to keep them off the back of the guerrilla, to pull us away from the populated area. . . . Their second . . . was . . . to cause as many casualties as possible on the United States forces so as to, quote, make headlines in the United States, unquote.

Concerning the Recon patrols along the DMZ, General Walt is quoted as saying:

I got better intelligence on the penetration through the DMZ area probably than anywhere else. . . . I had a lot of patrols of my own out, and through other intelligence means. The first time they came across with the division [the 324B] . . . in the summer of 1966—we knew that division was coming across. It was at that time that the Hastings battle started . . . we landed our battalions back of . . . their battalions . . .

and really chopped the division [324B] up in short order. So our intel-
ligence in that area was good. *

Operation Hastings ended on August 3, 1966. Contact with the enemy had been heavy, resulting in 574 Marines wounded or killed and
an estimated 700 NVA killed. Hill 208 had been determined to be the
command post for the entire 324B Division, rather than for just one of
its regiments. However, though the Marines of Task Force Delta had
made contact with elements of all three of 324B's regiments, as Best
and Buhl discovered a few miles south of the battle, not all 324B battalions were around Hill 208. However, by August 3, the 324B had
disappeared. It was thought that it had either returned across the border or had slipped farther into the higher hills and jungle to the west
to lick its wounds. General English disbanded the task force but left
one of the infantry battalions—2nd Battalion, 4th Marines (2/4)—at
Dong Ha. That battalion, together with the detachment from 3rd Recon Battalion, was to remain in the DMZ area to watch for enemy
troop movements in that very vulnerable area of South Vietnam. The
next phase of the operation in which the Recon Battalion was to participate along the DMZ was dubbed Operation Prairie.

Even though Hastings was terminated and the 324B was "chopped
up," the fighting remained tough and the enemy was still present in
significant numbers. On August 6, Team Groucho Marx from Major
Colby's command, led by S.Sgt. Billy Donaldson, was sent out on a
Stingray mission north of the Rockpile. On August 8–9, the patrol observed North Vietnamese soldiers and called for a reaction force to attempt to capture some. The tables were quickly turned, however, and
the one infantry platoon flown in by helicopter and the Recon team
were pinned down by heavy enemy fire from a nearby ridge. Due to
the heavy casualties, Staff Sergeant Donaldson took command of all
Marines until he was also severely wounded. The twenty-four-hour
battle resulted in five Marines dead and twenty-seven wounded as
they withstood attacks from at least a company-size force. One of the
enemy dead was the company commander. The heroics of the
Marines who battled against superior forces resulted in the award of
one Medal of Honor and one Navy Cross.

At this time, Lieutenant Vetter was leading his first patrol onto the
top of Charlie Ridge, and with action also occurring in the Phu Bai
sector, the battalion had its units engaged with significant concentrations of the enemy in all its RAORs.

Following Donaldson's patrol, an additional infantry battalion and

*This interview is on file at the LBJ Library in Austin, Texas.

supporting units were relocated to Dong Ha. But at the same time, Major Colby had finished his tour of duty and was replaced by Maj. William Lowry. It was at that point that Lt. Ron Hoover and his platoon were attached to the Recon detachment at Dong Ha.

Like Bill Buhl, Lieutenant Hoover was a mustang who had risen through the ranks to become an officer and Recon platoon commander. He reported to the 3rd Recon Battalion at the time that Terry Terrebonne and Bill Buhl were leaving. His platoon in Alpha Company became known as Hoover's Hunters, and the lieutenant was one of those whose face appeared on Vietcong/NVA wanted posters.

Hoover broke his platoon into four five-man teams, with him and his platoon sergeant each leading a team and corporals in command of the other two. The five-man team began to be more suitable because of the advent of the Huey "slick" transport chopper, which could much more quickly and quietly insert a five-man team into heavy jungle.

On September 9, Hoover led a team into the hills between the Rockpile and Khe Sanh, about twenty miles west of Dong Ha. They left at first light, and their mission was one of reconnaissance and observation. A captain from Division G-2 accompanied the team. Ron said, "All I remember about him was that he did pretty well, and that he was a jock type from Texas A & M."

As soon as they were inserted, they radioed back to the base that they had located a significant trail. Hoover said:

Although we were supposed to sit in an OP, the boss radioed to check out the trail. We did, and were on the move all day. That night we set up a harbor site and throughout the darktime we heard noises and smelled odors coming from ahead. Although I shouldn't have, I reconnoitered out of the harbor site around midnight. It was more difficult than I thought it would be, but at least I established the location of the sounds and odors. Getting back to the team was not easy. You worry about getting your dumb butt blown off by one of your own guys.

The team was northwest of where the future LZ Studd Camp Vandergrift would be, and just southeast of the foot of a mile-high mountain the Vietnamese called Tiger Mountain. The enemy camp was near Hill 492. It was the first time the area had been reconned, but it remained a significantly dangerous place, and members of the battalion were killed within a short distance of the location just weeks before 3rd Recon was to be shipped out of the country in 1969.

On Hoover's second day, the patrol quietly slipped up to the near side of the camp that he had located about 500 meters away on a knoll in the jungle. The vegetation was pretty thick, but the ground continued to rise into higher jungle beyond that hill. There were hootches with cooking utensils around, and a lot of fighting positions. Some of these were foxholes dug into the side of the hill like little caves. Each could hold one or two people, and the inside of each was covered with leaves like a matting. None of this was visible from the air. The patrol set itself in the jungle growth and watched the camp. In the part of the camp that they could observe no people were to be seen. The platoon then moved into the camp to investigate, but shortly found themselves in a tight bind.

Hoover said:

As we were checking out the camp, we heard voices coming up a ravine behind us. There was another trail that intersected with the one we had used at the edge of the camp, and the people coming were using that one. We believed that these guys might have left camp earlier to attend some classes farther down the slope. I got my team into these holes dug into the side of the hill in something of an L-shaped ambush inside their camp, and we waited.

We heard 'em laughing and joking, and I remember being surprised that they apparently didn't have a clue that we were around. The choppers had landed us only about a klick away the previous day. They got about twenty meters from us, and we had five of 'em in our sights, and although more were coming, we couldn't wait any longer. We dropped those front five with a quick burst of fire, and we heard scrambling back in the bush behind them. I expected to see them get on line and assault us, but they didn't—maybe they just didn't know what or how many we were.

Then Hoover and Andy Anderson jumped out of their holes and quickly checked out the bodies, grabbing some documents and weapons. The team started out for the high ground away from the camp. They would move for about ten minutes and then sit quietly, listening. Below them they heard someone shouting orders and people moving up the slope following them.

The patrol leader knew he was in a fix. There didn't seem to be any place for choppers to get in to pick up his team, they were being followed by an unknown number of enemy soldiers, and there were likely more in the area. They were on an uphill climb in the middle of jungle, and with only six people, counting the captain, if they took one wounded, it would have made things even more deadly.

Hoover described how the patrol attempted to keep ahead of the NVA and to be very careful:

I zigzagged the team uphill, always stopping and listening. The NVA kept close to us but still did not attack. The trees were fifty to seventy feet tall and too thick for any landing zones, and I knew that we had to have an LZ to get choppers in to extract us. When I tried to call in artillery for support, as well as to blast down some trees to make an LZ, I was told that it was not possible as General Krulak was flying in the area and artillery might hit his chopper. I felt that if Krulak had heard that, he would have gone and ripped somebody a new one for exposing a Recon team unnecessarily and using him as an excuse.

Anyway, we kept on the move, and they kept following but not making contact. That night, I set the team in a star defensive position, still under the canopy. You could hear 'em out there signaling to each other by beating bamboo sticks together. But they still did not attack— I never figured that out.

The next A.M. I knew we had to blast out an LZ. This couldn't last much longer—our luck was still holding, but for how long? I called in again for arty, and I got the same message: "The general is still flying around, you'll have to wait a couple of hours."

Finally the team got an artillery fire mission called, and it began to rip the area, shattering trees near the Marines. Then the NVA decided to start the battle, and from then until the birds came down and snatched the team out of their hole, they were under fire.

Lieutenant Hoover said:

After a clearing had been created by the 155 guns, Army Huey gunships came in. I was in contact with the lead pilot, and after we crawled into one of the holes blasted out by an arty round and he got our position, he told us to keep our heads down—to hide and watch.

There were four gunships flying in formation. First, they came from east to west and strafed the place. Then, they came north to south and did the same. They kept repeating the firing maneuver. After about thirty minutes, the pilot told me that they would pick us up one at a time, not staying for more than five seconds over our hole. That's exactly what happened. I told the G-2 captain to go out in the first bird. He was from Division Intelligence, and I felt that he needed to get out before there was any chance of him being captured. Finally, I was the last, but all told it wasn't long. Those Army birds did it beautifully: five seconds each, and we were jumping in one at a time.

The team was safely returned to its base at Dong Ha.

Each patrol was given a few days back at Dong Ha before going out again. The shorter their time in the field on their last patrol the shorter the length of time to their next patrol.

Another of Hoover's teams that was shortly to return to the same area just left by Hoover was led by Cpl. George Neville. He had been in Vietnam with Alpha Company since April. He, Ray Strohl, Al Rooney, Bob Young, and Robert Albach had all come across the Pacific by ship together, and they were among those who volunteered for Recon while sitting in the Marine replacement facility at the Da Nang airstrip. Albach ended up in Charlie Company and spent time patrolling Charlie Ridge. The others were sent to Company A, and Neville had been with Best and Buhl from Elephant Valley, northwest of Da Nang, to the DMZ. They had encountered enemy units prior to the DMZ patrols, including ones being led or accompanied by non-Orientals.

Two weeks after Hoover's patrol to Hill 492, Major Lowry, now in command of the Recon detachment, sent Neville's team back to recheck the area. Hoover had seen only a part of the camp, and no one knew for sure just how big it was or how many NVA were really out there.

The five-man Neville patrol, in addition to Neville, consisted of L.Cpl. James Grimm, Pfc. Alvin Stokes, Pfc. Stanley Paynter, and Pfc. Dennis Stahn. It would be awarded two Silver Stars and three Bronze Stars.

Neville described what happened:

We were inserted by Hueys, and as soon as we hit the deck, we knew we were in the big middle of beaucoup bad guys. We landed on a little knoll about twenty to thirty meters wide. Actually, the choppers didn't set down, and we had to jump from about four or five feet. Then, they were gone, and we immediately moved into the thickets. But as soon as the noise of the choppers was gone, we began hearing sounds from all directions. Hiding in the brush, we heard North Vietnamese voices, trees being chopped, and people breaking through the brush nearby. It seemed like those that were closest to the choppers had run. I don't know why, 'cuz we were sitting ducks. They must have been shocked and didn't stop to think. There were huts and signs of activity all around. Campfires still burned, with pots and pans cooking food, but no people. There were shelters, but I think the people had run away in the opposite direction, and now we took off in the other.

Before they departed Dong Ha, Neville had preset artillery on-call missions near their LZ just in case they ended up in the situation they now found themselves in. He immediately radioed for one of those on-calls to be fired.

He said:

As we set up in our little perimeter, barrage after barrage began to scream [in] like trucks tearing through the air. The terrain was all torn to hell around us. Then after that the fixed-wing came in. We communicated through an aerial observer flying overhead. He coordinated the whole air show. We had been inserted at about 0800 on September 23, and we called in artillery and air strikes until 1900 hours that evening. The NVA knew we were around but hadn't yet seen us.

So far undetected, the team of Reconners was maneuvering through a hornet's nest of NVA, more than Hoover had estimated to be at the enemy base camp his team had discovered not far away. The enemy was spread over a large area and in all probability consisted of several companies. Neville's team observed fortifications both finished and under construction. As the hours passed, the NVA regrouped and started their own search-and-destroy operation against the five young Americans, but Neville and his team continued to evade, calling in artillery and air strikes. He also called for an emergency extraction but was denied. The NVA had not yet seen any of the Marines, and the new commanding officer at Dong Ha decided that the team should remain and attempt to gain more information.

Neville stated:

We had to spend the night in another location, and we crawled through the brush to try to find the best possible harbor site. After finding one and setting ourselves up as best as possible, I planned new on-call artillery missions, including H & I rounds to keep the enemy off balance during the night. I felt that they would have just as hard a time moving in the night to find us as we would have.

We could hear 'em near us during the night. It sounded like they were building and digging all around, but fortunately there was no attempt to assault us during the night. The next morning we tried to move into a more defensible position. But I felt the whole mission at this point was compromised. We could not move without exposing ourselves to the enemy that waited. We knew they were around, but weren't sure just where, and they probably were in the same situation, except that by now they realized we were just one small team and knew that we were on this hill and had a good idea of just about where.

I now called back to the base for helicopters to extract us. Our request was again denied, and we were instructed to continue to use supporting arms and report observations.

Unfortunately, many Recon teams throughout the war were confronted with situations in which the rear command would direct them to continue to operate regardless of the fact that the team was in close contact with enemy units. There were numerous occasions when the command in charge of the fate of these small teams would order: "Break contact and continue your mission."

Shortly after the team was denied helicopters for an extraction, a group of fifteen to twenty uniformed NVA moved into position across the team's front. They maneuvered professionally and without fear, and prepared for an assault on the team.

Neville said:

Then, there was noise all around us. My point man pointed out another unit of ten to fifteen NVA setting up, preparing to attack. But it was like they knew we saw them, and it didn't worry them at all. They went about their business, surrounding us and preparing to attack. The terrain was not jungle, but a lot of thick brush and rolling hills. We set up a defensive perimeter as best we could, but we were surrounded and outnumbered by a hell of a lot. It was scary—like a little Alamo.

In ten minutes, we were hit by rifle fire from all sides. Then, suddenly, we saw about thirty to forty of 'em get up and attack from my right. They were pros, using fire team rushes like the Marine Corps teaches. They would use low crawls, and I could hear the commanding officer among them shouting orders. They seemed to have good command and control and were well disciplined.

The Marines fought back, but they were outnumbered ten or more to one. "We were under constant fire," Neville said, "but were fighting back for all we were worth. Stokes was shot in the arm but kept firing. We called for gunships, and they came in like avenging angels to pound the enemy for the second straight day."

The Marine Corps had finally gotten a unit of Huey slicks and gunships, and the Marine Reconners had begun to use both the Marine Hueys and the Army's. However, the Hueys were never available to the Marines in the numbers available to similar Army units.

Neville then communicated through an aerial observer overhead and called in Phantoms. If the Marines were to survive, it would only be if their radio was not destroyed and the jets and gunships were accurate. Nevertheless, Neville called in a ring of steel close around his men:

I talked 'em in on top of the NVA, who were only a few meters away, and a lot of enemy were caught in the open grass. Then the AO told me that we had to find a way to get the hell out of there as the F-4s were going to drop napalm. So I told him to have the jets make a run over the target to fix the location, and then as they climbed high to swing back over to dive for the bombing run, we would be running off the back side of that hill and hoping that we didn't run into any enemy in that direction. And then they came screaming over our heads about a hundred feet up, and as they climbed back up again, we ran.

The bush was thick, and the Marines—including the wounded Stokes—shoved their way through the thick tangle and ran as fast as they could to get past the crest. As they stumbled and ran down the opposite side of that piece of high ground they felt and heard the explosions of silver napalm canisters behind them. Each canister contained 125 gallons of jellied gas and spread death over an area the length of a football field, consuming the oxygen and burning or choking to death anyone in the way.

Neville said:

We had gotten far enough to survive the blast, but we still felt the heat and the burning smoke as it drifted over us. Then the AO called to us that we had to go back up to where we had been to get extracted because the terrain was too bad and steep where we were. We just hoped that everybody was fried up there so we wouldn't get shot to hell as soon as we were back up there.

The five Reconners climbed back up to a usable LZ and called in the Huey slick. The bird dropped down. It wasn't a gunship, but all hands aboard were firing their weapons into NVA teams that had regrouped from the bombing runs and were now trying to bring down the chopper.

The bird could get only one skid on the slope, and as the crew fired in all directions the Marines jumped for the hatch. They hoisted each other on board as the pilot pulled back up to try to reach the safety of the skies. One bullet exploded through the metal skin of the chopper inches behind the pilot's head, and several came up from below and whistled between the Marines' legs; one round partially severed a fuel line, which leaked on the Marines under it. But the Huey rapidly pulled away while supporting gunships strafed the enemy.

That Recon team had come very close to being five KIA, and probably KIA–BNR (killed in action—body not recovered).

A few days later the *Stars and Stripes*, in an account less modest than Neville's, reported:

> The Marines met the assault. They poured automatic fire into the attackers' skirmish line. Six enemy soldiers fell under the initial burst. The enemy kept coming until the five men hurled grenades to stop the advance. . . . The North Vietnamese took more casualties and stopped to regroup for a new assault—this time from three sides with a larger force. . . . The Marines fought desperately against the closing walls of enemy fire. They killed several more with rifles and grenades as they continued down the hill. . . . Pfc. Stanley Paynter shot one enemy with his rifle. When two more came to drag the body off, Paynter fired his M-79, hitting one in the chest, killing both. . . . The five men with painted faces had held off more than a company of North Vietnamese regulars. They killed 20 in their battle for life.

For his "exceptional presence of mind and courage in leading his men against the enemy and in gathering valuable intelligence information," George Neville was awarded the Silver Star for this patrol. Pfc. Alvin Stokes also received the Silver Star, and L.Cpl. James Grimm, Pfc. Stanley Paynter, and Pfc. Dennis Stahn all received the Bronze Star.

Patrols led by Hoover and Neville in the same general area less than two weeks apart had found encampments that could hold a company of NVA each. The eighteen- and nineteen-year-old Marine-boot-camp-trained Reconners operating along the DMZ had faced the tough professionals of the North Vietnamese regular army and were gaining a healthy respect for the new forces with whom they did battle.

However, there were also some new Recon forces joining the battle along the DMZ. At the time of the Hoover patrol, Operation Deckhouse IV was commencing in a ship-to-shore assault along the coast between the Cua Viet River and the DMZ. Battalion Landing Team 1/26 was the assault element. Attached were units from 3rd Force Recon and the 5th Recon Battalion that had arrived from the United States and were to become operationally and administratively attached to the 3rd Recon Battalion. For a short time 3rd Recon had as part of its command both 1st Force Recon Company and four platoons from 3rd Force Recon Company. The latter remained attached to the battalion until 3rd Recon received its orders to ship back to the United States in 1969. The one platoon from the 5th Recon Battalion was absorbed into the battalion structure. However, 1st Force was to shortly be reassigned to operate with the 1st Recon Battalion in the Da Nang area.

The arrival of the 3rd Force platoons reunited the new commanding officer of the 3rd Recon Battalion, Gary Wilder, and units of his former command in the United States. The 3rd Force Company had been created in November 1965 with Major Wilder as its CO. Its headquarters was at Camp Lejeune, North Carolina. Prior to that, Wilder had been with the scouting and patrolling branch of the Basic School, Quantico, Virginia. He brought a number of his staff with him to his new company. Other officers were selected from the infantry battalions, NCOs and staff NCOs were picked from existing reconnaissance units, and lance corporals and below were to be honor men from Infantry Training Regiment classes after boot camp.

Ken Jordan was then a lieutenant with 3rd Battalion, 2nd Marines, but received orders transferring him to the new unit. "Our mission was to organize and prepare for service with the Fleet Marine Force Pacific," he said. "We worked out of Camp Geiger alongside the 2nd Force Recon Company. However, their mission focused them on support for the Fleet Marine Force Atlantic."

The circumstances surrounding the initial failures of the 1st Force Company in Vietnam had been transmitted to the command of the new unit, and Major Wilder wanted his unit to do less jumping out of planes and less rubber boat and submarine training. According to Ken Jordan, the key words were now "shoot, move, and communicate." According to Jordan, they still jumped on the weekends when they could.

About five months after their creation, on April 25, 1966, three platoons from the company received their orders to ship out for Vietnam aboard the U.S.S. *Boxer*. There was no detachment headquarters, but Ken Jordan had just been promoted to captain and was the senior platoon commander, with responsibility for the three platoons. The other two platoon commanders were Lt. Doug O'Donnell and Lt. Jeff Ketterson. The remaining three platoons and the company headquarters stayed at Camp Geiger.

The *Boxer* sailed east through the Suez Canal and arrived in Vietnam on May 20. The platoons were attached to the 9th Marine Amphibious Brigade (9th MAB), then under the command of Brig. Gen. Michael Ryan. However, they spent only a few days in Vietnam before being shipped to Okinawa. Within days of their arrival, Jordan had to send Lieutenant O'Donnell's platoon into Vietnam to join Major Colby's detachment as they prepared for those first DMZ patrols. For the next two months Jordan's and Ketterson's platoons trained in Okinawa. During this time, Major Wilder came through the island on his way into country to take command of the 3rd Recon Battalion.

Finally, on August 1, 1966, the two platoons were shipped from Okinawa to Vietnam and assigned to the command of the 1st Battalion, 26th Marines (1/26), as part of the Special Landing Force. However, they did not immediately go to the DMZ and the 3rd Recon Battalion, but instead participated with 1/26 in Operation Deckhouse III, just north of Saigon. Ken Jordan said about that experience: "Except for a beach reconnaissance, where we went in by rubber boats from a submarine, we were used incorrectly. But frankly, that was my opinion about the use of other Recon units in Vietnam. No one understood the mission of Recon and how to use us. It was like we were another rifle platoon but a little further out front."

Three weeks later, the Reconners were near the DMZ, hitting the beach as part of Operation Deckhouse IV. By then the Recon element had been joined by a platoon of the 5th Recon Battalion from Camp Pendleton commanded by Lt. Judd Spainhour. On September 11, Jordan had his teams inland and to the right flank of the attacking BLT 1/26, and Spainhour was with his platoon to the left front of the Battalion Landing Team. The teams were inserted about 5,000 to 6,000 meters inland and the grunts crossed the beach behind them. The land was primarily rolling sand dunes, and the Recon teams, acting as an infantry screen in this type of terrain, were placed in an obvious combat mission role rather than one of reconnaissance. Intelligence had estimated that the enemy was more likely to hit the Marines from the right. The Cua Viet River and the Dong Ha base were a few miles to the Marines' left, but it was from this side that the Spainhour platoon was hit.

According to Ken Jordan:

Both Judd's platoon and mine were on a common Recon net with the battalion S-2. On September 15, my radio operator signaled me over and I heard firsthand the firefight that Judd's platoon had gotten into. Then I heard their platoon sergeant come on the air using code words indicating that Judd had been killed. A week later I lost one of my men, Dale Bradley, when we were hit by mortars.

The concept of our operations was one in which we set up a platoon patrol base, and teams would move out in different directions from there.

On September 25, the Recon teams backloaded and sailed south, finally ending their trek at Phu Bai, where they were attached to the 3rd Recon Battalion, then under Major Wilder's command. One more platoon from 3rd Force joined the battalion in October when Lt. George Stern brought his platoon ashore. In all, four platoons from 3rd Force Recon were attached to the 3rd Recon Battalion, while the headquarters and the remaining platoons left in the States relocated to Camp Pendleton and were reconstituted there to a full six-platoon Force Recon Company. There were now two 3rd Recon companies in the Corps, with four platoons attached to the 3rd Recon Battalion and the new company at Camp Pendleton.

Ken Jordan said that his most difficult moment in Recon happened on October 21, 1966: "I was in a Huey on an overflight when I got a message that Doug O'Donnell was killed nearby. He was shot through the heart as he ran out of a chopper on a team insert. They had rejoined us two days earlier from their detachment to 1st Force."

There later was to develop concern over the loss of officers on patrol with their teams. There were times when there were not only few officers, but the teams of Reconners rarely saw an officer. However, Jordan was adamant about the role of Recon officers. He stated:

> Lieutenants went out as patrol leaders, and it was October 6 that for the first time I sent my platoon out without me. Then in November, I was given the additional duty of battalion S-3, and I know firsthand how we were directed to patrol. We had orders to send out a certain number of patrols in specific sectors. It was simple math. There [were] not enough officers to maintain officer patrol leadership. For example, each Force platoon had two patrols, and I had a platoon commander and platoon sergeant in charge of each one. Then at Khe Sanh the situation became aggravated, and we were often without officers and staff NCOs as patrol leaders. The battalion teams operated in much the same way, with the platoon commander and platoon sergeant being patrol leaders of the two squads in each platoon. Marine Corps officers receive better training to be field leaders of their troops than is given officer candidates in other military services around the world. That is where they should be: *leading* Marines.

Major Colby was very proud of the Marines of his Recon detachment who initiated the DMZ battles. He stated that he had prepared a recommendation for the Presidential Unit Citation for his Recon unit and personally gave three copies of the recommendation to General English, who commanded the task force at Dong Ha. But, he said, "After that, they disappeared—never to be seen again. General English was always reserved about our work. I still feel that the job Recon did in that area was never fully appreciated."

The DMZ war that had started with Colby and his Reconners and the increased tempo of the fighting throughout South Vietnam was reflected in the questions being raised and the decisions being put into action within the office of the commander in chief. The secretary of defense had departed from his earlier belief that it would take only 200,000 American soldiers and two years to win the war, and by the end of 1966 he wanted the president to "seek a political settlement." The president himself asked his chairman of the Joint Chiefs of Staff, Gen. Earle Wheeler, and the MACV commanding general, William Westmoreland, "When we add divisions, can't the enemy add divisions? . . . Where does it all end?"

During the Vietnam battles of 1966, the battalion's teams had sighted, if all the enemy soldiers and workers counted are assembled together, approximately one entire enemy division with supporting units. The most notable and threatening year, however, was still to come.

During the twelve months of 1967, reconnaissance teams from 3rd Recon, in the northern two provinces of South Vietnam, observed and found themselves in the middle of twice what they had seen the previous year. It was a deadly year for both sides, but the one most astounding patrol began in the last days of 1966 and continued to January 2, 1967. It will be forever known as the Siler patrol.

CHAPTER NINE

The Co Bi–Thanh Tan

"During that year [1966], U.S. and South Vietnamese forces captured documents revealing enemy plans, strategic guidance, tactical doctrine, personnel rosters, and evaluations of U.S. and South Vietnamese forces. . . . Information, most of which was gained through . . . penetrations of enemy base areas . . . In many cases, individuals who performed in intelligence missions displayed courage, brilliance, and unparalleled dedication. According to numerous accounts many of these individuals outperformed the system by a wide margin . . . the quality of human-source information collected and the resulting intelligence suffered for the lack of proper management. The human-source collection effort . . . far exceeded the capabilities of the analysts, who were deluged. . . . Thus, analysts fell behind by three to six months in processing raw reports into a useful data base."—The BDM Corporation's Study of the Vietnam War, commissioned by the U.S. Army.

Although 1966 saw the 3rd Recon Battalion thrown, sometimes alone, into the teeth of the North Vietnamese Army's first major invasion across the DMZ, and although 1968 was the year of the massive Vietcong/NVA Tet Offensive, 1967 was the major killer of the war. During those twelve months, 3rd Recon patrols counted 14,121 VC/NVA in the northern two provinces of Quang Tri and Thua Thien. By comparison, the entire 324B NVA Division had an estimated strength of 8,000 soldiers. Over the two provinces, those same small Recon teams were responsible for killing or wounding an estimated 2,692 enemy, primarily by the use of supporting arms called in on their targets, although many were accounted for by the use of their own small arms fire. But these battles took a toll on the battalion.

During 1967 the average number of Reconners from the four line companies and from 3rd Force either on patrol or back in camp and preparing to return to the bush on patrol was just under 300 men. For that one year, the battalion suffered 284 Marines wounded and 46 killed, plus 4 Navy Corpsmen killed and 19 wounded. The casualties were at times horrific. However, the one mission that found a Recon team potentially in more danger than any other ended with no casualties being suffered at the hands of the enemy.

Lt. Jerry Siler's patrol northwest of the city of Hue over New Year's Eve and New Year's Day, 1966–67, was flown out from the new battalion headquarters at Phu Bai. The command post had moved to that location in the latter part of 1966 to help meet the increasing threat from the North Vietnamese. At the same time, the 1st Recon Battalion had moved into Camp Reasoner at Da Nang from its old post farther south in Chu Lai. The initial Recon command at Phu Bai was spearheaded by Bravo Company under the command of Capt. James Compton and, later, Capt. Sam Owens. However, Jerry Siler had been a platoon commander in Charlie Company at Da Nang. After the losses suffered during Operation Allegheny on Charlie Ridge, the platoon had been sent to Okinawa for refitting and training. But its stay was cut short, and the platoon was quickly brought back to Vietnam. This time it was sent ashore at Phu Bai and attached to Bravo Company.

Fifteen miles northwest of the city of Hue was the Co Bi–Thanh Tan, a valley named after two nearby hamlets. Running east to west, it was bracketed on the south by mountains and ridgelines and on the north by very low brushy hills that were no more than 40 meters high and dotted with streams and rice fields. The mountains bordering the south side of the valley were only about five miles from Highway One. The valley was about 4,000 meters wide. The coastline lay only six to seven miles northeast of the highway and paralleled that Street Without Joy all the way into North Vietnam, about forty miles away. The Co Bi–Thanh Tan Valley and ridges were to become a unique and storied battleground for the 3rd Recon Battalion.

The Co Bi–Thanh Tan Valley could easily be reached by trails and roads from the A Shau to the west and southwest and other NVA strongpoints to the northwest. It was a major avenue of approach to Hue City and to the fertile rice-growing plains between Highway One and the sea. Large cart paths crossed it, both from the mountains toward the sea, and also along the valley's east-west axis from the Bo River and Route 554 on the east to Route 601 on the west. The eastern part of the valley had cultivated rice fields; the western part was thickly overgrown with brush and vines, and some areas had heavy tree growth. The villages in the valley were so dominated by the Vietcong that the South Vietnamese government had relocated the villagers and designated the valley as a free-fire zone. Even so, many peasants had escaped from the relocation camps and had returned to their old homelands and ancestral burial grounds.

On December 10, 1966, main force enemy units struck in coordinated attacks on the Phong Dien District Headquarters, three miles to the north of the valley, and the An Lao Bridge, across the Bo River to the south. The Marine command felt that this was evidence that the 6th NVA Regiment—an estimated 1,500 men based in the mountains west of the Co Bi–Thanh Tan—was attempting to move into the populated rice-growing areas in the lowlands. On December 17, the 3rd Battalion, 26th Marines, was moved from the Dong Ha area to positions near Phong Dien and immediately began to encounter the enemy. On December 22 and 23, the enemy hit 3/26 with mortar barrages and ground probes of their lines, and then withdrew.

On December 23, Maj. Gen. Wood B. Kyle ordered the 2nd Battalion, 26th Marines, to join the 3rd Battalion in Operation Chinook, just west of Phong Dien along the O Lau River. He also moved the 4th Marines Headquarters from Dong Ha to take command of the operation. However, because of the monsoon rains and the maneuverability of enemy forces, the Marine infantry found little evidence of the elusive 6th NVA Regiment.

But the operation did produce evidence that in addition to the 6th NVA, the 802nd Battalion of the 1st Provisional VC Regiment was in the area with another 300 to 400 men. This indicated the possibility that the balance of that regiment was also in the area. It was suspected that the regiments' combined strength of about 2,500 soldiers was being directed at the U.S. and ARVN forces in the area of the Co Bi–Thanh Tan. In all likelihood their objective was twofold: (1) disrupt Allied lines of communication, and (2) attempt to appropriate their share of the rice supply from the fertile lands either near the valley or between Highway One and the sea.

Three other independent NVA battalions—the 808th, the 810th, and the 814th—each carrying on its rolls between 350 and 400 men, had recently been confirmed operating in the twenty-mile area between Quang Tri and the Bo River. In December, III MAF intelligence reports stated: "Noteworthy from the standpoint of enemy effort was the heavy and sustained mortar fire brought to bear against the 3rd Battalion, 26th Marines, on 21 through 23 December and the continuity of enemy action which was maintained for this three-day period. . . . A captured VC stated during interrogation that the 6th Regiment, consisting of four battalions, was located in the area." This location was approximately 4,000 to 5,000 meters west of the Co Bi–Thanh Tan Valley, an easy march.

Finally, four provincial and district VC companies with about 100 men each had been determined to be active in the same area. None of these enemy order-of-battle counts included either the local militia forces or the vast underground sea occupied by the "shadow government" and administrative support forces that worked and lived in their own hamlets and villages.

So, excluding these latter and excluding the 95th NVA Regiment, which had disappeared after its successes in the A Shau, III MAF intelligence in December 1966 estimated enemy main force units operating in or not far from the Co Bi–Thanh Tan at a possible accumulated strength of 4,000 soldiers. The III MAF commanding general, Lewis Walt, and the 3rd Marine Division CG, Major General Kyle, had reason to be concerned.

In this situation, Recon patrols were sent to penetrate the valley and surrounding mountains and hills in order to monitor enemy activities. Unfortunately, they were not given the G-2 information that would lead them to anticipate what was about to happen.

Lieutenant Siler was an intense mustang lieutenant with a driving desire to get the job done while watching out for all details. His experiences had made him a believer in the nine-man team because it was small enough to function as an effective Recon patrol but large enough to be able to defend and fight for itself in case of contact with the enemy. He felt that smaller patrols had much greater difficulty in taking care of their wounded while combating a superior enemy force. He emphasized training for all his Marines, requiring that everyone in the patrol know radio equipment and procedures, know how to call in supporting arms, and know how to read the compass and map and navigate the terrain with confidence. On December 30, 1966, Lieutenant Siler and his patrol were tested to their limits and beyond.

As a prelude to that experience, Siler's team had been on a post-Christmas patrol on the west side of the Co Bi–Thanh Tan Valley in the mountains. Siler said:

> It was just like the Charlie Ridge patrols. The S-3 gave us about a three-grid-square area, and we were to recon the place within that box. We carried an M-60 machine gun with us—our experience out there was that we had better have plenty of firepower.
>
> On the second day of that patrol we pulled off an ambush when a VC patrol walked right in front of us and took a break. In fact, I was in the middle of calling in a fire mission on a VC patrol in the valley

below us on the other side of the ridge when this other bunch of VC walked in front of us. It was composed of seven men and had a white Caucasian in the lead, and there was a black non-Oriental in the patrol also. They were all armed, but when they stopped for that break, they disappeared behind the bush. They were downhill in the brush and rock about thirty meters away. In fact, I had a two-man team down very close to them.

I had my guys trained to fire the first round on semiautomatic and then switch to automatic fire. If possible, they were also to aim in on the VC that corresponded to their number in the patrol. The number-one man would sight on the first man in the enemy team, and so forth. This would keep all of us from aiming in on the same one or two.

At Siler's command, his team initiated the ambush, then quickly moved through the thick brush and boulders into the ambush site. They found three bodies and blood trails but did not locate either of the non-Orientals.

Dale Sare was running point for Jerry Siler. Sare was a veteran of Charlie Ridge and Operations Taut Bow and Allegheny, and he was nearing the end of his tour of duty in Vietnam. Siler said:

You know it takes a special individual to be a Recon Marine, and it takes someone who is extra special to be a Recon point man. Dale Sare was one of those. The good point man is born with the natural instincts; you just don't train it into a person. When I say we pulled nineteen patrols with Dale Sare as point without losing a man, that speaks to how good he was. You can't put a value on something like that.

Siler continued the account of that first patrol: "After the ambush, we moved away from our previous location and down into the valley, and you know it was a free-fire zone. All the civilians were supposed to have been relocated out of there, and planes could drop their bombs freely without clearance. But, hell, we knew a lot of those farmers had come back to their lands and were mixed up with the VC."

Dale Sare then picked up the story:

We came out of the hills and were skirting the edge of the valley. First, Puff the Magic Dragon almost blew us away, strafing the valley with his coaxial-mounted Mike 60s, but we made it through that. Then we found ourselves very damn near a roadway. It was a well-used, hard-packed earthen roadway about five meters wide, and it seemed like the whole valley had suddenly come alive with people trooping down that road in one direction or the other. The vegetation was thick, preventing us from getting a good view of all the traffic, but I didn't notice any uniforms on any of the people. But being holed up in the bush trying not to get caught didn't give us a complete view of all that was happening. They were probably a mixed group of both civilians and VC, all in their black pajamas.

Siler was on the radio, calling in the reports to the battalion S-3. Very shortly a decision was made to extract the team; B-52s were to hit the valley with an arc light bombing run. The team carefully pulled back off the valley floor into the first higher ground and was picked up by helicopters.

The B-52s flew silently high over the valley on December 29, 1966, but their bombs screamed into the valley, boring into the earth and exploding it almost from the inside out. The thundering devastation could be felt and heard for miles. As the B-52s were attempting the complete demolition of the valley, Siler was told to get a team ready for a one-day bomb-assessment patrol on the thirtieth.

Siler said:

It was just supposed to be for one day—go out early and come back at about 1700 hours. The choppers were due in to our CP before 0800 in the morning. It was still the rainy season, but we hadn't had any for a few days. So just for that one day, we were going to travel lightly. One canteen, no chow—we would have breakfast and supper back in camp, no extra gear except for all the photographic equipment. Of course, we had our two PRC-25s and weapons. They wanted a body count, an analysis of the craters, any other effects of the bombs, and they gave me a big shopping list of things to look for.

Led by a Corporal Rubio, one other team from the platoon was out on the Co Bi–Thanh Tan ridge at that time, and it was only a few klicks away from where Siler was to take his team.

The bomb run paralleled the hills, cratering the valley floor from east to west. Siler said:

When I got out there and saw the craters and terrain, I knew there was a problem. It was devastating. The craters were as deep as fifty feet— maybe a hundred feet across. Trees had been picked up and thrown. The trees and undergrowth in places were so thick that it took us forty-five minutes to work our way around one of those monsters.

I wanted the patrol to be able to crisscross the valley floor, but I knew that to do an adequate assessment of what had happened would take a week or more.

Sare added: "We would send a guy into the crater to get pictures. There were bunkers blasted apart. Ammo boxes and weapons' parts, including mortars, were lying around. It was amazing to see how much had been hidden down in that valley. You could've walked right past 'em and never seen 'em before that B-52 arc light."

Siler continued: "We were at least two klicks from the hills but in real rough stuff—lots of bush, trees, and vines, and a lot of that blown into a twisted mass by the bombs. I think they used 250-, 500-, and 1,000-pound bombs."

However, Siler received an emergency call from Rubio, who was in the hills 2,000 to 3,000 meters away. His patrol had been hit from above by an NVA ambush, and two of his men were wounded, leaving the team with seven healthy Marines but facing machine gun fire from the high ground. Siler quickly made the only decision he could: he would take his team on a run through the bush and up onto the ridge to relieve his corporal.

"We took a straight path toward them, and I was running point," said Sare. "Jerry pointed, and I took off running to the southwest toward that knoll that Rubio was stuck on. We ran, jumped, climbed—whatever it took to get to 'em."

NVA gunners swept the field with automatic fire as Siler's Marines came running through the low bush to get to Rubio's team. The Marines, running and stumbling, fought just-a-minute vines and their own fears to help their buddies. They made the final dash and hit the dirt with their friends—all of them now pinned down by the machine gun above.

Two Marines from Rubio's team had been wounded before Siler threw his body alongside his corporal. The lieutenant quickly assessed the situation and determined that there was one enemy machine gun position, with probably three or four men, above them and about 50 meters away on a knoll. He felt that there were no other enemy. But then another Marine went down. Medevac choppers were called, and Siler quickly positioned his Marines to fight back; he had to act fast or more Marines would be hurt in their very vulnerable position. He had the combined teams lay down a base of fire on the enemy-held knoll above and sent Sare and two men to assault the NVA position, right into the face of that machine gun.

Sare said:

You never like to think about jumping up into that kind of hostile fire. So you just don't think—you do. I took two men, and we crouched low, ready to jump and run like hell at that gun position that was about fifty meters away above us on a knoll, and the damn terrain was pretty open. We had to depend on the covering fire of the rest of the patrol to keep Charlie's head down and his guns quiet; otherwise, our asses would have been burnt. Then our buddies poured it on 'em, and we were scrambling, running, dodging, and I don't remember praying, but there was probably some of that, too. I could feel my heart pounding out my ears, but I noticed that the machine gun had gone silent. We made it to the top and found five empty foxholes, which we jumped into. Then above us, less than one hundred yards away, we saw several enemy troops disappearing into the jungle. The jungle rose up like a giant wall at that point and just swallowed 'em, and they were gone.

The terrain had leveled off above the machine gun position, and the Marines had not been able to see the enemy soldiers move back toward the protection of that canopy. Using the terrain as a visual and protective block, they were able to escape the team without being seen. They did leave behind blood in the holes.

Siler stated:

The birds were on their way, and I called for artillery to blast away at the front of the jungle where those Charlie had disappeared. Then, within ten minutes, the choppers were above us. They dropped down, coming in fast, then picked up our wounded, flew off just as fast, and we were alone again.

I had to reorganize the remaining members of both teams. I had to take Sare and the other five of our team back down into the valley. So I told Rubio to wait until after we left and then to move through the bush on an oblique toward the higher ground off to the northwest. There they were to watch the valley floor and cover our backsides. Then my team moved back down into the valley and continued our mission of checking out the bomb damage.

The weather was still sunny, but clouds were starting to drift in from the sea. The team was to be out of there by 1700 hours that afternoon, but there was no way they could do an adequate bomb damage assessment in that amount of time. It was already just past noon, and Siler knew that he had a problem. They would have to get as far as they could, but they had carried no packs, no food, and only one canteen of water each for the one-day mission. They couldn't stay any longer than planned. The rain gods of Vietnam, however, had other plans for the Marines.

Siler's men tried to crisscross the valley, but it wasn't simply a matter of walking around bomb craters. The tangled bush, vines, and torn and twisted trees blocked their path. The B-52s had taken the earth and turned it upside down and sideways, thoroughly fouling the terrain. The Marines found partially buried logs that had been used for fortifications. There were ammo cans and other evidence of enemy positions ripped open and exposed. However, rolling in from the sea, a few miles away, was an ominous cloud bank, bringing the dark and wet monsoon-driven skies behind.

In that part of Vietnam, December and January are the peak months of monsoon rains, and the Marines had been experiencing a freak dry period for a few days; it was normal at that time of year to endure thirty inches of rain and more in one month.

Siler said:

> Before our pickup time, we were socked in, and it started raining like it only could in this part of the world. I knew we were dead in the water. No choppers could get to us now. We went out for an eight-hour patrol in the sun without raingear and food, and now who the hell knew what was going to happen. The rain drenched us to our bones. The next day was New Year's Eve, and our U.S.-declared two-day New Year's truce would begin.

By that time, the Marines had gotten into a flat area, but it was fast turning into mudflats. The trees were some distance away, and it was mostly brush and open land round the team's location. The dusk of evening was made even darker by the hard rain. Siler decided to try to find the best harbor site he could given the situation. Rain-drenched and increasingly caked in mud, the men came to a slight rise in the ground that was home to a thick clump of bushes. It wasn't far from a dirt roadway, which gave Siler some cause for concern, but the rain was too much, and it was getting late. In wind-driven rain that felt like hail, the men set up as best they could.

That night, Lt. Tim Huff, who had been on Charlie Ridge in August on ojt patrols with Lieutenant Vetter, was patrol leader of a team southwest of Siler and the Co Bi–Thanh Tan. The rain had stopped short of his position, but the cloud cover overhead made the night very dark. During the night, Huff's team sighted long lines of lights. They were some distance away, but he said the lights resembled lanterns moving along paths through the narrow valleys toward the Co Bi–Thanh Tan. He reported the lights to the battalion, but the sighting had already been reported by another Recon team. The next day, Huff's team would be extracted, but Siler's was bogged down and cut off.

Sare described the next morning:

> On the thirty-first, we woke up to real misery, if you can call what we had been doing sleeping. We were soaked cold, and nobody had any

food, raingear, or enough cleaning gear for the weapons. We were on this little rise in the ground that was nothing more than about ten-foot tall near a roadway—well, it was an unpaved cart path I guess, about four or five meters wide. It was very early yet. The terrain was open with about three-foot grass, except on this ten-foot-tall bump in the ground where there was a lot of thick brush. It was only about twenty feet from that roadway.

Siler's seven-man team stayed in the cover of the brush and prepared to sit out the rain. Soaked by hours of rain and mud, the skin on their hands and feet began to wrinkle and hurt. They were trapped by the storm, but a more dangerous enemy was approaching.

"You could hear 'em coming," Jerry Siler said. "They didn't have any idea a crazy team of Marine Recon was holed up in the bushes, in the storm, only a few feet from the trail."

Despite the rain, the sounds of weapons and gear banging around, and the talking and walking of an army in route-step-march, told the Marines what was descending down that wide trail out of the mountains right toward them. The NVA had no fear of marching down that road; they were covered not only by the rain, but also by the unilateral U.S. cease-fire.

Sare said:

Corporal Dean and I crawled a few feet through the bushes toward the trail to see what the hell was coming. Laying there in the mud, I parted the branches and just a few feet from me was an undamnbelievable scene. There was an endless column of North Vietnamese regulars. They had khaki uniforms, pith helmets, and I'll never forget the blue raingear. Weapons? They had it all—rifles, machine guns, 82-mm mortars. In fact, they seemed to be marching by type of unit. There were infantry soldiers, and then there would be heavy weapons, and then supply people, and so forth. But what scared me the most was the fact that they had flankers on either side of the route paralleling the road, which meant they had soldiers out beyond us. They came on four abreast and didn't stop coming. And they were so close they could have spit on me. We laid there for a while almost afraid to move. Then real carefully we slunk back to Jerry.

Siler continued:

We sat and hid in the thickets with the rain still falling, trying to figure this thing out. I was reporting by PRC-25 back to the battalion what we were seeing. But we had the main body in front of us continuing to march past like a parade, and their flankers were on our back side.

Some of 'em were stopping and talking, making head calls, and just whatever around our little brush-covered bump in the ground. I contacted Rubio up in the hills to find out what he could see. But the valley floor was socked in by fog and rain from his viewpoint, which was about a mile and a half away, and he couldn't see anything. I was afraid these soldiers would relieve themselves too close to us one of these times, and we'd be found and be in a real hurt locker. I sure didn't want to get into a fight now. I wouldn't have been able to call in artillery or air support for help because of the cease-fire. We would have been dead meat. I told Dale that we had to find another location farther away.

Dale led us crawling through the low grass and mud. I prayed that we wouldn't crawl into one of those flankers. At least the rain covered us, too.

Up to their butts in mud, the team crawled carefully to a position about thirty yards farther away. There, they could still keep the road and NVA under observation but felt a little safer. Being covered by both the weather and the cease-fire for the American New Year's celebration, the enemy seemed unworried.

Siler said:

As the time went by, the S-3 back at the battalion was pressing us for a head count. Sometimes when the rain slackened, we could see and count 'em better, but these NVA just kept coming—like a river. I knew that we couldn't tell them back at the battalion everything we were seeing, 'cuz they'd know we were out there chewing on beetlenut or something. Nobody would believe us. So I had Dale stick his eyeballs out of the bush and count the number of soldiers passing by a certain tree while I was using a watch to count the minutes. Every once in a while one of their flankers came pretty close to us. The first time Dale counted two hundred of the suckers in twenty minutes. Now just multiply that times all day and see what you come up with. They started coming in the morning early, and they were still at it late in the afternoon.

Siler finally told the S-3 that he could make his own estimate from the team's sporadic counts, but later that day he would agree to an estimate of about one thousand, although he felt that there were at least twice that.

Dale Sare clarified: "Sometimes, there were other Vietnamese mixed in with the NVA. There were occasional people in the standard black PJs walking or riding bikes, and sometimes the soldiers were not four abreast, one rank a step behind the next, but it was a pretty solid stream of them all day. I'd say there was at least a company of 'em passing by every half hour

The parade would continue all day, with no possible help from supporting arms due to the cease-fire. Dale Sare's estimate that a company passed his position every thirty minutes results in over a regiment of enemy soldiers passing by during the time that the seven Marines lay close to the road. It could easily have been the 6th NVA Regiment with the attached elements of the 1st Provisional VC Regiment that had been noted, just days earlier, in the northern reaches of the valley and hills only a few klicks away.

Siler said:

I ended up talking with the division G-3, not just the battalion S-3. We were told that, because of the cease-fire, III MAF was talking to MACV in Saigon and back to Washington to get clearance to fire artillery and call in air strikes. I gave them the coordinates of the road at the base of the hills near where we were and the coordinates of the village on the other side of the valley toward which the NVA were moving. I knew they were moving toward Highway One and maybe Phong Dien. The rain was too much for us to see more than about three hundred meters in any direction, but that was the area I felt they were headed toward. I also knew that there was friendly Marine infantry out in that direction. I told the G-3 that the NVA were moving in a column that was about four or more meters wide along that line, and that any air strikes should come in along the axis of their march right down that line. The valley was still covered by the rainstorm and fog, and it was that miserable way all day long.

However, no supporting arms were yet in the works. Communications were flying back and forth to higher commands for decisions; breaking the cease-fire would have to be decided by a very high level in the chain of command.

Sare continued:

It was just after dark, and still raining, when they gave clearance to fire, and we still had NVA all over the damn place. Then a radio transmission from G-3 said, "Move west." We said we couldn't because the enemy was there. Then they said, "Move south." And we answered the same. Then they radioed, "Move any way you can, but do it now." We knew what that meant.

There was a river not far to the east, about two hundred meters away, and we grabbed our backsides and whatever we had with us and jumped up and ran east. It was gray and raining, and when we jumped up it was almost in the middle of the NVA units. We ran stumbling, falling, slipping, and making too much damn noise, but we knew that the wrath of God was fixing to come out of the clouds and hail big goddamned hailstones, and we were in the middle of it along with all the enemy.

The seven Marines had jumped to run at the same time as the artillery was about to fire. However, the NVA didn't have time to figure out who was suddenly running away in the dark. The sounds of Mack trucks were quickly heard tearing through the skies, and the NVA started running, too.

"I know that the NVA heard us and probably saw us," Siler said, "but by then it was too late. We heard the heavy guns firing from a distance, and the rounds were smashing over our heads by the time we fell into the stream. And we *did* fall."

Closely followed by platoons of NVA, the seven Marines were running and sloshing through the mud in the dark. Out in front, but unknown to them, was a steep four-foot bank dropping down to the stream. By then the Reconners were so sodden with rain and mud that falling headlong into the water made no big difference. But that bank became a lifesaver. As Jerry Siler said, "We would've been cut to pieces by the artillery, and later the bombs that began to hammer away all night, if it hadn't been for that four feet of stream bank."

But the Marines weren't the only ones using the stream for protection; a good part of the NVA army had jumped in on either side of them, as everybody sought cover from the abrupt storm of artillery and bombs that had begun to pound the area.

Lieutenant Siler described the night:

We tucked ourselves into the bank and shivered all night in that water—all seven of us. I had the two Marines on either end standing guard, watching our flanks because we could hear the enemy jumping in the water and making noise up- and downstream from us. We were in the middle of the fire zone. It was really thick, and anybody who stuck his head up was probably going to lose it.

"It was a helluva unplanned New Year's Eve party," Sare added. "It lasted most of the night, with us up to our waists in cold water. The stream wasn't very big—about twenty feet across—but it had enough room for the NVA to join us up- and downstream, and I'm talking about pretty damn *near* us—just a few meters."

That evening back at the Phu Bai CP, Recon Marines were keeping track of the events, knowing that they had friends caught in the middle of serious problems out in the Co Bi–Thanh Tan. Lieutenant

Huff, just back from patrol, had been among the first to hear that authorization had been given to fire artillery in support of Siler and his team. Huff ran to the club and began to announce the news, but several friends cautioned him to be quiet because there were reporters in the building, and some were French. "We didn't trust them, particularly the French," Huff noted. "You know, there was a New Year's truce that we just broke, and we figured any French probably had ties back to Hanoi."

Drinks in their hands, all the men in the club quietly listened through the night as the thunder of the artillery batteries nearby announced that something had gone wrong with the cease-fire.

Out in the bush, however, one soaked-cold-to-the-bone Recon team crouched in the brush of the stream bank. Unbelievably tormenting, the rain continued to pummel the men. After all the artillery and bombs had stopped, the Marines remained in their dark stream bottom, afraid to move. By then, unseen in the dark and unfelt because of the constant rain and water, the blood was slowly oozing through small cracks in the wrinkled skin of their hands and feet. The effect was a relentless wet, chilling, overall agony that was worsened by the lack of food. Then it was the dawning of January 1, 1967.

"By the next morning," Sare said, "the bombing stopped, and the NVA moved out, leaving us by ourselves, huddled in the bushes against the muddy stream bank. It was still raining and foggy, too. I inched up to the top of the bank and noted a piece of higher ground not far away from the creek that we might try to get to when we felt a little safer, and then I slid back down into the water."

Jerry Siler was very concerned about the health of his team. He said:

> By now we all had immersion foot and hand. The dishpan-hand wrinkles had gotten so big and sore that our hands and feet were cracked and bleeding. I didn't know how well we could even defend ourselves if we had to. And now somebody up the chain of command had said that the bombing and artillery support could only be for that one night. So again, we had no help, and the weather was still too bad for the choppers to come out to pick us up. The enemy was still around but moving off in groups. And I was not about to try to pick a fight.

The team spent that day moving back and forth—relocating to the piece of higher ground spotted by Sare and then quickly skipping back into the stream when a group of NVA was spotted. The Marines were surprised by the lack of visible casualties. Their expectations had been that there would be death all around, but that wasn't the case.

With their rifles rusting, they had to await their fate, helpless against the weather, which by then was more of a problem than the NVA army. By the hundreds—and maybe by the thousands—the enemy had moved past them; now at least the tail end of the line was scattered into small groups. Many still found their way near the Marines. The men in Siler's team found their main sources of optimism in the facts that the enemy was suffering as badly as they and that a break in the weather would inevitably occur. Siler talked to the main Phu Bai base via his radio, which continued to function despite the weather and the bath it had suffered. He radioed back to the S-3 that command had to find a way to get the birds out to them. But the rain continued, alternating between a heavy, pounding torrent and light drizzle, and no relief was possible.

Sare said:

By the afternoon, the fog had begun to clear, and we could see a little farther, even with the rain. At times the rain slackened some, to a mist, but then it would come apouring again. There were some trees not far off that looked like they had been planted, and we crawled over there. We were so damn hungry and cold that we dug up the roots, skinned 'em, and tried to eat. They tasted like a cross between a turnip and a potato. I found out later that they were taro trees. It wasn't much of a blue-plate special, but it helped.

Siler said:

I was afraid all day that we would run into enemy, and that we were in too bad a shape to defend ourselves. You could still hear 'em trying to regroup and move away. We stayed in the same place all day and night, and so did the rain.

The next day, January 2, the orders came over the radio to try to walk out, but I told 'em we couldn't walk that far; besides, if we ran into the enemy, who I suspected to still be around, I didn't think we would fare too well, even though we could now call in artillery if needed. Later that morning, they called and told me that a company of grunts was going to be sweeping the valley to within four klicks of us, and they asked if we could get that far to link up with them. I told them that we would.

The unit of infantry that had been ordered to sweep the valley was a reinforced rifle company from the 3rd Battalion, 26th Marines. The

NVA had initiated them to the Co Bi–Thanh Tan area in the battle just prior to Christmas.

Siler continued his story:

It had stopped raining now, and we all said a little prayer of thanks as we moved to the northeast toward our infantry friends. Occasionally, we would see groups of NVA moving back to the southwest past us, away from the grunts. We managed to stay out of sight. They were only a small part of the enemy unit that had gone through on the thirty-first. But at least I now had radio comm with the infantry out in our front. I called 'em and told them that they were pushing the NVA past us, and that I would call in artillery on those we spotted. So I started sending fire missions back to the big guns.

The NVA were in small groups of about ten or twelve. If you could picture us, we were out in the flat, brushy land that was now a lake. There were some bushes, but the road was on a higher level. We avoided it because the enemy used it, and I didn't want to stumble into them. Sometimes, we would be near the road in the bushes, and we could see the enemy from the waist up. Finally, there was this one group coming up on us, and I decided that we were going to hit them ourselves. We could see our infantry unit not far off, and I had artillery support, and I just felt more confident. So I had everybody aim in on their number man in the enemy column. I was the number-three man in the patrol, so I sighted in on the number-three man in the NVA column. When I initiated the firing, each Marine fired his first shot on semiautomatic, and then we switched to automatic. But after that first shot only one weapon fired. After three days and nights in water, the M-14s were just too rusted.

Sare added:

Everybody was so frustrated, hurting, and ticked off by now that they wanted to take out their anger on these guys. I remember that one of the NVA was wearing a black derby hat instead of the pith helmet—he was my number. But when we started to fire, my rifle was the only one that kept firing after the first round. The NVA threw grenades—some exploded and some didn't, but none of us were hit. One grenade bounced off a Marine and fell into the mud—a dud. Those NVA that didn't go down, ran. Then they were gone, and when we, with our jammed rifles, went up to count bodies, there were three of 'em lying there in that muddy road. The derby looked like a dead beaver in the mud. Then, looking out to the east, we could see the grunts coming on not far away, sloshing through the water and mud. The sun had started to shine, and they were only fifteen minutes away.

Siler continued:

When we finally linked up with the grunts, there was a great feeling of relief. I told the commander that he needed a blocking force on the other side of the valley, 'cuz all the NVA were getting away from him to the west. There were hundreds of 'em in small groups moving to the west ahead of the grunts. Then, instead of [the commander's] calling in medevac choppers for us, we had to continue to sweep across the valley with the infantry. I hadn't experienced action like that before. Every once in a while, a sniper shot would crack in the daylight, and a Marine would go down with a head wound. You couldn't see the sniper but had to just keep sweeping on line. That was frustrating. But Recon was hurting so bad at that point I just wanted to get my guys out of there. They needed medication for their hands and feet—they needed food—they needed rest. What really ticked me off was that they sent a chopper out to get me, along with some of the dead Marines, because they wanted a report ASAP. However, my Recon team ended up walking back out with the infantry. Wading through the muddy slime, and their feet were swollen, cracked, and bleeding! I just didn't know what those headquarters people understood and didn't about what we went through out there.

Sare continued:

Well, they must have appreciated some of what we went through, because the division commander, General Kyle, met us when we got back, and he had the cook make steak, and he had Seagram's whiskey waiting for us. It was pitiful, though. We all were so sick that we couldn't drink the liquor and couldn't eat the steak. A couple of bites and that was it. We were so completely, physically shot—I remember that the walk-out with the grunts was one of the longest of my life. You can't describe what your bleeding feet felt like. It was after dark when we got back. There were reporters also waiting to talk to us—I could only mumble things that I don't really remember. We were kinda drifting along through a painful fog at that point. I only vaguely remember General Kyle meeting us and promoting every last one of us on the spot. That was how I became a sergeant.

Jerry Siler was taken to the G-3 at Phu Bai and debriefed. Even General Kyle came to see him. Siler said:

For the first time, I told them every dadgum thing we had been seeing. Until that point, I didn't want to tell them we were seeing thousands, 'cuz I knew they would never believe it. I told 'em that there had to have been more than a regiment of NVA. I don't know for sure whether they believed me then, but General Kyle did seem to appreciate our situation. I must have looked pretty rough. He was shocked when he looked at me, and said, "What in the world is wrong with your hands?" They were all cracked and bleeding—swollen up. And I looked at him and replied, "Sir, this is just from all the rain and water out there. It's not unusual, but I guess this is worse than normal. It's immersion hands, and the feet are the same way." You had to push the fingers to get them to open up, and if they dried out, you couldn't even pry them open.

Well, the general called his Navy captain, a chief medical officer, over to look at my hands and asked him what you do for this. The captain looked at my hands and said it was immersion hand and that they would prescribe a lanolin cream.

The general asked where that cream was, and the captain said there was a storage of some back on Okinawa, but that he didn't think they had any available in-country right then. Well, let me tell you, that cream took only a few hours to make the trip with a hot two-star general reading the riot act to some people. I think that I was shocked that the division commanding general was unfamiliar with what we had to go through in the field, but I also appreciated his reaction and concern after he found out.

Then, after the debriefing was over, the general's aide came up to me and asked me to come to the general's tent. When we got there, General Kyle broke out the brandy and gave me a glass. He told me he was promoting all my Recon team that evening when they got in, and I was to get the Silver Star. Then he asked if there was anything else he could do for me. I thanked him and said, "Yes sir, I was supposed to go on R & R yesterday and meet my beautiful wife in Hawaii. She's been there for a couple of days without any word from me. She's gotta be the finest wife a Marine could ever hope to have, but I know she's gotta be worried to death. Any help you can give me to get to her—I'd sure appreciate it." He told me he'd take care of everything and sent me back to my tent to get some sleep that night, and said he'd handle the problem.

The next morning the general's aide called on Siler and asked, "Can you be ready in about a half hour to go to Hawaii?"

Siler responded, "You better believe it!"

The aide made sure that the Recon lieutenant got his seat on the next available aircraft, and Jerry Siler was on his R & R trip to Hawaii the day after coming out from the middle of a reinforced NVA regiment.

* * *

Lee Klein was a lieutenant and the intelligence officer (S-2) for 3/26, and he was with the company of Marines that came out to find Siler's team on January 2. He was to have more experience with 3rd Recon Battalion patrols later at Khe Sanh, but on this day he had his first encounter with a Recon team. Klein said that the company from his unit sweeping the Co Bi–Thanh Tan Valley was strongly reinforced, and that Ontos were attached for additional firepower. But he also said that even though he was the battalion S-2 he had not been advised of the reports Siler had been forwarding to the G-3, and that he was not aware of the "thousand" enemy sighted, as had been reported from the field.

He added:

> When we swept across the valley, we had no contact with any NVA, except for occasional snipers. Then, after we picked up the Recon team, we turned around and came on back in. If there had been a regiment of NVA out there, they were sure gone now. I remember meeting Jerry Siler in a tent back at the headquarters, and I'll never forget how shot to hell he looked. I hadn't realized yet what kind of experience that Recon team had been through. He still seemed very nervous.

However, Klein stated, in regard to Jerry Siler's feeling that no one would have believed him: "I know when I was G-2 Forward, working out of Khe Sanh in 1967, that no one believed, or maybe wanted to believe, the Recon team reports of enemy headlights on the roadways and the sounds of enemy tanks in the night. Yet they proved to be correct. So I can understand why Jerry thought that he wouldn't be believed."

An end-of-1966 III MAF analysis of enemy activity stated:

> ... there was a substantial increase in enemy activity in the eastern Thua Thien Province (this includes the Co Bi–Thanh Tan area). Enemy initiated incidents included platoon, company, and two incidents of battalion size attacks against (ARVN) security elements located along Highway 1. . . . These attacks were preceded by light to moderate mortar fire. When compared to the month of November, the incidence of enemy action in Thua Thien would certainly seem to conform with his mission of attacking, where possible, our lines of communication. . . . Noteworthy from the standpoint of enemy effort was the heavy and sustained mortar fire brought to bear against the 3rd Battalion, 26th Marines on 21 through 23 December and the continuity of enemy action which was maintained for this three day period. . . . On 31 December a major sighting of approximately 1,000 well armed VC were reported in the vicinity. . . . In addition to small

arms the enemy was reported to be carrying mortars and machine guns. This concentrated enemy group was held under observation for several hours and at 1900 artillery and air strikes were called. Results were undetermined. . . .

However, during the last days of 1966 and the early days of 1967, other Recon teams from the battalion were also experiencing the onslaught of the North Vietnamese in the northwest frontier of South Vietnam. The battalion continued to spread its companies among the camps at Phu Bai, Dong Ha, and Khe Sanh.

Based upon changed intelligence reports concerning the enemy order of battle in early 1967, General Westmoreland requested 200,000 additional U.S. troops. He had dispatched to the chairman of the Joint Chiefs of Staff in Washington, D.C., messages addressing the increasing number of enemy units and the estimates made by the Central Intelligence Agency of enemy forces that doubled the previous enemy order-of-battle counts. The reply he received from General Earle Wheeler was contained in two cables.

The first cable read:

1. I have just been made aware of the figures you now report for battalion and large size enemy-initiated actions. . . .
2. If these figures should reach the public domain, they would blow the lid off of Washington.
3. Please do whatever is necessary to insure these figures are not repeat not released to News Media or otherwise exposed to public knowledge.

The second cable read:

The implications are major and serious. Large scale enemy initiatives have been used as a major element in assessing the status of the war for the President, secretary of defense, in Washington. These figures have been used to illustrate the success of our current strategy as well as over-all progress in Vietnam. . . . Your new figures change the picture drastically. . . . I can only interpret the new figures to mean that despite the (U.S.) force buildup, despite our many successful . . . attacks . . . VC/NVA combat capability and offensive activity throughout 1966 and now in 1967 has been increasing steadily. . . .

I cannot go to the President and tell him that, contrary to my reports and those of the other Chiefs as to the progress of the war . . . the situation is such that we are not sure who has the initiative in South

Vietnam. Moreover, the effect of surfacing this major and significant discrepancy would be dynamite. . . . Urgent action is required. . . .*

The confusion regarding strategy at the highest levels of the American military and political command translated into further dangers to be faced by Recon teams. The count of enemy forces was only one issue. There continued to be a battle between the Army and the Marine Corps regarding tactics: the Marine command advocated working with and protecting the citizens of South Vietnam in the populated areas; the Army command advocated the search-and-destroy concept. The latter would employ the mobility of American forces to conduct operations in the mountainous jungles of the borderlands in attempts to destroy the main force NVA and Vietcong units. Possibly because of these conflicts between philosophies, the III Marine Amphibious Force command remained reluctant to accept Recon reports of large-scale enemy units, some with tanks, that were sighted or heard in the deep reaches of the northwestern quadrant of South Vietnam. To acknowledge those reports would give the MACV (Army) command more arguments to use in its effort to push the Marines away from their enclaves and into battle with the main force units.

General Walt seemed not to fear the NVA. However, he was reluctant to accept information identifying large enemy units. If they did come across the border, he felt the Marine infantry battalions would make short work of them. Consequently, despite the experience of the disbelieved 3rd Recon reports concerning the 324B NVA Division prior to Operation Hastings in mid-1966, there again developed differences between the Marine CGs opinion and that of his Recon teams.

---

*1. Bruce E. Jones. *War Without Windows.* New York: Berkley Books, 1987, pages xvii-xviii.

2. *The Pentagon Papers,* as published by *The New York Times.*

3. CIA Memorandum, 2 January 1967. A copy is held in the LBJ Library, Austin, Texas.

CHAPTER TEN

The Beginning Khe Sanh Warfare and Problems with III MAF Continue

During 1967, the Marine Corps had in the field in I Corps eighteen to twenty-one infantry battalions numbering about 1,000 Marines each. These units were from the 1st and 3rd divisions and the 26th Marine Regiment. Prior to the end of 1967, the U.S. Army's Americal Division and one brigade from the 1st Cavalry Division were relocated to I Corps, increasing the American maneuver battalion strength in those provinces by about one third. There were, in addition, three battalions of Korean Marines and units from the Army of South Vietnam (ARVN). However, MACV intelligence estimated, in the same I Corps area, that by the end of the year there were fifty-six NVA/VC combat infantry battalions averaging approximately 600 men in each. MACV's count of the enemy order of battle did not include combat-support units or local guerrilla combat units.

On March 20, 1967, Capt. Tim Huff, by then the Charlie Company commander with the Recon detachment at Dong Ha, participated in a briefing for General Walt, commanding general of the III Marine Amphibious Force. Huff said:

> I was a Recon company commander at Dong Ha during the first part of 1967. For whatever the reasons, I ended up giving a Recon brief for General Walt as part of a larger briefing. Brigadier General Ryan was also there as CG of the 3rd Marine Division Forward. They heard presentations from each of the units. When it was my turn, I stood up and pointed to the map, indicating the locations of seven patrols that we had out at that time from west of Highway One to Khe Sanh. Three of those patrols had recent contact with the enemy near Khe Sanh.
> He, General Walt, asked me why we had those patrols near Khe

Sanh. I explained about the increasing amount of contact we were having with NVA units, and how we wanted to try to investigate. Walt said that he was trying to show Westmoreland (MACV commanding general) that he was wrong about the NVA coming across the DMZ in big numbers, and that he wanted patrols inserted between the Rockpile and the DMZ. He really didn't want to hear what I was trying to say.

I looked at General Ryan, and his look said, You're just a captain; keep your mouth shut. But I started to say something anyway, and they cut me off and went to the next unit's report.

Then, when the briefing was finished, I was grabbed and taken to a back room. There was a small group of the command around Walt and me. A smaller map was whipped out, and the briefing was continued for only Recon—that is, me. Walt reiterated that the NVA was not infiltrating, and said he was going to prove it. I really was getting frustrated, and said, "The NVA have been in these mountains since 1964. It's their home away from home."

He looked at me and asked, "You've been here longer than I have, Captain?"

He didn't remember me because in 1964 he personally had sent me from Okinawa to Vietnam with my Air Delivery platoon. So I told him that I had been in-country in '64 and had made drops and jumps into the jungle to Special Forces and elsewhere, and that this was my second tour.

Walt continued to interrupt Captain Huff and disagree with his report. Finally, exasperated with Huff, Walt said, "I want you to put a patrol in there tomorrow morning." He had pointed at an area of jungled mountains on the DMZ way north of the Rockpile. Huff argued with him, saying that there were no landing zones in that area and it just wasn't a good place to try to insert Recon.

Walt's voice became tougher, and he said, "That's the trouble with the Marine Corps today—they're too damn reliant on the helicopter!" Then he ordered Captain Huff out the next morning to insert two patrols by truck between Cam Lo and the Rockpile, and the Recon captain was dismissed.

Huff said:

So at about three A.M. the next morning, my driver and me in our jeep, and a six-by with two patrols in it, headed out of Dong Ha for the Rockpile. It was about a fifteen-mile one-way trip in the dark. I kept telling myself this was stupid—nobody drives out at night along Route 9. The only way we would make it is if the NVA thought we were one of their trucks. I couldn't understand Walt. Charlie owned the place out there.

So we made it past Cam Lo, and about halfway from there to the Rockpile, we dropped off the first team, trying to keep the trucks rolling so that no one would think we had stopped. Then we kept going for that one big hill that rose up out of a valley in the moonlight all by itself. It was off to the northwest of us. Hell, I was hanging on to my M-16 and praying my Hail Marys. I know what Ichabod Crane felt like in Sleepy Hollow.

I couldn't believe that we made it down that road and got close to the Rockpile, but we hadn't had any problems yet. It wasn't easy to drop off a patrol, go away farther, and turn around and head back without making it sound like that's exactly what you were doing. Anyway, we then got pointed back in the direction of Dong Ha and moved as fast as trucks can on Route 9 at three A.M. without lights.

I knew the patrols would be working their way to the north and trying to hide for the rest of the night, but after we had passed the place where we had dropped off the first team, gunshots broke out—the first team was in contact.

The drivers of the two vehicles pushed their accelerators as far as they could in that situation, trying to get back to the Dong Ha base. Huff planned to get helicopter support back to the team if needed. They were in off-and-on contact but had taken no casualties yet. Huff wanted to extract the team or drop it ammo resupply as the case warranted.

About an hour before daybreak the two vehicles bounced into camp. Huff said:

I had some ammo resupply tied down on pallets with the intent to drop them by chopper to my team if that was what we needed to do. We went out in a CH-46. The pilot was in contact with the patrol, and I was talking with him from the rear of the bird, but I had no radio contact myself with the team. My gunny was with me. When we got near the team, apparently it had been clear of the enemy for a little while, but the pilot was talking with the team leader, not me. It was difficult for me to really be sure of what was going on. The pilot called for yellow smoke to mark the team's location so he could go in to pick 'em up. They were not in sight yet. Then the smoke popped, and I watched below as we quickly dropped down. Thank God we hadn't started to hover, because it wasn't our team. The NVA must have had our radio frequency, and it was their smoke grenade suckering us down. The chopper flashed through a hostile LZ with .50-caliber machine gun fire raking its bottom. We were about fifty meters up and the pilot was hauling ass. The gunny yelled he was hit in the foot.

I felt a sting in my leg, and looking down I saw a wound beside my shin, but it didn't look like much. In fact, as the pilot raced back to Dong Ha, the gunny and me joked together about getting a decent wound that would take us out of the war zone for a while. What I didn't see was that the damn bullet had exploded out the back of my calf, taking most of my flesh and muscle with it. The leg just wouldn't work, but there wasn't much pain until later, back in the hospital at Da Nang, when they started to clean out the wound. That was it for my second trip to Vietnam, but I'll never understand why General Walt was so obstinate.

During those same weeks in March and on into April, a detachment of 3rd Force was working out of the Khe Sanh combat base and ran into similar problems. These were the patrols that Huff had been trying to explain to Walt and about which the general wouldn't listen. James Capers, Larry Keen, Chuck Harris, Greg Menary, and Alastair "Scotty" Scott were but a few members of that Force Recon detachment, and it was now these Reconners who began to locate the significant numbers of NVA that early in 1967 had begun to move into positions in the hills near Khe Sanh.

The Reconners were not aware of the big picture and the battle between Walt and Westmoreland, nor of how they were affected by it. What they were able to see from the ground level was that their patrols were encountering more and more NVA. Often their teams were not able to insert because of heavy enemy fire. Menary was a sergeant and a patrol leader. He said:

When I think about it, it still sends shivers down my spine. I came across the lower slopes of Hill 881 with my team, and we must've moved under the noses of the NVA on that hill. The team that was sent in immediately after us in the same general area was hit. The grunts went out as a reaction force, and they were pinned down. The fight was on. Our infantry caught holy hell up there. I remember wondering if hundreds of AKs or SKSs were aimed at us but let us go by.

There was no doubt among us who were patrolling out there that the NVA were in those hills in force. Sometimes at night on patrol, we would see long columns of lights that looked like Coleman lanterns. But nobody would believe you back at the base except other Marines in Recon or those from the infantry who had been on patrol out there.

In a few weeks, Lee Klein was stationed at Khe Sanh as the G-2 Forward, and he confirms that no one would believe the Recon team reports of tanks heard at night and long columns of enemy soldiers.

There was a mind-set against accepting the idea of large numbers of enemy units, and consequently the reconnaissance teams suffered.

Scotty remembers one patrol that failed to insert because of enemy fire. He was injured in the battle. When the chopper, riddled with bullet holes, returned to the base, Scott found himself standing with blood dripping down his face, talking not only to the colonel in command of the base but also with Generals Walt and Westmoreland, who were there on a whirlwind tour. When he tried to tell the commanding generals that the hills were crawling with NVA, the colonel contradicted him and said there were only a few (the base commander was not held in great esteem by the Reconners).

Scotty said, "The colonel there was more interested in keeping the place looking like a Stateside base than he was in finding and fighting the NVA. He just wouldn't believe us."

Greg Menary added, "We were painting rocks and painting shell casings to make flower beds when we should've been digging trenches around that base."

However, even intelligence that was received and processed at the higher levels of command was not routinely passed down to the battalion level. So whether it was the Recon Battalion or the infantry units, the people on the fighting level were often without a good picture of the enemy situation. While serving as the intelligence officer for the 3rd Battalion, 26th Marines, Lt. Lee Klein stated in a taped letter sent home in early 1967, "The Marine Corps is not very good at intelligence. . . . Up in the division level they hoard the information. They don't pass it down to you."

Another incident that occurred during this time period, shortly before Tim Huff's encounter with General Walt, adds to the picture being painted by Recon teams.

On February 27, 1967, 5,000 meters west-northwest of Cam Lo and about the same distance east of the Rockpile, a team from the 3rd Recon Battalion surprised both the NVA and themselves. That recon zone was not far from where Tim Huff was shot, and was approximately in the same grid square as Lieutenant Terrebonne's sixth patrol seven months earlier. This February 27 patrol exploited an ambush of opportunity and killed four North Vietnamese soldiers. However, the hard facts of life then quickly descended on its eight Marines: they had just ambushed the point of the 812th Regiment, 324B Division! That part of the division that had to be refurbished due to the casualties taken on Operation Hastings was now back in-country and looking for a fight. Outnumbered by about 200 to 1, the Marines quickly maneuvered their way to safer positions while radioing for help. Assistance was delayed and was committed piecemeal. The size of the enemy force was not understood by the command.

The first infantry unit sent to their aid was Company L (Lima Company), 3rd Battalion, 4th Marines, minus one platoon but reinforced with a platoon of tanks. It would have numbered about 150 to 200 men, while the NVA had about 1,500 entrenched in the area. The men of Company L were ordered to cover the five klicks to the Recon team on the ground, but heavy brush up to twelve feet in height held them back.

At that moment the 2nd Battalion, 3rd Marines, was involved in a shore-to-ship movement in order to go afloat for a while out of the war zone to Okinawa. The battalion headquarters, Company G, and about half of Company F were still ashore at Camp Carroll, about four miles southwest of Cam Lo. With the sudden turn of events, 2/3's battalion commander, Lt. Col. Victor Ohanesian (who had been with Charlie Company Recon on Operation Allegheny) was ordered into the battle by the 3rd Marines CO, Col. John Lanigan. Company L was by then involved in heavy fighting with well-prepared enemy troops. Lima was defending one of its tanks that had thrown a track.

The Reconners fought alone until just before midnight, when Golf Company of 2/3 linked up with it. Capt. Carl Bockewitz led the combined unit.

Early the next morning, Lieutenant Colonel Ohanesian started to lead his command group and the remainder of Company F across the last several hills to link up with Company G and the Recon team, which had been assigned to the operational control of 2/3. He had planned to sweep back against the NVA using Lima Company as a blocking force. That meant that slightly more than half a battalion of Marine infantry was trying to move from different directions into at least a three-battalion enemy unit that was waiting for it.

But on the morning of the twenty-eighth, Company L, the blocking force, was hit by massive mortar, antitank, and infantry attacks. This forced Ohanesian to change direction to go to the aid of Company L. Golf Company, with the Recon team, was then ordered by Colonel Lanigan to displace to Hill 124, 2,000 meters to the northwest of the battle that had threatened to overrun Lima Company. The company (plus Recon) moved forward and up the hill. Awaiting them was a two-sided NVA ambush, and the Marines were pushing hard right into it when enemy fire ripped both flanks. The fighting was so intense that the Marines who were battling uphill were not able to retrieve the bodies of those killed for hours. The heroism of the men of that unit in taking Hill 124 cannot be overstated. Among the bodies brought back was that of Capt. Carl Bockewitz.

Colonel Lanigan then ordered Mike Company 3/4 into the fight. It was to outflank the NVA hammering Golf Company Mike Company was helicoptered to Hill 162, about one mile northwest of Hill 124. This was the first time in the battle that a Marine unit was transported by helicopter. They encountered what was described as light contact.

Then Lieutenant Colonel Ohanesian, along with his battalion head-quarters and that part of Company F that was with him, was ordered to move forward northwest about 2,000 meters from Lima Company to link up with Golf. If ever there was a trail marked by death and bloody guts, this was it. Major Sheridan, the battalion S-3, reported that they knew that their orders would take them into a trap, but they had orders. The Marines were outmanned, outgunned, and in terrible terrain. They were hardly outside Lima Company's perimeter when they were decimated by the NVA from the front and both flanks. NVA mortar attacks walked up and down their column. The battalion commander and sergeant major were both killed.

Sheridan stated, "Moving the dead and wounded out of the killing zone required feats of bravery beyond comprehension. Lieutenant Colonel Ohanesian was carrying the last of the wounded Marines . . . when an explosion mortally wounded him, [plus] three other Marines and myself [were wounded]."

Their pugnacious bravery and gung ho spirit kept those few Marines from being crushed by the overwhelming force of the 812th NVA Regiment. The battle continued until the enemy began to with-draw on March 1.

Lee Klein was soon to make captain, and had already been transferred to the Division G-2 Forward in Dong Ha. Two days after this battle had begun, he recorded his thoughts about what was happening:

> Two days ago we had an eight-man Recon team get into trouble. They sent a rifle company to bail 'em out, but the company was taking too long to get there. So, they sent in another rifle company. They thought they could make it quicker. Both these rifle companies made heavy contact, and one suffered a tremendous number of casualties. Because these two got hit, they sent in one more rifle company. Then yesterday, they flew out another rifle company. In a matter of twenty-four hours, they committed five rifle companies to a combat area. They were in three separate areas.
>
> The whole thing has turned into a big fiasco. Right now, General Walt, General Kyle, General Ryan, and an ARVN general are up here trying to decide what to do. The whole thing has been mishandled

badly. . . . They threw five rifle companies into a zone where they knew they were going to make contact. Threw 'em in at separate times, at separate locations. . . . You just don't do something like that.

It was a bad play. We're just getting the results in now. I think the final count of wounded [Marines] is 135, and 20 dead. The only thing we can account for as NVA kills right now is four [the four by Recon in the initial moments]. This is probably one of the worst beatings the Marine Corps has taken in Vietnam. We lost this ball game completely. . . . We don't know if the NVA have fled north. If they have, it's a wise thing [on their part].

The NVA had indeed begun to withdraw at the same time the Corps had gotten its act together and moved two new battalions, 3/3 and 1/9, against the enemy. The odds were closer to even then. On March 3, maneuvering back through the hills and jungles toward the relative safety of the DMZ, some of the 812th Regiment's units were spotted by an aerial observer. Artillery and air strikes were called in, and later 1/9 found more than 200 NVA dead.

Maybe some of Recon's questions about the attitude of General Walt and his command toward the NVA can be answered by the official III MAF analysis of enemy activity for the month of February 1967. The total account for the February 27–March 3 action, which was initiated by a Recon team and in which Lieutenant Colonel Ohanesian lost his life, reads as follows:

The most significant contacts in north central Quang Tri took place approximately two weeks after the truce period and were precipitated by a USMC reconnaissance patrol ambush sprung on 27 February which resulted in 4 NVA KIA (Confirmed). Shortly thereafter an enemy unit estimated to be of company size attempted to surround the patrol resulting in the patrol withdrawing to the south toward friendly lines. Within a short time, elements of the 2nd Battalion, 3rd Marines and the 3rd Battalion, 4th Marines became heavily engaged with elements of estimated regimental size enemy forces, with at least two battalions of the 812th Regiment of the 324B Division in contact, reinforced with engineer and artillery (mortar) elements. After initially engaging friendly units from well fortified positions and inflicting moderate friendly casualties, primarily as a result of 82mm mortar fires, the enemy was eventually driven off toward his sanctuary in the DMZ by concentrated air, artillery and USMC infantry pressure, abetted by the 39th ARVN Ranger Battalion occupying a blocking position to the northeast. During the pursuit, the enemy left numerous bodies behind, some of them booby-trapped and many of them stripped of all clothing and weapons. Casualties among the disorganized enemy continued to mount and after six days of contact totaled some 536 KIA (Confirmed) and 312 KIA (Probable). Captured weapons and equipment included both 82mm and 60mm mortars, several light machine guns, one .50 caliber machine gun, gas masks, grenades, mines, and blasting caps.

Understanding that it was never the NVA's tactic to hit U.S. units and hold the battleground, but to hit and maneuver, the NVA likely were following their own policies when they battered the Marine units and then withdrew. The III MAF accounts, if they were truly believed by the authors and commanding generals, would perpetuate the belief that we again had driven the enemy from the battlefield and that he had suffered almost 50 percent casualties. Instead, it is far more probable that the NVA did just what its tactical policies dictated: leave before the full power of American air and artillery could punish it too severely. The casualties suffered by the NVA unit as reported in the day-to-day accounts do not indicate that the enemy suffered what the final reports stated.

If the Marine command believed what was very likely an enemy-KIA account inflated by about 40 to 50 percent, it was no wonder that less than a month later General Walt was not going to accept stories about serious problems along the DMZ. From the reports in his hands, he had learned that the NVA had suffered tremendous casualties and that every time they came across they were punished severely again.

However, if the enemy-KIA figures were actually 10 to 20 percent, as is more likely, a very different picture emerges. The unit was not put out of action and was still a serious danger to the Recon teams sent deep into its territory.

CHAPTER ELEVEN

Team Breaker

"I am concerned about I Corps.... The proximity of North Vietnam and available infiltration routes make it easy for troops from the North to pour into the I Corps area in almost any numbers required. I feel during the next couple of months there will be a major attack across the DMZ which will force Walt to concentrate additional troops which will so weaken his bases along the coast that the enemy can undo a lot of the good work that has been done ..."
—*General Westmoreland, January 1967*

On May 9, 1967, the seven men of Team Breaker flew out of the Khe Sanh combat base (KSCB) to land by helicopter in a small valley about nine miles northwest of the base. The first bloody battle of Khe Sanh was tapering off, and that patrol's zone went well beyond the heavy fighting that had been close to the KSCB. The patrol came from 3rd Recon's Alpha Company at Khe Sanh, and was attached to the Marine infantry unit there. Team Breaker's mission was to conduct reconnaissance and surveillance to determine the extent of suspected NVA troop movements in the area and to assess the results of a recent bombing run. The valley was a branch of an infiltration route from Laos, which was only six miles away to the west. The patrol's zone was about that same distance south of the DMZ. 2nd Lt. Heinz Alhmeyer was the new platoon commander, on his first patrol to learn on the job. Sgt. James Tycz was an experienced NCO and was the patrol leader. L.Cpl. Sam Sharp was assistant patrol leader. "Doc" Malcolm Miller was the corpsman. None of the four made it back.

On August 3, 1966, Operation Hastings had ended, and January 31, 1967, saw the end of the follow-up operation—Prairie I. The 1st Battalion, 3rd Marines, had been at the Khe Sanh combat base during the latter operation. Three main trail complexes joined on the Khe Sanh "plateau." The most southerly was along Route 9 and ran generally west to east from Laos into Vietnam, looping to the south to avoid the mountains. The next traversed ridgelines under jungle canopy from the west-northwest in a southeasterly direction past Hills 881 North, 881 South, and 861. The most northerly route was from the northwest through the valleys of the Rao Quan River and its tributaries. Dense elephant grass and bamboo thickets in the valley bordered by great mountains and ridges provided concealment. During Operation Prairie, units from the 3rd Recon Battalion operated out of Khe Sanh and patrolled out to a maximum of approximately 10,000 meters. Artillery support was from 105s and 155s at Khe Sanh with maximum ranges of 11,000 and 14,600 meters, respectively. However, with the end of Prairie, 1/3 (the 1st Battalion, 3rd Marines) left, leaving one company of infantry, one platoon of Recon (3rd Force), and supporting artillery at the base. Reconnaissance patrolling was the primary function remaining to both the infantry and to Recon. Teams from the latter were to patrol out to the maximum range of the artillery.

Although General Walt was determined to prove to General Westmoreland that the NVA were not crossing the border in significant numbers, in one two-week period in February, five Recon patrols made contact with NVA units near Khe Sanh and had to be extracted under fire. Hills 881 North, 881 South, and 861 were noted by the 3rd Force to have significant enemy activity. Hill 881 North was the farthest from the base, about 9,000 meters away; 861 was only about 5,000 meters away. As information was gathered from multiple sources, a picture developed that outlined the shadow of a new NVA division in South Vietnam—the 325C. This intelligence indicated that at least two regiments of 325C were in the area, numbering 3,000 to 4,000 men. A second Marine infantry company was based at KSCB, bringing the total American strength at Khe Sanh to about 1,000. Then Alpha Company replaced 3rd Force as the 3rd Recon Battalion detachment at the base.

After months of bloody foreplay between reconnaissance patrols and the NVA, the first battle of Khe Sanh began on April 24, 1967. Savage, gutty, and violent warfare raged on until May 10. The 3rd Battalion, 3rd Marines, was committed to the battle on April 25 under the command of Lt. Col. Gary Wilder, who had commanded the 3rd Recon Battalion throughout the latter half of 1966. Elements of the 9th Marines joined Wilder's forces, and the fighting was so brutal that at times entire Marine companies, or what was left of them, were prepared to die to the last man on bombed-out pieces of real estate around Hills 881 North, 881 South, and 861. Marines who were still able carried their dead or seriously wounded off the hills in poncho litters.

On April 26, Division CG Bruno Hochmuth jerked the 2nd Battalion, 3rd Marines, out of another operation north of Hue City and helicoptered it to Khe Sanh, where they soon learned of NVA tenacity and professionalism from the battle-weary Marines who'd been fighting them. During the last assault by the eighteen- and nineteen-year-old Americans against Hill 861 on April 28, they were greeted by silence and found the enemy gone. Battered heavily by artillery and airpower, the NVA had nevertheless completely policed the area and left "no equipment or anything of intelligence value" behind. Their withdrawal was professional. Twenty-five bunkers and 400 fighting holes were found on that one hill alone. All were laid out with interlocking fire zones, which had decimated the Marines who fought for every last foot of that hill.

In the battle to take the nearby Hill 881 North on April 30, Marines fought bunker to bunker against men from the North. In one bunker, two enemy soldiers fought against the Marines. The Americans threw grenades, killing one soldier, but the second sat on another grenade, which blew off parts of his body but did not kill him. The first Marine to go into the bunker was wounded by the same NVA. The next Marine was killed by the dying NVA soldier. Tear gas wouldn't budge the man, and only after several more grenades did the enemy soldier give up the ghost.*

Heavy battles continued through May 5, after which there was a three-day lull. Then, on May 9, two companies of Marines fought the last of their infantry encounters with the NVA about three klicks north of Hill 881 North. During the two-week battle, U.S. artillery fired more than 25,000 rounds in support of the Marines, and over 1,900 tons of bombs were dropped by supporting aircraft. Marines killed or wounded totaled 580, and 940 enemy were counted as KIA.

However, it had been Reconnaissance patrols that had initiated the first contacts with the North Vietnamese Army that began the battle, and it was also a Reconnaissance patrol—Team Breaker—that was involved in the last official action of the first battle of Khe Sanh. On May 9, the team was sent to check the results of bomb strikes on suspected enemy locations that lay far beyond the horrific fighting at KSCB. The patrol's mission took it 15,000 meters up the Rao Quan River and five miles past 881 North.

The seven- to eight-man patrol concept was becoming the norm. In order to place more patrols in the field, as required, the battalion had to start reducing the number of men per patrol. That also meant that fewer officers and staff NCOs served as patrol leaders. There would

---

U.S. Marines in Vietnam, 1966.

be a minimum of six teams per company, and sometimes the teams would be reduced in strength so that nine teams could be sent out to the field. It was not unusual for there to be only one, and at most two, officers who acted as patrol leaders per company. That meant that as few as one, and possibly none, of the nine patrols from one company would be led by a lieutenant. The same might be true for staff NCOs. Therefore, most patrols were led by corporals, and sometimes a lance corporal was assigned to be a patrol leader.

Second Lieutenant Alhmeyer checked in at the Alpha Recon detachment at the combat base just before the May 9 patrol. He was very shortly directed to accompany Team Breaker on its patrol, not to be in charge but to learn on the job from Sergeant Tycz, the patrol leader. Tycz was only days from the end of his tour, and other members of his platoon tried to talk him out of taking the mission, but he felt it was his responsibility.

The team was originally scheduled to be inserted in the morning and conduct a one-day bomb assessment and check of the area. However, the flight time was delayed until 1600 hours.

The afternoon of May 9 was hot and humid, and later that night light rain would be in the area. Most of Vietnam was by and large influenced by weather patterns coming off the sea to the east, but in the higher terrain near the Laotian border, the climate was controlled equally by those blowing in from the westerly lands of Laos and Thailand.

The Marines put on their packs, loaded their weapons, and followed their sergeant, James Tycz. Cpl. Ted Biszko was coming back from a mission to the north of the KSCB and had landed just minutes before. Prior to receiving orders that took them to Alpha Company, 3rd Recon Battalion, in Vietnam, Biszko and Tycz had been together at Camp Pendleton, helping to initiate the 5th Recon Battalion. Biszko had great respect for Tycz. In his mind, if Tycz was the patrol leader, your odds of accomplishing the mission and getting back safely were greatly increased.

Biszko said:

I was "hot" coming back in that day, because we had taken friendly artillery fire near our patrol, and I wanted to go speak to somebody about that. Then I saw Tycz going out with a bunch of new faces I didn't recognize. I asked, "Hey, Tycz, where the hell are you going?" He said, "I got a new patrol, and I'm going north of where you were. How was your area?" I told him nothing but friendly fire was happening where I had been, but if he was going north of that to kiss his ass good-bye. That was the way we talked—we were losing so many people. Then he jumped into the air and spun his legs like the roadrunner and said, "Beep-beep." That was our way of saying that "Charlie" Coyote wouldn't catch us.

Team Breaker boarded the helicopters at about 1600 hours in the afternoon. Earlier that day, an aerial observer had found evidence that the North Vietnamese were still near the hill complexes, and another battle was again raging. The birds then took to the air and flew up the river valley to the northwest. Hill 861 was to their immediate left as they departed Khe Sanh. Then there was 881 North a little farther to their left, and then the site of the new battle that day at Hill 778. The Marine infantry suffered twenty-four dead and nineteen wounded in taking the hill that day. Thirty-one NVA bodies were found.

The birds continued past the battle raging some 4,000 meters to their portside. At 3,330 feet, Hill 1015, Dong Tri, was the highest hill in the immediate Khe Sanh area, and the patrol flew past it to their starboard. Still farther out, past the limits of the team's other patrols, the choppers flew below Dong Pa Thien, which towered up to 5,000 feet and blocked the team from the artillery support of the Army's 175 guns at Camp Carroll.

About 2,000 meters farther north, the river below them forked; one branch came down straight from the DMZ; the other ran west-east. It was up this latter branch that the birds flew. Covered by jungle from midway up, the mountains behind them now rose to about 5,580 feet. Those that paralleled the north side of the narrow valley up which the team was being taken scaled heights almost the same—Hills 1572, 1613, 1488, 1418, 1335, 1198 (measured in meters). The landing zone was on the south side of the valley, where the stream narrowed and became shallow.

The hills framing the south side of the valley floor rose up just as steeply but not to the same heights as their kin opposite—the tallest being Hill 665 (2,182 feet), which stared straight down on the landing zone, about 540 feet below it. The LZ was about 400 meters above sea level, which put it at about the same elevation as the Khe Sanh "plateau," over 9.3 miles behind them to the southeast. The distance was important because the team was well beyond the range of the 105-mm howitzers at the combat base but was just on the outer edge of the range of its 155s.

There was no time for the Marines to take in the natural beauty of the landscape, however, as the birds quickly closed on the LZ ahead. From the mouth of the little valley, it was only 1,200 meters to the drop-off point, within easy sight of the small village of Nguon Rao. The LZ was on a low finger that jutted from Hill 665 like a thumb extending into the valley. Sandwiched between the stream to the north and the jungled slopes of 665 to the south, the thumblike knoll was hardly more than two football fields long and covered by grass with a few clumps of trees.

No signs of human activity were seen as the birds quickly dropped. The transport chopper hit the deck, tailgate down, and the Marines quickly ran out and dropped into security positions as the helicopter rose and rapidly disappeared down the valley. In a matter of minutes, Sergeant Tycz had organized the team and started to move through the still afternoon air that enveloped them. They were in the open, with the jungled Hill 665 staring down on them. For a Recon Marine, however, jungles are more comforting than an open valley or the knoll on which Team Breaker found itself.

Before the team could move very far, the men began to see evidence of the NVA. Freshly turned dirt was noted, so the Marines pulled out their entrenching tools and began to dig.

Rice storage was found, and to the disgust of the team, their "E" tools sank into "cat holes" obviously dug and used by Vietnamese soldiers. Fighting positions, including bunkers, were also found. As the time the team spent searching turned into hours, the Marines grew uneasy. Sergeant Tycz knew the standard Recon principle: move quickly away from the LZ; always assume that you have been seen going in or that the choppers were heard; never use the LZ as a harbor site—go anywhere, but don't harbor there.

Tycz took L.Cpl. Clarence "Tubby" Carlson, "Doc" Malcom Miller, and L.Cpl. Sam Sharp to search the finger in one direction and instructed Lieutenant Alhmeyer, Pfc. Steven Lopez, and Pfc. Carl "Britt" Friery to stay put. After they had gone, however, Friery stated, "Lieutenant Alhmeyer started to wander off through the three-to-four-foot grass. We tried to tell him to stay, but he wouldn't listen. Then Lopez and me talked about going after him but decided that we'd better obey what Tycz had told us and stay hidden in the grass where Sergeant Tycz could find us and the radios if he needed them. I also had the grenade launcher."

When the patrol leader returned, the lieutenant wasn't back yet. Before Tycz could put together a team to go find him, Alhmeyer walked back up to the team. The sergeant's anger exploded at the lieutenant and they had "words." Shortly after the incident, the patrol leader radioed a report and asked for the extraction that they had anticipated. However, he was instructed to set up a harbor site for the night, and told that aircraft would be out to pick them up in the morning.

Friery stated, "Tycz and the lieutenant went off about ten to fifteen meters to study the maps. We could hear them arguing." When the patrol leader returned, Friery said that he got the impression that the lieutenant had pulled rank on him (Tycz) and ordered that they would stay in this same spot for the night. The team had a secondary LZ, and Carlson had thought that was where they would move for the night. With Tycz reporting a bunker complex and tree platforms nearby, he didn't feel comfortable.

Carlson stated, "I remember Sergeant Tycz was on the radio and then arguing with the lieutenant about where we should harbor. It seemed to me that the lieutenant wanted to stay there and continue searching in the morning." No one heard the actual conversation—but they stayed. Carlson adds, "It's kinda like Tycz knew, and I knew it, too, that we were gonna get hit. We were sitting ducks." So the patrol rolled up in ponchos, hiding in the grass. One man was on watch at all times with the radio beside him.

Then, shortly after midnight, there was movement in the bush all around the team. It was dark, with a 1,000-foot ceiling of murky, gray clouds. The NVA was searching for the team and seemed to know where it was hidden.

Carlson said:

> When those NVA came up that night, they knew exactly where we were at. I could hear 'em all around us, and they just walked right up to us. I think they might have put a perimeter around us to make sure we didn't sneak off. . . . One of the other things I heard was one of our patrol trying to get his magazines out or something making clanking noises. Then I knew they, the NVA, were going to open up, and I laid flat. Then all hell broke loose. They had fire superiority right off the bat. I remember the moaning and groaning [from wounded patrol members]. I didn't know who was hit. Then I remember I could see what was going on. I don't know if the NVA were using illumination or what. Sergeant Tycz and somebody else were just to the right of me. Doc Miller was to my left, and Britt Friery and Lopez on the other side of Tycz. Sam Sharp was also in their area. But the NVA were all around, and I remember hearing them talking to each other. Tycz pulled a pin on a grenade, held it for a few seconds, and lobbed it a short distance in front of us. The enemy was very close. The grenade exploded, taking enemy casualties. You could hear them in pain. We continued to fire and throw grenades.

Friery had been sleeping, and Lopez was up and close to him. The first thing Friery remembered was Lopez firing over him at the approaching NVA. He said:

There were two NVA who had walked into us. I think Lopez was about to wake me when they did, and he started firing right above me. The first NVA was killed, firing an automatic burst as he fell. The second never got off a shot. Sharp told me to throw grenades and fire only on semiautomatic at the rifle flashes. The more we fired, it seemed to draw more fire from the enemy.

Alhmeyer and Tycz were both hit in that first burst of fire. The lieutenant was moaning, but Tycz must not've been hit badly. The [NVA] started throwing grenades at the sounds Alhmeyer was making, and Tycz was throwing them back. Then one got him, and I heard him moan and I started to move over to where he was. But Carlson was there first to help him.

Carlson described from his perspective what had been happening:

Sergeant Tycz was on the radio calling for helicopters. Then a grenade came in, and, by God, he went for that grenade. He grabbed it and threw it back at the enemy. It went off.... I can't remember exactly, but it was like Tycz was trying to protect a Marine who had gone down. It might have been Lieutenant Alhmeyer. Then another grenade came in, and he went for that one, too. That one went off in his hand. It got me, too, in the right arm. All hell was still happening—small arms fire, grenades. Then I was with Tycz, and he was mumbling that he needed morphine. I gave him some. He won the Medal of Honor twice that night.

Tycz had been on the radio, and I picked up the handset, but it wasn't connected to the radio. Grenades were then coming in from everywhere.

The Marines had set claymore mines around their positions, and in the initial fighting these were triggered and took down many of the NVA. However, it was difficult for the Americans to fight back. Grenades were thrown back and forth, but the volume of small arms fire, while at times heavy, was becoming sporadic. Most of the NVA attacks seemed to be coming from the east, carried out by, perhaps, a company of more than 100 men. The volume of AK-47 rifle fire from the east was horrendous. Marines who rose to a kneeling position were soon dead or wounded, and even lying prone didn't save them from grenade explosions. Tycz had gotten a radio transmission through before he and the radio were hit, but then both radios were out of commission and Lance Corporal Carlson was crawling around on his stomach trying to piece a radio together from their remains. He took a good handset from one dead unit and replaced the destroyed handset on the other with it. Finally, they could speak again to the help that was coming. The few meters that separated individual Marines seemed like miles. How many were still alive and able to fight? No one knew for sure.

Friery said:

Sharp was facing northeast when he was hit in the head. He fired an automatic burst into the ground as he went down. I told Carlson, and he told me to see about Sharp. When I checked him he was dead. The next morning I saw a hole the size of a silver dollar in the back of his head. He must have been killed instantly. At the time Sharp was hit I think Miller was still alive. I know that Carlson was trying to put a radio together, and he was calling for artillery, but none ever came.

Carlson stated that he thought that artillery fired, but was not effectual and would not fire for effect. Carlson at one point gave the radio to Lopez, who in a taped interview after the battle is quoted as saying, "We kept asking for artillery to come in closer and closer because the enemy was within ten meters of us, and it seemed as though the artillery batteries wouldn't cooperate. They wouldn't bring rounds in for us. And, we kept calling in for a 'Fire for effect,' and they wouldn't fire for effect."

A Marine air wing account of the alert given to its flight crews immediately upon getting the distress call from the team stated, ". . . the team was beyond artillery range and no fixed wing was available due to the weather."

The team was so far out from the base that the 155 howitzers were 15,000 meters away, and the big 175 guns were 29,000 meters off at Camp Carroll. However, that meant that either because of the distance or the intervening hills and mountains, the artillery could not adequately reach them, and for the first hour of the fight, these young 18- and 19-year-old Americans were in reality on their own, bleeding, fighting, fearing, and trying to hold on to life.

Carl Friery said, "Everybody was dead now except for Doc Miller, Carlson, and Lopez who were a little away from me. I was the only one facing to the north, and I remember feeling very alone."

After about an hour of desperation and fighting back, the Recon team finally heard help arrive overhead. UH-1E Huey gunships ripped into the valley, made contact with the team, and sighted the enemy within fifteen feet of the Americans. Under flares, the birds dove repeatedly out of the sky and machine-gunned the enemy. On the ground, Carlson was hit again by grenade fragments. Pfc. Lopez was trying to fight off the enemy from his position, but was himself wounded, and Friery was the only one still not wounded.

Back at Khe Sanh, within minutes after the initial contact, Maj. Arthur Colbert and his copilot, 1st Lt. Gerald Roberts, were awakened. They were briefed on Breaker's situation. At 0120, Major Colbert and Lieutenant Roberts, plus wingman Capt. Douglas Manz and his copilot, 1st Lt. Jack Lower, launched out of the Khe Sanh combat base and flew northwest in CH-46s. About four miles from the action, the aircraft crews saw flares in the distance. The ceiling was low, and hills partially masked the lights. It was an eerie scene under the ghostlike white-gray canopy of the clouds. Puff the Magic Dragon was now on-station, blasting NVA positions with its gatling guns. (Puff we also called Spooky, if it was dropping flares, and sometimes just Dragonship. It was a converted C-47 fixed-wing aircraft with three sets of six-barreled machine guns capable of accurately firing 3,000 to 6,000 rounds per minute into a small area. The ship dropped flares to light the target area, and the pilot then banked the plane and fired the guns himself. What resulted was a Fourth of July spectacle in the dark of the night that could do extraordinary damage to exposed ground targets. It should be noted that other aircraft were similarly used. The AC 119 flareship could be called Spooky, and a C-130 modified as a gunship was nicknamed The Spectre.)

Carlson said that there were lulls in the battle. In retrospect, he felt that the NVA had decided that the best bet was to keep the pressure on the Recon team, to use them as bait to trap the incoming rescue choppers. It would be no small victory for them to knock a helicopter or two out of the sky.

"We entered a valley where the team was located," Lieutenant Roberts said. "Contact was made with the gunship, and after several orbits the team was located on a hilltop next to a bomb crater. We made contact with the team, and they said they were ready to come out. . . . We commenced our approach, and I turned off all outside lights. . . ." (However, the area was lit by flares, so the aircraft was still very visible.)

There was a bomb crater within fifteen to twenty feet of the team, and this was used by the aircraft for a guide. Lieutenant Roberts continued: "We approached the ground and came to hover over the lip of the bomb crater. At this instant, we began receiving fire from all directions. The aircraft seemed to shudder and then the major added power and moved off to the right and started climbing . . . a round came up through the right heel rest and into my right foot. . . ."

Major Colbert was able to pull the chopper out of the fire zone and make it back to Khe Sanh. However, three of the four crew members had been wounded. The 46, the old, rugged, slow-moving "tank," had taken fifty-three hits and had lost a hydraulic boost system, engine oil pressure, transmission oil pressure, its generators, and its radio.

On the ground, Lance Corporal Carlson watched the 46 come in to try for the rescue:

> This chopper was close, but then it came under heavy small arms fire. Sparks were flying off its bottom where the rounds were hitting. Then Doc Miller was shot. I was with him trying to help. He kept saying that he was hit in the femur artery. I tried to tie a bandage around the leg and stop the bleeding. Then I heard a grenade land behind me. I didn't think; all I remember is rolling my back over it. But it never went off. Another grenade landed, and we were both hit again. Then Doc Miller asked me to put a backpack against him as a prop so he could face the NVA and protect the rear. I did, but then he slumped over dead.

Overhead, even though Major Colbert's rescue attempt had almost ended in disaster, the gunships were still exposing themselves to strafe the NVA positions. Flares drifted downward, their light reflecting off the clouds above and casting a flickering yellow glow on the ground. Then Puff was again overhead, adding a big new source of power from the heavens. The NVA backed away from that mighty dragon.

However, the NVA knew that if enough pressure was kept on the Marines and a couple were still alive, other Americans would do whatever it took to help. So they watched, waited, and occasionally probed the remaining Marines, lobbing grenades and firing their AKs.

At 0235 Capt. P. T. Looney and his copilot, 1st Lt. John Roots, launched out of Khe Sanh on the second rescue attempt. They flew out on a heading of 320 degrees. It took ten minutes for the flight. All Marine aircraft in the skies over the Recon team coordinated the next maneuvers. One Huey swooped down over the team on a marking run, dropping a smoke grenade. Sergeant Reese, Looney's crew chief, noted the smoke and pointed it out to his skipper. He then learned that the gunships had expended their ammo and couldn't help. Regardless, Captain Looney informed them that he was beginning his approach.

Lieutenant Roots shut off the exterior lights, but as Major Colbert's aircraft had been, the 46 was illuminated by the flares. Looney had his craft only a few feet off the deck and only 100 meters from the LZ, probably within spitting distance of enemy soldiers lying in wait. He pulled up, hovering, near the bomb crater and radioed the Recon team for a strobe light. He reported seeing the light only a few meters ahead.

Carlson heard the call for the strobe light, but having none, he popped a willy-peter grenade. His intention was to throw it a little distance in front of him. However, his wounded right arm was virtually useless, and his throw was awkward; the grenade landed just in front of him. With the big 46 beating a storm and coming in a short distance away, Carlson began to say the Lord's Prayer. When he heard later that Looney had spotted a flashing light, Carlson didn't know where it had come from. No one knows whether the light observed by Looney was the WP grenade or whether the NVA had the Marine radio frequency and had itself responded to Captain Looney's request, trying to draw the chopper in farther. Although they seemed to take an eternity, these events transpired in the space of only a minute or so.

Friery said:

I remember the first and second chopper attempts to reach us. The NVA were cross-firing machine guns at them. Right after one of their attempts to pick us up, a grenade landed next to me, and I threw it back. Then I got hit. My legs and groin were covered in blood, but it didn't hurt. I was scared to look. I thought parts of me were blown off. I was still trying to fight when Carlson accidentally threw a white phosphorus grenade only five feet in front of me. I was covered in that WP residue and remember yelling at Carlson and him apologizing.

Suddenly, that second rescue bird was hit by blasts of rifle and machine gun fire from a 360-degree ambush. It was like being engulfed—totally immersed—in a metal hailstorm with no shelter, no direction offering protection.

The NVA blasted the Plexiglas windscreen on the pilot's side, spraying glass around the cockpit. The bird shuddered. Captain Looney, Sergeant Reese, and the corpsman, Doc Bridges, were hit. Looney was mortally wounded in the upper chest, but fought off death as he attempted to control the ship. Lieutenant Roots had somehow been spared the initial onslaught, and he grabbed the controls, turned the bird to the portside, and climbed. Looney pulled himself out of his seat and struggled to the rear. Another Marine, Cpl. Steven Remo, was on board. He had been trying to help the crew chief and corpsman. Roots called him forward to the cockpit to help pilot the ship. First Remo helped his skipper lie down. Then Doc regained consciousness and, despite his wounds, helped Captain Looney and Sergeant Reese.

Lieutenant Roots managed to fly the battered bird back to Khe Sanh. Again, an old, slow warhorse of a CH-46 had flown into a massive barrage of enemy fire from point-blank range. Due to the skill and courage of its crew, the helicopter made it back. It landed at 0308 hours.

The corpsman had shrapnel in his hip and rear. Sergeant Reese had a shattered left arm. The skipper, Captain Looney, died about fifteen minutes after landing.

Out in the horror, however, the surviving Marines continued to battle against the odds. Only Lopez and Carlson were able to continue the fight, and both of them had more than one serious wound. Britt Friery was alive but unconscious.

Carlson recollects:

> I remember them [the helicopter gunships] firing quite a way from us. I was trying to throw a grenade when I was shot again in the arm. I looked down, and the grenade was inches in front of me. I grabbed it and tossed it behind me. It exploded, and I caught shrapnel in the back of my head. I fired my rifle at the NVA, but it "took off" on me because of my right arm. I had to try to cradle my rifle. I remember giving myself a shot of morphine. Then I was shot in the right leg. I thought everything was hopeless. In that state of mind, it was funny that all of a sudden the fear seemed to go and I accepted death. I just thought to call for our position to be bombed out of sight and to try to take as many NVA with us as possible. I radioed for artillery, but none came. I do remember praying and thinking that I would never have another cup of coffee.

There were four dead Marines around Carlson, and he didn't know if anybody else was alive. A few meters away, Pfc. Lopez was, in fact, still alive, but felt the same as Carlson—that he might be the only one left. But at least one other body still had a pumping heart. Britt Friery, wounded earlier in the fighting, had passed out. He recalled:

> I was shot about one and a half hours after the battle started. I was shot in the abdomen. About thirty minutes later, a grenade landed near me. I tried to find it, and then I tried to get away from it. Carlson yelled to me to move, but there was no strength in my legs, and I slumped over my pack. I was hit in the back, and Carlson was yelling out to me, but I felt myself sliding from consciousness. I prayed, "God, if you'll just get me out of here alive, I'm yours forever." Then, before I passed out, I experienced a feeling of invincibility, an awesome power like I was in a [protective] bubble. After that I do not know what happened.

Somehow the remaining Marines stayed alive, and the NVA again backed away. Carlson said that there are portions of the battle of which he remembers nothing. One of those "blank" times was from somewhere around 0330 or 0400 to daylight.

At daylight, new friendlies were in the skies overhead, and the NVA made additional attacks on the Marines. Maj. Richard Sancho, piloting a Huey gunship, stated, "Debris and bodies could be seen throughout the entire area. All hands were determined to defend the team and eventually extract them. The entire area was mottled with camouflaged bunkers and spider holes."

Capt. Rodney Alley and Sancho flew their gunships (UH-1Es) into the area at 0645 to relieve those on-station. Each of the new birds was well armed with external and internal guns and with rockets. The Recon team made radio contact with the new help. Captain Alley's UH-1E was armed with quad 60s (four external M-60s), rockets, two crew-fired M-60s, and the new TAT 101E. The latter was a turret-housed machine gun mounted under the nose of the helicopter. This modification was not found on the Army's Hueys although theirs included grenade launchers similarly mounted under the bird's nose. The gunships' arsenal allowed pinpoint accuracy and delivered devastating fire on the enemy, many of whom were concealed only by elephant grass. Still, the birds received heavy ground fire.

At daylight Carlson realized that Lopez and Friery were still alive. It was also when he first saw jets making runs, dropping napalm, and shaking the ground very close by. He remembered, "One pilot waved at me." But the napalm started a fire that became a danger to both sides. From daybreak till about 0900 the fixed-wings and Hueys continued to make low-level bombing and strafing runs, covering all sides of the team's position.

In the early-morning hours, Cpl. Ted Biszko was awakened and told that Tycz was being annihilated. Biszko said:

> Tycz was good in the bush. I couldn't see that happening to him. He wouldn't have been stupid enough to set a harbor site in a place like that. I turned on a radio to his frequency and heard a voice calling for help. Then later somebody asked me to get my team ready to go out with the choppers and try a rescue mission. I told him they didn't have to ask. Tycz was my best friend. It was a suicide mission, but so many were.

At approximately 0900, a CH-46 picked up Biszko and his five Marines. Biszko said:

> I told my guys to take all the ammo and grenades they could, and told the pilot if we couldn't get 'em out, we'd stay with 'em. I said to go in

with the jet and gunship cover like a motherfucker and to not even stop. Just keep the tailgate lowered, and we'd jump and roll. I told my guys we weren't leaving anybody behind.

Then we were out there, and the pilot gave me the thumbs-up as he was getting close. I got the team at the back of the chopper ready to jump, and it was then that the bird started taking big hits. A .50-caliber round went right through the deck and top of the chopper right beside me. Rounds were coming through the chopper. It started to roll around, and it was like we were spinning out of control. There was no chance to get close enough. But we got back to Khe Sanh—I don't know how. The bird landed, and we went running out, afraid that the 46 would blow up.

The company commander was waiting and yelling for us to run into another chopper that was getting ready to take off. This time I went running up to the front and emphasized to this pilot that he couldn't make the same mistake as the last one. He had to let the jets go in first and drop their bombs. Then he should be in as the dust was just starting to settle and drop us off.

Then we got out there again, and I saw the jets drop their bombs, but then the chopper started taking hits. A big hole blew through the bird and hit the fuel line. We were soaked in fuel, and the 46 was wobbling all over the sky. We got back to Khe Sanh again, and I couldn't believe that we were still alive. Then I started crying. We let 'em down. We couldn't get to 'em.

Then began a three-hour period of final, desperate battle. Lopez, Carlson, and Friery fought despite their wounds. The gunships overhead were refueled and rearmed in rotation, always providing the saving firepower because the Marine pilots just would not give up. Even when only one bird was up, because the others had to refuel or rearm, that one bird made continuous circling runs just over ground level. Maj. Richard Sancho, Capt. Rodney Alley, 1st Lt. Edward Lord, 2nd Lt. Richard Gregson, and their gunners and crew chiefs, Cpl. Larry Zimpfer, Cpl. James Holland, and L.Cpl. David Vermilion, never gave up.

The Recon team below kept radio contact with the pilots. The NVA closed and maneuvered, but a new menace was by then threatening everyone on the ground: the grass fire was building into a raging conflagration. At one point Carlson saw "an enemy soldier [who] suddenly appeared out of the brush behind me. I saw Lopez swing his rifle around in my direction, and I dropped. Lopez shot the guy. He was inside our perimeter. But the fire was that close, too, and I saw the flames burn his skin off."

Back at KSCB, Maj. Charles Reynolds, the pilot for the division commanding general, Bruno Hochmuth, had arrived in his unarmed Huey slick. It was now his turn, but two helicopter crews were combined. L.Cpl. Ronald Zaczek was crew chief. Major Sancho, First Lieutenant Lord, Captain Alley, Second Lieutenant Gregson, First Lieutenant Mumfurd, and First Lieutenant Schnick would be aboard two gunships and two 46s. The latter would act as decoys.

Friery says that Carlson saw Sam Sharp's body start to smolder in the fire and yelled at him to pour canteen water over it. Carlson said, "I did it, and as I was pouring the water, a rifle shot impacted only about three feet away. Then another hit Sam's body. By this time my legs were starting to work again, and I jumped up and fired a magazine on automatic at the sniper's position. Carlson was then yelling that another rescue bird was coming in." The Recon team radioed the approaching pilots that they would be dead soon, either because of the NVA or the fire.

The gunships led Major Reynolds in, but heavy fire from their west beat them off. Reynolds then made a second approach from farther to the north. An equal volume from that direction drove them off.

The 46s came into play and made diversion runs, receiving small arms fire. The gunships also dived and gunned the area. Major Reynolds—his copilot, 1st Lt. David Myers, calling out obstacles—then directed the aircraft for the team from a third direction, along the valley floor. In seconds, as they reached the knoll and the team, the UH-1E gunships flew near to the unarmed slick, firing from as close as 20 meters to Reynolds, Myers, and their crew, Lance Corporals Acosta and Zaczek. With enemy and friendly fire on all sides, the bird slipped in and quickly hovered near the team.

"When the chopper came in from the east and came up from the bottom of the valley floor up to where we were," Carlson said, "we spotted him and all three of us ran for the chopper. It didn't matter about the wounds—we ran." Acosta and Zaczek pulled, and the wounded Marines scrambled aboard in the middle of enemy fire.

Friery said, "I took about two running strides and threw my shoulders into the hatch. They grabbed my arms. I had absolutely no strength to hold on. Then we took off with them holding me and trying to pull me the rest of the way in."

"I remember," said Carlson, "lying on the floor of the chopper, looking the pilot in the eye, and the pilot giving me a thumbs-up."

Major Reynolds reported seeing the bodies of the three dead Marines, but no sign of the seventh team member. After a tragic and terrible ordeal, three Recon Marines had struggled through the long night and next morning. Four others gave their lives, and undoubtedly their sacrifice helped save Lopez, Carlson, and Friery.

Several CH-46s were shot to hell, and Captain Looney, the pilot of one, had been killed. Captain Manz wrote:

Captain Looney—pilot of the second attempt lead aircraft—he paid the supreme sacrifice for God and country. What more can a man do? In his twelve months in country, Captain Looney had contributed a great deal to the . . . success of his squadron. On this particular occasion, he was again contributing his professional flying skill and the combat knowledge of his many past experiences. His approach was perfect, but the situation was far from it. He took a fatal round and died thirty minutes later. His courage and professionalism were always in the highest tradition of the United States Marine Corps.

Captain Looney and Sgt. James Tycz were both at the ends of their tours of duty and would have gone home in a matter of days.

Sergeant Tycz and Pfc. Lopez were each awarded the Navy Cross, and Lance Corporal Carlson the Silver Star. The bodies of Tycz, Alhmeyer, Miller, and Sharp were never recovered. Corporal Biszko and his small team of Reconners had risked their lives, ready to jump into what they knew might be their graves, for the chance to save their friends, but their choppers had been turned back to Khe Sanh by the heavy enemy fire. They felt helpless.

Lt. Gen. Lewis Walt, the commanding general of the III Marine Amphibious Force, was transferred to Stateside duty within weeks of that patrol and the last of the heavy 1967 Khe Sanh battles. At one point, Walt commented on the beginning of the American commitment to create the KSCB, saying:

If I had had the troops out there [in northern I Corps], I would never have established Khe Sanh because I would always have had enough troops I could throw in. But I didn't have that many at that time, and when you're short of troops you've got to use firepower. And that's what I used. I put artillery and troops in there at Khe Sanh and by patrolling out from Khe Sanh we controlled the area.

The Recon Stingray patrol had taken on the major challenge of controlling the onslaught of regiment- and division-size NVA forces. However, that tactic cannot and did not work in the face of very large numbers of enemy units. Teams attempting insertions were shot out of one LZ after another, and when they made it in, the Marines would often find themselves in a running battle with superior enemy forces. Often, desperate patrol leaders radioing for help and extraction were simply told, "Break contact and continue mission."

CHAPTER TWELVE

Team Striker

On May 19, 1967, nine days after the death of the four Marines from Team Breaker, Secretary of Defense Robert McNamara sent a memo to the president recommending that two basic principles be clearly defined in regard to the policies and actions of the United States in Vietnam. Those were: "(1) Our commitment is only to see that the people of South Vietnam are permitted to determine their own future. (2) This commitment ceases if the country ceases to help itself." He further stated that the U.S. commitment was not "to insist that the independent South Vietnam remain separate from North Vietnam (though in the short run we would prefer it that way)."

The commitment of the individual Reconner was to his Corps and his Country. While he had long since lost faith in the ability of average ARVN soldiers to defend their own country, that was not of particular importance to him. The Marine was still from the old school of thought—that is, in his hands was a very special trust and responsibility given to him by America. Probably no Marine in Vietnam would have defined himself as a hero, but all were taught that they had to fight an international Communist movement in Vietnam, and those eighteen- and nineteen-year-old Americans believed and trusted in that commission.

By June 1967, after the bloody hill fights in the first Khe Sanh battle, Alpha Company was shifted from Khe Sanh to Phu Bai, and Bravo Company replaced them at the KSCB. The 3rd Force operated from Dong Ha along with Delta Company. Charlie Company was with Alpha and the battalion headquarters at Phu Bai. Lee Klein was still serving as the G-2 Forward at the Khe Sanh combat base. However, there were two intelligence sections at the base: one was Lee

Klein and the 3rd Division G-2 Forward, and the other was the S-2 section of the 26th Marines. Klein says there were often conflicts between the two, that the intelligence officer of the 26th Marines was "a track jock who had never before worked in real life." Klein told of a time when after a patrol a "Recon team leader was being debriefed by this S-2. The Recon leader stated that the team had heard Vietnamese voices all around the team. The S-2 then asked him if the voices were those of North or South Vietnamese. The young Recon sergeant just stood up and walked out in disgust." Klein pleaded in his 1967 comments, "We need to get people up here who know what they're doing."

At Phu Bai, Recon's primary focus was toward the western and northwestern approaches to the city of Hue that included the Co Bi–Thanh Tan. However, there were also concentrations of enemy forces in most directions around the old imperial capital of Hue City. It was during the summer of 1967 that the Hanoi command developed the plans for a general offensive, to occur on their New Year's celebration (Tet) that would begin 1968. It was the city of Hue that would be taken by the NVA and VC forces for a temporary time, and it was the Recon teams in the outlying hills who saw it coming.

Highway One paralleled the coast between Phu Bai and Da Nang, and another, more primitive, road roughly paralleled the main highway about ten miles farther inland. Mountains that reached three-quarters of a mile in height rose from their sea level bases and towered over both roads. The inland road began its southward path by branching off Highway One just below Phu Bai. About thirty miles later it entered Elephant Valley and then rejoined Highway One north of Da Nang. That roadway also branched into the southern reaches of the A Shau. The Co Bi–Thanh Tan was the main route for enemy forces coming toward the city of Hue from the northwest; the primitive road was the same for those coming from the southwest.

The mountains between the two roads into which Team Striker was to be inserted formed a horseshoe facing east and the South China Sea. From the mountaintops on one side to the tops on the other side was about five miles; the valley floor was about one mile across. Up the middle of this valley (in reality, a wide box canyon) ran a cart path, and next to that was a stream. The upper end of this valley was about eight miles from Highway One, and that was the destination for Team Striker. Intelligence estimates placed two Vietcong battalions—the 804th and the 804B, consisting of some 400 infantry each—in the vicinity of the team's insertion LZ. But the team was not told.

Mariano "Junior" Guy; his brother, Willie Acosta; and Jeff Savelkoul were all in Alpha Company and had survived Khe Sanh and those hill patrols. Savelkoul said, "When we patrolled those hills like 881 before the fighting started you knew they [the enemy main forces] were around. You could feel their eyes boring holes in you, but they were not choosing to hit you just yet." However, the Hue–Phu Bai area was to be an even worse experience for him and his teammates.

On June 29, there was a planned "flip-flop" of patrols in the same LZ in this valley south of Phu Bai. Willie Acosta was out with the team in the field, and his brother, Mariano "Junior," was on the team going out to take its place. Acosta's team had no trouble during its days in the higher jungle. The team had been patrolling the high ridge under the jungle canopy and hadn't encountered enemy units until it surfaced in the exposed lowland where the LZ was located.

The plan was for the CH-46 to drop off Junior's team, pick up the waiting team, and quickly depart. The incoming team was led by Cpl. Eugene "Cass" Castaneda, and Junior ran point. Savelkoul was a radio operator. The LZ was an open flat piece of ground near the edge of a ridgeline that jutted out into the valley from the higher mountains. Acosta's team had slipped down that jungled ridge to the edge of the LZ.

However, as Acosta and his team saw the helicopters coming in for the planned flip-flop, they were surprised by nearby small arms fire directed at the bird. They couldn't locate the source of the fire, but the CH-46 was on its way in and landed to drop off and pick up the teams. Inside, Junior was at point and hadn't heard the firing, nor had other members of the team inside the noisy helicopter. As was his custom, Junior leapt from the bird, followed by the rest of the team, looking for cover. Events were happening fast, and Acosta's team had run aboard and the bird had taken off before the pilots realized that they would have to drop back into the zone and retrieve the team that had just landed.

As the first bird rose into the air, both the chopper and the team on the ground were subjected to enemy fire. Savelkoul said, "Bullets were impacting all around and spraying dirt in my face. There was no cover except where there were enemy."

Corporal Castaneda radioed the choppers and asked for an immediate extraction. The second 46 that had accompanied the planned flip-flop braved enemy fire and dropped into the LZ. Under fire, the team of Marines ran for the bird, and the chopper laboriously lifted its way back into the sky and away from the peppering fire from below.

When it returned to the base, Corporal Castaneda's team was ordered back out the next day into the same general area. Although the LZ would be slightly different the next day, the result would be much worse. Junior would still be at point with his rifle and machete, and Savelkoul, the communication specialist, would still be on the radio. A recently acquired corpsman, "Doc" Michael Judd, had replaced "Doc" Zink, who was then serving at the Alpha Medical Company in Phu Bai. Other team members included Merlin Allen, John Killen III, Glyn Runnels, and Dennis Perry.

On June 30, the team was again in the air, heading back in the same direction, but this time it was preceded by fixed-wing aircraft that bombed and strafed the landing zone area. Members of the team didn't understand why jets would strafe the LZ and announce their coming, but theirs was "not to reason why."

As soon as the jets were finished with their runs, the lumbering 46 flew down toward the landing zone. Junior was positioning himself to be the first out and saw the tall elephant grass in the valley floor fast approaching. Savelkoul was back farther in the patrol, adjusting the extra weight of the radio on his pack.

When the chopper was within a few feet of the ground and Junior was about to leap and run, he was knocked off his feet by a sudden rocking and shaking of the aircraft. Still inside the chopper, the Marines sensed their first nervous fear; they knew that their helicopter had dropped into an ambush and was being battered by heavy weapons. Enemy fire penetrated the metal skin and ripped past the Marines inside.

As the helicopter lurched and shuddered, the pilot fought for control and tried to pull the aircraft out of the kill zone.

Savelkoul said:

I was toward the rear end, and I felt the chopper try to rise and turn around. As we went up higher, we were knocking out the portholes and firing our weapons or dropping grenades through them, trying to aim where we thought the VC were. The chopper was taking a lot of hits. Then I saw the round that took us down. I saw it fire from the ground and like a tracer streak toward us. It exploded a ten-inch hole through the side of the aircraft right next to me, and it caused a loud cracking noise. It exited through the roof and shattered a fuel line. But it was like the fuel pump was still surging and spraying its fuel through the broken line out onto us. The fuel ignited, and we were in the middle of this firestorm, and there wasn't anywhere to hide from it.

Junior stated that he and "Cass," the patrol leader, had run to the front and were firing out of the window next to the gunner. He said, "I heard guys in the chopper screaming. The fire was burning up the place, and Marines were on fire."

Even though 46s had survived severe damage in other battles, this old sky tank had been hit by an antitank round and it was starting to break up. The chopper was fatally wounded but struggled upward about two hundred feet. Stuck in the rear, Jeff Savelkoul was being enveloped by fire and smoke and was gasping for air. Savelkoul stated:

I needed to get air and stuck my head out of one of the broken windows. I got the air, but a piece of burning Plexiglas stabbed into my face. Then I heard somebody yelling, "Get up to the front; we're going down!"

I had to run through that wall of fire. I remember throwing off my pack because it was on fire. All my clothes were burned off except for one boot and my cartridge belt. In the confusion, I didn't realize that my hat was on fire, but when I finally knocked it off, my head was badly burned. My backside was particularly burned from my heels to my head. It was chaos. We were taking enemy fire through the chopper as well, and there was just nowhere to hide. I remember seeing a pile of bodies on the floor and Cass and Junior to one side.

The pilot, Capt. John A. House II, was struggling with the craft, trying to reach the top of a hogback ridge very close by and away from the VC. But it couldn't be. The surviving Marines saw daylight through the roof of the chopper, and then the back section of the helicopter cracked completely off and fell away from the front. The front section of the aircraft crashed into the top level of ninety-foot-tall trees. Captain House had made it about three-fourths of the way to the top of the ridge and had given the team's survivors some breathing room. But he was dead and his copilot wounded.

Junior said, "We hit those ninety-foot trees and really went into an uncontrolled crash, falling through the trees. We were frantic to get out of there and started pushing out through the windows on the right side."

Savelkoul, Junior Guy, Castaneda, and Perry leaped into the air out of the falling, burning wreck, but they were still high up in the trees. Each plummeted, being battered, spun around, and flipped by branches. They hit the ground hard. Savelkoul said he remembered seeing Junior stumbling around dazed for a moment, trying to get his bearings. "The helicopter smashed into the ground nearby and looked like a watermelon that you had dropped on the sidewalk. It just splattered on the jungle floor."

The wounded Marines found themselves on a jungle hillside. Junior and Castaneda were in the best shape, and they tried to help Savelkoul and Perry up the hill. Savelkoul and Perry were burned badly, raw and charred flesh hanging off them. Finally the two healthy Reconners struggled to the hilltop with Savelkoul and Perry, then started back down the hill to see if they could find more survivors. Of course, the VC were coming up, firing at the rescue helicopters that hovered and buzzed over the tall jungle canopy, trying to catch sight of any survivors.

Savelkoul explained:

Junior and Cass pulled Perry and me away and started us up the hill, and then they ran back down. Perry was in really critical condition. I was trying to pull him and hand-over-hand pull us up the steep slope. It hurt! The skin on my hands was pretty much burned off, my ears and hair were also burned off, and all down my back and legs my body just screamed.

You could hear the VC down below us shooting, and you could hear our choppers over the tops of the trees. I guess the desire to live keeps you going.

Junior Guy continued:

Cass got to the cockpit and crawled through the burning wreck to rescue the pilot. But he was slumped over, strapped in and covered by the fire. It was no use, but we managed to help the copilot, who was wounded and banged up, away from the burning wreck. Everything else was just obliterated. Everybody was dead.

We got back up to Jeff and Perry with the copilot, but wanted to go back down and try to find some weapons. Our rifles had melted, but maybe there was something to fight with. The VC were making their way uphill through the jungle toward us, and we were having to rush. We had one .38 pistol from the copilot and one grenade. Cass took the .38.

Before he and Castaneda went back down the hill to the wreckage, Junior took the one grenade, put it into Savelkoul's hand, and pulled the pin. He told Savelkoul not to dare let it go, but to use it in a final fight against the VC if they got up to them.

Savelkoul explained his feelings at that moment: "My hand was burned raw. The nerve endings must've been exposed. When Junior wrapped my fingers around that grenade and pulled the pin, the pain was fierce. Perry was lying in my lap. I watched Junior and Cass running from tree to tree, trying to get back to the wreck without running into any VC."

They made it down, but there were no more weapons to be found, and time was running out. They climbed back up, but had no radio on which to call for help. Then Cass found pen flares on the copilot and started firing them through the canopy overhead, trying to signal the rescue birds above. By a stroke of fortune he was able to hit one of the ships on the windshield. It was a Huey slick, which did a dip-nose-down signal to let the Marines on the ground know that he had received their message. The crew immediately lowered a sling through the trees toward the Marines. The enemy could still be heard, and they were closer.

The race for survival was not going to be easy; there was just no way that the ropes could descend through trees without getting hung up. Junior Guy still had his machete, so the young native of El Paso climbed the problem tree, hacking away at branches faster than the VC could climb the hill. He cleared a path for the slings, then slid back down. With the enemy closing and firing at the helicopters, trying to beat them to the team, the Reconners started their ascent. The copilot, Perry, and Savelkoul were each tied in tightly and went up one at a time. They were followed by Junior Guy and Cass—two in one loop. The last two stayed together, each not wanting the other to be the last on the ground.

"The sling was just a loop in a rope, and you had to tighten it so you wouldn't slip out," said Savelkoul. "That line dug deep into me. At the time, I couldn't see my back, but that rope made me feel how badly burned it was. It really hurt, but I held on as tight as I could."

By the time the VC clambered up to the crash site, the Marines were all safely aboard the Huey, and the birds swiftly turned and sped back to Phu Bai with the injured.

Back at the camp, during the time of the battle, Acosta, Junior's brother, was being kept away from emergency radio transmissions by well-meaning friends who knew that Junior was in deep trouble. But once the team had been pulled out and Junior was known to be among the survivors, Acosta was told, and he got over to the medical company as quickly as he could. Doc Zink was also there to receive his friends. He learned that his replacement, Doc Judd, had been killed, and it was an emotional experience for him. Perry, badly hurt, was carried in on a stretcher. He died two days later in a hospital in Japan. Jeff Savelkoul had burns over two thirds of his body, most third-degree. He hurt so much that he couldn't lie on a stretcher, so, naked, he walked away from the bird.

Savelkoul said, "The last thing I remember in Vietnam was talking to Doc Zink and asking him to take care of me. He gave me a glass of water and promised that he would. After that there was only a couple of vague moments that I remember before, two weeks later, I woke up in the burn unit of Brooks Army Medical Center in San Antonio, Texas."

Neither Eugene Castaneda nor Mariano "Junior" Guy was so severely injured that he had to be hospitalized. And although Junior was at first scheduled to go back to the bush in three days, the battalion decided to transfer him to Okinawa for the rest of his overseas tour. Corporal Castaneda was also transferred, but to another in-country unit working with the Vietnamese. On August 12, 1967, he was killed while on duty.

That June was the deadliest month of the war to date for the battalion. Striker had not been the only Recon team to get shot out of the skies in that month. On June 11, a 3rd Force team was being flown into the southern edge of the DMZ, two miles north of Helicopter Valley, when its CH-46 exploded in the air about 200 feet above the ground while descending to insert the team. All aboard were killed, including the seven-man team of Jim Moshier, Thomas Hanratty, Dennis Christie, Charles Chomel, Michael Havtanek, James Kooi, and John Foley III.

Five days before the Force team was blown out of the sky, a radio relay on a mountaintop two miles northeast of Khe Sanh was overrun. All three Recon men, David Sherrell, Howard Withey, and Dale Speir, were killed, along with three of the infantry who were with them. However, the NVA paid a heavy price, as the team called in 2,800 rounds of artillery and fought hard until they died fighting at close quarters.

One team operating near the DMZ northwest of the Rockpile observed two SAM missiles being fired from the middle of the DMZ—only about two and a half miles from their position. The team was able to silence the site with artillery and air strikes.

Battalion accounts record 1,393 enemy soldiers sighted during the month of June. However, none were counted for Team Striker, even though they probably landed in part of one of the two VC battalions suspected to be in the area; the team hadn't gotten a good view of any enemy soldiers.

Operating out of Dong Ha, Delta Company and Force together sighted 733 enemy during June, and estimated that they were able to kill 18 percent of those, primarily by calling in artillery missions that fired a total of 1,567 rounds. During this month, the three Recon companies along the DMZ accounted for two thirds of the battalion's sightings.

However, for that thirty-day period, fifteen Reconners were killed, thirty-nine were wounded, and one was listed as missing in action. The missing Marine was Di Ibanez, who, on June 5, walked out of his team's nighttime harbor site and never returned. Others had thought that he was going to make a "head call." They heard noises, but no weapons fired. After a search of the area, they could find nothing but teeth that apparently had been knocked out of someone's mouth. It was presumed that he had been captured. The next morning, the team found evidence of recently occupied enemy positions in the vicinity.

Marine Recon teams continued to note enemy activity in all parts of their RAORs, and the secretary of defense, in Washington, D.C., pressed the president to consider a decision to stop all bombing of North Vietnam and try to negotiate with the Vietcong and "split the VC off from Hanoi." However, the Joint Chiefs of Staff quickly countered the defense secretary, noting that this would be the American Dien Bien Phu. In a military briefing at the Pentagon, General Westmoreland also blasted the belief that the war was not achieving its objectives; he cited 1967 intelligence estimates that "approximately 45 percent" of the enemy units were considered to be "combat ineffective." He also added that he felt that the situation during 1967 was progressing so well that he expected to turn over the major share of the DMZ defense to the South Vietnamese Army.

However, 1967 would also see the attempt to create "Leatherneck Square" along the eastern half of the DMZ, and additionally would witness the return to many walk-out Recon patrols from those bases in the low rolling plains north and northeast of Cam Lo. There would be no turning over of the major share of the DMZ defense to the South Vietnamese Army.

CHAPTER THIRTEEN

The Summer of 1967

Throughout the summer, the secretary of defense and the chiefs of staff of the military waged a growing warfare of their own that was becoming more bitter as the battles in Vietnam became bloodier. Although this D.C. battlefield was virtually unknown to the Marine in the field, it significantly affected him. By the end of the summer, Secretary McNamara, not having convinced the president of the value of all of his beliefs, formulated his last attempt to change American policy in Vietnam. Among his proposals were: (1) to limit U.S. forces to 470,000; (2) to finish the barrier along the DMZ to help stop infiltration; (3) to keep the number of sorties flown against North Vietnam to a level of 12,000 a month; (4) to require drastic reform from the South Vietnamese government and military, and to pursue a vigorous pacification program among the people; and (5) to increase the credibility of U.S. peace gestures to the North Vietnamese and the Vietcong, and to try to split the VC from the North Vietnamese. The warfare in Vietnam was becoming increasingly mired in both monsoon and political mud, but the intensity was about to increase further. This time it would be directed toward the border frontiers of South Vietnam and Cambodia, Laos, and North Vietnam. The ante was increased, and the chips played were young American men.

After the lethal month of June, total sightings by the battalion's teams dropped to 951 enemy soldiers in July. The decrease was due in part to diminished enemy presence in the Khe Sanh area. However, during July, the NVA began to throw its weight toward Con Thien, near the DMZ, and the majority of the battalion's sightings during this month occurred in this sector, called "Leatherneck Square." Delta Company and 3rd Force, operating from Dong Ha, were involved there. The combat base at Con Thien was the northwest corner of Leatherneck Square. This was a part of the strong point obstacle system (SPOS)—although it was mostly referred to as the McNamara Line, after ͜ie secretary of defense, whose brainchild it was. The purpose of the system was to reduce infiltration through this section of the DMZ and force the NVA to travel the more difficult mountains to the west.

The 11th Engineer Battalion, operating under the III MAF command, had orders to construct the barrier, which was to consist of a cleared 600-foot-wide trace between strong points. That trace would then be wired, mined, and covered with sensors to detect movement. The trace would then be anchored by strong points, such as the one at Con Thien. Because of the vast effort required to build the SPOS, including the infantry needed to both protect the engineers and then man fixed positions, III MAF felt it would seriously diminish the flexibility of its infantry battalions. General Walt continually protested the plan. However, the work progressed in April and May, and on June 1, 1967, Lt. Gen. Lewis Walt gave up his command of III MAF to Lt. Gen. Robert Cushman. Walt returned to the States, and on January 1, 1968, he became deputy commandant of the Marine Corps.

As the work on the barrier system progressed, many thousands of Vietnamese were relocated from their home villages by the South Vietnamese Army to the Cam Lo temporary resettlement site. It was then that the North Vietnamese decided to assault the Con Thien area.

The first NVA attack was led by the 90th NVA Infantry Regiment, 324B NVA Division. On July 2, two battalions of the regiment executed a well-prepared ambush against Companies A and B of the 1st Battalion, 9th Marines. The location of the ambush was less than two miles northeast of Con Thien. The terrain was flat to rolling low hills with hedgerows, brush, and limited tree growth. The hills were hardly more than 50 meters high, except for Con Thien itself, which was only slightly higher at an elevation of 158 meters. It was a gradual, open ascent of only about 200 feet above the adjacent terrain. A streambed with protective cover extended south out of the DMZ to a point near the ambush site and served as one infiltration route for the NVA that offered cover and concealment.

Before the battle ended that day, other Marine units were committed, but the NVA controlled the situation and hammered the Marines with artillery as well as infantry attacks. At the end of that one day, the 1st Battalion, 9th Marines, had lost 84 killed, 190 wounded, and 9 missing in action. Only 27 Bravo Company Marines walked out of the battle.

However, Operation Buffalo then kicked into high gear, with the

9th Marine Regiment joined by two Battalion Landing Teams from the 3rd Marines in a hunt for the 90th NVA Regiment. Also attached to the infantry were patrols from the 3rd Recon Battalion. Two different teams from the Delta Company/3rd Force detachment at Dong Ha spent four and four and a half days, respectively, in the bush two klicks northeast of Con Thien. They were attached to the grunts and served as their forward eyes and ears. The teams slipped through the carnage and avoided serious problems to themselves. One team had a contact with five NVA, killing four. They reported, "Area is littered with enemy dead and equipment. Area is under constant mortar, rocket, and artillery barrage [enemy fire as well as USMC]."

The other team found enemy bunkers and had two contacts with a total of 200 enemy soldiers that resulted in 152 enemy killed by USMC artillery. They also reported the constant mortar and artillery barrages from both sides.

The Recon teams were used by the infantry to search into the DMZ in attempts to find the pathways used by the NVA in their forays south. One of those patrols spotted a 400-man NVA battalion moving toward the 3rd Battalion, 9th Marines. This report enabled Alpha Company 1/9, which had been badly mauled on the second, to take up ambush positions along the NVA route and rip them repeatedly, then withdraw just before the NVA retaliated with artillery fire. (One of the many problems with the McNamara Line was that it was within artillery range of the NVA from their side of the border.)

Although Operation Buffalo ended on July 14, the Recon teams sent into the area later still found ample evidence of the enemy. The day before the operation officially ended, while patrolling only two klicks west of Con Thien, one patrol lasted only fifteen hours and had three sightings and a contact with one NVA company. On the twenty-fourth, another team ran into a platoon of NVA less than a mile outside of the Con Thien base. The team suffered nine Marines wounded, and the scout dog was also hit. However, they counted eighteen NVA bodies before they were extracted.

Another team operated from July 23 to 26 just inside the DMZ and about two and a half miles west of Con Thien. Those Reconners had numerous sightings of both lights and NVA. One Marine was wounded in the fighting, but an estimated thirty-seven NVA were killed, either confirmed or probable.

Immediately after Operation Buffalo ended, Operation Kingfisher was initiated in the same area. On July 28, Lt. Col. Bill Kent's 2nd Battalion, 9th Marines, was sent with armored vehicles to attack through the southern half of the DMZ and push to the Ben Hai River, on the border. That border between the two Vietnams had been established in 1954 as a temporary boundary until nationwide elections could be held in 1956 (they never were). The DMZ was to be demilitarized for about two or three miles on each side of the river.

The battalion (2/9) had little contact before reaching the Ben Hai, but the NVA knew the area well and planned to counterattack the battalion on its way back out. Lieutenant Colonel Kent stated, "We actually were given very little intelligence information about the situation we would be facing. And we received no Recon patrol reports."

The armored vehicles, tanks and amtracks, proved to be more of a hindrance than an assistance. The terrain was so difficult that the vehicles had to stay on the road, so the infantry soldiers had to stay close to protect them. The battalion was forced to maneuver in column formation, trying to fight its way back from the Ben Hai. At one point toward the end of the battle, Kent took command of a reinforcing company from the 3rd Battalion, 4th Marines, and fought back to rescue two squads from his Echo Company that had become isolated and were holding out against NVA attacks. The battalion lost 23 Marines killed and 251 wounded. Neither before nor after 2/9's "armored thrust into the DMZ" did American infantry units spend much time within the DMZ. Operation Kingfisher was more proof that mechanized vehicles were not suited for combat in this terrain.

At about this time, but farther to the west, near Khe Sanh, there were conflicts that ominously foretold the future of that base. The 3rd Battalion, 3rd Marines, was responsible for keeping a portion of Route 9 open from Dong Ha to Khe Sanh for resupply. One platoon of Company M of that battalion was sweeping the road from Ca Lu toward Khe Sanh. About five kilometers out, the platoon ran into what was thought to be an NVA soldier urinating beside the road. The Marines had apparently caught him with his trousers in the wrong position, but the platoon was also shocked. As they advanced and opened fire on the lone ranger, they quickly were caught in a cross fire between the high ground to their north and a tree line to their south.

At first believing he had engaged a platoon of NVA in ambush, the platoon commander took appropriate action, only to discover very soon that he was alone and facing an NVA battalion-size ambush. The parent Marine company with supporting arms came to the rescue and enabled all Marines to disengage and return to Ca Lu. The next day 3/3 attacked those ambush positions only to find the NVA gone. However, what was found might have been the site of a major ambush for the next Rough Rider convoy, which had been following not far behind the platoon. One hundred and fifty well-camouflaged fighting holes were positioned near the ambush site. In addition, an NVA base camp was located close by and included 200 fighting holes and two-to-four-man log bunkers that were concealed with dirt and grass. Sleeping and cooking huts were also found. The premature ambush might have prevented a horror show for the Rough Rider convoy, but the tenuous situation in which Route 9 lay was also made known.

Despite the enemy contact in July, no Recon choppers were shot down and no Recon KIAs were suffered, but thirty-nine Reconners were wounded. However, the enemy's use of artillery was a concern. During Operation Buffalo, an enemy 152-mm howitzer round hit the 1/9 command bunker, penetrating five feet of sandbags, loose dirt, and twelve-by-twelve timbers, and killed the intelligence officer and wounded eighteen, including the battalion commander.

As July turned to August, the teams of the battalion saw an increase of activity near the Hue–Phu Bai zone. Enemy soldiers seen by Recon teams near the old imperial capital rose to 45 percent of the battalion's total. But while there seemed to be a slow increase in clandestine enemy movement around Hue–Phu Bai, the enemy's overt show of force along the DMZ continued. The first three weeks of August seemed to be the quiet before the storm, as the enemy units went about stockpiling supplies and ammunition and getting their grunt units ready again. Then their artillery and rockets began to blast pathways across the skies from out of the DMZ and from beyond that. Although Con Thien was to become the primary target, Dong Ha was also hit repeatedly. On August 26, 150 rocket and artillery rounds hit the base. Two choppers were destroyed and twenty-four were damaged. Less than two weeks later, the base was hit again by a shower of artillery rounds that damaged seventeen helicopters and destroyed the ammo storage area and bulk fuel farm.

The decision had just been made to stop the Rough Rider convoys to Khe Sanh, and now the main supply base for the KSCB was in jeopardy. The Marine Corps response was to immediately fly the helicopters back to the Marble Mountain facility at Da Nang, and III MAF started the construction of a new forward base and helicopter facility at Quang Tri, farther southeast of Dong Ha by five to six miles and just out of range of the enemy artillery that had been placed in or near the border.

However, farther south and southwest of Quang Tri and Hue City, Recon teams made heavy contact with the NVA and VC forces in August. These contacts were reported by battalion teams patrolling into the A Shau and closer, in the Co Bi–Thanh Tan.

Two Alpha Company teams ran concurrent patrols only two grid squares apart adjacent to the A Shau Valley in the first two days of August. On August 1, 1967, a team was inserted in the southern edge of the valley with the call sign Party Line One. 1st Lt. Bill McBride was the patrol leader. A day later the second team, Mono Type II, commanded by 2nd Lt. Al Weh, was inserted about 1,500 meters to the east, farther away from the main valley. The terrain was mountainous, with smaller valleys branching off the main A Shau. Montagnard tribes still inhabited the area, although many had evacuated voluntarily or had been moved by force from the area. One of the difficulties facing American forces operating in the area was that these tribes acted as the eyes and ears for the North Vietnamese.

The missions would take the Marines close to the Be Loung village and valley. Be Loung was near the junction of two major trails. One was a branch of Route 548 that ran down the center of the A Shau, and the second found its way from the northeast and Hue. This second trail ran north, twisting around mountains for about eighteen miles before passing the battalion's Whiskey radio relay site. However, to the south, the first trail joined with 548 in Laos (although with the Laotian name of Route 923) and then about five miles later reentered Vietnam, from where it made connections to Happy Valley and Charlie Ridge, southwest of Da Nang.

The ridgeline between the A Shau and the Be Loung valleys had been the site of several NVA antiaircraft batteries when they overran the Special Forces camp in 1966. Lieutenant McBride's team was to attempt to come down into the valley behind this ridgeline, which previously had been the AA battery site. Al Weh's patrol was to see if it could determine enemy activity in a suspected base camp between it and McBride, and to take notes on the weather.

Lieutenant Weh stated, "I went over to a Navy weather station at Phu Bai and was given instructions about clouds, et cetera, in order to report better about the weather. There was to be an infantry operation in the valley coming in on our heels, and they wanted to have accurate weather reports on the ground."

Although both teams were from Company A, they were not designed to work in tandem. They were independently set up and on their own. In fact, Party Line One was given very short notice for the patrol, as another team from another company had to cancel its scheduled insert for the same mission. It would be Lieutenant McBride, six Marines, and one corpsman. The scheduled time for the insertion was 1300 hours. McBride quickly worked with the pilot to select an LZ in an area that didn't offer much to choose from. Everybody was nervous about the mission. The A Shau was legendary. It was the main shipment route for NVA men and materials down the Ho Chi Minh Trail, with side roads to Hue and then on to Da Nang and points farther south. Special Operations Group teams had reportedly vanished in the area. Later, in 1969, Marine reconnaissance aircraft reported sightings of 1,000 NVA vehicles a day, and unidentified helicopters were also noted. It was a busy enemy-held area.

Then, shortly after noon on August 1, the CH-46 carrying Party Line One was in the air. The flight lasted thirty minutes, and then quickly the chopper descended toward a hilltop covered by elephant grass. The first problem then occurred. The grass was ten to twelve feet tall. The chopper had to use its tailgate to smash down the tough and tall weedy jungle below them. It wasn't something they had wanted to do. The extra delay would allow unfriendlies in the vicinity to get a bearing on the team. But finally they were in and trying to push through a dense matting of razor-sharp blades. McBride and his radioman tried to establish communications, and the result wasn't good. Because of the terrain a whip antenna had to be used. Comm was to be established with a C-130, call sign Rain Belt. The C-130 was on station, but as the big turboprop aircraft moved in and out of the area the quality of the radio comm varied.

As the team struggled through grass thickets, the men heard two shots not more than a half mile to their north—close enough for whoever it was to have seen the bird come into the LZ.

For the first 500 meters, the team pushed to the northeast. It took two and a half hours to make that short leg of the route. At that point, the Marines reached a finger that extended down from Hill 745; McBride's route would take him to the southeast and then south, making a 180-degree turn from their start. However, the Reconners then discovered a trail about a meter wide. It was well used, but there were no indications it had been used in the past few days. The team's method of movement was for the two men at point to carefully move down the trail while the other six remained at the ready behind them in a stationary position. After a short distance, the point would stop and watch and listen. Then one of the two would return to bring forward the rest. Then the process would be repeated. Using the trail was not high on the list of things they liked to do, but with thick elephant grass to both sides, it was felt to be the lesser of two evils.

The team found evidence of Montagnard animal runs, and they still were forced to use the whip antenna, which was not good for movement through the bush. However, as the team approached Hill 745, comm improved with one of the ground radio relay stations.

Lieutenant McBride said:

At about 1800 hours, we reached Hill 745. It was the site of an abandoned Montagnard camp. There were animal runs and trenches for protection from air raids. In fact, I suspect that they vacated the area in order to relocate their camp for better protection from American aircraft. The old camp was about one hundred meters square. We found lean-tos, old radio batteries, and cans. With the high ground and good comm, I decided that this would be our harbor site for the night.

About thirty minutes later, single weapon shots were heard from the valley below. The Marines situated themselves in the most defensible positions they could find and registered artillery concentrations to be on-call. During the night, the team reported hearing about thirty rifle shots that they felt were signals coming from the valley.

McBride stated:

We had two out of the eight awake all the time. I think we all had adrenaline pumping, and I don't know how well anybody slept. Then at 0445 hours, there was an arc light strike about five thousand meters away in the A Shau and the whole hillside shook like an earthquake.

The next morning we ate chow early and started our descent into the valley. We began to lose communication with our relays, and Rain Belt, flying above somewhere, had a hard time hearing our whispers. We did not want to talk any louder than we had to. Our radio link was good only about one third of the time. We moved down the trail very slowly. We made security halts frequently and just listened. The brush was still thick and visibility wasn't much. About two hundred meters down the trail, we heard wood-chopping from about a quarter mile ahead. Then we moved to the side in an old bomb crater and could see a part of the valley, but nothing significant was observed. The chopping had stopped, and we waited.

Finally we moved down the trail again, and after a little we could again hear chopping and now voices. They were about where we had heard the first noises. I sent the point team down farther. Then, very shortly, we received their signal that they had encountered enemy. The patrol halted as the point reported back that two women and two teenage boys had been coming up the trail with axes—they were Montagnards. The point did not fire his weapon, and the four turned around and ran back down the trail. He reported that the women were wearing wraparound cloths with trousers and the two boys had on only loincloths. We did not want to start firing and let everybody know what our strength was. But now, being detected, we obviously had a problem to deal with. So I directed the team off the trail to the west, and we moved in a circle through the bush back around to the north.

It was at about this time that Lieutenant Weh and his team were in the air on their way to a landing zone only about a mile away. The lieutenant had been concerned by his intelligence briefings, which indicated that he should expect the Montagnards to be watching obvious LZs. So, he said:

> I took my guys over to a water tower and we practiced rappelling. My objective was to find a location in the jungle some distance from my objective and rappel into it. But what I really wanted to do was to find a "depression" in the jungle canopy that was lesser in height than the surrounding jungle. If I could find a place like that, then the jungle would help mask the chopper as it hovered within that bowl and let us drop down through the trees.

Weh explained to the pilot what he wanted, and together they were able to locate a jungle depression not far from their recon zone. With the chopper hovering, the team lowered themselves, one at a time, through the tops of the lower canopy to the jungle floor. This LZ was 2,000 meters from the one into which Party Line One had set down. Weh said:

> My primary mission . . . was to be out there to broadcast weather conditions. I was told that the 1st Battalion, 4th Marines, two ARVN Ranger battalions, and one Marine artillery unit were preparing to invade the old airstrip at A Shau, and I was to report the weather. And I had to educate myself about weather conditions and terminology. The op order objectives had little bearing on reality.

Weh's team landed on the slope of a hill that was about 700 meters tall. There was no enemy contact, nor were gunshots fired, but it did take a while to rappel down. Weh stated:

> My platoon sergeant, Goodwin, was the only one of us who had experience rappelling out of choppers, so we took our time. Once we got in, there was no serious undergrowth to fight and the going was pretty easy. We moved about five hundred meters up the slope, and found a trail on the top. There we turned to the south and followed the ridge as it pointed toward the village of Be Loung, which was also an area we were to watch.

As the team was moving downhill, gunshots erupted from the direction of Bill McBride's Party Line One, not far away. The Marines of Party Line One had moved off the trail after their first encounter with the Montagnard women and the boys with axes. The Reconners had moved in a circle with over a 300-meter diameter, ending up within 40 meters of the same trail but farther uphill. They stopped and listened, but it was quiet—too quiet. McBride said:

I took three people, without our packs, and moved back to the trail and cautiously retraced our steps downhill to try to find out what was happening. Then my point spotted two men in uniform. They wore light-colored uniforms, bush hats, and had bandoliers of ammo across their chests, but there were no weapons visible. The point carefully returned to the rest of us, but then we saw the two run down the trail.

I decided to get the rest of the patrol and move uphill. By the time we got back, and the point man was down the trail a short distance, watching from there, we started taking fire. The point was returning the fire, and I called him back. Then we started to move to higher ground, but were hit from above. The point was shot in the hand. Another round had hit him but was stopped by his magazines; otherwise, he would have been down.

My radioman was in contact with Rain Belt, and they advised that if we could get to an LZ they were going to have extraction choppers out to get us. But we couldn't go either up or down the trail, and dropping off the narrow finger that we were on into the draws or valleys below didn't seem like a good idea, nor did I think we could find much in the way of LZs along the slopes.

So I set out security—we weren't under fire at that point—and we started to cut trees to clear an LZ right where we were. The trees were not huge, but between two and eight inches thick. We used our claymores to blow them and were making headway, and I thought a chopper could get in.

However, when the 46 came over he said it was not adequate and directed me toward an alternate zone to the southeast. Then we had to beat through very difficult and steep terrain. Previous artillery and bomb strikes in the area had left a tangled mess, and we couldn't make more than about 100 meters an hour. We only had a little time. I felt the NVA would be able to bring in more guns against us, and I didn't want to have to try to harbor out there overnight.

Then it was about 1900 hours when we reached the site that the chopper pilot wanted us to reach, and then they were debating whether they could pick us because it was getting dark. Finally, they called it off and told us they would be back in the morning. We had not been under fire for some hours now, but that delay really hurt us. We found a bomb crater and set a harbor site in it. Normally, I would have moved off somewhere else, but this was our only LZ. It was not a good situation at all.

Throughout the night, we heard movement on the finger and ridge to the south and west, and more in the tree line behind us to the east. I called in 175 guns all night, but their value was limited due to the difficult terrain, and it was hard to adjust. However, there was no contact during the night.

There was a significantly different night in progress for the other team, only a little over a mile away. Weh said:

> We harbored about six hundred meters away from the OP position we were heading for. We had heard sporadic fire coming from Bill's location, but so far we saw nothing that looked like we might have been seen or heard. However, we did have one "contact" that night in the harbor site. Some animal, and I still don't know what it was, came running through our position in the middle of the dark. I heard it and was watching, but couldn't see anything. Then all of a sudden there were four paws in my face. I was up and flailing away with my hands and arms in combat with *what* I didn't have a clue, and then it was running off over others, and I'm trying to whisper "It's all right. It's just some animal." I was real glad no one shot at it.
>
> Then the next day we moved into position on a little hill overlooking the valley floor by only two hundred meters. It had to have been an old Special Forces helipad. There was an eroding macadam surface and a trench surrounding part of it and a bunker. The NVA had stuck antihelo poles in the surface of the ground as a barrier against possible helicopters. But that's where we set up for the day. However, I was thinking that the patrol's only real value was going to be as a weather watch because the jungles were so thick around us that we couldn't see worth a lick into the valleys.

However, while Weh and his Marines were sitting in their OP, Party Line One was in a world of hurt not far away. They had got through the night without incident, and at first light, fixed-wing aircraft and gunships were overhead to strafe the area surrounding the zone. While that was happening, the team was trying to clear off some trees with their survival axes and saws. However, the pilot radioed for the team to move farther to the southeast to a zone that looked better. What would have happened at the first two possible LZs no one knows, but it could hardly have been worse than what happened when they finally got to where they were directed.

They moved 200 meters farther down the slope to the southeast. A Huey marked the LZ by flying over and firing into it. It was a large field, about 100 by 150 meters, that had been cleared by the Montagnards. It was much more gently sloping, and it was ringed by a four-feet-high wood fence. There was one bunker nearby. Then the Hueys dropped green smoke to mark the pickup spot, and the team moved from concealment as quickly as they could to get ready for the chopper.

McBride stated:

> Then the 46 came down, but couldn't sit down flat. I got four people in, and then the bird lurched out of position and took another thirty seconds to recover and set back down for the rest of us. I was the last to jump in, but as I was going to the chopper, it took a hit and a two-inch hole blasted open above the left wheel. Then I was being pulled aboard as the chopper was trying to take off. It got about ten to fifteen feet in the air and started dancing around side to side, and then plunged back to the earth. It hit on its right side and rolled over one and a half times. It had taken other hits, and the hydraulic fluid line was ruptured, and we were sprayed with the red liquid. Fuel lines were also shattered, and fuel was shooting out everywhere. We had seriously wounded, and people were trying to help each other out. The crew chief was killed. I had to cut the corpsman's bag off him to get him out of the tangled mess. I was concerned about fire and explosion.

The situation had turned into a chaotic nightmare. Lieutenant McBride was desperately trying to reorganize and take care of the wounded. The helicopter crew was now on the ground, also needing rescue, and the NVA had guns waiting for their next kill.

McBride continued:

> Then the guys had security set up outside, the pilots were helping with the wounded, and my radioman had reestablished comm. The second 46 was now coming in to pick us up, and it set down close by. We were under fire and trying to carry the wounded and the dead crew chief on board. It was difficult going, and my radio operator was hit seriously. We were still under fire, and at about twenty feet off the deck, we were hit again and the aircraft shuddered. But it continued to pick up momentum and we were able to get back to Alpha Med. Three of the team were seriously wounded, and three more died of their wounds. My secondary point man and myself had slight wounds. From the chopper, the crew chief was killed, and one other member of the crew was wounded.

Those Reconners lost were John Nahan III, Jack Wolpe, and "Doc" James McGrath.

However, the Weh team had been sitting silently on its OP position, and it heard the radio transmissions and gunfire coming from the other side of the hill, about a mile away. It always twists the guts of a Recon team to listen to another team's being shot to hell the way Party Line was. The men of the second team were sobered by it and wondered what might happen next. They sat tight, watched, and listened. They had no place to go, except back up the ridge they had come from or down into the valley that they knew had beaucoup bad guys. So they harbored in the OP, using the trenches built years earlier by Special Forces.

Weh said:

> Sometime past midnight we received word via the radio that our extraction time had been moved forward to first light. Later, I was to learn that the command had canceled the infantry operation into the valley, and I don't know whether that was the reason that they extracted us early or if it had something to do with the problems Bill had had, or some combination of the two. So I had the team take down those antihelo poles and make out of them the letters *USMC* on the ground.

Between 0330 and 0530 hours the Marines heard troop movement around the hillside. They reported this via their radio along with the weather conditions. Although Weh was starting to worry that the NVA had their radio frequency and had started to figure out where the transmissions were coming from, they made it through the night.

Weh said, "Anyway, we stayed put, and at 0700 we had the word that the choppers were on the way. Then about 0720, a round cranked off in the valley just below us. My stomach was speaking to me. It was a gut sense that the enemy was really closer than that. I knew it, and we were on the alert."

At 0730 the big chopper was overhead, and within ten minutes it was coming in to the LZ. Weh was on the radio with the pilot, telling him to turn around and put his tailgate toward the team as he settled into the zone. Then the jungle erupted with small arms fire. The Marines were racing for the chopper, except Weh and his radioman, Pfc. Harry Kenck.

Weh said:

> I looked at the tree line and then back at the chopper, and the other six Marines were running up the ramp of the bird, and my radio operator and myself are still standing in the trench twenty meters away. Well, the two of us hauled ass, and as we jumped in the bird was lifting off.
>
> Then Pfc. Dodd was standing right next to me, and I see this pained look go across his face. And a split second later I was on my face on the chopper deck. I had taken a round; maybe it was the same round that hit Dodd. A couple of my guys kept me alive, but the round that hit me cut a major vein in my leg, and I was down. They got the blood stopped or slowed enough to save my hide. Anyway, the Professor [Dodd] and I were the only ones seriously hit. There were two with minor wounds.

Lieutenant Weh later said about his men, "I have a lot of respect for those Marines: Sergeant Goodwin, who was my APL [assistant patrol leader]; Lance Corporal Gerdan, my rear point; Pfc. Kenck, my radio operator; Pfc. Gauthier; Pfc. Carter; Doc Earl; and Pfc. Dodd."

The A Shau was about fifty miles away on a straight line from Con Thien, and the next real move by the NVA came in that corner of Leatherneck Square. In the time leading to the planned Tet Offensive, the NVA design was to initiate major battles along the frontier. Still, although the DMZ, including Khe Sanh and Con Thien, was developing as the focus of Allied attention in I Corps, Reconnaissance teams had an increasing percentage of sightings near the old imperial capital, Hue City. In September 1967, of all Recon's enemy sightings, 57 percent were a result of patrols near Hue.

A III MAF report dated September 1967 stated, ". . . during the period 1 May–30 September 57% of all enemy losses [killed] in RVN [all of South Vietnam] occurred in I CTZ, and 56% of all US losses in RVN have also occurred in I CTZ." I CTZ (I Corps) was made up of the northern five provinces of South Vietnam, and it was the responsibility of the III Marine Amphibious Force. Most of the action in Vietnam was by then concentrated in the Marine tactical area of responsibility, and most of that was in the northern reaches, where 3rd Recon patrols continued to penetrate deep into enemy-dominated areas.

During the first six months of 1967, the teams of the 3rd Recon Battalion had sighted 7,911 VC/NVA troops—more than in all of 1966—and those reports continued very close to the same level, peaking in December with 1,905 enemy. However, in September all CH-46s had been grounded; on August 31, one had disintegrated in the air on a medevac mission, killing all aboard. That meant that except for Army Hueys, only seventy-three UH-34s, twenty-three CH-53s, and seventeen 34s aboard ships were available to all Marine units in Vietnam. Even before the loss of the 46s, the muster of Marine helicopters in Vietnam totaled only 189. In contrast, the Army's 1st Air Cav Division had 434 helicopters (the better Hueys) when it first fought in the Ta Drang Valley in 1965. One of General Westmoreland's biggest complaints about the method of operation employed by Marines in Vietnam was the Marine Corps' lack of enthusiasm for the helicopter.

Recon teams were initiating walk-out patrols more and more frequently. Some walked out with infantry patrols, and then one or the other would peel off in another direction. The Recon team would drop out of the patrol and hide in the brush somewhere, watching the situation until it was safe to continue toward its recon zone. It was hoped that any enemy units watching had kept their eyes on the infantry and had not yet realized that the patrol had lost a number of its members somewhere along the path. One such patrol occurred in the first part of September 1967 and was led by Cpl. John T. Morrissey from 3rd Force. Composed of eight men, the team's call sign was Spring Wheat Two. The route of the patrol was to begin at the Ca Lu outpost and work west toward Khe Sanh along Route 9 to a point near the ambush site of five weeks earlier on the same road.

Morrissey said:

> Right before the start of this patrol, I was visiting a 106-mm recoilless rifle position on a little high ground guarding the base, trying to educate myself on the weapon. Then I saw a sight that will always be imprinted in my memory. As I looked to the west, I saw this jet streaking in our direction flying low. My knee-jerk reaction was that it was Communist because it didn't look like one of ours—it was sort of Korean War vintage, like the one Ted Williams had flown. Then as it flew past, like about a mile per second, I realized that it was American, but then I saw the shocker. A red-hot SAM antiaircraft missile just about had its nose stuck up that jet's tailpipe, and the two disappeared over the hills like bats out of hell. I don't think that the missile ever caught the jet, because I never heard any explosion. I would have loved to have heard that pilot's stories around the club that night.

It was about that time that Morrissey decided to check in with his team's "seer." If there were any enemy missiles being fired at U.S. planes in this neck of the woods, he wanted some prognostication about the patrol's welfare, and he knew a person who had the "gift." Cpl. Bernie Allen was a member of the team, and whether he liked it or not, Bernie could normally see beforehand what was going to happen to the patrol. Morrissey said, "I would go to Bernie and ask what's going to happen this time, and he'd hit it on the head. His answers would be 'No contact on this one, John' or 'Yes, John, we're going to be fighting' or, there had been one answer 'John, you don't want to know.'"

That last response had caught the patrol leader's attention. He had then pried out of Allen that he, Morrissey, would be shot. And he was! However, he had mended, and he was now back leading his team. So he went to Allen again and asked what he saw for the planned patrol. Allen replied, "John, we're going to be running."

Morrissey thought to himself, Well, that's a helluva lot better than "John, you don't want to know."

On September 4, 1967, carrying M-14s (they still didn't trust the M-16s), one M-60, and one M-79, the team walked west along Route 9 with an infantry squad. About 1,000 meters out they dropped off, and the grunts circled to the south and back toward the base. Morrissey decided to wait where he was until the sun went farther behind the hills before continuing along the road. Route 9 paralleled a river, the Quang Tri, to its south. The Quang Tri ran from 100 to 200 meters off the road. Framing the right-hand (north) side of the road were sharp hills that rose about 200 meters.

Morrissey said:

> We weren't there long before we saw five to six NVA walking the skyline above us, and we called in mortars. Then just before we left the position, Pfc. Shear went down to a stream to fill canteens. It wasn't far off, but he reached the place about the same time as four NVA. He dropped one with his M-60 and ran back to our position. We immediately established a base of fire on the enemy, chasing them off, with one or more of them being killed, this time by an M-79 round. I thought that they may have been the point for a larger unit. Then we carefully moved west.

Later that afternoon, Morrissey was informed that a convoy between the Rockpile and Ca Lu, a few klicks to their north, had been ambushed, and that the battalion-size NVA ambushing unit was on the move in his direction. It wasn't long before Spring Wheat Two spotted two groups of enemy soldiers moving among the nearby hills. They totaled about fifty soldiers, and the Marines called in an aerial observer to try to get a better fix on them.

Sunlight was going to be in short supply very soon, so Morrissey wanted to relocate from his position between the road and the hilltops. He sent his team packing back down to the road, while he covered the rear. Then he started running to catch them. As he entered the roadway, lumbering toward the east, away from the setting sun, a sudden burst of automatic weapons fire kicked up dirt behind him. Morrissey remembers:

> I ran after the patrol, and the automatic fire was drilling up little clouds of dust just missing me—like the movies. And like in the movies, I'm firing my weapon behind me while running in the opposite direction. And I was laughing, thinking about Bernie's vision of us running. He didn't say "John, you're gonna be shot." And I believed him.

Morrissey quickly disappeared into the shadows, hoping that the NVA were moving in the opposite direction. The team's trauma, however, was only beginning.

He continued:

> It was getting late, and we had to find a decent harbor site, but there wasn't much to choose from. Finally, we settled into some brush between the road and the river as it was getting dark. But it just wasn't good in the way of either cover or concealment. We hadn't been there long when a whole unit of NVA started moving through the brush around us. We were worried they were looking for us, but at the same time, they seemed so casual about the situation that I didn't think they knew we were there. Then they set up camp around us. They lit fires, cooked, laughed, farted, and just acted like they owned the place, and we were in the middle of it within spitting distance of them.

The patrol leader sometimes truly earns his paycheck, and this would be one occasion that challenged Morrissey to deserve his $200 a month base pay. He quickly realized that to hide where he was until daylight very easily could mean that his patrol's death sentence would arrive with the sun—and possibly before. So he very quietly gathered his team together and whispered his suggestion. He said, "Look, we can't stay here, and there's no way to get out without being seen. So, I recommend that we wait until a particularly dark moment and just stand up and walk out of here. They'll see us, but they'll think we are some of their own." The team quietly agreed. The NVA were still rattling pans and laughing around them.

A couple of hours went by, and finally Morrissey knew their time had come. They shook each other awake and held their breaths as they rose out of the bushes and, not wasting any time, headed for the road—a hundred-yard, "mile-long" walk away. There were a few comments or questions thrown in their direction from the lounging Vietnamese shadows, but the Marines just grunted and kept walking. Soft bush hats and camouflaged faces helped them blend into the Vietnamese around them.

It was a bold move, but they walked through the NVA without incident and reached Route 9. However, the road was not necessarily a place of safety. The night and part of the day were owned by the enemy forces. Walking down that road at night could very easily lead them past an NVA patrol or into an enemy checkpoint. If they made it past those dangers, there was always the risk of "friendly fire" as they approached the Ca Lu post.

Morrissey stated, "Because we maintained silence and looked like

Charlie Company, Headquarters at Dong Ha. The Captain D. R. Gardner, then commanding, retired as a lieutenant general.

Charlie Company area at Camp Reasoner, Da Nang, with Cpl. William Knight in the foreground.

A Rough Rider convoy on Highway 9 west of Cam Lo. It also doubled as a truck insert of a Recon Team. Note that the Bush extends right up to the edge of the highway.

Landing Zone Finch at Camp Reasoner, CH-34s in residence.

Charlie Company patrol just after being dropped off by a truck alongside Route 9 at the foot of the Rockpile.

The Rockpile.

The view from the Rockpile.

Bravo Company reconner in the old village of Khe Sanh in 1969.

Team from Bravo Company on patrol in the vicinity of the old village of Khe Sanh in 1969. Note the interval between men and the conditions of the march.

Old French resort on top of Ba Na (4500 feet up) about 10 miles southwest of Da Nang.

Force Recon Team Springwheat (3rd Force Recon Company) in the summer of 1967. Front row: John Morrisey. Second row (left to right): Gary Gruerman, Glen Cannon, William Kress. Third row: Bernie Allen, James Shear, Jon Godwin, James Kuhl.

The author during a reconnaissance overflight by helicopter the day before a patrol.

Pfc. George Green (left) and Cpl. Tom Renard during Operation Taut Bow, before the fight at the bamboo wall.

Vietnamese, I believe we made it unchallenged, but then as we came close to Ca Lu, I had to break the quiet and call on the radio to insure that any Marine guard positions or ambushes would know we were coming in. We made it, but it was no stroll."

Whatever the strength of the enemy that threatened the DMZ area, there still was an almost unnoticed increase in enemy sightings and contacts in the vicinity of Hue. However, it wasn't unnoticed by the Recon teams operating in Thua Thien Province (the Hue–Phu Bai area).

The 5th and 6th NVA regiments, each consisting of more than 1,500 soldiers, were suspected to be west and northwest of Hue. Also, somewhere in the same vicinity was the NVA regional headquarters. Intelligence had also estimated that one independent NVA battalion was located closer to the city on its west side. Operating to the west and northwest of the city was the 6th Vietcong Regiment. The two previously noted VC battalions, 804 and 804B, the likely causes of Team Striker's being shot down, were still located to the south of Phu Bai. In addition, eight independent VC companies, about 500 troops, were known to be headquartered in the province. The total number of enemy infantry in Thua Thien was estimated at about 3,785. Combat-service and administrative units consisted of another 2,199, and 2,900 guerrilla militia were also counted. Still, there were an estimated 20,589 enemy farther north, near the DMZ, and that was where Allied infantry started to be concentrated. Only three Marine infantry battalions were in Thua Thien Province, compared to the ten along the DMZ. There were some units of the 1st ARVN Division and some from the South Vietnamese Marine Brigade in the province, but only the latter was developing into a combat-worthy unit.

However, discounting for the moment the ARVN units that might have been present in the 3rd Marine Division TAOR, which was made up of the two northern provinces of Quang Tri and Thua Thien, thirty-six enemy infantry battalions were maneuvering against thirteen Marine infantry battalions.

Of course, those statistics were not available to the Recon Marine. Two of those Reconners, who joined the battalion in the summer of '67, were Pfc. Bobby Hall and Pfc. Darrell Eriksen. Each, in addition to basic training, had attended scout/sniper familiarization, mapping, artillery, and air-support courses, and a three-week Recon school at Camp Pendleton after boot camp. Their orders were for the 3rd Recon Battalion. There was still a supply shortage, there were no training patrols near the camp, and they learned on the job.

Hall said, "I remember times when we were short of 782 gear, and when a Marine was killed, we had to split up the gear for the rest of

us. . . . On my first patrol, it was so hot and humid that the sweat made it hard to see. I just tried to follow the others and learn from them."
Eriksen added:

> We operated in eight-man patrols, although on occasions we used six or seven men. There were very few staff NCOs and officers, and our leadership came primarily from corporals. We had briefings from the battalion S-2 about the enemy situation from the information he had, and we had scuttlebutt from the other patrols, but we were really some-what short on information about the enemy.

According to Hall, prior to one September patrol, when it had be-come too boring in camp and too tempting elsewhere, he, Cpl. Randy Stahlberg, and Pfc. Fred Schultz used the battalion executive officer's jeep without permission to recon the nightlife of Phu Bai. That night the three were hidden inside a dark bunker from American MPs by bar girls. But to no avail; they were pulled out of their little fortifica-tion at gunpoint and packed off to a local lockup. Punishment was swift—the loss of a stripe and back out on patrol within two days to the Co Bi–Thanh Tan and its environs. But Stahlberg was too good a patrol leader to lose both leadership responsibility and a stripe. The patrol consisted of seven enlisted Marines, one Navy corpsman, and one scout dog, which was to prove of questionable value. Stahlberg was the patrol leader.

On the eleventh of September, at thirty minutes past noon, Stahlberg's team was flown about seventeen miles northwest of Phu Bai and six miles west of Hue. The location was about five klicks southwest of the Co Bi–Thanh Tan and the Bo River. The S-2 brief-ing had told them that enemy activity had been building up to the west of Hue, but had given them nothing specific about their area. That's what they were to find out. Previous patrols had invariably com-mented that because of the heavy NVA/VC activity in the area, en-emy base camps were suspected to be in the vicinity.

The patrol carried two PRC-25 radios and its special weapons in-cluded one M-79 grenade launcher and one M-60 machine gun. Erik-sen ran point and carried an M-14. Not only was the M-14 felt to be a better weapon than the M-16, but it was better for the point to break a trail with if he had to. Each man carried six to eight canteens of wa-ter, which included water for the dog. Their mission statement read:

> Determine the nature of enemy activity developing along the natural infiltration routes that could be used by VC/NVA and enemy base camp areas. Pay particular attention to size and direction of enemy

movement. Act as a forward observer for artillery on targets of opportunity of at least 15 or more enemy. Make every attempt to capture a prisoner by ambush.

The team was flown to the LZ, a narrow saddle in a ridgeline, in UH-34s. The ground rose more than 100 meters to both front and rear. They were dropped into open terrain, but triple-canopy jungle covered the ridges above them. As quickly as they landed, the Marines moved up the ridge, seeking the cover of the jungle. Trails covered their entire route. Where possible the team avoided the paths, but the ridge was narrow and trails were the rule. As they cautiously moved toward the higher ground, the radio operator noted hearing Vietnamese voices on their radio frequency.

With a few exceptions, the first day and a half was uneventful. One of the exceptions was a dog event. While climbing a tree to get a better bearing on their location, Stahlberg exposed his low-hanging rear end to the dog, which promptly leaped and locked his teeth onto the back side of Stahlberg's trousers—fortunately, flesh was not included. There hung Stahlberg, trying not to make noise but clinging desperately to the tree with feet and hands and shaking his backside to rid it of the animal. Finally, the rear end of his trousers tore out, and the dog dropped to the ground.

That hadn't been the team's only shaky experience with the dog. Earlier, the dog handler had brought the animal into their hootch back at the base, hoping to get him used to the patrol members. At some point in the tête-à-tête, Hall had knocked an ashtray over and leaned down to pick it up. The dog was instantly at his throat, with the handler straining back at the leash, yelling for Hall not to move. Bent over, knowing his throat was inches from being shredded, Hall froze. The dog finally backed away at the command of his handler.

Eriksen also had an encounter with the dog; his happened in the dark of night while on the ridge in the harbor site. At one point he reached out to wake the next man who was to stand radio watch. His hand came to rest on the dog's nose. Eriksen's blood went cold. The dog didn't wake, but it took Eriksen ten minutes to carefully withdraw his hand.

The second day found the team moving through jungle undergrowth. At about 1330, the patrol heard elephants a few hundred meters away in the lower terrain. The noises lasted for about five minutes, and the team marked the map coordinates. Then, about two and a half hours later, the patrol picked up the voices of two or three Vietnamese moving through the bush not too far off but on a route taking them away from the team. At 1730 the Marines felt and heard the impacts of nine artillery rounds about 1,300 meters to their east. However, they could not find out who had fired the rounds.

The second night out, the team had to position its harbor site near a trail as it was hard to avoid them all. The Marines hadn't met any unfriendlies, except for the dog, yet. The nighttime site was always approached in a double move. First, at about dusk, they located themselves in one spot, and then, as it became darker, they relocated—although the second spot couldn't be too far away. That was just a precaution in case they were being followed.

Two of the men were up every forty-five minutes, and each hour on the hour, the battalion COC would call each patrol in turn and ask the radio operators to click their handsets if all was "alpha sierra"— all secure.

That very black night, Hall found himself lying so near a trail he was almost in it and hoping that it wouldn't be used that evening. But it wasn't long after the patrol had set in that the whole hillside lit up— "like New York City," according to Hall. Hall and Eriksen agreed that the lights looked like lanterns, and in addition, there were the sounds of a generator. The ridge that the Marines were on was roughly T-shaped. Over an area spanning about 1,000 meters and all around their position the Marines noted three groups of lights, with each having ten to fourteen individual lights. The people behind the lights appeared to be searching the area, and the Reconners wondered if they might be the objects of that search. Hall saw one enemy soldier with a light not far down the trail that ran beside his position. It appeared that the VC was directing his light in their direction. Quickly, the patrol radioed for the on-call artillery they had plotted around themselves. In minutes, several rounds landed approximately 50 meters from the team—the patrol leader had planned the on-calls close by, and 50 meters was *very* close.

Significantly, the Marines noted that when the artillery gave the call over the radio that the rounds had been fired, the lights went out and stayed out until the fire mission was over. However, screams were heard from one of the areas where the arty had impacted.

Later, the team still heard enemy around them and called for Puff the Magic Dragon.

Whether it was artillery or air support, and particularly when it was night, Recon teams were always concerned about the accuracy of fire missions. It was a science, and sometimes an art, to properly plan supporting arms for a small team in the jungle, miles away from friendly bases. In this situation, the team was in the middle of the fire zone, and its men moved into a tight group and held their strobe light so that it pointed straight up into the sky—in the hope that the enemy would not be able to see it but that Spooky would note their position. It worked.

The Dragonship's fire was directed onto enemy positions around the team. Throughout the first three passes of the well-gunned bird, the patrol noted yells and screams from the nearby Vietnamese. The rounds were so close that some tree branches ripped by the ship's eighteen machine gun barrels fell on them. There were also ten secondary explosions, including some in the area where the elephants had been noted earlier in the day. Then there was stillness.

The balance of the night saw the team on 100 percent alert. Each Marine laid his magazines, filled with hundreds of rounds of ammo, in front of him, ready to reload as needed. A short rain hit the area. Then, at 0245 hours, another light was seen in the area where the previous lights had been noted. The patrol again called in artillery, and again the light went out. The team had no further contact with the enemy for the rest of the night.

It can be confidently stated that the safety and effectiveness of this patrol was due to having the artillery on immediate call, with the air wing arriving sixty to ninety minutes later. The big guns were the only constantly available fire support that could be on target within five to ten minutes, and that was the norm. Under Randy Stahlberg's leadership, the Marines maintained their discipline and did not fire their weapons, thereby avoiding potential disaster.

The next afternoon at 1400 hours, the patrol was extracted without incident—except that the dog wouldn't get on the chopper. The animal was between Hall and Eriksen with the enemy not far away. The stern warnings of the team ringing in his ears, the dog handler had to carry the animal onboard. The dog was of questionable value to the team. In an area so heavily infested with enemy, the animal was constantly alerting. As well, there were no water sources available for the animal so the members of the team had to carry its supply, which cut down their mobility and decreased the amount of supplies they could carry for themselves.

Results of the patrol's actions were not known. There were no reported enemy KIAs, and since the contact was at night, no estimates could accurately be made about enemy casualties. It is, however, true to say that the enemy units realized that somewhere painfully close to them was a small team of Marines.

During September, battalion teams averaged 3.9 days per patrol, 8.6 men per mission. This included all units: Companies A, B, C, D, and the 3rd Force Recon Company. Although most people thought that Force patrols carried only four or five men per team, 3rd Force was operating similarly to the battalion Recon companies, with a standard of eight men per patrol. During the month, the battalion's teams participated in six infantry operations and sighted 852 enemy, killing (confirmed and probable) 187 of those enemy soldiers. However, these figures didn't reflect the times when, although a patrol was in the middle of enemy units (as the Stahlberg patrol had been), no counts were able to be confirmed and none were listed.

It was not an easy month for the Recon teams: five Marines were killed, twenty-three wounded. Two corpsmen and one Kit Carson scout were wounded. One corpsman was missing in action. (Near where the Jeff Savelkoul/Mariano "Junior" Guy patrol had made contact with the enemy, a team also in contact with the enemy had one Marine killed and three wounded. Its corpsman was also wounded, and while he was being hoisted into the medevac chopper, a sudden lurch in the rescue bird threw the wounded man out of the hoist and into the jungle some distance away and downhill from the team. He was never found.)

During the month the battalion experimented with the use of the Starlight scope. A new sniper platoon attached to the battalion recorded thirteen enemy killed, one sampan sunk, and one damaged. Since all those actions occurred at night, they would not have been possible without the scope and the snipers. Regarding fire support, battalion teams called in fifty-nine artillery missions shooting an average of fifty-seven rounds per mission.

However, there wasn't enough Marine Recon in the eyes of General Westmoreland. The Army CG urged the Marine Corps to reorganize, do away with the Ontos battalion because those vehicles were not suited for deployment in much of the Vietnamese terrain. He also did not like the 3.5-inch rocket launcher platoon. If these types of units were eliminated, in Westmoreland's mind, the Corps could increase the number of other units that he felt to be much more valuable. He urged the Marine command to create a new Recon battalion. He also pushed the president for another 200,000 troops (which would bring the total American commitment to 665,000), indicating that the war might be over in two years if he had the additional forces. By Defense Department calculations, however, this would mean a call-up of the Reserves, and this was not considered acceptable for several reasons. It was agreed that a lesser number of 55,000 would be sent.

Regardless, the American infantry battalions were facing the borders, and the command was particularly concerned about the increasing threat along the DMZ. Over the next three months, as the battles for Con Thien ended and the ones for Khe Sanh began, however, Recon teams counted the building presence of enemy forces moving in the direction of the city of Hue.

CHAPTER FOURTEEN

Buildup to Tet—The Intelligence "Black Hole"

The summer of 1967 had seen another battle in Vietnam, and it concerned intelligence data. In part, the Recon battalions were responsible for gathering this data, but the battle was far removed from their level or knowledge. The antagonists were the MACV Intelligence Section (J-2) and the Central Intelligence Agency (CIA). Both agencies had refused to be placed under one unified command, and their estimates of the enemy order of battle varied by up to 100 percent. The CIA estimated that the enemy could have as many total soldiers in South Vietnam as the United States had—and possibly significantly more. In large part, the reason for the diverging opinions was that MACV had focused primarily on main force units and excluded the guerrillas and VC infrastructure from their counts. In addition, since the beginning of the war, the lower estimates had been used; to double the number of enemy estimated to be in South Vietnam would cause a political explosion in Washington, D.C. Regardless of the exclusion of the guerrillas and VC infrastructure from the count, black-PJ-clad enemy fighters would lead the way in many of the forthcoming Tet Offensive battles. Recon teams counted them alongside the uniformed main force units, and they were on the move.

While the minds of the American military and political leaderships were focused on the outlying border battles of Con Thien, Loc Ninh, and Dak To between September and December, Recon teams began to see a disturbing trend. There were three Recon companies along the DMZ and only two near the Hue–Phu Bai area, yet the two near Hue were sighting more enemy than the three along the DMZ. Enemy units were seen moving in ever-increasing and significant numbers, particularly in the Co Bi–Thanh Tan. The Siler patrol had seen them moving north, toward the rice fields near the coast, but these new reports showed them moving east, toward the city.

Don Karoski had only joined the battalion in August and had been designated a radio operator. He had not gone to communication school, but he had been through infantry and Recon schools and Vietnamese-language training. Even without radio school, he could hump one on his back. The battalion had many corpsmen who were Marine-green through and through. Bob Sutherland was one, and he was the "Doc" for the first part of Don Karoski's tour. Together they would experience the bush from Hue–Phu Bai to the DMZ. More particularly, in October they would see the pickup in VC and NVA activity in the Co Bi–Thanh Tan.

Sutherland had been serving as a corpsman on Recon patrols for two months by the time Karoski arrived, but the gung ho Doc was establishing a reputation for himself that would eventually lead to the unique promotion—for a *Navy* corpsman—to assistant patrol leader. It was a designation that he wore with pride. He and Karoski were in the middle of what each had set his eyes on when he enlisted: Marine Recon.

On October 12, 1967, the two were a part of a team, call sign Empress Alice, led by Sgt. Kevin Connelly, a former infantry Marine who had transferred into Recon. The patrol was composed of nine men and operated similarly to other such teams—a three-man point team; then the patrol leader, radio operator, and corpsman in the command team; and the three-man rear team. Most of the men had canned the M-16 and carried the M-14. An M-60 was along for heavier firepower, but that wasn't unusual for where they were headed: the Co Bi–Thanh Tan.

The team flew out in Hueys because the battalion had been able to replace the lost CH-46s with some of the more maneuverable, speedy, and Recon-compatible birds the Army had been accustomed to for years. Their destination was very near the Bo River, but just on the east side of the river and a couple of klicks from the main Co Bi–Thanh Tan Valley. The LZ was in a small three-sided cup facing the Bo. Except for Hill 285, the surrounding high ground that boxed in the LZ was all less than 200 meters in height. It was not jungle-covered terrain, but there were elephant grass and scattered clumps of trees and bushes.

Immediately after the Recon team landed, it came under intense small arms fire, so Connelly radioed the birds to get back down and extract the team. The helicopter pilots braved the fire to return to rescue the Marines. With heavy fire ripping holes in the choppers, it was a miracle that no one was wounded or killed.

Back in the main base, the team was told not to unpack; it was going to be returned the next day. Karoski and Sutherland reported that their company commander in the rear expressed doubt that the team had actually encountered heavy enemy resistance. This situation was faced every so often by the Recon teams; some men in the rear head-quarters did not understand the situation in the field. In part, this might have been so because intelligence data regarding the enemy or-der of battle, even if didn't count the guerrilla and Vietcong infra-structure (VCI), was not getting down to the battalion level.

However, the next day, prior to the patrol's return to the same gen-eral area, the same officer had to rethink his position. He had to obtain endorsement signatures from members of the patrol for the helicopter squadron, which was recommending the Distinguished Flying Cross for its pilots. The squadron's evidence included statements from the pilots and crews and physical evidence—helicopters shot full of holes. The choppers were so riddled by bullets and the rotor mecha-nisms were so badly shot up that the squadron didn't know how they flew. A repeat of the June horror stories was narrowly missed.

On October 13, the same Marine team was on board different choppers flying toward the Co Bi–Thanh Tan ridge. They would be landing on the opposite side of the river from their first LZ and on the back side of the ridgeline. There the river carved a narrow 500-meter-long canyon through the ridge. To the southwest the river came down through the hills in a series of sharp bends and curves. Hill 165 was at the end of the ridge within their Recon zone, a last major promontory before the ridge plunged down to the river. There were trees along the river, then sand flats, and just at the foot of the hill was a small stream that was also lined with trees. The ridge itself was covered primarily by short grass and scattered clumps of bushes.

The choppers landed the Recon team in the brushy sand flats be-tween the river and the ridge. They had a 1,000-meter hump to cross before they reached the ridge, and then a steep climb to get to the top. The Bo would normally be a highway for boat traffic, and it was only a short distance behind them. The ridge was in front. The team mem-bers hoped that their early-afternoon landing would take place during VC siesta time.

The choppers swooped down, kicking up the sand into a heavy windstorm. Quickly, the Marines jumped out and ran for cover, but they encountered no evidence of the enemy. Just 1,500 meters from the previous day's try, so far so good for the team.

The Marines had to get to the high ground as quickly as they could, and yet the flats across which they now carefully pushed their way were filled with potential dangers. The team, camouflaged and quiet, slipped through the thick brush past a vacant VC base camp hidden near the foot of the ridge and arrived at the small stream it had to cross

before the ridge could be climbed. Then they moved into water that
was deep enough to require them to float their gear and weapons
across. It was alive with leeches, and all Marines on the team were
jumped by the little critters.

It was a hot and sweaty march, but Connelly didn't want to stop until they got to the comparative safety of the hilltop that stared down on
them. They climbed toward their goal through the late afternoon, and
there was still no evidence that they had been seen. But they would
have to be very cautious while they were moving on the high ground,
where there was only the short grass and scattered clumps of bush for
concealment. They would have to depend on luck, hoping that no
enemy would be passing along the river and look up to see nine men
climbing up the hill only 1,000 meters away.

Finally, after about four hours of sweaty humping, the Marines
reached the hilltop with about an hour of daylight left. They took a
break and hid in three teams under clumps of bush. The breather was
sorely needed. Newcomer Karoski, his hot, itchy body crawling with
leeches, huddled under a bush and ripped his green utility blouse off
so he could pick the suckers off. Thus he brought down upon himself
the wrath of his patrol leader. Connelly, lips tight, advised his radio
operator that his lily-white skin could be seen for two miles and
threatened the team with having to move again. But it wouldn't; in
that last hour of daylight, and just after reaching the hilltop, the
Marines began to see small columns of uniformed soldiers mixed
with civilian-appearing, black-pajama types traveling through the
middle of the valley on a road that had a hard surface, but was not
paved, and was about two lanes wide. The map labeled it "#554." It
ran west-east toward the Bo, which ran north-south along the eastern
end of the valley. A plantation of palm trees was located near the river
and the road. The flat land, filled with rice-growing areas and villages,
continued on the east side of the Bo, but broadened into a wide expanse of populated areas that led to the doorstep of the city of Hue.
The river followed its pathway to the north for about four miles and
then turned east to intersect with the Huong River (the Perfume
River) just north of Hue. The rivers and their nearby villages served
as the main avenues of approach to the city.

With the Marines now on the highest piece of real estate for two or
three miles in all directions, Connelly was reluctant to leave. The
team cautiously remained off the skyline and set up a 360-degree
perimeter for the night. Claymore mines were placed on all sides.

Then the patrol leader calculated his on-call artillery missions
within 500 meters on four points around the team. He had the M-60
and all the M-14s set to give maximum interlocking fires. His posi-

tion would not be an easy one for any enemy force to take. They settled into their harbor site—and they made it through the night.

The next day began as the day before had ended. The Marines started counting the groups of Charlie marching down Route 554. They were all in small groups of from two to twelve, but they carried rifles and were heading in the direction of the Bo River. They were in columns, and even though most were in uniform, they seemed to be unconcerned about marching down the middle of the valley in the open. By this time, the enemy forces were well aware that Recon teams were challenging their right of uncontested passage through the area, and the Marines on top of Hill 165 wondered about the temerity of their foe down below. They didn't seem concerned; they were moving on a mission.

The smaller teams of enemy, two or three soldiers each, were allowed to proceed, but the bigger groups were repeatedly hit by artillery called in by the Reconners. Doc Sutherland stated, "The view from where we were was just incredible. They weren't but about a thousand to fifteen hundred meters away and just lollygagging down the road. We'd drop a few rounds on them, and they'd jump out of sight beside the roadway, and then after the fire mission was over, they would get up and move out again."

Rusty Kenyon, who was big enough to pack the M-60 up the hills, was set up behind brush, peering over the sights of his weapon, and noticed the numbers of the enemy who were camouflaged with brush as they moved in the valley. Jimmy Taylor watched the enemy skirt the plantation that spread out below him.

Karoski said:

It was strange how they'd keep coming every day. I remember distinctly how I called in artillery for Connelly, adjusting the rounds up the road toward the NVA, and they just kept marching down the road and at the last minute would jump into trenches beside the road. Then we'd call in air support. I don't know how many of them we may have killed, or whether they carried off any bodies at night, but the next day they were back walking down the road. If they hadn't taken the bodies away, they would've been stepping over them.

Connelly decided to continue the same OP and take his chances of being spotted, although that might keep them dangerously long in one spot. There just wasn't any better position around. So they stayed put, kept off the skyline, and watched, concealed, from the bushes. Then each morning, early, the team checked the claymores to insure that no enemy soldier had slipped up during the night to turn them around to face the Marines. There wasn't any evidence yet that they had been located. All day on the fourteenth and fifteenth, the team stayed and counted the eastbound groups of enemy soldiers traveling the road in front of them. And each day the enemy left some dead behind in the ditches.

Then late in the afternoon of October 16, an F-4 Phantom streaking overhead on call for the Marines made a turn that brought him around the back of the hill on which the Reconners were positioned. Sutherland said, "The pilot radioed us, 'Be advised that the back side of your hill is alive with Charlie.' Don was on the pilot's radio frequency. The pilot then began to make strafing runs to blast the Charlie off the slopes."

Sutherland said, "When he began his bombing runs, he was so close we could read the writing on the bombs."

Karoski added:

He was streaking past us close enough that it got to where I knew the number of flips that each bomb would take before impacting. In between the fighting, I stopped to take pictures of the jet diving right across our noses. From what we were told by the pilot and from what we could count ourselves, I believe that there was from fifty to seventy VC coming up the hill. I know we were holding our breaths that they hadn't seen us that first day, but after they didn't come after us right away, we figured they hadn't seen us.

Now we weren't sure whether they could've spotted somebody on top of the hill; picked up our trail from a few days earlier; possibly had radio direction finders; or just got over their case of the dumb-ass and figured out that we had to be up where we were lobbing artillery in the same area every day.

But the fight was on. With close air support overhead, the Marines threw grenades down the hillside, and every time enemy soldiers were spotted, the Marines opened up with their M-14s—except for Rusty Kenyon, who rattled them with his M-60 machine gun. For the moment, the Marines held the advantage, but how long would that hold out? The sun was rapidly blazing its trail downward, and darkness was just over the next mountain. The Marines radioed the battalion base and requested an emergency extraction.

The enemy was close enough that the claymores had taken their toll. (The AO had counted twenty-seven bodies strewn on the hillside before dark.) Then the last mine was detonated and the last grenade was thrown, but the Marines still fought from the advantage of the hilltop. They continued the battle into the night—all the while continuing to push headquarters for an emergency extraction. There was some debate back at the base about leaving the team out until the next morning, when an infantry sweep into the valley could use it as a blocking force, but wiser heads prevailed. Without the claymores, without grenades, and low on ammo, the Reconners would likely have been overrun and killed during the night.

Finally, the Hueys were on the way, and in the blackness of night, Kevin Connelly used the strobe lights to bring the birds down and take the team away. Empress Alice had been in and out of two hot spots over five days and, although the first patrol had resulted in severe damage to a helicopter, the team had not suffered one casualty. But the enemy had suffered considerably.

Sutherland, Karoski, Kenyon, and Taylor expressed their anger with those in the rear headquarters who did not have "bush experience" yet questioned the team's reports. All four men from Empress Alice stated that morale suffered when an officer disbelieved reports of enemy sightings or thought that small Recon teams could stay in the field overnight after being attacked by superior units of the NVA.

However, October was just the beginning. During November, three of every four enemy soldiers spotted by battalion teams were seen by Reconners operating in the Hue–Phu Bai recon zone. This happened despite the fact that three companies from the battalion were operating in the DMZ area and only two were responsible for the RAOR around Hue. While sightings were still voluminous in the Co Bi–Thanh Tan, patrols were also running into enemy activity elsewhere in this sector.

One eight-man patrol landed on a ridge south of Phu Bai, about five and a half miles east of the location where the Striker team had been shot out of the air. Throughout October, patrols that had penetrated this area had significant finds that gave ample evidence of VC and their camp areas. Other intelligence sources also indicated the presence of a 400- to 500-man enemy unit. One two-day patrol into that zone on November 3 began with almost immediate sightings. The team went in at 0900 hours, and by 1200 had discovered a VC base camp approximately 300 meters in diameter. It was nestled in the fork of a stream and had a small dam on the main stream just outside the camp's perimeter. A trail paralleled the stream into the camp. The vegetation was thick and there was a forty-foot jungle canopy overhead. The patrol, led by Sgt. J. W. Monise, hid in the thick undergrowth and adjusted artillery on the camp, which they estimated contained some fifty VC. The enemy left the area running, and the Marines moved deeper into the jungle.

On the morning of November 5, the Reconners made contact with several small groups of VC, which resulted in a series of armed clashes between the Marines and the VC and between the enemy and the armed gunships that came out to assist the Recon team. The Marines were extracted under emergency conditions at 1130 hours, having taken one prisoner, but with one of their own wounded. The patrol report stated:

> Recommendations: No other patrols should be inserted in this area because of the extensive enemy activity ... bombing should be conducted. .... Heavy new enemy buildup and extensive enemy activity ... Patrol feels that this is an area being used by a large well armed VC unit because of the two patrols conducted by this team, what they have found, and the volume of fire which was delivered at the helicopter on the last occasion.

How well this intelligence data was received by the higher commands is a subject of concern. Many in the battalion felt that Recon reports were not being taken seriously. In addition, intelligence analyses from higher commands were not readily available to the battalions in the field, including Recon.

Within days of Sergeant Monise's patrol, the battalion received a new commanding officer. Lt. Col. Bill Kent took over the reins of the battalion teams on the Marine Corps' birthday, November 10, 1967. Prior to his time as Recon battalion commander, he had spent the summer with the 2nd Battalion, 9th Marines. On September 12, during Operation Kingfisher, in and near the DMZ, an early-morning mortar attack ripped through his battalion CP, and Kent lost his infantry command when he received a serious knee wound. He spent two months on the U.S.S. *Sanctuary*, offshore, recovering. Then, on November 10, he flew off the ship and walked into the 3rd Marine Division Headquarters looking for a job. His old battalion had a new CO, and he was worried that with his lingering knee problems he would be assigned to some staff or logistics job. As he walked down the 3rd MarDiv Headquarters' main passageway, he ran into the commanding general, Bruno Hochmuth. It was from Hochmuth, directly, that Kent discovered that he was the new CO of the 3rd Recon Battalion. However, within four days General Hochmuth was killed, and Kent had to deal with generals who didn't trust or appreciate the value of the Recon teams—a situation that may have contributed to the difficulty Recon reports apparently encountered on their way through the chain of command.

Brigadier Generals English and Metzger were assistant division commanders of the 3rd MarDiv, and Metzger took over for two weeks as the CG in November when General Hochmuth was killed. Lieutenant Colonel Kent stated:

> I took the watch on November 10, 1967, and General Hochmuth was killed four days later. While I didn't get to work directly for him as his Recon officer very long, I had known him earlier. My combined experience with him gave me the sense that I could have gone to that old Texas Aggie at any time, and he would have listened and given credit to my reports. He was a hard ass—hard charger, but at the same time, honest and straightforward.
>
> Gen. Louis Metzger took over after Hochmuth went down, and he didn't trust Recon from his chair to the end of his desk. When I was CO of 2/9, he told me he had a bad experience with a Recon patrol. He said he was driving on Route 9 one day and saw a patrol that he believed to be Recon screwing off near the road. He felt the team was misreporting where it was supposed to be, and correct or not, that colored his opinion the rest of the time that I knew him. He told me, "I don't believe Recon one minute."
>
> Major General Thompkins, who took over the division after Metzger's two weeks, didn't pay a lot of attention to Recon. He seemed to be preoccupied with minor details and Khe Sanh.

The military and political pressures were then seriously focusing on the developing siege of Khe Sanh, and less attention would be paid to events near the old capital city of Hue.

However, on the same Marine Corps birthday during which Lieutenant Colonel Kent assumed command, one of the 3rd Recon teams out in the Co Bi–Thanh Tan saw an eye-opening movement of enemy troops, again toward Hue City. As Marine and Army infantry were being pulled away to the borders, behind them units of the NVA and VC slipped toward the population centers. They moved undetected—almost. Recon teams noted the increased activity and the direction of the enemy movement, but Bill Kent would say, "My general impression was that our reports were going into a big black hole. . . . You never got any feedback, so you never knew if you were producing any intelligence that anyone appreciated."

That Marine Corps birthday patrol was led by Sgt. Norm Karkos. According to Jim Barnes, a Karkos-trained patrol leader and a career Marine like his mentor, Karkos earned the reputation of the "ultimate warrior" because he never turned from a challenge. He was out to get his job accomplished, to eliminate mistakes, and to get back home alive. He pushed his teams across their recon zones until they knew the territory about as well as the enemy, sometimes better. He had been medevacked from the battalion the previous December; returned in the summer; later went to a Provisional Reconnaissance Unit (PRU) working out of the Phoenix Program, and then transferred to 1st Force Recon because he saw the PRUs as too incompetent.

However, on this November 10, the day Lieutenant Colonel Kent was taking over the battalion, Karkos and his team were in the Co Bi–Thanh Tan. It was an eight-man team, and its recon zone covered part of the area patrolled by the Empress Alice patrol led by Kevin Connelly. Its LZ was only several hundred meters away, near the ridge.

The team landed not far from the Bo River, with mountains to its left and the lower Co Bi–Thanh Tan ridge to the right. The main valley was on the opposite side of the ridge. The team moved quickly out of its landing zone on the southern side of the ridge. The patrol moved up the ridge and crisscrossed the crest from east to west, away from the river. There were a few breaks in the ridge where streams had gouged narrow gorges. For the first five and a half klicks to the west of the Bo, the highest points were Hill 165 and a few similar elevations farther west. The team's zone included the ridge and the edge of the valley floor. Karkos's intention, as his point, Jim Barnes, stated, was "to patrol the whole six klicks and not to sit in observation posts. Some might have sat in OPs, but Karkos pushed us through the whole area on foot looking for evidence of the enemy. It wasn't a surprise that if Karkos couldn't find anything in the assigned RZ, he would ask for the zone to be extended so he could hunt further."

The team moved out with Sergeant Karkos in the middle with his radio operator, Cpl. Charles Lutz. Karkos would rotate the point and the rear. He didn't want to let anyone, especially the point, get too tired or too mechanical at what he was doing. At night, the eight men sat in a harbor site in a tight circle with on-call artillery missions plotted around them within 500 meters. Two men were to be awake all the time, with one on the radio. Every hour on the hour, the man on the radio had to key the handset twice if everything was "alpha sierra"—all secure. However, there were times after pushing hard all day long when sleeping was too easy.

Barnes remembers one such occasion:

> I had radio watch one hour, and my eyes gave up the battle and closed. My brain-housing group drifted off. The next thing I remember was that my eyeballs were wide open, my brain was racing at two to three thousand rpm, my heart was pumping like crazy, and the cool metal of a knife was firmly against my throat. And I had to listen to a whispered lecture from my patrol leader that the knife could have very easily be-

longed to a VC, and both myself and the rest of the team could be dead. Well, I never had the sleeping problem again, but on the other hand, it was somewhat comforting to know that Karkos was on our side—night or day. Still, the word got around, and if the terrain and cover allowed, I think everybody started to stand up on watch. Sitting could mean sleeping, and sleeping meant either Karkos or the VC.

The first day of the patrol was November 5, and for the first five days there were no contacts and no sightings. But there were signs. The patrol was extended to six days because of heavy overcast and rain. During that time, Karkos led his patrol, sometimes running point himself, crossing and recrossing the ridge, searching for enemy.

Charles Lutz described the first days of the patrol:

We walked down a stream on the back side of the Co Bi–Thanh Tan ridge and found VC harbor sites and footprints all around, but not much else. Then, on the morning of the eighth, we were on the ridge watching the valleys, and there was this sight of a whole hillside area and parts of the valley below us just filled with smoke like from campfires. We called in artillery. Then later we checked the place out and found those fires were really hot springs. The whole place was filled with little springs of hot water. But we also found fresh trails and footprints that looked like they had just been made that day. So Sergeant Karkos set us in an ambush along one of the trails that evening. That night we sat tight and heard Vietnamese voices, but they never got closer than a hundred feet and never knew we were there.

Karkos kept the team moving and crossed the stream, carefully traversing the low ground in the direction of the main Co Bi–Thanh Tan Valley. The stream was heavily covered with vegetation and hidden on its banks were more pathways. Lutz described the situation: "The next day, we crossed this stream. It had a lot of trees and bushes that concealed whatever may have been in it. Along the stream, we found another well-used trail and again a lot of fresh footprints in the mud."

Over a distance of about seven and a half miles, the ridgeline had five breaks in it where streams flowed through from higher elevations. These streams were easy pathways for the Vietcong and their North Vietnamese brothers. These same routes approaching the city of Hue from the west were only about eighteen miles straight-line distance from the northern portion of the A Shau Valley, which remained a significant staging area for the North Vietnamese.

However, following the stream and trail, the Karkos patrol pushed through the cut in the ridge out into the valley to the north. Lutz stated, "We followed it until we came out of the stream and through a graveyard. Out to our front was the open valley, and the ridge was just behind us. The stream was just a short distance away. We had found fighting holes in and near the graves, and that's where we set up an ambush for the night. I was the radio operator and in the same hole with Sergeant Karkos."

For a few hours, there was nothing but incessant mosquitoes. Then, Lutz stated, "At about 2300, we heard movement crossing the stream. It sounded like people wading across. We radioed Barnie [Jim Barnes], who had the secondary radio and was on the other end of our ambush. He heard the noise, too."

Rusty Kenyon ran point for as many patrols as he could. He liked it up front, and he was there on this one with Karkos. On this night, though, he was sharing a foxhole with a Kit Carson scout, and said, "I about throttled the guy. He was always trying to rub insect repellent on himself because of the mosquitoes, and I knew the VC could smell the damn stuff. They were damn near us, maybe fifty yards away or less, going down the stream."

Lutz continued, "Nothing happened, though. The VC never came closer, and we just had to put up with all the mosquitoes. A couple of 'em bit me on the lip, and it stung so much I thought a scorpion had bitten me. My lip swelled up to twice its size."

Then the rain started, and the Marines knew that they would likely be stuck out in the bush without helicopters. They stayed at the bottom of the ridge throughout the Marine Corps birthday in 1967, with the monsoon winds and rains whistling their salute. But whatever or whoever had passed the Marines in the stream only fifty meters away during the night was out somewhere in the valley or beyond by the morning. It was likely that they had crossed the open during the night or under cover of the rainstorms that swept the valley. These Marines had not heard of the New Year's Jerry Siler patrol, eleven months earlier, but they were very near the same location.

The stream near their ambush site, where they had heard the enemy troop movements during the night, ran out into the center of the valley and under a small bridge on Route 554. As the rain started to clear in the afternoon, Charles Lutz said:

There were these helicopters flying for some grunts not too far away, and we heard shots from a tree line in the valley. Then two minutes later, Rusty Kenyon, our point, spotted this VC running across the open ground down that road from one tree line toward another about five hundred meters away. I saw him, too. Then we saw about ten more come out of the trees. They ran across after the lead guy. Then about twenty took off running, and these guys were carrying mortars. We watched through our binoculars—they were only about seven hundred meters away. We then figured that these guys were NVA and not VC.

Then there was another twenty, and we called for arty, but they couldn't fire for us. There was some check-fire holding the artillery support. I think it was because there were helicopters in the line of fire. When the count reached two hundred and fifty VC, they finally got the rounds out. We counted about two hundred and seventy-five to three hundred NVA running toward the river and tree line to the east, and figured there must have been a battalion of 'em.

How many more of the enemy had crossed the open at night or with the rain shielding them earlier in the day is not known. There was a lot of time under that cover for them to move across the open. By the time the artillery was able to fire, most of the enemy had disappeared into the tree line. Only thirty-seven rounds of artillery were fired.

However, when the artillery was "on the way," Karkos moved his team to the higher ground along the ridgeline to get a better view and to be in a more defensible position. The VC/NVA had been within 500 to 700 meters of the team, and the Marines didn't want to have to fight out of a graveyard if they were found. By the time the team had worked its way up the hillside, the last of the artillery was descending on the target. The team was extracted within an hour.

After that morning, there was never a doubt for the members of the Karkos team that the movement during the night in the stream must have been part of the same unit. The enemy had used extraordinarily sound discipline. The Reconners had heard no clanking of rifles, canteens, cooking gear, or other objects. The enemy had also avoided the trail on which the Marines had waited in ambush. Most NVA and VC units were aware of the possible presence of Marine Recon teams and used good discipline even though they were out in their own backyard.

Five days later, a team operating in the same area, but closer to Hill 165, sighted 275 to 280 enemy soldiers and heavy sampan traffic on the river. During November, throughout the battalion's areas of responsibility there was a decrease in sightings near the DMZ but an increase in the Co Bi–Thanh Tan and other areas around Hue. In the 3rd Recon Battalion command chronologies, it was said of the Co Bi–Thanh Tan, "This area continues to show heavy enemy movement. . . . Area reveals new buildup . . . and heavy enemy activity."

Seventy-seven percent of the enemy sighted by the battalion

throughout northern I Corps in that one month occurred in the Hue–Phu Bai area. This followed the trend. For the last six months of 1967, the number of enemy sighted by the 3rd Recon Battalion outside the old imperial capital had steadily increased from 30 percent of total battalion sightings to 77 percent. Then, in December, the count of enemy doubled. And while the sightings along the DMZ increased, December sightings near Hue–Phu Bai skyrocketed to 1,470 NVA or Vietcong.

Lieutenant Colonel Kent described one December patrol:

> During the Christmas truce, we had one of our best patrol leaders out with a team in the Co Bi–Thanh Tan. He was Sgt. Walter Zawistowski—"Ski." They went out on Christmas Eve and returned on the day after Christmas. That team sat on the Co Bi–Thanh Tan ridgeline on Christmas and started counting enemy soldiers crossing the valley, heading for the Song Bo and in the direction of Hue City. The VC were apparently confident in the American holiday truce. I stood in the COC and listened to the radio reports coming in from Ski. The number of VC was getting so high that I advised Ski to call a fire mission and screw the truce. He already had.
>
> But getting a fire mission approved on this Christmas truce was like pissing up a rope. I could hear Ski on the radio, showing his exasperation with the whole thing, and that's when I ran out of our CP the short distance to the division command and started yelling at the people in the division headquarters. But it took the Saigon MACV headquarters to approve. Division had to get the go-ahead from III MAF, and they had to get the sanction from MACV. All we could do was fuss and cuss and listen to Ski describe a battalion and more of enemy moving across the open, heading toward the old capital.

Finally, after a couple of wasted hours, approval came in. A fire mission of over 1,000 rounds followed, and it was in turn followed by several air strikes. While the large majority of the enemy had reached cover along the Bo River, the team did do some damage to the enemy. Bodies were seen lying in the rice paddies, and twenty-two secondary explosions were observed. However, an enemy unit of more than 600 soldiers had seemed to escape the supporting arms. They were noted moving at about the same location where the two November patrols had each seen 250 to 300 troops. However, reports by Recon teams near Hue showing a significant escalation in enemy troop movements seemed to cause no concern. Preparations continued to be made for the division—including the 3rd Recon Battalion—to move away from the Hue–Phu Bai area to the Quang Tri camp, closer to the DMZ. The American and South Vietnamese commands just couldn't accept the fact that the enemy might be planning a major offensive against the population centers along the coast. In Saigon, MACV's chief intelligence officer said later, about the idea of NVA and VC attacks across the length of the country against urban centers, that ". . . it was so preposterous that I probably would have been unable to sell it to anybody . . ."

American attention was directed at the DMZ, and particularly at Khe Sanh, where the president and his command personnel were fearful that another Dien Bien Phu would occur. Formerly classified documents reveal a litany of concerns about the DMZ and Khe Sanh, but not very much about Hue. Some of the messages that flashed back and forth between commands show that preoccupation:

- "There has been an extensive buildup of North Vietnamese forces near Khe Sanh . . ."
- "COMUSMACV desires a thorough military analysis of the Dien Bien Phu battle to ascertain that we are taking all countering actions possible in relationship to the analogous Khe Sanh situation."
- ". . . deploy the 3rd Brigade of the 1st Air Cavalry Division . . . deploy the 2nd Brigade of the 101st Airborne Division . . . to Hue/Phu Bai for attachment to the 1st Cavalry Division . . ." (Actually, the location was north of Hue, about halfway to Quang Tri. The focus was always to the north.)
- "It is directed the III MAF [Marine Corps] make available to the 7th Air Force all tactical bomber sorties . . . The serious threat we face in I Corps and Khe Sanh in particular, demands this."

Using Bill Kent's analogy, it was like "pissing up a rope" to get the command to see the danger around Hue—even though Recon teams were noting enemy units in strength moving from the northwest and west toward the city. In his appeals at the division CP, Bill Kent had pleaded, "Hey, we got something going here. We're missing the world's greatest opportunity." However, no one had ears for what Recon was saying.

By Christmas Norm Karkos had been laid low by intestinal parasites and was temporarily out of action, and others in the team had been reassigned to different squads and patrols. Sgt. Gus Gustafson, formerly an assistant patrol leader, had been given a patrol himself. Charles Lutz was still with the team.

The team went out on December 27 and returned on December 30. Whiskey Relay was about eight miles due west of Phu Bai. The relay had been taking sniper fire for days, and within twenty hours of the return of Ski's patrol, Lutz was following the lead of Gustafson on a

Rough Rider insertion. Lutz said the trucks traveled the rugged roads out past Whiskey Relay with the Marines bouncing their rear ends into bruises from trying to sit on the benches inside the six-bys. Not far past the relay station, the Marines were dropped off to finish the route by foot. The trucks disappeared in the distance as the Marines tried to quickly move across open terrain. It was late afternoon. The rains had slacked off, and the team pushed across paddies and through elephant grass. The hills toward which it trooped were not the tall mountains that loomed over the skyline in the far distance, but the lower foothills. Scattered clumps of trees on the hilltops offered observation positions and concealment to the Marines, and that was where they were headed. However, the draws and valleys also contained tree lines through which the VC and NVA were suspected to be traveling. It would be easy to have an unfriendly encounter with NVA and VC between the road and the hills.

Through the late afternoon the Reconners slogged their way and finally arrived undetected on a small hilltop on which a clump of pines broke the skyline. They tucked themselves into the trees and didn't have long to wait. Just as they were setting into positions, Charles Lutz said, "I saw a VC going up this hill only about four hundred meters away. Then there were two others, and they had a surveyor's transit with them. They used it to sight in on our positions back at the bases. Well, we called in artillery and disrupted their plans. I don't think we hit them, but they left in a hurry."

The team then moved to a steeper hill not far away. Again, they hadn't time to take off their packs before they sighted enemy. Lutz whispered to Gus to come check out what he was seeing. Five VC were moving in the low ground to their front. They were well camouflaged and using the trees as cover. The Marines watched and waited to see if there were others. The draw through which the enemy soldiers were coming was only 500 meters away. Then the team spotted the rest cautiously moving behind their point. Lutz was on the radio, reporting what he was seeing back to Whiskey. In a play-by-play account, Lutz had to keep changing the story to fit the events. The count of VC/NVA rose to fifty; then to one hundred; then fifty more; and they finally counted over two hundred. The enemy carried rifles, machine guns, mortars, and rice and firewood. There was a mix of uniforms in the main body. Some wore black PJ bottoms and blue shirts; some had green ponchos; and some had regulation uniforms.

The team called in air strikes and had an AO come on station to help coordinate. Sixteen sorties were flown, blasting and burning an area 1,000 meters by 2,000 meters. The bombs hit so close to the Marines that Lutz said, "We watched one five-hundred-pounder drop on one side of us and flip through the air just over our heads. We could've read the serial number on it. It blasted about three hundred meters from us, and rocks and debris rained down on our heads. We huddled tight to the trees."

The team dug in for the night. They called in H & I artillery fire all night, and rain came along with the artillery. The wind blew, and the Marines were wet and cold. The next day, Lutz said:

> A major called us and wanted us to go down and count bodies. We told him he was out of his mind. I know I had seen five more NVA the next day, and I know they were there to police the battlefield—picking up weapons and carrying off dead and wounded. But there was still a lot of trees to hide whatever all they had down there. For us to go down would have been suicide. To top it off, the rain was still falling, and if we had run into enemy down there, no choppers could've come out to help us.

The team did not go down into the valley to count the NVA bodies, and returned from the mission in a cold but somewhat healthy state on December 30. They walked back while Whiskey Relay guided them with reports every twenty minutes; another three companies of NVA were said to be between the relay station and the team. The Reconners went into a "no-fire" zone at one point on their return, checking out a pagoda mausoleum for ancient Vietnamese kings. They waded chest-deep through leech-filled, rain-swollen rice paddies, and shivered in the cold wind, but they got back to the road and their extraction trucks.

For several more weeks 3rd Recon teams probed the hills and valleys around Hue, and their reports continued to show the increase of enemy activity, but as Bill Kent said, that information seemed to be sucked into some black hole. By mid-January the teams of 3rd Recon were being consolidated at the new command post farther to the north of Quang Tri. While it is true that Charlie Company and 1st Force Recon from the 1st Recon Battalion came up to Phu Bai from their base in Da Nang at the end of January 1968, those units could not be expected to understand the situation and the terrain in the few short days prior to the "General Offensive and Uprising" that was launched into the urban centers of South Vietnam at the end of the month.

One officer in the Army Intelligence section of MACV, Bruce Jones, is quoted in his book *War Without Windows* as follows: "The battle of Hue proved to be a sobering experience for the allied command . . . [D]espite forewarnings of a possible multibattalion attack at Tet, American and South Vietnamese forces had been taken by surprise. Even more disturbing was the discovery made by the 3rd Brigade of the U.S. 1st Cavalry Division after the battle had begun."

The attack against the city of Hue began at 0340 hours on the morning of January 31, 1968. Two battalions of the 6th NVA Regiment charged from the west into the old Citadel. Another battalion of that regiment set up blocking positions on Highway One leading from the northwest into the city. At the same time two battalions of the 4th NVA Regiment assaulted from the south into the MACV detachment compound and other areas on the south side of the Perfume River. The third battalion of that regiment established blocking positions along Highway One from the south into the city. Then the independent 12th Sapper Battalion appeared and took over the area on the north bank near the Imperial Palace of Peace. An uncounted number of guerrilla units and VCI appeared within the city, and the battle was on. The surprise was so complete that, not understanding the gravity of the situation, the new Marine command, which had just days earlier replaced the 3rd Division at its Phu Bai headquarters just south of the city, sent only one infantry company to relieve the besieged city.

Jones had mentioned the disturbing news that the 3rd Brigade, 1st Cavalry Division, had generated when it was ordered south from its camp halfway to Quang Tri. It was to counterattack the NVA who were inside the old city. However, maneuvering south, it ran into elements of three additional NVA regiments: the 24th Regiment, 304th Division; the 29th Regiment, 325C Division; and the 99th Regiment, 324B Division. These three, if they were at full strength, would have constituted a division-size force. Previously, they had been reported by MACV and Marine Intelligence to be located around or near Khe Sanh. During the past days, however, they had slipped away from Khe Sanh without detection to reappear just north of Hue, more than fifty miles away.

From January 1 to December 31, 1967, the battalion had sent 1,327 patrols to the field. Those teams sighted 14,121 NVA and VC. An estimated 2,692 enemy were killed or wounded by Recon teams, primarily through the use of supporting arms. Fifty-three Reconners were killed, 451 wounded.

Despite Recon sightings that should have warned of a major enemy move against the city of Hue, the MACV and III MAF command had decided to relocate the battalion as well as the 3rd Marine Division Headquarters to the new base under construction at Quang Tri, about thirty-five miles closer to the border and away from Hue.

CHAPTER FIFTEEN

The Year of the Monkey

Gen. William Westmoreland stated that the climactic battle of the Tet Offensive was at Khe Sanh; he even established a study group to consider the use of tactical nuclear weapons there. However, at least a portion of the Khe Sanh paranoia was a result of the fear of the president of the United States. Lyndon Johnson insisted on a "signed in blood" paper from the Joint Chiefs of Staff that Khe Sanh would not be lost. Fifty percent of the total U.S. maneuver battalions were shifted into I Corps, which did much to deplete the rest of the country of needed infantry.

During June 1967, the battalion had suffered fifteen deaths and forty wounded, until then its bloodiest month. January 1968 was more than twice as deadly; in thirty-one days, thirty-four Reconners were killed and seventy-two were wounded. During January, the four letter companies and the 3rd Force Company conducted 126 patrols, averaging 8.5 men per patrol. Sixty-three percent of the battalion's 106 casualties were sustained by Bravo Company at Khe Sanh, where it was forced into the bunkers for much of the month: twelve Bravo Reconners were killed and fifty-six wounded during those thirty-one days, most as a result of the continuous enemy rocket, mortar, and artillery attacks.

When the battalion moved to Quang Tri on January 26, Charlie Company and 3rd Force were in Dong Ha, and Bravo was at Khe Sanh. On January 13, Delta Company moved to the new command post to help build the camp. Alpha Company and Headquarters and Service Company remained at Phu Bai until January 26, when they then also relocated to Quang Tri. They were replaced at Phu Bai by elements of the 1st Recon Battalion, coming up from Da Nang.

On January 30–31, 1968, the Vietcong attacked 36 of South Vietnam's provincial capitals, approximately 30 percent of the 245 district capitals, five of the six autonomous cities, all the major air bases, and numbers of other bases. The shift in command locations just days earlier undoubtedly played into the hands of the NVA strategy, and with an estimated 30,000 spies throughout South Vietnam, the NVA leadership was probably well aware of the shift of U.S. forces.

On January 2, 1968, a patrol was inserted on the ridge overlooking the Co Bi–Thanh Tan Valley and very close to the site of Sergeant Ski's Christmas patrol a few days earlier (sighting 674 enemy moving toward Hue). It was also the same recon zone in which Sergeant Karkos had patrolled on November 10–11 and had sighted approximately 250 enemy troops moving toward Hue—and the team was sure that more had passed during the night. The January patrol's team leader, Sgt. Francis Houdashelt, was new to the battalion and had no Recon experience. The patrol was also announced to the entire area by the helicopters' machine gunning the landing zone immediately prior to and after landing the team. Another major problem was that the team was landed on the skyline and not along the backside of the ridge in the smaller valley. The combination of inexperience and the aerial announcement to the nearby world was enough to allow the enemy to seek, fix, find, and destroy the patrol.

The team left Camp Evans at 0900 hours on January 2, 1968. The CH-46 in which it rode circled above the valley as jet aircraft and gunships strafed the ridge on which it was to be inserted. Then, at about 0930, the chopper dropped into the LZ and the Marines jumped out and ran to set up a quick three-sixty. Later, Pfc. Underdue and Pfc. Brown reported that the troop-carrying helicopter fired its machine guns as it entered and left the LZ. Underdue was quoted: "As we were setting down, the crew chiefs on the 46s, I believe, made a mistake in prepping the zone on the way in with M-60s. This was a dead giveaway. We actually couldn't set up a good three-sixty because as we were leaving the chopper, they were still firing."

The team moved a short distance along the ridge, but remained close to the LZ. Within ten minutes of insertion, Pfc. Underdue, the radio operator, advised the gunship that it could leave.

The ridge was very narrow and open, rising about 100 to 120 meters from the valley floor. On the south and opposite side of the ridge, the terrain dropped about 80 meters just as abruptly and then quickly rose again to hilltops that looked down on the ridge from 500 to 700 feet above it. One hundred or so meters to the east along the ridge was a slight rise. Five hundred meters to the west the ridge rose about 50 meters over the patrol's location. The area was covered only by grass but had a good view of the Co Bi–Thanh Tan Valley. Trees and thick brush grew farther down the slopes.

The team's mission was to determine the nature of the enemy movement along the infiltration routes and to check the area for VC base camps. For reasons unknown, Sergeant Houdashelt immediately set the team into an OP position very near the LZ. Brown and Underdue were taped by the 3rd Marine Division general staff shortly after their rescue. Each was taped separately.*

Pfc. Underdue stated, "About one-half hour later, we spotted one VC filling his canteen. Some time later five more were spotted." These enemy soldiers were located about 300 meters below the team, on the back side of the ridge.

Pfc. Brown said, "We called to see if we could call a fire mission and were instructed that we couldn't have it 'cuz they wanted a better sighting."

Brown stated, "Our PL [patrol leader] passed the word that we were to leave our gear and move down one man. Take his rifle and move down. One man could eat, and the other be on watch."

The patrol stayed in the same position for the balance of the day without incident. At approximately 1700 hours, Sergeant Houdashelt passed the word that the team would pull into a tighter three-sixty for a harbor site. At that time the eight men were still in pairs in a wide four-point star position, maintaining observation in the different directions. It is not known just what the intentions of the patrol leader were, but it had been the practice of other patrols to move into an initial harbor site position and then to relocate after dusk. Whatever his intentions, the VC hit before the team could get set as the sergeant wanted.

Underdue had been paired with Pfc. Miller, who carried the M-79 grenade launcher. Miller had just left to move toward his place, and Underdue was moving closer to Pfc. Pitts. Brown said that no sooner had Houdashelt given the order to move in tighter than " . . . our point man with the M-60 yelled out, 'Gooks.' About the same time there was a burst of automatic fire, and the point man was hit."

Underdue described the initial burst of fire:

> Our point man, Peppi, was hit about three times, but managed to yell, "Enemy, I'm hit." Then he fired his M-60, but it jammed and he was hit again, and this time he was killed.

*Their accounts were taken from the patrol report and from tapes—supplied by former company clerk Max O'Canas—made by Division ISO on January 4, 1968.

Pfc. Pitts, next to me, shouted, "Where is the enemy?" I said, "We're surrounded. Keep your head down." He moved around beside me and got hit in the upper left forehead and slumped over.

On the north end of the patrol's position, farthest away from the attack, were Brown, Doc Jarvis, and Pfc. Harris. Brown stated, "Harris ran up to me and the Doc and told us he was going up front. As he took off, well, all I heard was a moan."

Underdue said, "I don't know what happened, but he never made it. I guess the sniper got him, too."

Rain clouds were moving over the sky, and with confusion and death engulfing the team, Doc Jarvis yelled at Brown that he was going to try to make it to the "front." Brown reported, "He grabbed his bag and ran up front, too. That's the last I heard from the Doc."

Underdue described the scene: "At this time the Doc ran up, and we never heard a word outa him. Then Sergeant Houdashelt was hit—I believe shrapnel in the leg from a grenade. He shouted, 'Underdue, I'm hit.' So I grabbed my cartridge belt, and as I was spinning around I received an incoming round grazing my forehead."

Brown said:

At this time I was running out of ammo 'cause my cartridge belt was over here when we moved around. I started to run over to get it, but the sergeant yelled for everybody to keep down. So I crawled up there to get it. When I got there, I was just behind—about even—with Pfc. Underdue, Sergeant Houdashelt, and our point man, Peppi. That's when the M-79 man [Miller] got off one round. That's the last I heard from him. Then Peppi was hit again. Sergeant Houdashelt got hit with—I believe it was a grenade. He was still on the radio. I don't think he was hurt too bad.

Brown indicated that Houdashelt had gotten on the radio after Underdue had been hit. He said, "Pfc. Underdue moved over to help, and that's when a round grazed him in the head. At this time, the sergeant yelled out for everyone to fire. So I commenced firing, and that's when I realized that my rifle was the only one going."

Peppi Gauthier, at point, was down. Pfc. Pitts, who had been next to Underdue, was shot in the head. Pfc. Harris, the assistant patrol leader, had been shot trying to get from the rear to the front, as had Doc Jarvis. Pfc. Miller, with the M-79, had gotten off one round when he was hit. According to the patrol report, all this had happened in less than ten minutes. The only three left were Sergeant Houdashelt, who had received grenade wounds, Pfc. Underdue, who had been temporarily knocked unconscious by a forehead wound, and Pfc. Brown.

Three Marines were left on the ridge, and two of those were wounded. Incoming fire was deadly and accurate. The rounds, at least some of which were shots to the head, were well aimed and were picking off the Marines. This would support the belief of the survivors that there was an enemy soldier in a nearby sniper position. Since there was a slight rise only about 100 to 150 meters south of the Marines, it is probable that a sniper was located there.

Then, Brown stated, "Pfc. Underdue came to—he had been knocked out for a few seconds. Sergeant Houdashelt asked if he could still shoot. Pfc. Underdue said 'Yes,' and continued shooting. Sergeant Houdashelt kept on the radio."

As Underdue described it: "A few minutes later I got to Sergeant Houdashelt. He asked if I could shoot. I told him I was okay. Then I said, 'Jerry, put the radio down. You got the medevac coming in. Start throwing grenades.' "

Their position was getting worse—from ten to fifteen enemy soldiers were closing on the three remaining Marines—and Underdue yelled at the sergeant, "Pull back, we're getting overrun." Then Underdue said, "No sooner had I started moving back than a grenade landed on top or next to him. The grenade went off. I hollered out twice [for Houdashelt] with no answer."

Brown remembered:

Sergeant Houdashelt kept on the radio. He said something about having to get the pack. Pfc. Underdue said there wasn't time. Then Chicom grenades went off. You could hear them making a funny noise. One of those went off, landing right by or on the sergeant. Underdue had yelled 'Incoming.' He [Houdashelt] couldn't get out of the way. It hit him. That's all we heard from the sergeant. Pfc. Underdue, I thought he was dead, too, then [he] crawled over to where I was. I just kept shooting. I never did manage to get back to all my gear—ammo and grenades. I got ahold of Doc's, and I was shooting his ammo. Underdue crawled to where I was, and he started throwing grenades. I kept shooting. After throwing five or six grenades, we moved off the hill to the north side.

Everybody else was dead. We think there must have been a sniper on another part of the ridge. His shots were hitting right in there. Pfc. Pitts was hit right between the eyes, and Pfc. Harris only moaned for a couple of seconds. We estimated that between ten and fifteen soldiers attacked us, plus there was a sniper, and whatever they had farther down the hill. Then we moved through the brush and into the canopy, about one hundred to two hundred meters down the hill.

It was at this time that the rain really engulfed the valley. Brown stated that "it was raining pretty hard." The two survivors crawled downhill through heavy brush and into canopy on the edge of the valley floor near a creek. That was where Sergeant Karkos's patrol two months earlier had positioned itself and spotted more than 200 enemy.

Helicopters arrived over the ridgeline above the two Marines, and one even landed for a few seconds at their old position; however, the Marines could not be seen, and enemy forces drove the choppers away. Underdue and Brown managed to move across the valley floor and evade detection. They had neither map nor compass, but followed the sounds of artillery booming from the distant Camp Evans. The following day the two were picked up near Hill 51 by a patrol from Bravo Company, 1st Battalion, 9th Marines, and were returned to the battalion.

The battalion commander, Lieutenant Colonel Kent, stated that this patrol leader was new and had made a mistake when he stayed in the same location at which the team had been inserted. He commented on the patrol:

> They were hit in a counterrecon move. That was the mission of that enemy unit—to look for Marine Recon teams. I don't think there's any doubt about that.
>
> It was a helluva thing. I don't understand why people would stay in one spot like that. I know that under the leadership of other, more experienced, patrol leaders the team would be on the move and very careful. The harbor site, for example, would not be moved into until after a feint. The team would locate temporarily in a site at dusk. Then after it would be a little darker, they would move out of that site to another just in case they had been spotted. It was a thing you were taught and learned. If you wanted to get the job done and live, you had to take that kind of extra effort.

However, shortly after the January 2 patrol, Delta Company was sent to Quang Tri to begin construction of the new battalion command post, and the battalion CP Forward, with Kent in command, was shifted for the interim to Dong Ha. Basically, for most of the month of January, the Hue–Phu Bai area was left with only one Recon "letter" company, Alpha, and the "rear" battalion command.

At the Khe Sanh Combat Base (KSCB), after about January 20, the ability of Bravo Company to send out patrols was severely limited by the heavy enemy activity, and at times no patrols were allowed. Kent said, "Colonel Lownds [commanding officer of the 26th Marines at the KSCB] wouldn't send them out. We thought about the possibility of jumping the Force people in deep beyond the immediate Khe Sanh fighting perimeter. We practiced them parachuting near Quang Tri. Although we never used it, we wanted to be ready in case we had to." Colonel Kent had also unsuccessfully argued that since it could no longer fulfill a reconnaissance mission at the KSCB, Bravo Company should be relocated back to the Quang Tri CP.

During the time period leading up to the initiation of the "General Offensive and Uprising" on January 30–31, Recon teams continued to operate along the infiltration routes near the DMZ. On October 3, 1967, Charlie Company had moved from Phu Bai to Dong Ha, joining the 3rd Force to patrol that sector. One of the dictated-from-on-high tactical efforts to stem the flow of the North Vietnamese across the Demilitarized Zone was the strong point obstacle system (SPOS)—the McNamara Line. To build the actual barrier of wire and mines, the Marine Corps command had estimated that 672 Marines would be killed and 3,788 wounded. This estimate was based on initial experiences with the first phases of the project. As a result, MACV ordered the construction of the strong points first. The project caused serious command difficulties because General Westmoreland was never satisfied with progress on the project. Despite heavy rains and enemy activity, the engineers of the 11th Engineer Battalion pushed through with the construction of Route 561 from Cam Lo, through C-2, past Con Thien and to the barrier parallel to the DMZ. Gravel had to be trucked fifteen miles from near Camp Carroll. Interest was so intense from Washington, D.C., and MACV in Saigon that Westmoreland ordered General Cushman, CG of III MAF, to take immediate steps to correct deficiencies and to exert better quality control. As a result, Cushman assigned Maj. Gen. Raymond Murray to oversee the project.

By mid-December, significant progress had been made. All bunkers for the fortified camps at A-2, C-2, and C-4 were in place. The engineers had also completed the gravel-base construction of Route 561 from Cam Lo to Con Thien. Although not asphalted, the route could now handle 60-ton truck traffic during the rains, and it didn't turn into a complete sucking quagmire. Since 3rd Recon did not have sufficient helicopters, the new roadway allowed it to send out patrols by truck during the monsoons. However, this also meant that quite often the teams served as foot patrols in the immediate vicinity of the newly fortified strong points, such as C-2, while the infantry worked on the fortifications. Both 3rd Force and Charlie companies ran the teams from Dong Ha. The routine consisted of an early-morning truck trip from Dong Ha out Route 9 to Cam Lo, then a turn up 561 to C-2. From there, the team walked out.

As Bobby Hall said, "The terrain was a Recon Marine's worst nightmare. It was flat and open, with tree lines located occasionally to give the patrol the feeling that they were being watched."

Roy Sykes, a Charlie Company team member with Hall, added, "You were seen from everywhere out there. They knew where we were."

The terrain was so flat for so long that it was about 7,000 meters (4.3 miles) before one could find a small hill noted on the maps as 162 (162 meters, 531 feet, above sea level). However, even though the terrain was relatively flat, there were numerous thickets and draws for concealment. It had been easy traveling for the NVA moving into South Vietnam. But just what the on-the-ground enemy situation was remained unknown for the Marines being sent to patrol the area. Both Hall and Sykes stated that they had no idea what to expect.

On January 12, 1968, Cpl. Roberto Navarrete led a patrol west of the C-2 area with Hall, Sykes, L.Cpl. James Alderman, "Doc" Jerry Peterson, Lance Corporal Sheehan, Pfc. Thompson, and Pfc. Wright. The team was trucked from Dong Ha to C-2 early and moved out from there at about 0800 hours. During that first day the team moved about 2,000 meters toward the west, carefully walking through the bush across the low, rolling terrain, trying to stay hidden among the thickets, but feeling very exposed.

Sometime in the afternoon of that first day, the team heard Vietnamese voices. The men stayed low in the bush and listened as the voices moved close around them. Not knowing exactly what they were hearing, the patrol leader called for artillery, hoping to flush whatever it might be out of the thick brush. The Marines stayed down, and the big guns slammed the neighborhood. At first the Vietnamese voices became louder, then they disappeared. However, no bodies were sighted.

The Recon team then carefully continued on its patrol route—doing its best to find cover and stay out of sight. There were no additional "sightings" that day; however, after the team was in its harbor site that evening, Vietnamese voices were heard again. The Reconners didn't know where the Vietnamese were going, or if the VC knew there was a Recon team on patrol. However, past patrols had taken casualties in the same general area.

Early the next morning, the Reconners moved out. There was no evidence of Vietnamese. All was quiet. The team was moving to the northwest. The brush was very tough to move through, but it wasn't long before the team encountered a wide path that could have been used to "drive a tank down," in the words of Bobby Hall. The patrol decided to avoid the heavy bush for a while and use the path. However, evidence of past action along the roadway was seen. Bobby Hall ran point, and he quietly led the team along the road. At one point, Hall carefully stepped around an American helmet in the path. No one touched it.

During that morning the team continued to encounter NVA patrols in the area. Navarrete stated that he felt the numbers of NVA patrols were indicative of a buildup to attack or harass C-2. The patrol leader received word to begin to maneuver out of the area back toward C-2.

The team then crossed a large path where it forked into two minor trails through the waist-high grass. In front of the Marines was a low knoll overgrown by grass and some thickets. To one side of it was a grove of trees. One fork of the trail led in front of the trees, between the team and the high ground; the other skirted the opposite side of the knoll. Hall began to carefully push down the trail that would have led the team between the trees and the knoll.

Lance Corporal Alderman was supposed to have been point man that day, and he had a full year's experience under his belt, but he was running second behind Hall. Intuition or whatever, Alderman was concerned about the patrol, and he damn sure wanted to get back to the States alive and healthy. At this point Hall said he felt Alderman grab him from behind and quietly motion him to lead the patrol to the opposite side of the trees. Walking down the path toward the trees, with the high ground on one side and the trees on the other, rubbed against his instincts. The veteran was right, but none knew for certain at that instant.

Hall said:

The trees were now on my left and a big open area, about the size of a football field, was on my right, and then another tree line appeared across our front ahead of us. I started to hug the cover provided by the trees on my left, and I was getting ready to move into the trees when I heard someone quietly call my name. Alderman was behind me, and it must have been him.

The bush was about chest-high on Hall, and the trees and thickets that rose well over his head were immediately to his left. Hall said that he didn't respond to the low voice behind him because at that moment he had stepped into a narrow path that he hadn't seen before. The thickets closed tightly on the trail that was only half a foot wide.

Hall looked to the right and left. The trail ran into the tree growth, and Hall was nervous.

Then, about ten feet away, Hall saw the back of a large NVA soldier who was standing in the trail. Sandwiched in the thick brush on the trail, Hall slowly and quietly squatted. The NVA was talking to someone else in the brush whom Hall couldn't see. The Recon team had moved quietly, and even though only ten feet from the Marines, the enemy hadn't heard them.

Hall said:

As I crouched low in the trail another NVA came out of the bush, and then two more. The four were standing in a circle talking and quietly laughing. I didn't know what they were saying, but I felt that they must have been discussing our patrol's location. I think they had an ambush set on the other side of the trees and were now in the process of adjusting its location since we hadn't accommodated them by walking into it. I think they were setting up a new ambush on this side of the tree line, but we had gotten there first.

He continued:

I glanced back for the rest of the patrol. But they weren't to be seen. What I didn't know was that they had already gotten low in the bush behind me. Kneeling in the trail, I could still see the NVA ahead of me. I'll never forget that they were wearing fresh, light-green, clean uniforms that caught a person's attention. The guy that stood with his back to me was big, broad-shouldered, and when he turned around I remember noticing that he had very white teeth and a red star in the middle of his helmet. The helmet had netting around it.

As Hall squatted in that narrow trail with the thickets almost covering him and NVA soldiers turning to walk toward him, only three paces away, he wondered who was going to die and if it would be him.

He continued:

Two of the soldiers ran off into the bush, and the other two started in my direction. I didn't know that Roy, who was our radio operator, was already in contact with our command center back in Dong Ha and sending out the warning that we were about to make contact. From my perspective, I was alone, getting ready to introduce myself to two NVA soldiers. One was the big guy, and the other had stars on both collars of his uniform.

Roy Sykes, on the PRC-25, was down in the weeds a few paces behind Hall. No one had to tell him what to do. The members of the patrol behind Hall were in a better position to see the NVA than the point man. They had seen the NVA first, but didn't know exactly how many there were nor just how wide the enemy position might be. It didn't make any difference to Sykes; he was quickly whispering through the radio back to the battalion COC. His words: "We're going to be in contact. We've just walked around one ambush and now are going into another."

Not knowing that the battalion headquarters was in touch with the team, and not even knowing for sure where the rest of the team was, Hall was crouched low in the trail. He said:

I believe that the training I received back in Camp Pendleton [California] saved my life on this day. What had happened at Pendleton involved a counterguerrilla warfare training exercise in which I stepped into a "native" hut and faced two important-looking "enemy" officer types. I didn't fire, and they pointed a gun at me and declared me dead. This time I stood up facing the two NVA walking toward me, and instinctively fired my rifle, hitting the big guy just in front of me. I watched his face show shock as he stared in disbelief at me. I fired two more times. Then his eyes rolled back, and it was like I could see the life leaving his body. Then he fell over on his rifle.

Sykes keyed the handset into the speaking position to allow the rear command group to listen to the gunshots so that the beginning of their battle could be audibly verified.

Hall said:

Then it seemed like the longest time that I stared face-to-face with the second NVA, the one with stars on his collar. He didn't have a weapon. He was looking steadily at me, and then he calmly bent over right in front of me and started to pull the big guy's weapon from under him. That's when I fired again and again. And he flipped over, and I watched his eyes go blank.

Sykes was now talking loudly on the radio: "Get the choppers out here and get us out."

In the meantime, Hall was hastily getting away from the trail and looking for his mates. He said:

Then I ran toward the patrol and found them just behind me. Immediately, a Chicom grenade flew over our heads and exploded behind us. It didn't hit anybody. Then I threw a grenade back, and it blew and was followed by screams. Corporal Navarrete threw another. It exploded, and the screams stopped. The NVA were firing their rifles in our direction but probably couldn't see us.

Navarrete had command of the situation and was issuing orders to Lance Corporal Alderman, giving directions to Hall concerning the direction they needed to take to get out of the danger zone.

Hall said, "Then Alderman told me that Navarrete wanted to pull away from the tree line back across the field behind us. The idea was to back off and call in supporting arms and get the hell out of there. So I took off to lead the patrol. As we got out into the field, the NVA started shooting at us, and now I figured they could see us."

The Marines zigzagged across the open, somehow not taking casualties. Then the patrol leader, realizing that he was missing a man, called a halt to their run.

Hall said:

Alderman grabbed me from behind and yelled at me to stop. All I wanted to do was to get across the open, because the grass was so short that it was like your front lawn. When I looked back to where Alderman was motioning, I saw Corporal Navarrete racing back through enemy fire to grab Thompson, who had become separated from us back near the tree line. So the rest of us set up covering fire for the two of them. Navarrete got to Thompson and was pulling him back to us, and we were firing like hell to protect them. Thank God Roy Sykes was still on the radio. As we had been running and firing, he was calling in air support.

During this firefight, the body of the Reconners battled with the enemy to keep them from being able to focus on Navarrete and Thompson, who were almost within a handshake of the NVA. It took tremendous courage for the patrol leader to do what he did. Hall was standing exposed to enemy fire while he kept his rifle blazing back at the enemy in the tree line.

Sykes hardly had time to fire his weapon, as he had the handset stuck to his head to get friendly air support to their position. The team was still close enough to the trees to hear the enemy call out orders to each other. Then Navarrete and Thompson raced back, and the patrol leader directed fire for Lance Corporal Sheehan, who was lobbing his M-79 grenades into the thicket. Doc Peterson, Pfc. Wright (rear point), and Alderman were also coordinating fire from their side of the defensive line. The Reconners were firing while circling their wagons, fearful that there could be more enemy coming from the opposite tree line. In the meantime, Sykes had brought in an AO above them, and between those two, helicopter gunship attacks on the enemy-held tree line were being coordinated. The battle lasted for an hour and a half before the rescue birds were able to reach the team.

Then a CH-46 dropped out of the sky and landed tailgate down near them. The Marines rushed for the bird while still under fire from the enemy force. Quickly inside, the Marines joined the chopper's gunner in returning a fusillade against the NVA. Taking hits, the chopper lifted into the safety of the distant skies and landed the team at the C-2 combat base less than 2,000 meters away. From there the team watched the fixed-wing attacks by F-4 Phantom jets. Sykes said the Phantoms cremated the place. The following day, the infantry reported finding eighteen enemy dead in the battlefield.

However, after a short time, the team was picked up by other helicopters and returned to Dong Ha. Both Sykes and Hall stated that they were surprised by some of the command criticism they received about their conduct of the patrol, and they were told that the patrol would return very shortly into the same area. Sykes stated, "The next patrol, we were sent out by helicopter into the same area, but we never even landed. We were shot out of the place by enemy fire. Even though, it was all burned off—there was nothing left. We still got shot out of there before we could get out of the helicopters. The NVA were still thick as flies out there. There really seemed to be a major buildup."

Hall added, "The enemy soldiers I saw seemed to be fresh and in good spirits."

Navarrete stated that two patrols later his team found an NVA base camp and field hospital in the same area. This was immediately prior to the Tet Offensive, but the Reconners did not know of the massive nationwide Vietcong and NVA offensive that was to kick off within days.

As a result of the action, Hall got a stripe back that he had lost in Phu Bai, receiving a meritorious promotion to lance corporal. Roy Sykes received a Bronze Star for his radio work. The Marines continued to patrol the Leatherneck Square area encompassed by the SPOS: McNamara's Line.

The NVA were coming across the DMZ in preparation for the Tet Offensive, and because they did not want to be located, they might occasionally have seen some Recon teams and let them pass. The teams were dropped off or picked up by truck, or walked out in terrain that was flat to rolling with open, grassy areas. This allowed for any enemy located in observation positions in the few tree groves or other positions on the limited plots of high ground to see the teams coming. The NVA could navigate the terrain at night, and by using the dry streambeds and the cover offered in those and other locations, they could pass through the area more easily than they could travel in the mountains. The distance from the DMZ to Route 9 at Cam Lo was only about eight miles.

At this time much of the Marine infantry was being used as sand-baggers and construction laborers to build the strongpoints along the SPOS. The system called for the construction of four company strongpoints and two battalion base areas, all within the 9th Marines' TAOR. Only one reinforced Marine regiment between Quang Tri and the DMZ and the ARVN units in the area had the responsibility of both conducting offensive operations against enemy units and assisting in the construction of the barrier. The Marines were fixed into static positions located within striking distance of NVA artillery.

Regardless, construction of the SPOS continued, and Recon patrols walked out from the individual combat bases doing short-range, infantry-type reconnaissance missions nearby, while the grunts filled sandbags and dodged incoming artillery. The Reconners invariably felt the presence of enemy eyes boring holes into their backs, and some of these walk-out patrols from the Leatherneck Square bases had deadly results.

On February 15, 1968, a 3rd Force team of eight Marines led by Lt. Terry Graves walked out from approximately the same location as Sykes and Hall. However, their orders took them east instead of west. Soon after the start of the patrol, Lieutenant Graves and his Marines ambushed and killed seven NVA but found themselves immediately surrounded by an estimated company of NVA infantry. The Marines suffered five killed, three wounded, and one helicopter shot down.

The bravery and sacrifice of one Reconner for another cannot be better shown than in the actions of Lieutenant Graves, Cpl. Danny Slocum, and Pfc. James Honeycutt. As one UH-34 tried to rescue the eight Marines and was overloading its capabilities while being shot full of holes by point-blank NVA fire, Lieutenant Graves, alone on the ground and under enemy fire, waved off the chopper. He knew the chopper would have a difficult enough time getting off the ground without him; it definitely would not make it with him. By himself, and already wounded, he stayed to defend the attempts to take off. Then the wounded Slocum and Honeycutt realized what the lieutenant was doing and jumped out of the bird to face what was likely to be their deaths also. They would die with their lieutenant in the hope that the others might make it. The pilot was reluctant to leave them, but with every second bringing more destruction to his metal bird, he lifted the shattered chopper into the air.

The chopper was able to return with the five Reconners, but three died of their wounds. Of the three who remained on the ground, only Danny Slocum survived. Posthumously, Lieutenant Graves received the Medal of Honor; James Honeycutt, the Navy Cross; and Cpl. Robert Thomson the Silver Star. Corporal Slocum and Doc Thompson also received the Silver Star. Five Reconners were killed, including Adrian Lopez and Steven Emrick, and three were wounded, including Michael Nation.

Many Recon teams were encountering enemy forces during the period just before Tet. During January, while Bravo Company suffered the most casualties at Khe Sanh, Charlie and Delta companies each took eight KIA, and Alpha suffered six deaths. Of the eight KIAs sustained by Company C, six were killed on one patrol north of the Rockpile in the third week of the month, just prior to Lieutenant Graves's last patrol. It was another walk-out patrol, but this time from near the Rockpile. The history of the battalion was filled many times over with lessons learned about walk-out patrols, particularly in the open and in the daylight. However, the lessons were ignored or forgotten by those in command, possibly due to the pressing need to get more patrols in the field but without sufficient helicopters available.

This team's call sign was Little Gull. The op order stated, "Patrol will not be extracted until the RZ (recon zone) is sufficiently covered." It was rough terrain, and the eight-man team took four days to make a four-mile trip. The team was dropped off by truck at a river just below the friendly positions near the foot of that tall mass of rock that jutted out of the valley floor like a lonely cliff to the left of the Reconners as they worked to the north. Not far past the Rockpile, and easily visible to the northwest, was the Razorback, which rose up out of the earth like the armored back of some prehistoric dinosaur. The team started at sea level near the Trinh Hin River, just off Route 9, moved across brushland in the midday, and slowly climbed higher into the jungled hills. The Nui Cay Tre was Hill 484, and it was the last point on the team's patrol route. Somewhere along their route enemy soldiers had sighted them, and they watched and waited for the Marines.

On day four, January 19, the team was still trying to fulfill its orders by covering the entire RZ. They had now reached the top of Hill 484. The Marines tried to cross the summit, which was about 400 by 100 meters, carefully and reach a suitable landing zone. They had been told to relocate to another spot that would be better than where they initially set up. Then the eight Marines were caught in a platoon-size ambush. The Vietnamese were well armed, using U.S. M-79s, M-26 (U.S.-made) grenades, and automatic weapons to cut the Marines down from as close as 20 to 30 meters. Four Americans lay dead in the first seconds. The point and a Vietnamese Kit Carson scout were in advance and not hit. The point shouted to his teammates (only three of whom were still alive) that he was coming back to help. The three were returning fire with their M-16s and grenades. After the point shouted, and as he was attempting to get back through the elephant grass, a long burst of automatic weapons fire sounded from his direction. That was the last they heard from the point man. The Vietnamese Kit Carson scout had disappeared. Later he would return to Marine lines reporting that he had been captured by the enemy but had overpowered his captors and escaped through the NVA positions.

The secondary radio operator was wounded, but crawled to the one working radio and attempted to notify the battalion of the situation. At that time, he was about 20 meters from the other two surviving Reconners, who could hear his voice shouting on the radio above the firing. Then he was hit again, and killed. The two Marines remaining kept firing for thirty more minutes. Three NVA were killed by the two as they tried to attack the Marines. Then the Reconners, one of whom was wounded, maneuvered back downhill in the direction of the Rockpile, a long four miles in the distance. The enemy tried to cut them off, but the Marines continued to move and evade. They managed to avoid the enemy until darkness provided them the concealment they desperately needed. During the morning of the twentieth, they were able to signal an AO, and were shortly picked up by a helicopter.

Mike Englebert, a member of the Little Gull team until this patrol, was just returning from recuperation for a back injury when he saw the team ready to board the truck for its Rough Rider insertion. He ran to pack his gear to go with the team, but was too late. Englebert said that he did not understand the composition of Little Gull for that patrol because only the patrol leader, Retshulte, and one other member were experienced. The rest were new to the battalion.

In the weeks leading to the Tet Offensive, as 3rd Recon patrols were being hammered or were themselves raining American artillery and air support down on enemy units, the Allied command did not understand that many of the enemy units the patrols were supposed to be blocking were, in fact, already behind them, in the urban centers. Except for the battle for Hue City, most of the Tet Offensive was borne by units of the Vietcong that had previously been thought to be decimated.

The Vietcong Tet Offensive also seemed to surprise some North Vietnamese. A Vietnamese with the 304th NVA Division stated:

> Until then, even most of the North Vietnamese officers thought that the Vietcong was severely decimated. Even after the beginning of the Vietcong uprising all over the country, there are still very different opinions within the North Vietnamese officer corps. It is not at all clear to them what the actual strength of the Vietcong is. . . . To be sure, the Vietcong and the North Vietnamese are the closest of allies and each depends upon the other. But, nonetheless, each seems to distrust the other.*

In the BDM Corporation study of the war, General Westmoreland is quoted on the surprise of the Tet Offensive:

> As General Davidson (MACV J-2) put it to me later: "Even had I known exactly what was to take place, it was so preposterous that I probably would have been unable to sell it to anybody. Why would the enemy give away his major advantage, which was his ability to be elusive and avoid heavy casualties?"
> He was no doubt right. When I asked Jack Seaman, commander of the II Field Force, in the summer of 1966 to prepare a war game based around the worst possible contingency in the region around Saigon, his staff had come up with almost exactly what did happen in 1968, but even though the appraisal alerted us to the possibility, we deemed it at the time unlikely.

Therefore, despite certain intelligence data—including that gathered by Recon teams near Hue—indicating that the enemy was preparing for a major attack on the country's population centers, the U.S. and ARVN commands did not consider the NVA/VC capable of launching this attack, and they disregarded Hanoi's long-standing intentions.

The 50 percent estimated enemy battle casualties were in large part suffered by the Vietcong and not by the units of the North Vietnamese Army, and those casualty figures may well have been grossly wrong.

*The author of this article, which appeared in *Weser Kurier* in Bremen, Germany, on February 15, 1968, two weeks after the beginning of that offensive, also stated that he had asked General Giap if the impending attack on Khe Sanh was to be America's Dien Bien Phu. Morale among the NVA troops had been high, and the phrase Dien Bien Phu was a rallying point. He said that Giap smiled and answered, "One can in no phase of the fighting compare the situation of the Americans with that of the French fifteen years ago."

CHAPTER SIXTEEN

The Backyard

Enemy Order of Battle (OB) estimates published by the III Marine Amphibious Force during the first three months of 1968 and during the Tet Offensive give some indication of the miscalculations of the casualties suffered by the enemy. On January 1, 1968, there was an estimated total enemy strength throughout I Corps of 27,110. During that month, III MAF reported that 8,407 of the enemy were killed. On February 1, III MAF estimated that there was a total enemy strength in I Corps of 26,100. Then, during February, 14,344 enemy were reported killed. At the beginning of March, the estimated enemy OB listed 21,925 troops. Finally, during March, 9,203 more enemy dead were added to the KIA roster. However, by the end of March, the enemy was estimated as having 32,095 soldiers in the field in I Corps— more than he had at the beginning of January (27,110), but after he supposedly suffered the estimated 31,954 killed.

Battalion commander Bill Kent had described the intelligence situation as a "black hole," but he was also glad to be able to consolidate his units. He said:

> When 1967 closed, Recon Battalion was into some big organizational and geographical changes that were to have major impacts on how and where we operated in '68. Company E had been formed at Quang Tri with the numbers the battalion gained with the deactivation of the Antitank Battalion. I continued to operate the Battalion Command Post Forward from the Force Company Command Operations Center at Dong Ha and largely concerned myself with things going on north of Quang Tri and at Khe Sanh. Frank Baulch, my ExO, ran things at Phu Bai with H & S Company and Company A. Company C and

Force were at Dong Ha; Company D was working on the new camp at the Quang Tri airfield; and, of course, Company B (reinforced) was still attached to the 26th Marines and very busy at Khe Sanh. We were looking forward to the time when the camp and COC were to be completed at Quang Tri and the consolidation of effort that would bring. This view [looking forward to consolidation] was not necessarily shared by the companies—particularly Force. Company E departed for Okinawa to train before becoming operationally ready.

We continued to maintain Recon representatives with the infantry regiments, and they were our eyes and ears closest to the maneuver battalions. They played a major part in the construction of the Recon plan and kept me informed of what the regiments were thinking and doing on a day-to-day basis. They also kept the infantry S-3s and fire support coordinators informed of where our patrols were located.

Because December '67 had seen so much enemy activity in the Khe Sanh area, General Thompkins (3rd MarDiv CG) directed me to reinforce Company B at Khe Sanh with an additional platoon. I tried to convince him not only not to reinforce, but to ease Company B out and keep them in the Recon business, but it was a no-go. So Phil Reynolds [Bravo Company CO] and his guys got the long and shitty job of mostly sitting in the 5V ring [i.e., the center of the bull's-eye for the NVA artillery and rockets].

It was during February that Lt. Terry Graves won his Medal of Honor and was killed. A real shit sandwich that epitomized the nature of the fighting that went on in the greater Leatherneck Square area. It was a snapshot of what we found ourselves into in that area: a patrol loaded for bear and tasked with several alternative missions; a hard-charging new lieutenant; an area always full of bad guys who would stick to you like glue if you made contact; a surplus of supporting arms to the point of making it difficult to integrate their fires; and dwindling daylight. Lots of heroics, lots of everything except the ability to act directly to influence the action. What a helluva feeling. It still hurts.

At the end of January, as the Tet Offensive was about to explode on the scene, a patrol led by Cpl. Charles Achberger entered an area between Dong Ha and Quang Tri, about six klicks west of Highway One, in an area called the Backyard. The team's call sign was Hayride, and the team was largely composed of the same Marines who'd been part of Corporal Navarrete's team. Again Bobby Hall was on point and Roy Sykes was on the radio. It was standard for these patrols to be trucked out Route 9 from Dong Ha toward Cam Lo. Then they would be dropped off or the trucks would turn south off the main road and travel along dirt roads deeper into the Backyard. If the latter was the case the team would jump from the trucks near where the road (quite often Route 559) turned back to the east. From there the teams would move into their assigned recon zone, while the truck drove for its life out of the area. Sometimes the patrol's mission would take it by foot a long way, across the Vinh Phouc River and back to Highway One. That was the route used by Corporal Achberger's team.

On this day, the team moved the long distance south and crossed the Vinh Phouc to set into an afternoon observation position. The terrain was very open, and the Marines quickly noted enemy soldiers on Hill 58, near Route 604, which was on the pathway back to Highway One. The team was very near the river, and 604 paralleled the Vinh Phouc, which was only one or two klicks away. Hayride was in the field only three hours when an NVA unit of about fifteen men opened fire on the Marines from a small ridge not far away. They returned fire, called in helicopter gunships, and moved away into better concealment. They felt that they were still in terrain that was too open and their position could still be compromised.

Lance Corporal Sykes stated:

We called for an extraction but were denied—they felt the situation wasn't bad enough. . . . We figured we'd get hit that night, so we sat in some bushes until just before dark, when we moved about a hundred meters into another set of bushes. Well, just after dark, automatic weapons fire opened up all around us, but aimed at the area we had just left. They blew those bushes apart. We saw enemy walking the area with flashlights looking for us! We called for an extraction again, but it was a negative. They said it was too dark and there was too much enemy activity around. At one point, I guess the NVA were within about twenty feet of us, and I just laid there trying to keep it quiet on the radio. Then we heard all kinds of fire again. We called in gunships, but it was too dark, and they couldn't find us. So one gunship was going to come in low and was going to drop a flare, so we could direct him from the flare. He took a heavy volume of fire: M-79 or 40-mm fire, .50-caliber fire, .30-caliber, AK-47 fire, carbines. And he put out his lights and pulled back up to the other gunship. He and the other pilot were talking and decided to get the hell out of there because it was too hot. He advised us if we came under fire to get the hell out of there because the place was swarming with enemy. . . .

So we called in our on-call artillery around us and stayed down. All through the night we heard rockets being fired at Quang Tri, and some landed near us—I would say within seventy-five feet of us. We couldn't even stick up our heads—didn't dare stick up our heads—to try to find where they were. We just reported an azimuth to where we heard the rockets coming from. . . .

The next morning was foggy, and the team started to move out of the area, but as the morning overcast began to clear the team received some sniper fire. The Reconners continued to try to avoid the enemy, who seemed to still be around but not in the same numbers as the night before. That first day the Marine command had no idea how serious the situation was in many of the cities of South Vietnam as Vietcong and NVA units were attacking throughout the country.

Later that day, Hall saw one NVA soldier who waved at him but then realized Hall was an American and quickly disappeared. Sykes said, "So we kept moving and went down into a ville that we were going to search. We saw a bunker in this ville with two helmets sitting beside it, and a couple of bush covers hangin' on a tree."

As the Marines carefully moved forward, they sighted two VC near the bunker. However, before the Recon team could take them under fire, the enemy saw them and ran for cover out of the village. Sykes said:

> The bunker looked deep and was heavily fortified. It had a five-foot gun port. The ville was supposed to be abandoned. Everywhere we'd go around the ville we'd see Vietnamese. We'd walk up a hill, and there'd be NVA on top of it, so we'd go back down. We'd go up another hill and there'd be more up there. There'd be four or five or two or three at a time. They all had AK-47s and were dressed in green with camouflaged pith helmets. Everywhere we'd go there'd be NVA. Then we saw fifteen NVA walking toward where we'd just walked. We called for gunships, but we couldn't get them. They didn't have any available. Finally, an Army ship came over and started to fire on these NVA. As he fired, the NVA scattered for cover.

However, this gunship was not called by the Marines. He had spotted them and swung around for a run on what he apparently believed to be NVA, but they quickly held up an air panel and waved him off before he unleashed friendly fire on them. After escaping problems with the gunship, the team was told to walk back; on the way they would pass another Recon team set in ambush to cover their return.

More patrols followed this one into the Backyard. Typical patrol reports concluded with statements such as these:

> (1) Area covered by patrol reveals heavy movement to the northeast; there could be some type of tracked vehicles operating in the area; trails in the area reveal heavy, recent use; the enemy appears to be infiltrating through the area; (2) area covered by patrol reveals enemy troops living in the area, large enemy units observed in the area . . .

heavy enemy activity . . . team appears to have made contact with estimated company-size unit; this area has been the area of operations for
an enemy battalion for quite some time; Recon teams have made large
sightings and contacts throughout the area.

February and March were largely spent supporting the fight around
Leatherneck Square and getting ready for the relief of Khe Sanh. The
battalion paid more attention to areas around Camp Carroll, the Rockpile, the Ba Long Valley, and the new LZ Stud between the Rockpile
and Ca Lu. Task Force Hotel, under a new assistant division commander, General Hoffman, was put together to run the Marine part of
the relief of Khe Sanh from Stud, and Lieutenant Colonel Kent was
responsible for the creation of the supporting Recon plan. During that
period, 3rd Recon established a program to exchange patrol leaders
on a limited basis with the 1st Recon Battalion and the Army. Men
were also sent to the Army's LRRP Recondo School at Nha Trang,
and to scuba school at Subic Bay in the Philippines. Within the battalion, on selected patrols there was an increased use of dog teams,
Kit Carson scouts, and snipers. Force even began to arrange a few
practice jumps into zones secured at Quang Tri. Kent says, "I felt that
the new centralized camp at Quang Tri began to have a positive effect
on the command and control of battalion operations and training."

The battalion commander felt the Recon teams were doing good
work, but occasionally tragedy still struck. He said:

There was one case where the mistake was made worse by rear area decisions. It was a situation where a patrol located comm wire and followed it to a cave on a ridgeline overlooking Camp Carroll. The patrol
leader heard VC voices from within, and instead of laying low and
watching, he pops in a CS grenade. He stirred up a hornet's nest of enemy soldiers who outnumbered the team significantly. The donnybrook
that followed resulted in the loss of the patrol leader [Lt. Donald Ma-
tocha], and a Sparrow Hawk reaction force that was mauled by booby
traps and mortar fire. Since the patrol leader's body was not recovered,
the division CG tells me to go get the body. I tell him the job ought to
be done by an infantry sweep. But that doesn't sell. So I have to send
another patrol in, and they get their asses knocked off with two more
dead Reconners [Gary Meyers and Carlos Dominguez] and a wounded
Recon lieutenant [Lt. Edward Osborne]. Finally, months later, the remains of the dead patrol leader were recovered by an infantry sweep.

That first Recon patrol occurred on April 4–5, 1968, on a ridgeline
across the Cam Lo River from the village of the same name. It was the

same ridge in the same recon zone to which Captain Best and Lieutenant Buhl had led a combined patrol two years earlier and noted strong evidence of the enemy's presence. George Neville noted rock latrines built by enemy forces on that '66 patrol, and all members on the Recon team "smelled" bad news everywhere—and they were only a few thousand meters from Cam Lo.

Like the Best-Buhl patrol, the 1968 team went out afoot, crossing the river in about the same place as the 1966 team. There were ten men, including the new lieutenant, a Kit Carson scout, and a corpsman. This time, the Reconners suffered one killed—the lieutenant—and five wounded. Their patrol report states:

> Patrol moving up toward the top of a hill . . . found a two-foot-wide trail . . . appeared to be well used . . . found comm wire running along next to the trail . . . spliced in several places . . . observed a portion of an 82-mm mortar tube . . . also observed two-man fighting holes as they moved up the hill . . . heard talking and observed what appeared to be the opening of a bunker built into the back of the rocks . . . point threw a CS grenade into the opening . . . 4–5 NVA ran from the opening. . . . The patrol initiated SAF [small arms fire] resulting in 4 NVA KIA (confirmed) . . . enemy began to exit bunker from another entrance and patrol also received some SAF . . . and grenades [from] an estimated 15 NVA.

The patrol continued the firefight, tried to maneuver to a better position, and called for extraction; however, the team had one KIA and five WIA, one of whom was missing (the Kit Carson scout received a minor wound and made his way out of the area; he was safely rescued by another Recon team).

The patrol report continues: "Transport helos came in to extract the patrol . . . wounded were hoisted . . . Patrol could not find KCS [nor] recover body of KIA . . . Assistant Patrol Leader checked the area . . . remaining members of the patrol were hoisted into transport helos . . . were receiving sporadic SAF during the extraction . . ." The final conclusions were that the bunker appeared to be a forward observer position. It had "an outstanding view of the Camp Carroll–Cam Lo area."

Lieutenant Colonel Kent stated:

> During this time I think that division was getting its full value from Recon. We were more flexible and economical with our resources. The battalion won a Navy Unit Citation for its actions during the '67–'68 time period. After Khe Sanh was abandoned, in May and June the battalion camp at Quang Tri really filled out. All the companies were

brought back to it, except for Force. We patrolled the old Khe Sanh areas with small patrols, and it was during this time that the NVA began to use the Quang Tri River west of the city.

As with all good Marine outfits that stick in your memory, it is the people who make it what it is. People who did more than what they were asked to do as a rule rather than as an exception. In my view, 3rd Recon—reinforced with the Force companies at different times—made a chunk of Marine Corps history, and they have every right to be damned proud of that fact. The Corps said go do it, and, by God, they did it proper!

During the entire period in which the battalion served its country in Vietnam, Marine and Army pilots and crews continuously braved enemy fire to support and rescue Reconnaissance teams battling overwhelming odds. The Army had many more of the better choppers, and their warrant officer pilots were extraordinarily fearless, but the Marine pilots were the mainstay of the Reconnaissance inserts and extractions. In the months prefacing the Tet Offensive, then during those battles and after, many Recon teams were lifted out of deadly situations on ridgelines, deep within the jungle, and in fog-enshrouded valleys by one Marine pilot who should be especially noted in the annals of 3rd Recon Battalion history. That Marine pilot was Maj. David Althoff.

Althoff was awarded the 1968 Alfred A. Cunningham Trophy as the Marine aviator of the year. John Glenn had won the award in 1962, but while Glenn was challenging the comparatively unknown dangers of space flight, Althoff knew exactly the deadly risks he took. Many times his odds were worse than fifty-fifty, but what counted most in his mind were the lives of those Reconners on the ground battling against huge odds and under siege by the North Vietnamese forces. He piloted his CH-46 through horrendous enemy fire and was awarded three Silver Stars, three Distinguished Flying Crosses, fifty-three Air Medals, and one Bronze Star. All three Silver Stars came as a result of Recon team battles.

One such battle took place on February 2, 1968, when an eight-man Recon team, operating in the Backyard, about five miles southwest of Dong Ha, become engaged with an estimated 100 NVA. The team had been inserted in the morning, and the day got cold, wet, and foggy as the clock turned toward night. While the team was in an OP location, a company of NVA (100 to 125 men) passed within twenty-five meters of them. As the NVA disappeared into the brush ahead, the team called artillery on the enemy, who then began a series of skirmishes with the Marines. The team avoided casualties by calling in supporting artillery and gunships. However, once night began approaching, the team called for the rescue birds to get them out.

By the time the CH-46s arrived, the team was pinned down and surrounded. Without lights, Althoff flew the lead bird down through heavy overcast. As he broke out of the clouds from a 300-foot ceiling, the team heard and located him. They then used a single light to guide the bird in. The major directed his chopper straight into the small landing zone in the midst of heavy enemy fire. His aircraft received a heavy volume of small arms and .50-caliber fire from the nearby and enveloping NVA forces. The hydraulic system control closet located behind the pilot's head took six hits, and one hydraulic system immediately failed. The rear ramp was rendered inoperative, and the fuel gauge dropped to zero. As the chopper crew and the Reconners returned fire, the team managed to jump aboard, and Althoff flew his bird back to Dong Ha at tree-top level, concerned that they might not make it. There is no doubt that the Reconners would not have survived the night if Althoff hadn't gotten them out when he did. For that action the major received his first Silver Star.

On May 13, 1968, a four-man team was sent to retrieve the body of Lt. Donald Matocha, killed on the April 4–5 patrol discussed earlier.

The Echo Company team was led by 2nd Lt. Bruce Wilson with Gary Myers at point, Clark Christie as radio operator, and Carlos Dominguez as rear point and carrying claymores. Christie also carried the body bag with which to return the remains of Lieutenant Matocha. A reaction force of volunteer Charlie Company Reconners led by the company commander, 1st Lt. Edward Osborne, was ready to go to the team's assistance if needed.

The team walked out from a Marine outpost with a grunt patrol and then dropped out into the bush. On the second day it reached the objective: Dong Kio, a hilltop about 300 meters in height, located approximately three miles west of Cam Lo and within 1,000 meters of the Cam Lo River.

Immediately upon reaching the point where Lieutenant Matocha's body was believed to be located, the team encountered a fortified bunker and was hit by automatic fire. Myers and Dominguez were killed and Christie and Wilson were wounded. Christie was on the radio and trying to fight back at the same time. The NVA were not only in the bunker but also in nearby positions. Responding to Christie's call, two Huey gunships came overhead followed by two CH-46s with Lieutenant Osborne's ten-man team, which included Sgt. Roberto Navarrete, who was to take command of a portion of the team.

Christie became separated from Wilson, and the latter was knocked down the hill by an enemy round as he was trying to pull the severely wounded Myers out of the kill zone. The radio operator himself had been hit twice in the back by AK-47 fire, but returned fire and killed the NVA soldier firing on him from the bunker. He was later seriously wounded again by shrapnel from an NVA rocket.

Heroism by Reconners fighting to save their friends was the story of the moment. The teams were hit by NVA small arms fire from more than one bunker and by incoming rocket and mortar rounds. Sergeant Navarrete and Corporal Yee had maneuvered to attack and destroy an NVA gun emplacement that was causing havoc for the Marines, and they did so, with Navarrete standing in the face of the enemy's weaponry to fire a LAW (light antitank weapon, M79—an armor piercing rocket with a disposable launcher) into the aperture of one of the bunkers.

One reaction team member was trying to drag the now severely wounded Christie out of the line of fire, and he threw his body over the radio operator to protect him from incoming mortar rounds. Marines with Lieutenant Osborne ran downhill to rescue the wounded Lieutenant Wilson, but had to get him back up to higher ground through enemy fire. L.Cpl. James "Barnyard" Barnerd exposed himself to try to signal one of the 46s down and was severely wounded by a rocket blast only three feet away. Navarrete and Yee raced to Barnyard's aid, but the three were pinned down by the NVA, who were now maneuvering to envelop and overrun the Marines. A single rocket wounded Christie again and injured several of his rescuers.

Lieutenant Osborne stated that they were under heavy NVA fire, including mortars, and he called for the balance of the reaction team. Instead, it was decided to extract the teams.

Then Maj. David Althoff flew into the hailstorm of enemy fire. Mortar rounds landed within ten meters of the Reconners just in front of the Sea Knight helicopter, but the major came in with the 46 anyway. He stayed on the ground until the Marines were on board with their wounded. But Doc Bradford and one other Marine had somehow become separated from the other Marines still on the ground. Althoff flew his bird toward their position. His copilot, R. G. Canada, described Althoff's actions:

> [The two Reconners] were finally located . . . down the northern side of the ridgeline. With no place to land the aircraft, Major Althoff approached the ridgeline's northern slope and hovered his aircraft along-

side the hill until his rotor blades were just barely two feet from the side of the hill. The last group of Marines was able to embark the aircraft through the right-side door. This too was done under heavy weapons fire.

Lieutenant Osborne was on board the aircraft during the last rescue, and also noted that they were under extremely heavy fire and that the major's rotor blades were kicking up the earth.

Five days later another Recon team was in contact in horribly difficult terrain and against overwhelming odds. Althoff and his copilot, Kent Van Winckel, were on a resupply run to Marines near Khe Sanh when they were called for an emergency extraction of a Recon team code-named Sky Merchant, which had been patrolling for three days between the Rockpile and Khe Sanh. On May 17, Sky Merchant, an Echo Company patrol, had sighted several enemy strongholds and called artillery on them. However, the team then became the object of a counterrecon operation by the NVA. On May 18, the team's rear point fired on two NVA approaching the team's position. 1st Lt. Frank Sinagra, the patrol leader, then had his radioman call for the extraction choppers, and he moved the team out of the jungled high ground and down the slope through elephant grass to be picked up. They were near the foot of Tiger Mountain.

In the words of L.Cpl. Mark Kosterman, a member of the patrol:

While on an eight-man Recon patrol west of Dong Ha Combat Base near Ca Lu, my Recon team [3E3] made contact with two NVA. Shortly after that we came under heavy enemy attack by small arms and automatic weapons fire and began receiving 60-mm mortars. At the time we began taking mortars the UH-1E gunships had arrived and were circling overhead. However, we had difficulty showing them where the fire was coming from. Suddenly, the enemy mortars and small arms fire hit the team, and I was the only one not wounded or killed. Only myself and one other of the wounded could still fire our weapons. I called for a medevac ASAP. It seemed like the CH-46 took only a minute to arrive. He made one pass and headed right into our position for a landing.

It was Althoff, call sign Chatterbox 21-1.

Lieutenant Sinagra had called for an 8-inch howitzer artillery mission so close to his position that the artillery unit would not fire. In the meantime, the NVA had bracketed the team with its own mortars, and there was no time to lose if anyone was going to survive. Walter Ensign was the team's M-79 man, and he momentarily suppressed the initial enemy fire with his grenade launcher. David Padilla went out to place claymore mines. However, the enemy fire then increased and the lieutenant was hit in the head, elbow, and chest. The corpsman, Lanny Long, was shot in the arm, abdomen, and liver.

The team was on the edge of a steep cliff and, in what easily could have been its last radio message to the choppers, stated that if the birds couldn't come in right away they could forget it. It was then that Althoff made his move. However, once again the LZ was on the edge of a steep incline and he would not be able to land on all wheels.

Capt. Allen Monroe and 1st. Lt. J. M. Armstrong flew the Huey gunships in support of the patrol that day. Armstrong described what happened after Althoff descended to pick up the Marines on the ground: "After about three minutes it was evident that something was wrong, and we were told that the team was attempting to carry their wounded aboard through elephant grass. Chatterbox 21-1 called that he was receiving mortar fire from his two-o'clock and small arms fire from his nine-o'clock, but as the progress of the team was unknown, he elected to remain in the zone."

The fire and counterfire were so heavy while the Reconners struggled to get on board that the Hueys ran out of ammo. Althoff also was receiving small arms fire from his eleven-o'clock, so the firing was directed at him from approximately a 180-degree arc across his front. No longer having the gunships' help, he called the other transport bird to fly over and machine-gun the area with its .50-calibers. Althoff wasn't the only Air Wing Marine risking his life. Chandois Norton and one other gunner from Chatterbox 21-1 ran out the back end to help Kosterman carry on dead and wounded Marines. One had been hit directly by a mortar and his body was blown into fragments. Kosterman said, "We were forced to return empty-handed as the man we were trying to find had received a direct hit by an enemy mortar and could not be located."

For ten minutes, Althoff held his bird in a very vulnerable and unsteady position on the hillside with only his rear wheels on the ground. The lieutenant and corpsman, both seriously wounded, helped each other on board. Kosterman and the two helicopter crewmen ran through enemy fire to carry the bodies of four dead Reconners on board. Even though his chopper was ripped by the heavy incoming, Althoff was able to take off. He piloted his shattered bird and the Marines out of the kill zone. Van Winckel, the copilot, said the major lit up a cigarette and gave the controls to him on the flight back to their base. Van Winckel added that it wasn't unusual for birds from his squadron to be under heavy fire and in a bad spot while trying to pick up Recon teams. He said the difference with David Althoff was that he was *always* in that hot zone.

However, four Reconners from the Sky Merchant team were killed, and one was killed and his body not recovered. The dead were Walter Ensign, Jr., David Padilla, Neil Sullivan, Gary Thomas, and James Young. Lieutenant Sinagra and Corpsman Long were seriously wounded. And although he braved enemy fire repeatedly, Mark Kosterman survived without a wound. For bringing out the survivors and hovering in the face of enemy small arms and mortar fire, Major Althoff received his third Silver Star of his Vietnam tour.

Kent Van Winckel also commented on the bond that was established between the teams from 3rd Recon and his squadron. He stated that on one occasion, a 46 went down in enemy-held jungle without a Recon team on board, but a reaction force from the 3rd Recon Battalion immediately responded to the call for help and was on the way to surround and protect the chopper and its crew.

The war raged on through the mountains and along the border, but it also was happening closer to the bases. The Backyard was west of the battalion's new camp at the Quang Tri airfield. Covered by low brushy hills not higher than about 100 meters, and with certain treed areas primarily along streams, the Backyard became a prime location for dropping off Recon teams by truck. For the most part, the hills sharply punctuated terrain that was otherwise broken only occasionally by waterways. Dry-weather dirt roads numbered 557, 558, 559, and 604 crisscrossed the area. Routes 557 and 558 bordered the area on the south and west. Route 558 extended due south from Cam Lo to near the Thach Han River, and Route 557 stalked that river through the woods and finally into the paddies that entered the city of Quang Tri from the southwest. The region extended approximately sixteen klicks (about ten miles) west of Quang Tri and Highway One, and about twelve klicks (eight miles) south of Route 9, which ran west from Dong Ha to Cam Lo. Higher mountains framed the west side of Route 558. The Vinh Phouc River, smaller than the Thach Han, cut through the middle of the Backyard. Recon teams—including the Best-Buhl patrol—had, since 1966, patrolled into the higher mountains farther west, but with the battalion's relocation to Quang Tri, patrols began to be sent into the Backyard, nearer to the new base.

Three of those patrols took place in July. The first, from Bravo Company, was code-named Early Flower and ran from July 15 to July 19. It made two sightings of 110 enemy, avoided contact, and called in artillery on the NVA. The second patrol, lasting only twenty-six hours, was also from Bravo Company and carried the handle Deer Fern. This team had one contact with nine enemy and found documents, money, and gear. Both patrols operated adjacent to or near the Vinh Phouc River, about two miles west of Highway One.

Then, on July 22, 1968, the battalion sent a specially designed diving mission to investigate the Vinh Phouc from its headwaters to Highway One, through the heart of the Backyard. For two years American Intelligence had known that the city of Quang Tri was one of the objectives of the NVA. Possible routes for that attack included a western approach that paralleled the Vinh Phouc River and Route 557.

By the time of the third patrol, inserted at 0940 hours on July 22, 1968, the command situation had changed. Bill Kent had finished his tour of duty as battalion commander and been transferred back to the States on July 12. He was replaced by Lt. Col. D. R. Berg. In addition, First Lieutenant Dusenbury had taken over for First Lieutenant Nosal as Bravo Company CO. On July 19, First Lieutenant Noe had assumed command of Delta Company, replacing First Lieutenant McBride. First Lieutenant Myllymaki took the reins as Echo Company's commander from First Lieutenant Youngstrom on July 28. As well, during July the battalion received new S-2, S-4, and assistant S-3 officers. Lieutenants Petty and Osborne still commanded Alpha and Charlie companies. Lieutenant Noe and a new mustang lieutenant in H & S, Richard Harden, would shortly become involved with this river patrol by leading two different reaction forces to help the embattled Marines on the Vinh Phouc.

The river patrol was to be led by 1st Lt. Mike Waddell, who had been with Bravo Company at Khe Sanh. Waddell stated that the Khe Sanh experience had been difficult on morale. From mid-January, Recon teams at the KSCB were not allowed to patrol more than two klicks from the base. Enduring the constant mortar and rocket attacks that took so many lives was difficult. Bravo Company left Khe Sanh about two weeks after the siege was declared over in April. Lieutenant Waddell then was assigned to scuba school in Subic Bay. Until the river patrol, the use of divers had been primarily directed at bridge checks and training classes near the base.

The op order given to Mike Waddell for the patrol called for him to be in charge of five Recon teams—two on each side of the river and one diving team in the water. Waddell was to be in a boat in the middle of the water with an M-16 and a radio. The proposed plan was that four divers would patrol along the banks of the Vinh Phouc, two on each side, checking for enemy and caches of weapons and supplies along the river's edge. The fifth would have scuba gear and check the deeper parts for caches.

Waddell argued with the S-3 that command and control would be difficult to impossible in a situation where he was trying to coordinate the snorkelers on the sides of the river and the diver with the scuba gear while coordinating four teams paralleling the river beyond his sight—all in a potentially hostile situation. In addition, he was new to the area, having spent most of 1968 either at Khe Sanh or at scuba school. If he was going to be stuck in the middle of the river trying to coordinate the divers, he wanted to have platoon commanders with the teams on either side of the river. The lieutenant lost the debate; the S-3 didn't seem worried, giving Waddell the impression that the only enemy he might find would be a few individual Vietcong who wouldn't give the patrol any problems. However, the river was to be checked to determine how it might be used by these VC.

The teams' landing zone was near the river crossing of Route 559. As the crow flies, it was almost five miles to the bridge on Highway One. In real life it was at least twice that far. One great difficulty the teams faced was that there wasn't a reasonable way for them to maintain a clandestine presence. Down the river, ahead of them, any VC would certainly know they were coming. Their patrol route would not be in exactly the same recon zones as those of the previous patrols into the area, but it would be very near some of them, including the one taken by the January patrol of Corporal Achberger's team, which crossed theirs.

The four nondiving units were Teams Barrister, Selby, and Showcase—led by Corporals DeHaemers, Durning, and Shircliff, all from Delta Company—and Team Isthmus, commanded by Cpl. Frank Kehr from Charlie Company. Several of the more senior NCOs had been reassigned from their teams and given diving gear for the trip.

The teams and the divers landed on both sides of the river about ten klicks due west of their base at Quang Tri. Cpl. Dan DeHaemers, team leader of Barrister, said that 0940 was the latest any of his patrols had been inserted. "It took a while to load and unload the boat, the Aqua-Lung, and what they needed to go at least for the first day or two of diving without resupply," DeHaemers noted.

Louis Rose was a Navy Corpsman assigned to Delta Company (and one of the few scuba-qualified corpsmen in the battalion), and he accompanied other diving patrols for training and to retrieve bodies. The July 22 patrol was the only time in his experience that a Recon Battalion used divers to check miles of river deep inside enemy-held terrain. He said, "They took us out by CH-46 and landed us quite a way upriver, and we had to carry the boat I don't know how long 'cuz in some areas the water was so shallow."

Lieutenant Waddell reported that the concept of operations was that one team would be in advance on each side of the river, while the two remaining teams would be directly out from the divers and close enough to provide security. However, because the river bent and looped back on itself every few hundred meters, it was not possible to maintain that formation.

Kehr added:

> My team landed on the north bank of the river and provided a point security over there, while one other team, I believe it was Showcase, did the same on the south bank. Both of us moved out in security positions while the rest of the patrol with divers came in near the river behind us. It seemed to take a long time to get everybody and their gear in. At least a lot longer than the normal patrol would've taken.

The teams went out in four troop-carrying birds with gunship escorts. DeHaemers said that his team was in the chopper with the boat, and added, "The op order gave the general impression that this was going to be a walk in the park—a hot dog mission. We ran a pretty light mission as far as packing fighting gear was concerned. The patrol had only one M-79 and one M-60. We were running pretty light. Contact with the enemy didn't seem to be a concern."

Kehr stated:

> That attitude was shown when we made contact on that second day. The mission was compromised, but they would not extract us. We had divers in the river, and they were vulnerable. It was difficult to coordinate with one another as all the teams were in various locations on either bank of the river or in it. After the enemy obviously knew we were in the area, and we had one skirmish with them, I thought we should have been extracted.

DeHaemers said, "To get the boat out with all the scuba gear, we had to land in more open terrain on the south side of the river."

Kehr added, "My team was inserted on the north side. It was hilly and had tall grass over there, and we were in a point-security position. We were sitting a little higher on a low ridge watching what was happening below on the other side and thinking to ourselves that this whole operation was attracting too much attention to itself for a Recon patrol."

Each team was composed of seven Reconners; the diving team was made up of six divers and Lieutenant Waddell. The divers were primarily sergeants from the Delta Company teams and were more experienced. So in some cases it was the assistant squad leaders who ended up as patrol leaders for the Delta Company teams. "Lieutenant Waddell was a good lieutenant," DeHaemers said. "I think he picked the divers because their experience made them better able to handle an emergency in the river, and the danger increased as time went on. Because of that, the sergeants were in the water, and those of us who were normally the assistant patrol leaders led the teams on the riversides."

Then-Sgt. Butch Waddill, who retired a lieutenant colonel, said:

The "river patrol" stands out in my memory, not only because it was so unusual and so disastrous but also because it was my last patrol with 3rd Recon Battalion. I had spent this, my second of three tours in Vietnam, as a team leader in Delta Company. I was a sergeant at the time and was fortunate enough to have been trained as a Navy diver at the naval base at Subic Bay, Philippines earlier in my tour. Up to the time of the patrol, my tactical diving activity with the battalion consisted of inspecting the underwater structures of bridges for enemy sabotage activity and the occasional body-search-and-recovery. The river patrol was the first operation of its type that I know of where we actually swept a river with scuba divers looking for enemy positions and supply/weapons caches.

. I was one of four divers in the water along with Doc Rose, one of the corpsmen assigned to Delta Company, and two others. Lieutenant Waddell and one other diver followed us in a light aluminum bass-type boat, providing coordination and support for our activities. Doc Rose and I had been on many Recon patrols together, and we had a great deal of respect and confidence in each other's abilities. As it was the end of my tour, I had already been relieved of my responsibilities as a Recon team leader but was selected for the patrol because of my diving qualifications and Recon experience.

We were inserted upriver by helicopter and swept east toward Highway One, checking out the riverbanks and bottom en route. We were given very little in the way of mission intelligence and did not expect any significant enemy contact. Even the security on the banks was provided by Recon teams, which was not tactically sound nor in accordance with doctrine. The mission was definitely not clandestine, and the security was more appropriately the mission of the infantry.

The river was so shallow and narrow at the point where the teams landed that several Marines had to carry the green aluminum boat before being able to set it in the water about a klick downstream.

However, the teams moved fairly quickly during the first day. Lieutenant Waddell stayed in the boat on the river and coordinated the divers while maintaining radio contact with the Recon teams out in the bush on either side. The boat stayed near the diver with the scuba gear, who was checking the deeper parts of the river. The other divers worked near the riverbanks with snorkels.

Two teams flanked and preceded the divers on each side of the river. In a day and a half, the teams traveled about four klicks straight-line distance, but because of all the loops in the river, the actual distance was much more. Doc Rose said, "The second day we started to find holes just about eighteen inches above the waterline. They were small enough that a Vietnamese could crawl into them, and then they widened out inside so that two or three of them could sit on a flat floor with a domed roof. We found some sacks of rice and weapons, including M-1s."

Sergeant Waddill stated:

> Doc Rose and I were the lead team of divers at the time checking out the north bank, when we began finding spider holes just above the water line. They were spread out about fifty to one hundred meters apart, and their entrances were camouflaged with covers of woven vegetation. The first holes were completely empty, but as we continued we began finding holes with increasing amounts of discarded items of clothing and equipment. We had put our scuba gear in the boat and were now swimming along the bank.

At approximately 1730 hours on the afternoon of July 23, Isthmus set up on a small bluff on the north bank, about 20 meters above the downstream edge of a loop in the river. The divers were approximately 500 meters to the rear, in the bottom of the loop. Corporal De-Haemers's team, Barrister, was near the divers on the north bank. Teams Selby and Showcase were on the south bank. Trees lined the river, and behind them the land was much more open, with rolling hills covered by grasses and bush. The land between Isthmus and the others behind in the loop was open grass or paddies. Along the south side of the river and just ahead of the Marines, the terrain rolled into low hills with wooded areas closer to the river. Less than 1,000 meters away were Hill 58, Route 604, and the site of Corporal Achberger's patrol at the start of the Tet Offensive a few months earlier. It was also the same grid square where Deer Fern had made contact only a few days earlier.

Then, late in the afternoon, Corporal Kehr was grabbed by his radio operator, Cpl. Steve Lowery, who whispered, "There's a VC down there." Directly below them, but on the opposite bank of the river, about 20 meters away, was a uniformed enemy soldier. He was alert and cautiously moving upriver as if he was aware of the diving team farther down the river, behind Kehr and Lowery. Lowery later said that another NVA soldier, about 30 meters below, had spotted him, but obviously thinking that the Marine was one of his own, he had waved a signal. The Reconner returned the signal to the enemy, who continued his careful movement westward. When Kehr had repositioned himself, the two noticed another soldier in a green uniform carrying an M-1 carbine. He also had the look of a scout for a larger unit. Kehr got on the radio to check with the teams behind him and make sure that there weren't any friendlies in the area, and was assured that there were not. Immediately, three more enemy showed themselves below Isthmus; they were carrying AK-47s, light packs, helmets, and bandoliers, and were dressed in black and green. Then Lowery spotted another group. Kehr received permission to open fire and signaled his team to commence firing. The first rounds were fired on semiautomatic to insure an accurate first shot, and then the Marines flipped their selectors to automatic. The NVA/VC were moving through brush but were very visible to the Marines overlooking their path. In the first burst of fire, four enemy soldiers went down.

As these enemy were taken under fire by Isthmus, the Marines farther back in the loop of the river began to receive fire. DeHaemers said, "It was accurate fire. I was five feet from Sergeant Waddill and Hodges, and one round went right between us. That's when Beson was hit on the other side of the river. But we stayed put in order to give the divers protection. They had only one weapon each and wore swim trunks."

L.Cpl. Steven Shircliff had been leading Showcase along the south bank ahead, not far from the NVA soldiers seen by Isthmus. He had wanted the Reconners on the north bank to hold their fire until his team could get into position ahead of the NVA, but the firing broke out before Showcase was set up. The NVA had seen that the Reconners were moving to head them off, and they opened fire, hitting Rick Beson, who carried the M-60 and was at point.

Shircliff stated, "The rounds were ricocheting off the rocks and Beson suddenly fell facedown. I grabbed him and as I turned him over I saw he was shot through the neck. He was bleeding like a fire hydrant. I stuck my thumb in his wound to try to stop the bleeding."

Cpl. Bill Durning was acting as team leader of Selby because the normal squad leader, Sgt. Carl Hodges, was serving as one of the divers. Selby was also on the south bank, not far from Showcase.

After the first shots were fired, Corporal Kehr thought that the four

NVA were dead, and he told his squad members to cease firing. But when they did, he said:

> The firing continued, and then I realized that we were now being attacked by enemy on our side of the river, coming up our piece of high ground from the east. We were also taking some shots from the opposite side. I spread the team out into a half circle and told everybody to get a little separated, as I was worried about being mortared. Then I moved by myself to the northeast down a saddle into the brush to see if I could spot anything coming from that direction behind us. As I went down that saddle, just within fifty meters, I saw two NVA moving up to the slope through some woods to my right. I fired a magazine at them, and then immediately to my left a shot rang out. I ducked and looked at a bush about twenty feet away that had shaken and [I] saw a puff of smoke. I grabbed a frag, held it for four seconds, and threw it into the bush and killed that guy.
>
> Then I went back up to the team and was going to surround our position with artillery. But Steve Lowery had already been in contact with helicopter gunships and told me not to bother with the artillery since the choppers were coming in to blast the area.

DeHaemers said, "We were still holding fast where we were, but we had received rifle shots coming directly from our north. Some enemy were between Isthmus and ourselves. It was getting dark, and it had clouded over and started to drizzle. Selby had tried to go out to the east to help Isthmus, but three people had gotten wounded and had to come back."

At least one of those wounded had been hit by fire coming from near where Frank Kehr's team was.

Kehr stated, "I had an air panel placed out so the gunships could locate us. The pilot could see me and asked for me to point to where the Charlie was. I did, and he came flying about ten feet over our heads, really gunning the area to the south and east of us—between us and into the woods to our downstream side."

Not long after that, a thirty-man reaction force from H & S Company (from the 3rd Recon Battalion base at Quang Tri) led by Lieutenant Harden, came out and landed near Isthmus. The force included a medevac for Beson. The two teams spent the night near the bottom of the small ridge that Isthmus had been on earlier. Barrister and the divers were about 200 meters away on the north bank of the river, and Selby and Showcase were on the south side.

The night was clouded and drizzle fell most of the time. But it was quiet and the VC did not show themselves. The next morning, as

Lieutenant Harden led the reaction force down to link up with the teams at the river, the Marines found a booby-trapped artillery round lying in their pathway. The enemy might not have made a move on the Recon force, but he was obviously in the area and planning what to do next about the Marines.

After the enemy contacts, the patrol's mission was definitely compromised, and the continuation of it meant that the Reconners were in an extraordinarily vulnerable situation. However, Lieutenant Waddell was ordered to continue.

The next morning, Showcase continued to patrol the south bank area. Shircliff stated, "I had a Kit Carson scout named Khe walking point, and he was very efficient at locating booby traps. But then an explosion occurred behind us, and we found out that Perry (a Showcase Team member) had hit a booby trap and had his legs blown off."

DeHaemers said:

> The next morning Showcase started to move out on the south side and immediately hit a booby trap and Perry was hurt. Then the orders were given for the two teams, Isthmus and Barrister, on the north bank to cross the river to the south side. The reaction force stayed on the north bank. We spent probably the next hour involved in checking the area for booby traps and getting the chopper in to take Perry out.

Shircliff said that it seemed to take a long time to get the medevac in for Perry; when it left they continued cautiously moving upriver with Khe still at point. Then the Kit Carson scout stopped the patrol and sent word back that he had found another booby trap. It was a grenade in a can, and although L.Cpl. Idus Conner had pulled it out of the can by the time Shircliff reached him, the booby trap did not work. Shircliff said he had a serious discussion with Conner about moving the grenade and told him that they were just lucky it hadn't blown. Shortly after this, Showcase and Selby joined forces along the south side, Corporal Kehr took Isthmus on ahead, and Barrister and the divers brought up the rear.

The teams had used the boat to cross the river through the drizzle, which continued to fall, and now the mission was ordered to continue with all of the original teams on the south bank and the thirty men of the reaction force on the north bank. The six divers and the boat were told to continue their mission in the river.

Frank Kehr said that although the river looped to the north, they moved to the east, away from the water for a short distance, before coming back. By that time, the patrol was no longer operating as a reconnaissance mission, and Kehr's team reconned by fire as it went.

Route 604 was only about 1,000 meters to the south, and trails connected the road to the river, passing across Isthmus's route of advance. In fact, although the patrol didn't realize it, it was now crossing the path of the Deer Fern patrol and that of Corporal Achberger's patrol, the one that happened during the initiation of the Tet Offensive. Corporal Kehr called for an aerial observer, but the pilot saw nothing.

DeHaemers described the terrain: "All along the river for the next thousand meters was a tree line for about ten meters or so out from the river's edge. Then beyond that were rice paddies with scattered areas of tree growth and hedgerows."

Frank Kehr directed his team back toward the river but ahead of the others. It found no bodies of the soldiers the teams had shot. "Somebody had cleaned the place up," he said. "So we moved on down the river, and then we started to find things. The area that we had crossed to get back down to the river had several spider-trap-type fighting holes, and on down the river close to the bank, we found numerous small campsites—even clotheslines with enemy uniforms hanging on them." The Marines of Team Isthmus sensed danger all around and radioed warnings to those behind to be cautious.

DeHaemers said:

It had stopped drizzling about midmorning. We were coming behind Frank and the combined Shelby-Showcase team. We found holes and tunnels and began to frag them. On the north side, the bank was much steeper than where we were, and the river was deeper. The divers on the north side were in the water right next to the bluff. The Aqua-Lung diver and boat with the lieutenant [Waddell] were in the middle, and the divers on our side were from ten to twenty feet out from the bank. We were moving adjacent to them.

Doc Rose, who was in the water near the north bank, said:

We kept on finding holes just above the waterline and had counted twenty-two when I hit the one with a VC in it. There was a small ravine that fed down into the river. It was about fifteen to twenty feet wide where it converged with the river. The flanking security team had walked around that and were on ahead. At the mouth of the ravine, there was this hole just above the water and a little ledge about six inches below that. It was on the curve of the bluff that cut back into that ravine area. When I saw it, I swam over and pushed up on the ledge to look in. Then my heart jumped into my throat and my eyes must've gotten as wide as silver dollars, 'cuz I stared face-to-face with a Charlie. I think he was as shocked. He was eating rice and jerked up to stare back at me.

I pushed back into the water, and I swear my fins were moving at three thousand rpm. I had a burp gun. I had two eighteen-round banana clips taped back to back for that wire-handled .45-caliber gun. I believe it's one of the few weapons that you can fire without having to clear the chamber of water. The river was over my head, and I was treading water and trying to get back. Then I hollered for the security team, but the next thing I know is that Charlie is out of the hole and running down the ledge just above the water. I turned the burp gun sideways on automatic and fired at him. The recoil spun me like a top in the water. I think that I shot him in the leg with the first round. I know the security team got him. I found out later he had a big load of cash and a 9-mm pistol.

Sergeant Waddill also encountered an enemy in a hole. He said:

The support boat was out of sight behind the other team at the time. I had just spotted another spider hole and climbed inside to find an enemy soldier staring at me. I quickly pushed myself out of the hole and back into the river, yelling to the security force on the north bank that I found a VC in a hole at the waterline and to throw me an M-16 ASAP. As the security force on the bank was separated from the river's edge by the heavy vegetation, they had to toss the rifle over the bush without actually seeing where I was. It landed in the river. When I retrieved it and fired, it exploded because of the water that had gotten into it. The VC escaped, and when I got back to the hole, I found that he had left his 7.62 Tokarev pistol, cartridge belt with a red star buckle, and assorted other equipment.

The Tokarev had gone out of production in the Soviet Union in 1954; however, it was still being made in China. It was also called the TT-33, and probably was produced in larger numbers than any other automatic pistol made.

As the two divers crossed an inlet of the river to another portion of the riverbank, they noticed another hole, this time higher up the bank. Sergeant Waddill was in the lead with Doc Rose just behind him. Lieutenant Waddell had, by this time, moved his boat into position to help, and had attempted to knock some of the debris away from the hole before the sergeant climbed to it.

Less than 200 meters downstream and in front, Isthmus was now starting to find evidence of enemy camps. Kehr stated:

Where the river again looped to the south we ran into a big camp. It was right before noon. We would go back and forth from the riverbank to about twenty-five meters away from the river, trying to watch for people who might be to our right. In the bottom of this second loop as it turned again toward the northeast, a finger of a hill came down to near the edge of the river, and that's where the biggest camp was [this was only about 600 meters from Route 604, above them].

Barrister was closer to the divers but couldn't see the north side of the river very well. DeHaemers said:

> We had found booby traps, but none had been tripped since early that morning when Perry was hurt. Sergeant Waddill was in the water on the north bank along with Doc Rose, and they were finding holes in that bluff just above the waterline. Sometimes they would disappear in the brush along the edge of the river. But the bluff was too tall, and we didn't have sight of either the reaction force that was providing security on the north bank or our other teams, ahead of us on our side. On the opposite bank, the bluff rose twenty or more feet, and the river was wide and deep. We were worried about the divers' security way over there.

Ahead, Isthmus was investigating the campsite. Carved into the riverbank among the roots of large trees, the camp was protected from aerial view. One part of it included what was obviously a boat landing. A few inches below the waterline was a bamboo dock in the river. It could easily be used to load or off-load men or supplies and not be seen from the air. A guard's post was nearby, complete with a hammock, and there was other evidence that the position had only recently been vacated. The Marines found shelves filled with ammunition and grenades, and a large sack of rice. Dug into the high walls was a hearth with a two-and-a-half-foot black iron cooking pot. Brush obscured the entrance to a tunnel that burrowed into the abutting finger of a 100-foot-tall hill that crested at the roadway, 600 meters above. How far the tunnel went, the Marines never found out. Kehr contacted Lieutenant Waddell via the radio and informed him of the situation. At that point, Waddell was trying to help Doc Rose and Sergeant Waddill on the opposite bank some distance to Kehr's rear. The lieutenant told Kehr to stay in position until the rest of the patrol reached him.

Suddenly, the silence was shattered by an explosion, automatic weapons fire, and a Marine's scream for help. The eerie quietness of midday was ripped by enemy fire. Kehr could only be sure that a Marine behind him had been hurt and that small arms fire was coming across from the north bluff of the river. His team was out of the kill zone. Lowery, on the radio, was doing his best to find out what was happening.

The divers had begun to investigate the latest hole, and Sergeant Waddill fired his M-16 at the entrance from his position, a little lower on the bluff. Waddill said, "After firing into the entrance, I started to push myself up to the hole. But then the muzzle of a light machine gun appeared, firing a long burst that impacted in the river just in front of the boat."

Because Waddill was trying to get up the bluff to the hole, he was just out of the line of sight of whoever was in the hole. Doc Rose described the scene:

We had found nothing in that first hole. Then we saw another one behind a curve in a tree. The tree had grown out from the riverbank and then had curved up, and it was in that space that this other hole was. I was on one side and Sergeant Waddill on the other. The muddy water was about waist deep, but we were standing in the mud among banyan tree roots.

Then Hodges, standing in shallow water on the other side, started yelling he could see the enemy and was pointing just above us. We were hanging on to the curve in the tree with our feet in the mud. Then immediately, this machine gun opened up right near us. I could feel the percussion and saw the bullets leave a trail in the water and ripped right up to Hodges, and he was hit. He yelled, "I'm hit. Mother of God, help me."

Butch Waddill said:

It was at this point that the situation deteriorated completely. The VC in the hole had a clear view of our security forces on the opposite bank and began taking them under fire. I yelled across to alert them and tried to direct fire into the enemy position, but it was too well camouflaged and too well fortified for them to effectively engage. My rifle had blown up, so I threw a fragmentation grenade into the hole, but it was quickly thrown back and exploded in the river. At the time there was quite a bit of firing going, including other enemy weapons firing from somewhere nearby.

Doc Rose and the support pulled back upriver out of the line of fire, but I was in a position just downriver from the spider hole, and it was between me and the others. The bank was very steep, but I was able to hug it and climb down out of sight of the enemy gunners. I slipped into the river and swam upstream. The security teams had tried to knock out the enemy positions, but had been unable to do so. Finally somebody, I believe it was Lieutenant Waddell, called in a series of air strikes that knocked out the enemy gunfire.

Lieutenant Waddell described what was happening from his vantage point:

Once we saw the holes, we worked our way over to investigate them. Then, after the attempts to throw grenades down that one hole, I saw the barrel of a machine gun come out of another hole. He had me dead to rights. He was about twenty meters away, and the bullets ripped through the water right past me. I should've been dead. Sergeant Hodges was hit and screaming. He [the VC] hit others on the south bank, too. I jumped into the water and hung on to the boat with one hand while I fired my rifle with the other. And I kicked, trying to swim the boat out of the line of fire.

We got the boat to the shore, and Waddill, Rose, and myself determined to try to get up the bluff and come in on the VC from the land side. But then we started to take fire from the north, and we backed down the bank to find cover. I decided to call in supporting firepower.

DeHaemers described the scene from his perspective:

Sometime between 1100 and 1200 [hours], we were within ten to fifteen feet of the south riverbank and there were cracks from weapons fire. My point man, Babb, said, "Hey, De—I got hit."

He had gotten hit in the left bicep. At the same time, I saw Sergeant Waddill near that north bank jump back from the bluff in waist-deep water yelling there was a Charlie in a hole. The river was about thirty yards wide. All in that same instant, Hodges was hit in the river by a machine gun. He got hit in the groin and the leg, while he had been swimming in shallow water, trying to make the south bank. I called in a sitrep and told the headquarters that we had contact with an unknown force and two Marines were wounded and requested a medevac. I gave the radio to Foy and Babb, and then Bill Donnelly and myself ran across the killing zone to reach Hodges in the river. There was about a ten-yard open space we ran across, and automatic fire from the north bank was impacting around us. One of our difficulties was that we didn't know where the reaction force was on the north side of the river.

Hodges had been snorkeling near the middle of the river and had then swum closer to our side. He started to thrash in the water when they shot him and was about twenty feet offshore. Then they shot him again in the thigh. But their fire was now directed at my team, where Babb was on the radio and John Foy was laying down covering fire.

Donnelly had gotten the heel of his boot shot off running across the killing zone. So we hit the deck and crawled through the grass to about ten feet from where Hodges was. There was about a five-foot muddy drop to the water there.

We started to lay down a base of fire on the north bank to protect Hodges. Then John Wood from Showcase walked up. He was standing in the open and didn't see us. It was like he was unaware or didn't care. Later, I found out that John had just been told that his buddy—Conner—had been shot. But when he saw Hodges, he put his M-60 down and jumped down the slippery bank to help him. Hodges was in front of him, very close to the shore now.

Babb was wounded, and nearby, Foy had been shot and killed. Conner, like Donnelly, had joined Barrister after the Shelby-Showcase realignment.

Steven Shircliff was downstream, but not far away. As the wounded Hodges was trying to get out of the water, Shircliff was trying to organize the Showcase-Shelby combined team to lay down a base of fire on the bluff opposite them. He had the M-79 and was firing grenades at the spider holes across the river. John Wood had the M-60, and Shircliff was helping him with ammo. Shircliff sent Doc Tomlinson, Conner, and W. D. Cox to help the wounded from Barrister who were in the kill zone.

Then Hodges was hit for the third and last time. The round impacted in the back of his neck. He jerked up and fell facedown into the water. DeHaemers, Wood, Donnelly, and Shircliff were trying to get down the short, but steep and muddy, bank to get him up. Donnelly ripped off his web belt so Wood could use it to pull himself and Hodges back up the muddy slope. Then DeHaemers pulled on both of them, trying to get Hodges up the bank. Shircliff said, "Hodges looked at me with his mouth wide open, gasping for air. I remember trying to give him mouth-to-mouth. But it was too late."

DeHaemers added, "When we saw the neck wound, we knew that he was dead."

Just prior to this action, Corporal Lowery, of Isthmus, stayed on the radio while Kehr took the food out of his pack and loaded up with half the ammo from his team and two LAW rockets. He joined Shircliff and Wood as they moved down to the kill zone to try to help Barrister. The three Marines began to make their way back upriver through the trees. They moved quietly in the thickets overlooking the water. The bluff on the other side was significantly higher than they.

Before Hodges had been gotten out of the water, the three were in position to try to help. Kehr fired his LAWs into the opposite bluff and started firing his M-16 on automatic as Wood and Shircliff raced across the impact area to reach Hodges. It was at this time that Lieutenant Waddell was in the river, trying to swim the boat out of the line of fire.

Kehr now could see more clearly the enemy positions on the north bank. There was about forty yards of mostly river between him and them. He counted three or four positions from which the enemy was firing. Like cannons firing from an old man-of-war, they would alternate, each one in turn firing at the Marines and then withdrawing. Kehr continued to lay down heavy automatic fire into the holes.

Word was swiftly moving up and down the south bank that Hodges, Conner, and Foy were dead.

It wasn't long before Kehr's rifle began to glow in the shadows of the trees, and Kehr had to rest the piece. He didn't have any way of knowing about the heroics of Shircliff, Wood, DeHaemers, and Donnelly not far from him. While Kehr was overheating his M-16, most of Team Barrister, who had been joined by some members of Shelby-Showcase, was still pinned down in the killing zone. DeHaemers then leaped to his feet and began pouring automatic fire into the north bank.

The enemy fire had by then decreased significantly. Kehr was moving, but was stopped short by the sight of a dead Marine just in front of him. He didn't know who it was. Then he positioned himself to fire into the north bank once more. The enemy's fire had picked up. He fired until his rifle glowed red and he had to pause again. Then he saw a Marine, he presumed it to be one of the divers, in the water next to the boat, which was close to the north bank but farther upriver. He yelled at the man and asked if he could see the enemy. For the next few minutes, the Marine in the water shouted directions to Kehr as he adjusted his fire into the holes on the bluff on the north side. However, Kehr was also receiving incoming from the Charlie on the other side. The VC fighting holes were positioned to provide cover and concealment, but they couldn't fire to their right, the location of the diving team that had remained upriver from the cross fire.

DeHaemers stated:

Conner, who was with Shircliff's team, had made it to Barrister, but he was shot and killed. My team was still in the killing zone, lying behind a foot-tall dike with bullets flying over their heads. One of my people had been shot trying to help Foy. That's when I tried to crawl across the open space to see if I could get to the wounded. Then I was hit twice in the chest.

I heard somebody yell, "De's hit." Then another voice yelled, "Are you hit bad?" I said, "Yeah, I'm really fucked up." Then I don't think I laid there two minutes when I heard a voice say, "What the fuck are you doing here?" He asked me if I could move and I said, "No." He asked if I had any ammo, and I said, "No." Then he grabbed me and started to drag me out of the killing zone. He had gotten me to almost where Hodges lay when a round tore the rifle out of his hand and took a finger with it.

Although DeHaemers didn't recognize him, it was Frank Kehr who had pulled him out of the open.

Before Kehr started to drag DeHaemers to cover, he had one magazine filled with tracers left, and this he carefully aimed at the north bank and unloaded. Then, as fast as he could, he grabbed DeHaemers by the collar and started to pull him out of the kill zone. It seemed to take forever to reach cover, and just as they were reaching it, Kehr said, "I felt a pain in my right hand. Looking down, all I could say was, 'They shot my fucking finger off.' I looked at the jagged bone where the little finger of my right hand used to be and then I dove for cover." His ring finger was also hit and was bent and broken, and parts of the meat of his hand had been ripped away. Kehr said he just couldn't believe it. Shircliff and one other member of his team helped pull DeHaemers to safety.

"Then I realized," Kehr said, "the rifle was also gone, shot out of my hand. I took my bush hat and wrapped it around my hand."

DeHaemers stated, "I couldn't figure out how this VC was so lucky with the AK. Too many of us were getting picked off. After Frank had dragged me and he had gotten hit, the action was still going on. I think that maybe this guy on the other side had a scope with his rifle. Then two guys from Showcase dragged me farther away."

Some of the teams had made it to a partially destroyed building, and some to an old bomb crater. Bill Donnelly and Steven Shircliff were organizing the pullback of Barrister, Shelby, and Showcase. The clouds had returned. Kehr lay behind the paddy dike. He said:

I heard members of Isthmus shouting, asking if I needed help—should they come to get me? I was in the open, but behind a small rice paddy dike next to the woods. I yelled back for them to stay down where they were. I low-crawled back to them. There were rounds still being shot at us, but I made it to the crater and jumped in. Doc Fife was there, and he started to take care of my hand. He asked if I wanted a shot of morphine. I said, "Not till we get out of here."

Doc Fife, although a member of Isthmus, had been all over the battlefield, helping anybody who needed it. He earned a Bronze Star for his actions that day.

Now the rest of the Marines were pulling back to clear the area for the gunships to rip through. Wood marked the target, but Lowery, still on the radio, told Kehr that the gunships weren't coming. Kehr and Lowery then spoke with the people back at the base. Because of Kehr's fractured hand, Lowery had to key the handset for Kehr to talk. Kehr didn't know whom he was talking with, but the man stated he wanted to get a prisoner before the gunships were authorized to hit the area. In the crater with Kehr were wounded and dead Marines. The Isthmus team leader then had a one-way yelling match with the voice on the other end of the radio, attempting to explain to him that this was not a situation in which they could take the offensive to capture a prisoner and that they needed air support immediately and medevacs as soon as the NVA's guns were quiet.

Kehr won the argument. Then, from the open paddy, the Marines watched the gunships streak overhead and gun the riverbank. The divers, boat, and Lieutenant Harden's reaction force were still on the north side.

Lieutenant Waddell stated:

I didn't have radio contact until I got out of the water. Then I had to clear the line of the radio traffic from the teams in order to try to establish contact with Battalion. After I called in for support, I let the individual teams call in their situation and medevacs. I was out of direct contact with them, and it was easier and faster for them to call in their own medevacs and sitreps. Then I got back on the radio and coordinated the air support. They came in at a danger-close range.

After the air strikes had quieted the enemy, Sergeant Waddill said:

I returned to the enemy fighting positions by crawling through the vegetation which had been decimated by air strikes. I crawled right over the hole and not knowing the enemy situation, tossed another fragmentation grenade inside. When it detonated the entire roof caved in with me on top of it. I found myself inside the remains of the hole covered with dirt and surrounded by RPG rocket rounds that the VC had left behind. I searched what was left of the hole and recovered the rocket ammunition. We, the divers, continued to move cautiously downriver, finding a few more empty holes but experiencing no further enemy contact.

The cloud cover then thickened again, and Lowery reported that the medevac choppers couldn't see the ground. Kehr said:

I had Lowery key the handset and hold it for me while I talked to the pilot. I told him the ceiling was about fifty feet, and it sounded like they were directly over our heads. There was the small hilltop nearby, and he was afraid of crashing into that or the trees in front of us. I told him that we had dead and dying Marines, and that if he couldn't come in now, I didn't think we would come out at all.

Then he said, "Do you swear there's fifty feet of clearance?" I swore before God that there was at least forty. Then he said, "All right, son, hang tight and watch for us. As soon as you see us, let me know, and if we're near that hill make sure you let me know." I answered, "Aye, aye, sir."

When the chopper broke through the clouds, it was immediately over the Marines. The CH-46 dropped its rear tailgate next to the Americans, and Raul Reyes and others who weren't wounded helped the less able on board. Frank Kehr, his hand ripped apart, and Dan DeHaemers, with two chest wounds, were taken out on the same medevac.

DeHaemers said, "I was medevacked to Dong Ha, and Lieutenant Noe [his company commander] met me there and asked what was happening out near the river. I told him there were still Marines out there. Then he must have taken another reaction force out to help the rest of the patrol."

Three Marines had been killed and fourteen wounded. The Marines still out there included Lieutenant Waddell, Doc Rose, and Sergeant Waddill, who were with Lieutenant Harden's team on the north side of the river. The bodies of Conner and Foy remained somewhere on the south bank.

Doc Rose said his group pulled back and watched the air strikes blast the area as the afternoon faded into the clouds. He said, "It hit pretty hard to hear the scuttlebutt about guys being killed who you had patrolled with. Hodges, Foy, and Conner we knew were dead, and then others were also hit, but we didn't know for sure what their condition was, but we could see the medevac missions going on across the river."

Lieutenant Waddell said:

It was too hard to try to coordinate the teams on the one side, the reaction force on the other side, and the divers. There should have been a different command situation. I really had my hands full just taking care of the diving team. But that was my opinion from the time the warning order was given. We tried to direct the aerial bombardment into the holes, but they were hard to pinpoint. We, the diving team, just were wearing swim trunks. I had an M-16 with me, but it was hard for the divers to use weapons while they were in the water. There were some runs by the fixed-wing after it got dark.

Steven Shircliff was not wounded, and all the able-bodied had been extracted from the south bank along with the wounded and Hodges's body. Shircliff stated that after they had returned to Delta Med, the able-bodied were ordered back out to the same LZ they had just come from to await another reaction force. He said:

> I can still remember those insane words to return. Not only myself, but everyone else who was left were in tears, shock, and disbelief. It was unbelievable that we were being ordered back into the same hell we had just managed to survive. But we followed orders.
>
> We were inserted near this old building that was partly blown apart. It was there that we set up a 360-degree perimeter. There was a smoldering campfire and fresh rice and fishheads. The NVA had been using the place.

About an hour later, as it was getting dark, Lieutenant Noe arrived with a Recon reaction force. He was briefed by Shircliff, who told him where the bodies of the two dead Marines should be located. However, with darkness coming on, the team decided to stay where it was. Shortly after dark an NVA soldier walked up to the Marines in the building. One of the Reconners thought he was their Kit Carson scout and called for the team to hold its fire. Hearing the American voice, the NVA calmly turned on his heels and began to walk away. Then the Reconners opened up and dropped him, but no one ventured out. Later in the night, the west side of the team's perimeter was hit by small arms fire. Lieutenant Noe called in supporting aircraft, and the team had to keep flat as shrapnel knifed into the sides of the building.

The others, still on the north bank of the river, had also set into a night position. Doc Rose stated:

> That night we sat in a harbor site with the security team on that north bank. It was just Lieutenant Waddell, Sergeant Waddill, and myself from the diving team, and we linked up with the reaction force. I remember one action that happened that night was when a *chieu hoy* scout went out to relieve himself and came back in from a different direction and was killed by Marines who didn't know he was out there.

Why he came in from the opposite direction in the middle of the night, I don't know.

Sergeant Waddill stated:

As it was almost dark, we regrouped with the security forces on the north bank and harbored for the night in a small clearing next to the river. Later that night, we received incoming mortar or artillery near our position. I was slightly wounded in the shoulder by a piece of shrapnel, but the rounds were not close enough to us to do any significant damage. After the incoming, the remainder of the night was uneventful. The next day we continued down the river to the bridge at Highway One.

Our morale was poor. We had lost friends because of what we believed to be poor decisions in the rear. It was an inappropriate mission and had cost us dearly.

Upon his return to the United States a few days later, Sergeant Waddill received a promotion to second lieutenant.

Doc Rose described the last day of the patrol:

We sat in place until the next day. Then Lieutenant Waddell, Sergeant Waddill, and myself were told to get into the boat and take it downstream to the railroad bridge next to Highway One. That was a few miles away, and we flew down that river, the three of us in the boat. It was the Badlands, and there wasn't any delaying in our minds. We had the motor in high gear. There was a lot of talk about why we had to take that boat down the river in the open instead of taking it out by helicopter. The pucker-power factor was a real force in getting us downstream.

Across the river, sunlight brought to Lieutenant Noe's team the job of getting the bodies of Conner and Foy. Noe told Shircliff to take the men he felt he needed and search for the two bodies. Shircliff took four Marines, and they crawled toward the river with Lieutenant Noe's team providing cover as needed. They found Foy first, and pulled his body from the trees where it had lain back about thirty meters. Then they worked closer to the river. The Marines spotted the body of Idus Conner lying in the trees at the edge of the water next to a bomb crater. Corporal Wood had been with the team on the patrol and was a pal of Conner's. He told Shircliff that he would go into the open to bring back his friend's body. While the team watched the river and trees, Wood crawled down to the river. Then he grabbed the body, stood up, and pulled it onto his shoulders. Suddenly, an NVA machine gun started firing from one of the holes in the bluff. Wood was hit in the stomach, chest, and hand, but he ran with the body of his friend over his shoulder despite the wounds.

The team had started firing at the NVA to give Wood some protection. He carried his friend's body thirty feet while the Marines were locked in a firing duel with the stubborn NVA, who had probably been waiting on the other bank for an attempt to retrieve the body.

As the Marine ran into the friendly lines with Conner's body, he said to Shircliff, "Short-Round [Shircliff's nickname], the motherfuckers finally got me."

However, the team was able to pull back to Lieutenant Noe's position, taking no more casualties. Noe had called for more gunships to rock the opposite riverbank once Lieutenant Harden and the men on that side had moved downstream. A medevac bird came in for the bodies and Corporal Wood, who had been given morphine and was somewhat delirious. He was holding on to Shircliff, begging "Short-Round" to go with him. As they loaded Wood onto the bird, Shircliff helped, but the wounded Marine would not let go of his friend. As the aircraft lifted off, a member of its crew shoved Shircliff off with his boot. However, the drop was about thirty feet by then. The lance corporal stated, "I damn near broke my neck when I landed. After going through all that hell for three days and surviving, I nearly got killed being kicked out of one of our own choppers."

The Marines were ordered to walk back to Highway One, a distance of almost five miles, and they were a somber group. Shircliff said, "I can remember the mood was very dark and solemn. Some of the guys were just talking and shaking their heads in disbelief about what had taken place. I think we all were trying to figure out how things could have been done differently. I felt so guilty, and I still do. I've been to the Wall in Washington and looked at the names of Conner, Foy, and Hodges and asked 'Why?' "

Lieutenant Waddell added, "When we got back and were in the debrief, the S-3 turned very critical of me and basically blamed the ambush on me. That type of attitude was typical for him. I believe that some of the problems that the teams ran into were a result of inexperience on the part of those issuing the orders—that and their attitude that sometimes would not listen to the advice of the patrol leader in the field."

Lieutenant Osborne, the Charlie Company commander, stepped into what he saw as a potentially bad situation between the S-3 and the members of the Recon teams, some of whom were still bleeding. Osborne said, "The S-3 was trying to blame the screw-ups on the teams, and they were about ready to lock and load. I sent them out, after which I had my own tête-à-tête with the major. He was the one who had really designed a very bad mission. Any blame was his, not theirs."

It wasn't just in Vietnam that people were wondering what was going on. As Steven Shircliff and the other Reconners wondered "Why?" other Americans in places of high command responsibility were also wondering what to do. A presidential commission that included Gen. Maxwell Taylor concluded that neither the South Vietnamese Army nor its government "will rise to the challenge," and called for "a new strategy." A Defense Department analysis added, "We know that despite a massive influx of 500,000 U.S. troops, 1.2 million tons of bombs a year, 400,000 attack sorties per year, 200,000 enemy KIA in three years, 20,000 U.S. KIA, etc., our control of the countryside is now essentially at pre–August 1965 levels. We have achieved stalemate at a high commitment. A new strategy must be sought."

CHAPTER SEVENTEEN

1968 Comes to a Close

A 1968 report from the Defense Department stated, "While we have raised the price of NVA aggression and support of the VC, it shows no lack of capability or will to match each new U.S. escalation. Our strategy of 'attrition' has not worked. Adding 206,000 more U.S. men to a force of 525,000, gaining only 27 additional maneuver battalions and 270 tactical fighters at an added cost to the U.S. of $10 billion per year, raises the question of who is making it costly for whom. . . ."

General Westmoreland, MACV commander, researched just how he could increase the numbers of needed front-line units in his attempts to meet the enemy main force units head-on. He had urged the Marine Corps to trim the numbers of men in rifle companies to bring them down to a size more on par with the equivalent Army companies. He also encouraged the decommissioning of the Ontos (antitank) battalions. In their place he wanted the Corps to create a new Recon Battalion in each division. His plan was to create new Marine rifle companies and Recon Battalions without changing the total number of men in Vietnam. The Marine command finally agreed to the decommissioning of the Ontos units. However, it felt that a better way of achieving the objective of additional Recon teams in the field was: (1) to add a third squad to each platoon, and (2) to create one new company in each Recon Battalion.

In December 1967, Company E was created. New men were brought in, and some of the existing leadership was transferred to that company. However, the battalion commander felt that the company had to be trained at the Recon training area (the Northern Training Area—NTA) in Okinawa. For six weeks in January and February, Capt. J. W. Raymond headquartered the new Company E in Okinawa, and they were on their own to devise the training syllabus to ready the new unit. On February 20, Echo Company was "chopped" back to the operational control of the battalion at Quang Tri.

Throughout the balance of the year, except when attached to other units as was 3rd Force at Dong Ha, the battalion stayed together at Quang Tri. However, after August 12, when the Force company joined the battalion at Quang Tri, all companies operated from the Quang Tri base. Unlike the old base at Dong Ha, the 3rd Marine Division Headquarters, located near the Quang Tri airfield, was outside the range of North Vietnamese artillery and rockets launched in or near the DMZ. The main NVA artillery piece was the M46 130-mm field gun (vintage 1954 Soviet design). Within effective range of 27,000 meters, these guns could be entrenched and camouflaged beyond the northern boundary of the DMZ well into North Vietnam and still fire on the Dong Ha base; they would have had to be moved into South Vietnam to fire on Quang Tri.

Recon teams were sent near, and sometimes into, the Demilitarized Zone to search for the NVA they knew were utilizing the area as a route into South Vietnam and as a launching pad for rockets, missiles, and artillery. One of these patrols, a five-man team from Echo Company, was led by Sgt. Joseph Biber. Biber had experience and was always concerned about the proper patrolling techniques and discipline, but prior to this patrol, he evidenced a touch of extra worry.

It was a new team, code-named Coral Bush. Pfc. Robert Barnard was at point, Biber behind him, followed by radioman Pfc. Charles Kimble, Pfc. David Bennett, and Assistant Patrol Leader L.Cpl. Robert Arney running rear point. Barnard and Bennett were on their first patrol, although there had been countless hours of practice in the days leading to this mission, when Sergeant Biber had run the five through patrolling techniques, immediate-action drills, and map and compass work.

The team's recon zone was a several-grid-square rectangle centered on a ridge adjacent to the southern boundary of the DMZ, about twenty air miles northwest of their base at Quang Tri. The ridge that they were to recon was narrow and about 3,000 meters long. It rested about 1,500 meters south of and parallel to the DMZ. It was shrouded and shielded by tall jungled canopy. To get in, the team would have to land just to its north in a saddle "clearing" overgrown with elephant grass.

On September 19, 1968, the Marines had to wait in line for the helicopters; they were flown out at 1000 hours in a CH-46. As the chopper swung around the hills just below the DMZ to come in adjacent to the ridge where the LZ was planned, the team saw what at first it thought was a company of Marine infantry nearby. The unit in question was using cooking fires near foxholes on the edge of the forest in a small bowl 500 to 700 meters to the west of the team's saddle LZ. The infantry seen wore helmets and green utilities. Sergeant Biber, however, said that he hadn't been told of any friendly grunt units out in the team's recon zone. Then the birds dropped behind the higher ground and out of sight of the "infantry."

Jumping quickly from the tail end of the chopper, the patrol found itself on the edge of a bomb crater in the middle of tall razor grass. The men looked up at high ground layered by jungle on three sides. Cautiously, but as fast as was prudent, the Marines moved toward the seeming safety of the jungle on the slope of the ridge a short distance away. After ten minutes the razor grass gave way to the jungle. The team paused and listened. Pfc. Kimble, on the radio and next to Biber, called in their sighting of the nearby troops. Then, judging that they were not in any immediate danger, Kimble told the helicopter gunships still cruising overhead that they could shove off. The team then began a steep 200-meter ascent through jungle undergrowth so thick that despite their close spacing the Marines sometimes lost sight of each other. The full fury of the monsoon season had not yet arrived, and the humid heat of late summer made the climb even worse.

It wasn't long, however, before the team had reached the top of the ridge, where it found a trail running along the crest and perpendicular to the pathway that had brought it uphill. The top of the high ground was so narrow that Biber decided to follow the trail. To not do so yet patrol the ridge would mean the team would be in the thick brush on the sloping ridge sides, creating far too much noise. Bob Arney said, "We never used trails, but didn't have a choice in this case."

On top, the team turned to the right and began to carefully step to the west. A short distance down the path, Barnard, at point, found small saplings bent and tied together with string, forming a short tunnel over the trail. Not being certain about its meaning, the Marines went around this tunnel and then reentered the trail. Barnard stated, "I was cautious to begin with, but after that sign, or whatever it was, I was very concerned and anxious."

The Marines covered about 300 meters, going up, down, and up again over slight rises along the top of the ridge. The jungle was still very thick, and the canopy was at about 100 feet. Lance Corporal Arney, at the rear, couldn't see the first three men in the line. The only person he had a glimpse of was Bennett, who was slipping through the thick jungle ahead of him. Bennett was carrying the M-79 grenade launcher. Arney was constantly aware of his responsibility to watch the rear without losing sight of the men in front of him. In case of contact at the front, he would immediately step to the opposite side of the trail from the man in front of him and turn to cover the rear. Biber had insured that they trained enough so that this and other immediate-action techniques were ground into their memories.

Barnard said:

We really weren't on the trail very long. The saplings tied over the trail were behind us and not far away. Then we passed by a pile of four large stones that had been obviously stacked by someone. Just past that we stepped into the bush to take a break and simply to watch the area. My anxiety level was on high alert. Although we had been training for weeks before, and although I had Recon School at Camp Pendleton, this was my first patrol. Sergeant Biber was always near me—the second man in the team.

The patrol leader then put the team back onto the trail, and it moved out. Barnard was still at point: "We were going up another rise in the trail. The brush was still very thick, and the jungle grew very tall. Then there was a right-hand turn in the trail, and a log lay across it. We were trying to be very quiet, and I carefully stepped over."

The team had to push its way through the bush and vines. It was tough going. About ten meters or so from the first log was another, and between and beyond these logs the shadows and closeness of the jungle opened up to such a degree that the Marines could see ten or so meters ahead of them.

Barnard, the team point, had moved through the thick jungle without a sound. The utilities he wore were soaked in sweat, and the camouflage paint on his face was gradually deteriorating because of the heat and humidity.

Barnard said:

It was like I was coming into a clearing. At least the brush was not as thick, although the trees were still overhead. Maybe because of the easier going, I got a little bit ahead of Biber, behind me. But as the jungle cleared out, and as I stepped over the second log, I saw this young Vietnamese in uniform sitting on another log about ten yards in front of me. His mouth dropped wide open when he looked at me. He had a rifle, an AK-47, lying in his lap, but no pack or helmet. I always had my rifle on semiautomatic. Maybe I was afraid it would jam on automatic, but I started firing at the soldier in front of me, and he went down to the other side of the log.

Then the jungle opened up with bullets flying. It's still hard to be positive, but I know there were at least three automatic weapons firing from the sides of the trail and to my front. The only reason that I can believe they didn't hit me in those first moments was that in the confusion in the jungle they were focusing on the guys behind me. But as soon as they opened up with their automatic weapons, I dove down the side slope into an eroded space under the log I had just stepped over. I don't know how they didn't hit me. Anyway, I went into this bit of cover offered by the hollow under the log. I tried to return fire. Being somewhat below them on the side of the trail, I think that I had more protection than I realized at the time.

With Barnard a slight distance ahead, and now enemy small arms fire ripping through the jungle around them, the rest of the small team of Reconners quickly reacted as they had been trained to, but they were still in the dark about the situation. Sergeant Biber immediately was concerned about Barnard's situation ahead of him. He and Pfc. Charles Kimble had hit the jungle floor behind the first log when the firing started. Bob Arney had quickly jumped to one side of the trail, covering the rear, but hadn't a clue about the seriousness of the situation.
Arney stated:

Where I was, even though it wasn't far behind the point, it was like darkest Africa. The jungles were tight, and I couldn't see a thing. But immediately I covered the rear. I expected that the men in front of me would be breaking contact like we were supposed to do and coming back down the trail. My job was to cover the rear so we could move out in that direction, and so that we wouldn't be surprised from the rear. But there was no one coming in my direction.

Barnard had slid under the log and tried to return fire, but bullets buzzed in the air over his head and slammed into the log. Sergeant Biber, concerned for Barnard, was yelling up to his point to find out if he was okay.
Barnard said:

As soon as I yelled back that I was, the NVA opened up on us all. Bullets slashed over my head and blasted the log. I know that I had shot two of them: one on the log and one in the bush. I had seen a rifle come out of the thickets and had fired directly into the man behind the weapon and heard screaming and moaning from that position. But every time we yelled back and forth to each other that just caused us to receive more fire, and I tried to stay under the little protection that I had. They were within thirty feet of me.

Sergeant Biber was constantly concerned about Barnard, to his front. He hollered again for Barnie, and again the point answered from his washed-out position under the next log. And again automatic weapons fire erupted and impacted around the Marines. Dirt and wood showered on the Reconners, and they returned fire. Two small teams of enemy soldiers were locked in conflict in thick jungle, and neither knew the size of the enemy force it was facing. The NVA had two men down, but they were only about 800 meters from the enemy company that the Marines had seen when coming into the LZ. It was dawning on the Marines that the guys firing at them might be attached to that unit.

Kimble said, "I radioed for a reaction force because I had put two and two together and come up with the fact that these NVA shooting at us were really a part of that company we had seen when we were first flying in."

Barnard said, "I was lying under the log and returning fire. Every time Sergeant Biber yelled and I answered, it was like a swarm of killer bees were zipping over my head. So the next time he yelled, I didn't answer, but I tried to scoot under the log to surface on the other side, facing . . . Biber. As I did, more firing broke out."

When Biber couldn't hear a response, his reaction was immediate. Not waiting any longer, he jumped up to go after his point man. Kimble was on the radio sending a spot report back to the base and calling for air support. He said, ". . . and the next thing I knew, Sergeant Biber had jumped to his feet and was starting to leap over the log to go after Barnie. That's when they opened up again and cut Biber down. I then told 'em on the radio that we had a casualty, and I started to help Biber."

There was a lull in the fighting, and it is probable that the NVA began to pull away. At the rear, Bob Arney was still protecting that side, but his team did not come to him. He said, "No one came, and as soon as the sounds of gunfire stopped, I left my position and moved toward where the fighting had been. Then I heard that Sergeant Biber had been shot, and I wanted to get to him."

Arney was at Biber's side almost as quickly as Kimble, and he stated, "Sergeant Biber was struggling to slide back to our side of the log, and I helped him. He was hit in the leg and it was shaking fiercely, and he told me, 'I'm going to pass out.' Kimble was back on the radio, and Bennett was trying to drop some M-79 rounds onto the NVA position."

"I heard the NVA talking to each other and moving back through the bush away from us," Barnard said. "I was afraid we were in contact with the larger group that we had seen earlier. Then I scrambled back to the other side of the log with the others. I saw then that Biber was hit, and I heard him mumble something. Right after that he passed out."

The Marines tried to save their sergeant and worked desperately to get the flow of blood stopped; the wound was high in the groin, and it was obvious that an artery had been severed.

"I tried to put a battle dressing on Biber," Kimble said, "but the wound was high in the upper leg, in the groin area, and it was very difficult to get the wound dressed. The blood was just shooting out of him like a geyser. But then I got the word on the radio that the choppers were on the way. Before he passed out, I told him, 'Hang on, the choppers are on the way.' But then his eyes rolled back, and he was gone."

There was no corpsman on the patrol. Barnard said, "Biber's wound was so big and in such an awkward place that we really couldn't get a battlefield dressing around it. We stuffed the bandages into the wound and tried to give him mouth-to-mouth resuscitation. But he didn't respond, and I think he was dead right then."

"Barnard tried to carry him on his shoulder but that wasn't working. Then we made a poncho litter," Arney said. "Barnie and I carried Biber in that, and I was also trying to keep everybody together. Kimble and Bennett got farther ahead of us, trying to find a place where we could be extracted."

Kimble said, "The choppers came overhead, but we had tall jungle between us and them. I had contact with them over the radio, but they couldn't see us. I used a mirror to signal them, and they saw that. The pilot then directed us to a place ahead that from his perspective seemed like he might be able to drop a hoist through."

The Recon team moved along the top of the ridge, retracing its path. However, it did not go back down the hill. The chopper pilot was directing them to the opposite end of the ridge, about 2,000 meters from the point of contact. It was a struggle for the Marines trying to carry the body of their dead sergeant and Barnard was covered in Biber's blood from attempting to transport his sergeant over his shoulder in a fireman's carry.

Even in the jungle shadows, the heat of midday was overwhelming and the team was fortunate that the NVA had not yet decided to move after it. The enemy was likely trying to pull back with their casualties and determine who and how many had hit them. However, the Marines made it to the place just off the trail where the pilot was directing them, a small clearing made by an artillery round or a bomb. Still, the jungle reached close to 100 feet overhead. Hovering high over the treetops, the chopper lowered a sling. The process seemed to take an eternity. One Marine at a time was lifted up through the canopy—the body of Sergeant Biber first and then the others. Bob Arney had become the patrol leader, and he ordered the others up the lifeline ahead of him. The entire patrol lasted only two and a half hours, and forty-five minutes passed from the time of contact to the time of extraction.

When the entire team was finally aboard, the chopper took them to Camp Carroll, where they were debriefed—even the commanding general was there. When the team members discussed the initial sighting of the "company" uniformed in green near their LZ, the debriefers informed the Marines that there were no friendly forces in the area and that those had indeed been enemy soldiers. The team was at Camp Carroll for about an hour and a half before being lifted back to the base at Quang Tri.

Although Sergeant Biber died in combat, the number of Reconners on the killed-in-action roster began to diminish in the latter half of 1968. While fifty-five died in the service of their country from January 1 to July 1, that number was reduced to sixteen in the last six months of the year. In large part that was because no Recon company was being confined to the trenches in Khe Sanh, where Bravo Company had taken such a battering, losing twelve in January alone. However, the 1968 Tet Offensive had taken two high-ranking American casualties: the president of the United States had decided not to seek a second term; and on July 3, 1968, he reassigned the commander of American forces in Vietnam, General Westmoreland, to the United States, and replaced him with Gen. Creighton Abrams.

On October 31, 1968, President Johnson announced a complete bombing halt and the start of four-party negotiations among the United States, the South Vietnamese government, the National Liberation Front, and the North Vietnamese. Although the Vietcong and NVA had suffered serious casualties as a result of the Tet Offensive, according to the CIA, they still had a total troop strength in South Vietnam almost equal to that of the United States. In four years of warfare, the enemy had doubled its military strength in the country, had doubled its infiltration rate, retained control over at least 50 percent of the rural population, and set the tone for the fighting by choosing to engage when and where it wanted. President Johnson foresaw another decade of American commitment at a level that he was not prepared to accept. However, while negotiators were bickering over the shape and arrangement of tables at the peace talks in Paris, the military command sent Reconnaissance teams into the DMZ in attempts to capture a North Vietnamese soldier crossing the border into

South Vietnam: proof positive that the NVA were still infiltrating despite the peace talks and bombing halt.

During 1968, teams from the 3rd Recon Battalion captured eight prisoners of war, but none was more sought after than one who might be a showcase prisoner for the negotiators in Paris. Sandy Reid was a corporal in Bravo Company, an experienced patrol leader, and a recent graduate of Recondo School. One day a couple weeks before Christmas 1968, and between patrols, he walked into the command bunker at the battalion's Quang Tri base. On the situation map he noticed a series of eight recon zones scattered in the DMZ just below the Ben Hai. They were to be assigned to different teams in an attempt to capture a prisoner. Reid pointed to one four-grid-square zone and asked that it be reserved for his team. It was, but shortly thereafter Reid lost his only experienced point man before the team could get organized. As a result, Reid placed himself at point and handed over command of the team to L.Cpl. Lee Gaugler. Gaugler had run twenty-eight patrols with Reid, becoming a trusted and capable assistant patrol leader. Now Lee Gaugler was given the responsibility of commanding a team that was to be watched by his entire command structure to the highest levels.

Gaugler's team was the last of the eight to make the attempt. Each of the other seven had made contact with enemy forces in the DMZ, and after firefights, each had to be withdrawn without the hoped-for prisoner. One team had managed to grab a wounded NVA, but he had died a short time later; the objective was a live body. All eyes were focused on the final team: Lee Gaugler, Sandy Reid, Jim Consaul, Johnny Hood, Mike Posey, and Chuck Rains.

On December 10, at about dusk, the six-man team was flown out by CH-46 toward the DMZ. Preceding the team were fixed-wing aircraft that bombed off the top of a hill, making an LZ for the following choppers. Lee Gaugler says that the hilltop was still smoldering when they landed. Neither Reid nor Gaugler remembers strafing runs in other areas to confuse watching NVA. The nearby hilltops were covered by jungle and ranged from 300 to 400 meters in height. The only break in the canopy was where the jets had pounded out the LZ.

Immediately after being dropped in by the 46, the team unsuccessfully attempted to establish radio contact with command. The radios weren't functioning. Fortunately, the helicopters, which were disappearing in the darkening eastern sky, could still be contacted. Informing the pilot that they had radio problems, Gaugler asked them to return and extract the patrol. The pilot stated that he couldn't because he was running low on fuel. He said he would return.

Then, sitting alone on the hill in silence, with dark descending around them and small brushfires still giving off bits of light on their little corners of the hill, Gaugler said, "We heard below us a barking dog coming in our direction. Then there were Vietnamese voices with the dog. We all knew then that it was NVA searching for us and using at least one dog. They kept getting closer, and we were really alert in our perimeter. Suddenly, we had radio comm with an American."

In the first instant that was confusing to the Reconners, and then they quickly recognized it for what it was. Obviously, the NVA had raised the level of the counterrecon patrols to include not only dogs, but also an American—at least an English-speaking person—to contact the Marines on their radio frequency.

Gaugler said, "The voice was on the radio and he kept saying something to the effect, 'Why don't you guys come over here with us [the NVA side]? You'll see it's not that bad over here.' Then I had Jim Consaul, who was our radioman, put on the whip antenna and use it as a direction finder. Jim pointed the antenna in the direction that we thought the voice was coming from and moved the radio around to see where it came in stronger. We plotted his voice to the north of us, where the other Vietnamese voices and the dog were."

Then the helicopters were back out. It had taken about an hour. The team directed fire from the gunships to their north side—within 100 meters of the Marines. That was the best answer the Reconners could give to the "American" on the other end of the radio.

"While the 46 dropped in to pick us up," Gaugler stated, "the gunships continued to make runs on the area where we had plotted the enemy. But the choppers were taking fire. Tracer rounds were going in both directions."

However, the rescue bird was able to drop down on the smoldering hilltop to snatch them out. They made it safely back, but very quickly the team was back in the air—at about mid-morning the next day, December 11. This time the RZ was located to the east of the previous day's zone, approximately 2.8 miles due north of where Coral Bush (Sergeant Biber's patrol) had made contact with the enemy.

They landed on a hill named Dong Ong Cay. It was only about 200 meters tall and overlooked the Ben Hai River boundary between North and South Vietnam. The river was the northern boundary of the recon zone. A dirt road crossed the Ben Hai within 1,000 meters of their LZ and crossed their patrol route. It then paralleled the river for about 5,000 meters to the west. As it crossed into North Vietnam the road was named Route 1006. In part it served as a petroleum pipeline; taking advantage of the bombing halt, the North Vietnamese were rushing into service gasoline lines near the DMZ. The pipeline ran to a point about 4,000 meters north of the DMZ.

But on the Marines' side of the river, ravines and streams probed south from the Ben Hai into the team's RZ, and 50-foot canopy topped the higher ground; thick undergrowth concealed many of the lower draws. Much of the jungle had been defoliated; it was sparse and brown.

The landing zone was on a bombed-out 100- to 200-foot hill line that ran abreast of the river. It slowly descended toward the east. The last reaches of this high line descended to the Ben Hai itself. Sandy Reid said, "The thing that sticks in my mind was that brown was the predominant color. I felt very much exposed. There was evidence of a lot of bombing runs and a lot of trees were toppled. There was bush but not much leaves and a lot of barren branches. There was also evidence of previous military operations that had been conducted in the past. There were fighting holes, but none seemed to have been recently used."

The team passed through an area where shell casings and other remnants of bombing runs were strewn about, and everywhere were old fighting positions. Near the dirt roadway, the team found a disabled truck and an armored personnel carrier. Both were of Chinese or North Vietnamese origin. The team wondered why the vehicles hadn't been salvaged. They seemed to be in relatively decent shape.

The Marines carried M-16s and one M-79. Each man packed six canteens. For the balance of the first day—and the second—the team stuck to the high ground, working its way west to east. It then reached a spot overlooking a stream named Khe Nhi. This route brought the Marines out of the bombed area and into more undergrowth and canopy. Apparently the American planes had concentrated their bombing and defoliation runs on areas near the road. Now the Marines were in dense undergrowth. However, after two days, the water supply was low and they decided to drop off the high ground to the Khe Nhi to get water. The Ben Hai River was visible and within 300 meters.

The Marines cautiously made their way down the last of the finger near the river and approached the smaller stream. The land was steeper on their, the western, side of the creek than across it to the east. They decided to cross and approach the water from the opposite side. The stream was shallow, about fifteen meters wide. The six Marines crossed and crawled into the brush and reeds on the east side. They found a "tunnel" into the thickets and carefully made their way a little distance from the exposed edge of the stream, set up a defensive position, and listened.

Then Reid and Gaugler moved toward the stream to fill canteens, but they were halted by noises to both sides. An unknown number of Vietnamese were passing in front of them, unseen because of the thickets. One group passed them, but another was still coming.

The Reconners knew that there was a huge emphasis on snatching a POW, and so they needed to take certain risks they normally might not have taken. Gaugler and Reid untaped CS grenades from their web gear, pulled the pins, and lobbed the grenades into the middle of the voices on each side. Gaugler said, "The grenades blew and the gas hit 'em hard. You could hear them coughing and vomiting."

Reid added, "They were not happy campers."

But then the two Marines heard enemy moving through the thickets toward them. They were only a few meters off, and it sounded like there were three soldiers. The Marines estimated that the NVA were trying to get away from the gas and were making their way up the tunnel along the same path that the team had taken.

Gaugler said, "Sandy and I looked at each other and started moving forward in hopes of grabbing one of them."

Reid stated:

We were crawling through the thickets, but right before the stream started to thin out, we saw them stand up with their rifles in their hands. That's when we opened fire on them. The rest of our team was just about ten to fifteen meters behind us, and it was about the same distance in front of us to the stream and the NVA. Then we got quickly back to the others, and we all started to crawl back down the tunnel toward the stream and NVA. We found an 82-mm mortar tube and an NVA pack. Lee and I crawled farther toward the creek, but we heard Vietnamese voices ahead of us near the stream, and it seemed like they were yelling up at us.

Gaugler added that it sounded like at least a dozen soldiers ahead of them.

In fact, the team had split the NVA into two groups—one to each side of them. They had found no bodies, but there were blood trails on the path. Gaugler said, "We called the battalion and advised them of our contact and what we had. I requested that we be able to maneuver to a pickup LZ and that we be extracted. Our mission was now, I felt, too compromised for us to effectively achieve, and there would be unnecessary danger to the team. However, my request was denied, and we were told to continue with the mission."

The team then continued to move quietly in a southeasterly direction up a ravine toward some higher ground. Vietnamese voices below, near the stream, could still be heard. The team slowly and quietly moved away from the NVA near the stream.

Reid said:

> I was at point, and the terrain through which we were going was very thick brush. We had made contact in the middle of the afternoon, and it was getting on into the late afternoon now. I wanted to get to the high ground and was moving uphill, about three hundred meters now from the contact. Then, suddenly, the ground was no longer underfoot, and I was falling. The bush had been so thick that I had actually been walking on top of the thickets, and when I dropped through I went down out of sight into a well-beaten pathway below. There was a heckuva trail under me completely covered by the brush. I had been walking on top of that thick matting of brush and not known that I had left the ground.
>
> I would call the path a high-speed trail that led up to the higher ground. I quietly called to the rest to come on down, and they did.

They then made contact with an AO. Reid said, "He had been in the vicinity when we ran into the NVA, and we had him on the radio. His view of the situation and terrain was a hell of a lot better than ours. He told us that he could see fighting positions up higher, and the place looked like it had been real busy. In other words, continuing to go uphill did not look like the wise thing to do."

As a result, the patrol changed direction and went back down, but farther upstream than where they had previously made contact with the enemy unit. The Marines were able to move easily and quietly down a path that was wide enough for three people to walk abreast. Over their heads was a tight-knit mesh of brush and vines. Although a few trees grew, particularly along the stream, they were not in jungle. Both Reid and Gaugler commented about how easily enemy units could have moved for hundreds of meters on good wide paths under a complete umbrella of vegetation, and yet, there were few trees. However, the Marines were very much on alert. Enemy units were near them, and each knew approximately where the other was.

Both sides in this small battle of wits and wile were quiet, wondering just how many of their foe were nearby and what they were doing. Finally, the Marines were back at the creek. The trail was still concealed from aerial view. The team then turned to follow the path along the water and continued upstream, away from its previous contact. About 100 meters up the trail, some Vietnamese voices ahead of them called out from around a bend in the stream where a logjam had blocked the shallow waters. The voices came out of thick brush. The Marines halted, not sure whether the NVA were trying to determine if they were Americans or thought they were more of their own. The Marines crouched low beside a short embankment, trying to figure out how to answer. After a brief silence, the challenge came at them again.

Gaugler, trying to balance the team's needs to both stay healthy and get a POW if possible, used his most authoritative voice and the only Vietnamese words he could remember—he shouted, *"Chieu hoi. Chieu hoi."* ("Open arms"—a phrase used to entice enemy soldiers to defect from their side to ours.) Immediately, an American-made grenade was thrown out of the bush from about ten meters to his front, straight down at his face. Instinctively, he ducked, and the grenade slammed into the groin of the radio operator, Jim Consaul. As Consaul groaned and uttered an epithet, he lurched quickly backward, throwing the projectile over his head. It exploded harmlessly in the stream.

Reid stated, "I believe these guys were a part of the first group that had gone past us earlier, and they were separated from their main body. I don't believe that they knew for sure who we were until they heard Lee's voice. But the bit with the grenade definitely got the adrenaline flowing."

"I saw two NVA jump up," Gaugler said. "Both Sandy and I were at the front, and I opened up with my rifle and nailed 'em. I could hear one thrashing around, and the other was dead. I told Sandy and Johnny Hood to go up and bring back the wounded, and I started to call for the helicopters to come get us."

The Marines were in a potentially deadly situation, and it wasn't going to be made easier by trying to capture the wounded NVA and take him along. The rest of the NVA unit had to be somewhere nearby, but Reid and Hood had to crawl through the bush and were not sure about the NVA's condition or his weapons.

Reid said:

It was so thick that I left my rifle with the M-79 man and took his pistol to crawl up to find out what was happening with this wounded guy. I only had to crawl about ten or fifteen feet, and all of a sudden this guy's head popped up out of nowhere right in front of my face. Scared the hell out of me! I was able to grab his hair with one hand and jammed my .45 into his eye and commanded, *"Chieu hoi."*

I could see blood on his uniform from a gunshot wound to the shoulder, and his arm was under his body. I was afraid that he might have a grenade and told John to reach under him and see if he could find anything. He didn't find any, and then we dragged him to his feet and got him back to the rest of the patrol. By this time, Lee's talking to the command, and it seemed like they were really rushing to get us out, although it was primarily because of the POW.

The sun was then setting, and shadows had spread over the ravine. Gaugler said:

At this point, I didn't know whether they would be able to get us quickly enough. But I saw two Army helicopters flying over and contacted them through the AO, who was still a part of the ballgame above us. The Army pilots agreed to come down.

The AO then dropped a white phosphorus grenade just uphill from our position and noted to the choppers where we were in relation to the smoke. Then the birds swooped down and strafed the ravine we were in. They hit close. You could hear the machine gun fire ripping through the brush on all sides. But it was getting dark by the time that they actually dropped down to pick us up. In fact, there was no good opening except over the stream where a logjam was, and those logs became our LZ. They couldn't set down, and we had to push and pull each other from the top of the logs into the chopper.

Reid said:

We were just holding the POW up. He wasn't tied or anything. I think he was in shock. We pushed him on board, and then got the rest of us up, although Consaul was hard to pull up. He was pretty big, and it took a while to get him on board. We were getting pretty anxious about taking too much time and letting the NVA set up to blow us out of the sky. I remember looking up at the Army warrant officer in the cockpit and giving him the thumbs-up. He said in a slow drawl, "Y'all boys all aboard now?" He didn't seem concerned in the least, but I was yelling at him to get the hell out of there. He slowly turned around and then shot out of the streambed like a bolt of lightning.

The Army pilots took the team and its prisoner back to the small base at the foot of the Rockpile and stopped there for a while to check out a hit that the second chopper had taken. It was losing fuel, and they wanted to see if it could get back; after a short pause, they flew straight to Quang Tri.

Reid said:

When we landed at the base, there was all these people that came running out to us to see the POW. Even the chopper pilots, who would have normally flown back to their Army base, shut down their engines and climbed back to take a look. When we got this Vietnamese out, and he saw this horde of people running toward him, he just dropped down in a faint. But I think that part of the reason was his loss of blood and semishock.

Gaugler stated:

On our return trip with him, I put a compress on his wound and told him to hold it there, which he did. I gave him a cigarette and patted him on the head and said, "Everything's going to be okay now." Then we found a Chicom grenade still on him! That was quickly thrown out the hatch of the chopper. The next day we heard that the POW was patched up that night and the next day shipped off to Saigon.

A few months earlier the battalion had been offering an extra R & R to any team that could bring back a POW; by December 11, that policy was no longer being implemented. However, within five days, General Davis, 3rd Marine Division CG, awarded two Silver Stars, two Bronze Stars, and two Navy Commendation Medals to the six Reconners, presenting them at an official ceremony at the main base. Sandy Reid also received a meritorious promotion to sergeant.

CHAPTER EIGHTEEN

1969 Part One—The Last Year

The year 1968 had witnessed in large part the destruction of the Viet-cong as an effective fighting force, and by the end of the year the NVA and Vietcong losses for the previous four years were estimated at 500,000 to 600,000 men. But the North Vietnamese Army had taken over, almost exclusively, the conduct of the war, and there were an estimated eight divisions of NVA in South Vietnam. Four of those were located in Quang Tri Province, which was the RAOR for the 3rd Recon Battalion. The commitment and purpose of the Vietnamese Communist forces remained unchanged, and they had the flexibility to adjust their military strategy as needed. Where they made errors and suffered losses, they changed course. Where they won victories, they built on that base of success, both militarily and politically. As the U.S. forces withdrew from Vietnam, the NVA main force units were steadily developed into a more conventional military juggernaut designed to crush the South Vietnamese forces.

The teams of the 3rd Recon Battalion entered 1969, their last year of the war, facing NVA main force units of significant numbers, but those counts were small when compared to the North Vietnamese Army that was ready six years later to march through South Vietnam faster than Sherman through Georgia. By 1975, North Vietnam had built a force—200,000 men—that was designed to protect its home front. More importantly, an expeditionary force of twenty-two divisions backed by tanks, artillery, antiaircraft guns, missiles, and other independent tactical units was ready for the final assault on South Vietnam.

The battalion finished its four-and-one-half-year Vietnam deployment in 1969. The 3rd Marine Division was one of the first units withdrawn from Vietnam, and with it went the battalion. So although the first half of the year witnessed more Recon teams in the field than any January–June time period of the war (909 patrols were out during that time), from July to November, the number of patrols was reduced to 452. Charlie Company left Vietnam on August 13 with Regimental Landing Team (RLT) 9; Alpha left on October 7 with RLT-3; 3rd Force was transferred to III MAF on October 23 and remained as a fighting unit in Vietnam until March 10, 1970. After that, although carried on the rolls, 3rd Force had no Marines assigned to it; it was officially deactivated later in the year. Echo Company was deactivated on November 19, only three days prior to the battalion's departure from Vietnam, and its men were reassigned to other companies. The 3rd Recon Battalion was the last unit of the 3rd MarDiv to leave Vietnam. Most of the battalion left on November 22, 1969, and arrived in Camp Schwab, Okinawa, a week later. Only one small detachment of the unit remained, at the mouth of the Cua Viet, and it could not depart for a few days because of heavy storms. But it caught up. The redeployment was completed on December 6.

The 3rd Recon Battalion Command Chronology submitted to the commandant of the Marine Corps for the battalion's last two months in Vietnam stated that the battalion withdrew its operations from the western portion of the two northernmost provinces of South Vietnam and concentrated on protecting the flanks and rear of the division as it gradually withdrew from Vietnam:

> It was at this time that the Recon Battalion wrote the final pages to the 3rd Division's Vietnamese history as it became the last Marine organization to operate in the DMZ, Mutter's Ridge, Khe Sanh, the Da Krong and Ba Long valleys, and the never to be forgotten Rockpile.

It went on to state that when the division was staging out of Quang Tri and Dong Ha:

> . . . the Recon Battalion was given the task of reconnoitering the Backyard area in defense against rocket, mortar, and sapper attacks on the Division Headquarters and staging areas. As the division embarked, the Recon Battalion was given the mission of securing the north bank of the Cua Viet River by surveillance. After the departure of the division, the Recon Battalion became the Mobile Reserve in defense of the Quang Tri Combat Base, and it did not stand down until just eight hours before it embarked aboard the U.S.S. *Ogden* for Okinawa.

That's the end of the story, but before that there were still 1,361 missions. Those last-year teams sighted 5,245 enemy and had 336 contacts, which resulted in 30 Reconners killed, 173 wounded, and two Medals of Honor. The teams continued the 1968 trend—smaller patrols, averaging a little over six and a half men per mission.

The year began with the 3rd Marine Division along the DMZ, together with the 1st Brigade of the 5th Infantry Division (Mechanized) of the U.S. Army. Task Force Hotel operated in the northwest corner of South Vietnam, headquartered at the Vandegrift Combat Base. The Army's 101st Airborne Division and its XXIV Corps headquarters and XXIV Corps artillery were stationed in the Hue–Phu Bai area and at Dong Ha.

Enemy units in Quang Tri Province consisted of an estimated six regiments of the B-5 Front Headquarters and one regiment of the 7th Front. Some of those units were undergoing refitting within their sanctuary areas. Other NVA units had been pulled out of the country to get replacements and be reorganized. Yet it was estimated that 36,800 enemy soldiers, more than in 1968, were within Quang Tri Province. At the beginning of the year, enemy activity against U.S. forces was light. However, in February, Marine units began to find caches of arms and supplies that were forewarnings of pending enemy assaults.

During February, reconnaissance teams from the battalion and Marine infantry units covered the DMZ searching for additional supplies. Under the then-current rules of engagement—and because of the peace talks, which were under way—U.S. ground forces were prohibited from crossing into the DMZ without specific orders from MACV. However, defensive squad-size patrols were allowed. In late February, Fire Support Bases Neville and Russell (north and northeast of the former Khe Sanh Combat Base, respectively) were hit by NVA sapper units. The assaults by the NVA in the northwest quadrant of the province were met with Marine counterattacks. However, as the Marine infantry hit objectives along the DMZ north of Khe Sanh and the Rockpile, it was obvious that it had to secure its western flank.

There was an abandoned fire support base code-named Argonne on a mountain within 1,500 meters of Laos, about six klicks south of the DMZ. Trails that branched off to the west from the Ho Chi Minh Trail ran past Argonne into South Vietnam. The mountain was 1,308 meters tall (4,291 feet) and had good visibility into Laos. For weeks a new assault had been planned against the mountain to secure it and the western flank of the Marine operations farther to the east. Three companies of the 1st Battalion, 4th Marines (1/4), would conduct the assault. One company was to land on the top, while the other two would land in the valley to the north. The operation plan also called for a team from the 3rd Recon Battalion to lead the assault on the top of the mountain itself. This team would land first to check and secure the LZ, which had been cleared of trees by the Marines who had previously occupied the position. Now, however, it was anticipated that the reception might not be friendly.

That five-man team was Frostburg, and Cpl. James Taylor was team leader. Taylor had been in Vietnam, in Alpha Company, continuously for almost two and a half years. The Huey slick carrying the team had a pilot, copilot, and two gunners. The bird approached the LZ in absolutely clear weather and was only about fifteen feet off the ground when it was shattered by a heavy volume of ground fire. Taylor said:

> The chopper split in two. The head end went down with all of us still in it, while the ass end folded back nearby. The team was just behind the cockpit, and it was pulverized by fire. I can remember hitting the ground and the front end was skidding around with the rotors still spinning.
>
> Then the team jumped out and set up some kind of quick positions under fire. The NVA were hitting us hard. The Huey gunner was working out real good. His M-60 was blasting away at the NVA. The shell casings from his 60 were landing on my back. Normally I carried a shotgun but this time I had an M-16, but the damn thing jammed. The gunner handed me his 16, and I started using it, and I know I hit six of the NVA.
>
> There were old Marine positions around, and the NVA were using 'em. All we could use were our small arms. We couldn't lob grenades because the rotors were still rotating directly over our heads. They started coming in waves at us. I got hold of the radio and asked for Puff to get out there and blast the area, and he was out there real quick; I think he must have been on station somewhere close. He started working over the area, getting real close to us. Then fixed-wing came over and blew the hell out of the place. The air support was there so quick that we were in and out of there in thirty minutes.

The pilot had been killed in the initial blast that shattered the chopper, and the copilot was wounded. Taylor and his team had been perched on the edge, ready to jump and run on landing. With the first shots fired, Taylor had been hit in the left arm. The air support had been there for the grunt units following and was ready to help.

Taylor said:

We had a lot of air support, and that's when they brought in a 46 to pick us up. It dropped the tailgate, and everybody went for it. I checked the cockpit [of the Huey] and saw a bloody mess. The pilot and the copilot were hit. One of the gunners helped me carry the two to the 46. It was taking fire. I turned and fired at the NVA while the gunner pulled the last one, the copilot, on board. Then I turned to jump in, but the chopper was taking off. Everybody was on board except me, and the bird is off the ground getting the hell out of there. My team reached out over the tailgate, and I reached out to them. They pulled me into the bird as it was flying off. At that time, I still thought that the pilot was alive. I think I went into shock when I saw his face blown off. Later, I ended up at the main hospital at China Beach and then was shipped back to the States.

Corporal Taylor had served on Recon patrols from Alpha Company, 3rd Recon Battalion, since 1966 and was finally on his way home. It was time for that young man. Enough was enough.

After the team was extracted from the old fire base, the first transport chopper, with elements of the rifle company that was to land, tried to set down but couldn't. The Huey's wreckage, the rotor still spinning, prevented them. The battalion commander, Lt. Col. George T. Sargent, Jr., was with the lead bird. The choppers had to divert to a lower landing zone. Then Capt. Joe Green's Delta Company led the assault from the lower slope to the top of the mountain, clearing enemy out of old American bunkers one at a time. During the rest of that day, that night, and into the next day, the Marines battled for the mountain, withstanding enemy mortar attacks but suffering ten killed and twenty-one wounded in the first twenty-four hours, including Lieutenant Colonel Sargent and his S-2 officer.

The enemy mortar attack was originating from near the Laotian border, and the other companies of 1/4 landed in the valley below and searched toward Laos to drive away the tubes. However, some of those rounds were being fired from Hill 1154, within 300 meters of the border, on the South Vietnamese side, and just about 1,200 meters from Argonne. Marines from the battalion attacked Hill 1154 and found that it was fortified with bunkers housing an NVA platoon. After Company A, under the command of Capt. Buzz Buse, took those heights, the attacks against the Marines at Argonne significantly decreased.

Using a Recon team to secure a landing zone immediately in front of an infantry battalion, in effect running point for the battalion of grunts, is a highly questionable concept.

CHAPTER NINETEEN

1969 Part Two—Looking into Laos

During the first five months of 1969, two major infantry operations attacked the North Vietnamese west of the city of Hue in the valleys and mountains that served as the northern border between Vietnam and Laos. One, code-named Dewey Canyon, was spearheaded by the 3rd Marine Division into the Da Krong Valley, centered about forty miles west of Hue. The other, Apache Snow, was led by the Army's 101st Airborne Division into the northern A Shau Valley, which lay immediately to the south and southeast of the Da Krong. It was a rugged and beautiful setting of mountains, rivers, and valleys inhabited by Montagnard tribes and North Vietnamese Army. This portion of the Ho Chi Minh Trail entered Vietnam from Laos near the Co Ka Leuye ridge, primarily from Route 922 in Laos, which became Route 548 as it entered Vietnam. From the border, roads branched to the northeast toward the Vandegrift Combat Base, to the east toward Hue, and to the southeast into the A Shau. U.S. aircraft sighted as many as 1,000 trucks a day using the 548.*

To better understand the ability of the North Vietnamese to send both supplies and troops into South Vietnam, the following comments of a Vietnamese "contributor" to a German newspaper (Bremen's *Weser Kurier*) in 1968 need to be read. The contributor served with the 112th Special Battalion as it marched south on the Ho Chi Minh Trail to be attached to the 304th Division, operating near Khe Sanh.

*Charles R. Smith. *U.S. Marines in Vietnam: High Mobility and Standdown, 1969.* Washington, D.C.: Headquarters, U.S. Marine Corps, History and Museums Division, 1988, page 27.

During the previous weeks, guerrilla troops comprised of mountain tribes (Montagnards) had decimated and driven out Royal Laotian forces operating in east Laos and, thereby, cleared the way for larger North Vietnamese units on the Ho Chi Minh Trail. Whereas, on earlier marches, we had to keep close to the border area, this time we could swing wide to the west, which significantly lessened the annoyance of air attacks.

The march route, which up to now consisted of three to four branch routes and converged at certain bottlenecks, now had a dozen alternatives. But even if the American air attacks were tripled, the effect would be less than before because the North Vietnamese units now march all day. Before this, an advance was possible only at night. Up to now, I had gone three times . . . to the South. Each time, it was an unimaginable exertion. And casualties from attacks, illness, and accidents amounted to as much as a third of troop strength. This time it was almost a stroll, even though the Americans during this time flew more attacks against the supply route than against the North.*

In his book *Hamburger Hill*,** Samuel Zaffiri reports:

One night, while near the peak of Dong Ngai [a mountain in the A Shau, about sixteen miles due east of the Co Ka Leuye and in the northern reaches of the twenty-eight-mile-long A Shau Valley], and with fighting still going on all around him, Denholm [a platoon leader in the 101st] looked down into the heart of the A Shau five thousand feet below and saw what he estimated to be a convoy of at least forty trucks, all with their lights on, moving right down the center of the valley. When he got over the shock of the sight, the lieutenant called in artillery fire on the convoy, but the trucks turned off their lights and pulled off the road. For a number of nights afterwards, Denholm spotted similar large convoys and each time called artillery on them, though he doubted if he was causing any damage. One night he and another officer even saw the lights of what they were sure was a giant Russian helicopter flying back and forth from one end of the valley to the other . . .

Helicopters, both unidentified and Russian, were sighted operating in the border areas at other times. They were not numerous, but they were there. For example, in mid-1968 an MACV-G2 publication stated that sixteen such helicopters had been reported and some of those sighted were operating from the Cambodia-Vietnam border re-

*Copy obtained from the LBJ Library, Austin, Texas.
**New York: Pocket Books, 1988, page 8.

gion. Reports indicated that they could be used to carry raiding parties or to ferry high-ranking officials.

In Zaffiri's accounts, another platoon leader in the 101st "thought that the entire operation [Apache Snow] smacked of lunacy.... Every allied unit that had gone into the A Shau in the last four years had met disaster there . . ."

The route used by the trucks Lieutenant Denholm had seen turned to the west and branched as it neared Laos, each of the two roads passing 2,000 or 3,000 meters off either end of Co Ka Leuye Mountain. Route 548 served as the primary road link into the combat zone from Base Area 611, which sat astride both sides of the border and ran parallel to it. Intelligence had estimated that the area was the home for all or major elements of the 304th NVA Division, consisting of the 9B, 24B, and 66B Infantry regiments, the 68B Artillery Regiment, and the 83rd Engineer Regiment. Each of the regiments totaled approximately 2,000 men, plus headquarters and service personnel.

In January 1969, the 3rd Marine Division ordered a regimental-size operation into the southern Da Krong, with Col. Robert Barrow in command. It began as Operation Dawson River South and was renamed Dewey Canyon as it continued into February. Teams from the 3rd Recon Battalion preceded the infantry, checking LZs for mines and booby traps and being the point eyes and ears for the grunts coming behind.

The Co Ka Leuye ridge straddled the border at the southwestern end of the valley and mountain complex called the Da Krong. The border boundary actually ran down the middle of the top of the Co Ka Leuye. It was approximately 3,500 meters long and on the north end peaked at some 1,500 meters (approximately 5,000 feet) above sea level. The ridge was not flat over this expanse. The 1,500-meter north end was better described as a mountaintop with steep cliffs framing its east and northeast sides. However, it also dropped sharply down to the south and then abruptly rose again to an elevation of 1,360 meters on the south end. A dirt roadway branched off 922/548, traversing the lower southern slopes of the ridge itself before running abreast of a tributary of the Da Krong River at the foot of the eastern cliff side of the ridge. Once on top, Marines could walk back and forth from Vietnam to Laos and not leave the promontory. Tactically, it was an important position to hold, allowing observation of either country. However, it had been virgin territory for Marine units until the latter stages of the war. Recon teams were not the first Americans on top of Co Ka Leuye, and the initial herculean effort to go up by foot is best described by the commanding officer who took his 200-man infantry company to the top.

Capt. Dan Hitzelberger commanded Golf Company, 2nd Battalion, 9th Marines, on Dewey Canyon. He stated that in the first phase of the operation they had constant individual sniper contacts as they moved into what was called LZ Dallas. That was approximately three miles from the Co Ka Leuye. The territory was very mountainous and covered with jungle except where the mountain tribes had cleared hillside farming plots. After a day or two of patrolling around LZ Dallas, Hitzelberger received a warning order from the battalion CO to take the Co Ka Leuye. He looked across the valley at the seemingly vertical ascent of 3,000 feet or so from the valley below, and his immediate response was "You've got to be joking!" The sheer eastern face of the cliff had stared down at them for days. The thought of taking an entire infantry company with all its gear to the top was formidable, to say the least. Hitzelberger described the cliff as a "jagged tooth." He was told that there was no intelligence estimate that the mountain was being used by the enemy, but it so dominated the area that it was necessary to secure it.

"We came down steep slopes from LZ Dallas to cross the river between it and the lower slopes of Co Ka Leuye," Captain Hitzelberger stated. "The clouds had cleared, and I stepped out into a clearing on the lower finger coming down from Dallas. I wanted to get a good view of the mountainside we would have to go up."

Then a sniper round cracked from across the river, narrowly missing Hitzelberger, who immediately dove and rolled. A second shot from the sniper's position, which was above and on the other side of the river, actually drilled into the ground under the captain's face. The sniper was a good shot but, at that distance, was just a hair off.

Hitzelberger said, "The platoon behind me opened up on the sniper and took him out."

Once across the stream, the company began its steep ascent. Even on the easiest route selected by the company commander, the Marines were forced to move in a narrow column up a 35 percent grade on the northeast side. The jagged tooth still abruptly rose above the jungle ahead of them. Hitzelberger described how the rain had made the slopes muddy and his Marines found that one step up sometimes meant a slide back down. Hitzelberger said:

As we climbed, we started picking up animal calls from a short distance away, maybe a hundred to two hundred meters away. They would sound like chickens or roosters, but I grew up on a farm, and I knew that these were humans trying to imitate animals. It seemed like there would be one on either side of us, and one ahead. It was like they had tried to locate our position by forming a triangle of these recon scouts of theirs, and they would communicate through these animal calls. But I tried to avoid using trails and tried to stay high, and because of that we were able to surprise and take out one of their sniper teams before they could set up.

About 2,000 feet up from the stream, still heavily covered by double-growth canopy, the company found a four-strand, above-ground, comm wire system tied into the trees. "It was very well done," said Hitzelberger.

Superb quality, the workmanship was good, and the materials were excellent. It equaled anything we had, if not better. The communication system that they had was well camouflaged in the trees and couldn't have been seen from aircraft. The wire was taut, and they used insulators, and there was a good wide pathway that ran along underneath. The lines and the path ran from east to west across the mountainside. We reported this and received a message back not to disturb the line, as another of our units had found another leg of the same comm system farther to the east, and they had tapped it and were trying to decipher North Vietnamese messages. In fact, at that time we did hear Vietnamese voices on the ground not far away, but we settled into the mud and just remained quiet, hoping that they wouldn't realize just yet that we had found their comm lines. They seemed to be going west toward Laos along the trail under the lines.

Later that afternoon, we reached the base of the sharp rise to the top. Now this was not on the eastern side—that would have been impossible.

Still, the side they were attempting had a grade nearly twice that which the Marines had been struggling up so far—it was approximately 60 percent for the last 1,000 feet. Hitzelberger had each squad use a climbing rope. Climbing teams without packs, but with weapons, would go up, tying in different legs or stages of ropes behind them for the rest of the company below. Because of the heavy tree growth, they never saw daylight during this time. In some locations, the trees had diameters of four or more feet. Once he had a squad on top, the rest of the company climbed up.

By dusk, after a huge struggle, the 200 Marines and all their gear reached the crest. They found a mountaintop covered by thick jungle. Hitzelberger said, "You couldn't see anything, the foliage was so heavy. There were no signs that anyone had been using the top of that mountain for anything. It was virgin terrain."

Captain Hitzelberger stated:

That same night I was radioed with new orders to move my company
back down. After we had just spent so much effort climbing up, I almost cried. Then that next morning I looked around the place for
routes back down that were not the same as I had to take to get up. All
around the easterly side from the northeast to the southeast were very
steep cliffs, and there was no way to go down. There was a possible
route on the westerly side into Laos, but to go down there meant I
would've been masked by the mountain from my artillery and radio
support to the east. That left only one way: the way we had come up,
and retracing your path was always asking for trouble.

Late in the morning, Hitzelberger sent a reinforced fire team followed by a squad down the ropes first. They were to provide security
for the rest of the third platoon, the first to go down. As the lead elements of the platoon got down the first steep descent and moved over
to one of the few pieces of relatively flat ground, they spotted enemy
soldiers. The NVA were not trying to hide. It was as if they were
tempting the Marines into following.
Hitzelberger said:

I advised Browny, my third platoon commander, to go ahead and try to
take those NVA out, but to be very careful not to get sucked into an
ambush. But then they became very heavily engaged with about a
platoon-size NVA force. Then my second platoon was able to come to
the assistance of the third, and not long afterwards my first platoon was
down, and I had them swing to the left and break through the NVA on
that flank and force them back. The NVA just moved back to the dirt
roadway under the comm wire in the trees, and much more quickly
than we could, they disappeared to the west into Laos along that path.
It was a well-defined trail between four and eight feet in width and ran
parallel with the contours of the mountain.
    During that battle, Doc Burnstein had gone to give aid to several
Marines who had been hit, and he, too, was shot. He was doing what
he was trained to do: give aid to wounded Marines under fire from enemy forces. He was hit in the neck and had multiple wounds. Then
L.Cpl. Thomas Noonan jumped to their rescue. In rescuing his buddies, Noonan was killed. He was later awarded posthumously the
Medal of Honor.

The company had taken five killed and eighteen wounded, and
Hitzelberger had to use a reinforced platoon to carry the dead and
wounded down what was still a very steep and muddy slope under a

constant drizzle. They used the comm trail that the NVA had built, but went east instead of west. It was late in the afternoon, and the weather and canopy prevented choppers from getting to the Marines to extract the dead and wounded. The team moved into the night, through the dark. Airplanes dropped flares every so often under the clouds, and the company would move ten to thirty yards by the little light that each shed on the jungled slope. Then they would rest in the dark. It was very, very difficult terrain through which to carry the wounded and dead.

"I remember one Marine," Hitzelberger said, "whose nickname was Turtle, coming past me lying on a stretcher with about four or more other Marines carrying him. He was pretty severely wounded, and he asked me, 'Skipper, are you going to get me out of here?' I looked at him and said, 'I'll get you home, Turtle, and you'll make it.' He said, 'Thank you,' and rolled over and rested. I think that's when I decided to make the Corps a career."

Operation Dewey Canyon ended on March 18, two months after it started. It was a unique plan that worked well in the mountainous valleys of the Da Krong.

However, the casualty list was high, with Marines suffering a total of 1,050, of which 130 died. There were an estimated 1,617 NVA killed. The operation was judged to be a resounding success. However, despite the skill employed in this "mountain warfare," and in spite of the casualties inflicted on the enemy and the disruption of his operations, units of the 304th NVA Division were soon noted to still be in the area and just to its south, in the northern A Shau. With an engineer regiment to draw upon, the NVA were quickly at work repairing roads, building alternate routes, and it seemed to be simply not possible to permanently stop the tide that flowed from North Vietnam through the vast jungles and mountains. Captain Hitzelberger said that the NVA engineers had built roads as well as comm lines that were impossible to locate by aerial reconnaissance. He also said that their engineers were very good as basic infantry soldiers. Despite Dewey Canyon, NVA units, materials, and supplies were moving again into the Da Krong, the A Shau, and farther east, toward the Quang Tri–Hue–Phu Bai sector.

Then Operation Apache Snow kicked off on May 10, with two battalions of the 9th Marines returning to the Da Krong, serving primarily as a blocking force for the 101st Airborne, which assaulted into the northern A Shau a few miles to the east and southeast. The Army would eventually commit three of its battalions and one ARVN battalion in the fight for Hill 937, Dong Ap Bia. That 3,000-foot-tall mountain would be one of the last "body count battles." Controversy surrounded the commander's decision to battle face-to-face for the rugged terrain against an estimated enemy regimental headquarters, instead of pulling back and pounding the place with B-52s. The soldiers who fought and died for Hill 937, which they would leave in short order, irreverently named the real estate Hamburger Hill.

The attack had begun on May 10, and after a bloody and brutal battle, the Americans reached the top on May 20. The following day, at 1430 hours, a six-man team from the 3rd Recon Battalion landed atop the northern point of Co Ka Leuye ridge. They could spit into Laos and were less than an hour's ride by NVA truck from Hamburger Hill. Floyd Nagler was on that team, but it wasn't his first ride to the top of Co Ka Leuye. The previous month he had been on a reaction team that spent twenty-four hours on the mountain helping out a Recon team that had been there for two days, had been in contact with the NVA, and needed help. Both teams were extracted. Nagler stated, "On the May 21 patrol, I was literally behind the same boulder where I had been in April."

However, prior to the team's insertion on May 21, fixed-wing aircraft pummeled the ridge with bombs and napalm. From this and previous bombing, portions of the top of the ridge were barren except for the boulders and the trees denuded of their branches and greenery. Tree trunks impeded the descent of the choppers so that the last six or eight feet was a jump for the heavily packed Marines. The ground smoldered; old C-rat cans had been uprooted from their burial sites by the bombs. The team was led by Sgt. Scott Quinn. Sgt. Ernie "Preacher" Husted was APL; Hollis Stabler was rifleman and primary radio operator; Floyd Nagler was rifleman and the specialist in mines and booby traps; Ronnie Cox was rifleman; and the corpsman was Doc Denesevich. For a Recon mission, the team's members carried an extraordinary amount of ammo and mines, but they were to remain in the same location for the duration of the patrol, and they remembered the April encounter with NVA forces.

Just as Hitzelberger had found, the entire easterly side, from north to south, was protected by a cliff that dropped almost straight down for about half a mile, so their concern was primarily to the westerly side, in Laos. As had Golf Company, 9th Marines, the Recon team understood that any NVA coming up from Base Area 611 in Laos would be able to avoid U.S. artillery because the mountain masked them. But to the east, it was a wall of rock.

Nagler stated:

We couldn't have backed up more than ten feet, and we would've fallen off that cliff. And on the top, the Huey slicks couldn't land us because of the tree trunks and boulders. There was no canopy, but a lot of tree trunks and some of the rocks were ten or more feet in diameter. Immediately after landing, we went to work trying to clear some of those trunks for a decent LZ when we needed it. It's one thing to jump down but another to try to jump up to a chopper. We set up trip flares, claymores, and warning devices. There was no place to run if the NVA came up. If it was clear, the view was breathtaking, but if you had a fear of heights, it was no place to be.

"It was the best OP I was ever on," Stabler added. "I think we may have seen the battleship *New Jersey* out in the Gulf of Tonkin. But the position was not enviable in other respects, and Floyd worked hard at his self-taught specialty, with mines and booby traps."

Nagler said:

I set up three consecutive rings of mines and traps. The farthest away was about a hundred meters, which were the trip flares. The second ring were booby-trapped grenades, and I had shortened the fuses on the grenades to about two seconds. The third ring were the claymores. We strung these out from the north-northwest of our positions around the west to the south. We had brought in a hundred trip flares and I initially placed twenty-five out. We had carried in extra ammo that included three cases of M-60 ammo, a case of M-79 rounds, a case of frag grenades, and CS grenades. In addition, I had personally bought a modified M-16 from the Army LRRPs that included a 102 grenade launcher attachment with M3 silencer.

Later in the afternoon of that first day, the fog rolled in and the high-altitude wet cold settled on the Marines. They tried to set up housekeeping among roots still smoking from the bombing runs. Approximately two hours after dark, they observed what appeared to be antiaircraft fire coming from the east but could not obtain a fix on the position.

There were no immediate contacts with the NVA, but about two hours past midnight, at least one other enemy was trying to check them out. Stabler said:

I was sleeping between boulders, and a rat came right up to my face. I was sleeping and didn't realize what it was. It felt like a part of a dream. Then I jerked awake and had a brief fight with it, kicking it away. I tried to go back to sleep, but it was raining, and the wind was blowing across the top of that mountain like it was a wind tunnel. It was just miserably cold.

Then I'm sitting there, and I swear to God, a voice came to me and said, "Put your weapon down." It was one of those statements or commands that you don't even think about, just obey, and I leaned my rifle against a rock. Then the voice said, "Untape a grenade from your strap. Straighten the pin. Put your finger in the ring." Simultaneously, as I had the pin ready to pull out, a trip flare out to our west side went off, and I instinctively threw the grenade at the noise. The grenade exploded, and in the flash of light, I saw the silhouette of a man with a satchel charge in his hand. He turned and ran back down the hill.

I've got to tell you that the voice I heard was just as plain as talking to you. And I'll tell you no Marine will, at 0200 hours, without provocation, untape a grenade, straighten the pin, and put his finger in the ring like he was going to pull it. You just don't do that. But I did it when I heard the voice, and maybe that grenade helped to influence the enemy soldier to run back down the hill rather than to throw the satchel charge at us.

Nagler added, "A few moments later, we heard one of my booby traps go off farther down the hill. We were on alert the rest of the night."

The mountain was still socked in the next morning. Wet and cold, the Marines checked their defenses and kicked away more rats, and Preacher set about on a personal mission of trying to blow down more tree trunks with det-cord. By afternoon, the clouds had lifted, but they hung like a low ceiling not far above the Recon team. As the ground below became visible, the team saw activity around some tree houses on the Laotian side of the border not far above Route 922. They called in artillery but without serious effect.

Later a strange, huge bird, like a giant condor, swooped below the clouds over the valley not far from the Marines. Then there was nothing but a light drizzle, quiet and cold.

That night was a continuation of the quiet, rainy cold. The Marines had brought two-piece rain suits, but the cold penetrated to their bones. As had happened the night before, at about 2130 hours, the Marines observed the flashes of what appeared to be antiaircraft fire. By noting the time it took the sound of the guns to reach them, the team calculated that the weapons were from seven to eight miles away.

The same weather conditions continued the next day, May 23, and it was hard to observe anything. Then at 1310 on the twenty-fourth, Stabler and Doc Denesevich were on the back side of the position, sitting on a shelf a few feet below the top of the ridge. The two Reconners could sit there, bracing their feet against a tree that grew out from the cliff, looking down into Vietnam. All of a sudden, according to Stabler, "Doc leaned over and said, 'We're in the shit.' "

Stabler continued:

When Doc warned me, I heard shots and immediately radioed back to the battalion that we were in contact. I asked for an AO immediately. I stood up on that shelf and looked over the edge of the cliff back toward where the firing was coming from. I was trying to see where the enemy were, and only my head was poking up over the top next to a tree, and all of a sudden, there was an explosion, and the tree disappeared. It just blew up and splintered all over me. I dropped quick, very thankful that the guy's aim was off, wherever he was.

There was about twenty meters between me and Floyd, and I felt I needed to get up to them, so I jumped up on top and ran, sliding like into second base right behind the boulder with Floyd. He was reloading his rifle, Quinn was nearby, and Cox was aiming in to shoot. Doc stayed back off the edge of the cliff, and Preacher was just off to the south a little. Then Floyd and I got to our feet and were firing over the top of the boulder at the NVA. But as we were firing, we both watched this Chicom grenade come flying through. We both jumped down, and it blew up about six feet away.

Stabler wasn't hit, and he put another magazine into his rifle. Cox and Stabler then jumped up and started firing again. Sergeant Quinn leaped on top of a boulder, exposing himself to enemy fire and opening up with the M-60, then blew everything away. The NVA fire quieted.

"Then I dropped back down and looked at Floyd, who was still sitting," Stabler said. " 'Well, are you hit or not?' Then I put in another magazine, and Floyd finally answers, 'I think I'm hit.' " Because of the cold, windy climate, Floyd had on several layers of clothes and it took a while for him to discover just how or where he had been hit. It turned out that three pieces of shrapnel were lodged in his abdomen, but none seemed life-threatening.

Stabler said:

At that point, we figured that they had probed our position twice, and Floyd was wounded, and it was only a matter of a short time when they would come up the hill and hit us hard. I remembered on another patrol serving as a radio relay for a team that was totally wiped out, all Marines killed by the NVA, and it was hard to listen to their cries for help over the radio and not be able to do anything about it. The NVA would try to hit a team at night when they meant business, 'cuz they knew your chances for help in the dark were very limited. There was now no question in our minds but that they knew where we were and what our strength was. It was our third full day on the mountaintop, and we felt it was time to be extracted and called for the choppers. But the message that came back was that we wouldn't get it and to continue the mission.

Nagler continued:

We estimated that there had been ten to twelve NVA hitting us from two directions. The grenades came from I-don't-know-where. It was like they popped out of nowhere. They were just checking us out. They'd get serious later.

After the fight, which lasted only about ten or so minutes, we went out to reset our booby traps. We only had four claymores left, and that wasn't near enough to cover our west and south fronts. Preacher and I created our own version of a claymore. We took M-79 "firecracker" rounds and wrapped them with det-cord. They were hand detonated. We set up five of those to go with the four claymores. That made us feel only a little better, though; being only six, we felt vulnerable.

The rest of the twenty-fourth was quiet, and so was the night. The team busied itself cleaning weapons. The cold, windy, and misty mountain weather still harassed the Marines. Stabler also doubled as a radio relay for other Recon teams who needed one. The next day was more of the same. The team was scheduled to be extracted on May 26, just one more day, but the wait was ominous. The twenty-fifth was quiet, and the Marines hoped that they had been wrong about the NVA's coming after them in earnest. Then, on May 26 at 1000 hours, they received the news from the battalion that they were extended. Stabler asked for a resupply. He received an okay on the re-supply, but later that was canceled. No return flight, no resupply, but more misery from the wet and cold and wondering where the NVA were. They didn't have to debate that question for long. Three hours after they were told the choppers weren't coming, a lone AO flying over the Laotian side of the valley radioed the Marines that there were approximately three hundred soldiers, maybe two or three companies of NVA, maneuvering up the western and southwestern sides of the mountain toward the six Marines!

Nagler said, "I was on the radio with the pilot, as Hollis had gone out to the perimeter to check the booby traps. We got the word about the NVA to the battalion, and they said the choppers were coming to get us out."

"Floyd got word to us," Stabler responded, "to get our heads down because the enemy was coming up and the AO, an OV-10 Bronco, was going to strafe the area. We did, and he hit close to us. The NVA were closer than I would have liked."

The Bronco streaked from the east to the west, firing his miniguns and rockets, shooting downslope into Laos. The pilot made four strafing runs and reported down to the team that the extraction choppers should be on the way and to hang tight. Floyd said that the OV-10 pilot did all this on his own. He was flying over, knew the team was in the area, saw the danger, and then took it on himself to help. However, the team's guardian angel was soon out of ammo, and the choppers were still not on-station.

Five hours had passed since the first sighting by the AO, and still no friendly air was out to help the team. Finally, the Marines heard what they had been expecting from their west, the sounds of troop movement. They were still downslope a distance; the climb was tough.

In spite of his wounds, Nagler went with Cox to check the trip flares and booby traps. Before they could get very far, the two heard more movement around them—and closer. They quickly returned to their positions. Preacher and Quinn edged out to try to see what was happening. They saw NVA soldiers and opened fire, detonated the claymores, and threw grenades. By then Hueys were overhead, but it was already after 1800 hours.

One of the Huey slicks tried to get in on the top, but despite Preacher's det-cord tree trunk clearance efforts, there were still too many of the obstacles for the bird to land. The team was under fire and fighting back at the time, and the situation was too dangerous for the Hueys. By then the Marines were in a free-for-all battle.

"It seemed to me," Nagler said, "that the NVA were putting out more fire from the south where Hollis and Quinn were, and that was their base of fire. Then I believe their intent was to maneuver troops in on us from the west. Doc was still in the position on that shelf just down from the top, and Preacher and Cox were side by side with me. I think that we were getting hit by the lead point teams of the companies the AO had spotted."

The small team of young Americans was busy fighting against a numerically far superior force that was inexorably gaining the advantage of the terrain and forcing the Marines back to the cliff's edge. The Americans, battling for their lives, had a half-mile drop off the cliff at their backs and choppers that couldn't land to rescue them.

However, unknown to them, one of the old lumbering tanks of the sky, a CH-46, with typical Marine pilot bravery, had flown into the valley below on the Vietnam side. Using the cliff as cover, the huge bird rose vertically just off the face of the sheer rock wall. The NVA didn't see him coming, nor did the Marines. His rotor blades were dangerously close to the mountainside as he hugged the cliff and slowly rose to reach the embattled Recon team. Like a huge, thundering spacecraft, the 46 edged into view just behind the battling Marines, its rotor blades wopping in tune to the gunfire. Their rescue bird was there! Other than getting shot, there was one last obstacle: a mistimed jump into the helicopter from the rock outcropping meant a half-mile fall.

"It was a beautiful sight to see the big bird rise up just over the edge of the cliff," Nagler said. "He turned 180 degrees so his back side tailgate was able to rest on a rock outcropping. We had to jump about three feet to make it, and four of us did so. Preacher and Hollis were still firing as rear point, holding off the NVA. On the inside of the chopper, we had knocked out the Plexiglas windows and were firing through them."

The last two Marines on the cliff were firing their weapons, each motioning for the other to jump in first. Stabler said:

Then the bird, while it hovered, turned or shifted around a little, and for whatever reasons the tailgate closed, and Preacher and I were still outside. Then it set a wheel down on my foot, but I managed to jerk it free. The NVA were still coming when the bird swung into me and knocked me down to a lower ledge. If he would've hit me in the other direction, I'd have gone off into the valley. As it was, I fell about ten to twelve feet and landed on my knees. My knees were hurt and ripped up, but all I could think about was to get back up to the helicopter.

Preacher was yelling at me to get into the chopper, but I yelled back for him to get in first.

Stabler had the radio and felt he should be the last to jump aboard. If anyone was left behind, better the one with the radio—at least he could call artillery and fixed wing to rip the mountaintop. A number of enemy would go down with him.

Stabler continued:

Quinn was inside, yelling and motioning for us to jump on the wheel fender and climb through the window. Preacher jumped on the fender and shoved his pack through and followed it himself with the guys inside pulling on him. It was done very quickly.

I started to take my pack off, but then this NVA appears about thirty meters away on this rock. He instantaneously opens up on me with his rifle on automatic, and he's blasting the rock where I'm standing. Rock chips were hitting me, and at first, I thought I'd been hit. But just as quickly, I was returning fire on automatic and blew him off his rock. Then I turned and jumped for the chopper I landed on the wheel fender, but had to rip off my pack to go through the window.

By then the chopper had gotten the word that the last Marine was on board, and the pilot started to drop into the valley and away from the enemy fire as quickly as he could. However, Stabler was still coming through the window.

Stabler said:

I had gotten my head through the porthole, which was large enough to get through, but when you've got your backside hanging out of a moving chopper, things are a little more difficult. As we were pulling away, I saw two bullet holes blast through the opposite side wall of the bird, leaving big holes as they were exiting. I knew they had entered the chopper just beside me. The guys reached through the window and grabbed my six-day-old rotten trousers and tried to pull me through using that handhold. All they did was to rip them completely off me.

With the chopper flying fast to the east and lower, Hollis wasn't going to be left behind. With the NVA peppering the 46 with small arms fire, Hollis Stabler's bare backside hung out the window as his parting shot at the NVA. He said, "All I could think of at the moment was, These suckers are aiming at my butt, 'cuz that's what I'd be doing in their place."

The team returned safely, miraculously with only one wounded, that being Nagler, from the hit he took two days previously.

In a few months, the battalion would begin to leave Vietnam, but teams would still face challenges. And it would mean death for some. Thirty-five Reconners would give their lives during the last nine months of their war, when the companies received orders to depart Vietnam.

CHAPTER TWENTY

1969 Part Three—West of the Rockpile and Home

During the first months of 1969, enemy attacks and Marine contacts with the enemy increased. Then, during the early part of the summer, large-scale enemy activity diminished. However, that was not to be the case for Recon teams.

Late in the evening on May 28, a Company A team was inserted near the village of Khe Sanh, south of Route 9. During the next three days and the morning of the fourth, the Marines sighted over 100 NVA moving through an area that included the old French fort and coffee plantation just east of the vacant village site of Khe Sanh. The NVA wore green utilities, pith helmets, and carried AKs. Some hauled construction material, others carried stretchers with wounded. Many seemed to appear, literally, out of the ground, and the team concluded that there might be underground facilities in the area. On the morning of June 1, the Reconners were extracted after it was determined that they had been sighted and a team of NVA was maneuvering in their direction. Information gleaned by that patrol simulated a need to know more about what was happening in the vicinity of the "abandoned" village of Khe Sanh. So, on June 2, Team Flight Time from Delta Company was sent to investigate.

At about the same time, on May 30, 1969, Lt. Col. R. R. Burritt assumed command of the battalion from the outgoing Lt. Col. A. H. Perry, who had the battalion since taking command from D. R. Berg on December 13, 1967.

The third squad, third platoon, Delta Company, was to go to the north of Route 9 very near Hill 471 and close to what had been at one time an old Montagnard (Bru) hamlet on a hilltop about 300 meters south of Hill 471 and only 10 to 15 meters lower. Third squad overlooked Route 9 from about 500 meters south. The team was led by Cpl. William Buck, Jr., who was beginning an extension of his tour and was an experienced Reconner. Also on the patrol was Lt. Michael O'Conner, who was also experienced. Other members of the patrol were Douglas Barnitz, Robert Pearcy, Harold Skaggs, and William Wellman, Jr.

The team landed at 0930 hours on June 2 and immediately found "cooking gear still hot, helmets, and fresh banana peels" at that location. Within 10 meters the team found a bunker, and then: "two (2) bags of potatoes, two (2) bags of rice, two (2) helmets, one (1) cartridge belt, one (1) first aid kit, one (1) belt, one (1) pair tennis shoes, one (1) shirt, one (1) AK magazine, two (2) bush hats, six (6) fragmentation grenades, a bunch of bananas, one (1) document, and U.S. C rations."

However, after this initial landing and the finds made by the team, there is some confusion about what happened next; the patrol report skips to 1750 hours on June 3, when the team was back at the original LZ, the location where it had found "cooking gear still hot." It is not known whether it stayed in that spot the whole time or came back to it. Given the experience of the patrol leader and the lieutenant, it is inconceivable that they stayed in that one location, and it is almost as doubtful that they would have stayed close by. Standard operating procedures dictated that the team would not stay in its LZ, and the necessity of patrolling away was heavily underscored by a team's finding cooking gear still hot, etc. Some of the team members' friends have conjectured that they must have received orders to return to the site or to stay there.

After setting up a harbor site on the hilltop, the team sighted five enemy soldiers wearing utilities and helmets. No statement is made regarding the location of the enemy, only "no action taken." The night must have gone by quietly until 0250 hours. At that time the patrol was surprised by an enemy force of unknown size.

At the onset, the team was hit by small arms fire and Chicom grenades, taking one KIA immediately, and one serious WIA and four minor WIA. The team radioed for all on-call artillery fire, and at 0305 hours an aerial observer (AO) was overhead. He reported the battle raging within ten meters and on all sides of the Marines. The team requested a reaction force, calling back to the battalion: "Get us out of here." At 0315 the AO had fired his last ammunition. He had seen one secondary explosion. At 0320 radio communication was lost with the team. At 0400 the reaction force of twelve men was in the air. However, the next report, at 0620, stated:

Helicopter observed three (3) possibly five (5) members of the team and reported that the area looked like it had been hit with a flamethrower. 040700 reaction force found the six USMC KIAs . . . near Hill 471, five members of the team were in a trench and the sixth was approximately ten meters down the hill. On-site investigation indicates enemy came up the northeast side of the hill, team received RPGs, satchel charges, chi-com grenades, bangalore torpedoes, and small arms fire. The area was covered with powder burns from explosives. Reaction Team Leader stated that the marks on the ground and the way the equipment was scattered, the team must have been involved in hand-to-hand combat. (Lieutenant O'Conner was apparently shot while he slept, because his body was found still wrapped in a poncho liner.)

Lt. David Sipperly spoke with the reaction team leader, who amplified his feelings about the savagery of the fight. He said that Corporal Buck had been found ten meters away from the others with his K-Bar (knife) in his hand and had apparently gone down wounded and fighting hand-to-hand against numbers that overwhelmed him. The bodies of the Americans had been ripped by both small arms fire and explosives.

Flight Time—Marines Barnitz, Buck, O'Conner, Pearcy, Skaggs, and Wellman—was the last team to be totally lost by the battalion.

With the phased withdrawal of the 3rd Marine Division and the increasing reliance on the ARVN 1st Division in the DMZ area, enemy attacks accelerated again. Although Charlie Company, 3rd Recon Battalion, left in mid-August as a part of RLT-9, other units of the regiment had begun their departure a month earlier, with the 1st Battalion, 9th Marines, leaving on July 14. As they left, the 4th Marines' TAOR was extended in the west. This resulted in the division's changing its tactics from multibattalion search-and-destroy operations to small-unit patrols. The infantry had already begun work with its version of the Stingray patrol, and now its use was increased, the teams consisting of beefed-up squad patrols assigned to one grid square. They packed ammo and food for four days and used forward air controllers and forward observers to call and control air and artillery strikes. But then, in late July, the enemy picked up the pace again.

In early August, units of 2/4 encountered strong enemy resistance near LZ Mack (the site of the January 1968 Little Gull patrol ambush). Two companies of NVA in fortified positions were assaulted by Company F, 2/4. The enemy included units of the 304th NVA Division, which had recently returned from its own R & R. The NVA forced Foxtrot Company back down the slopes, but after a day of fighting, and with the aid of heavy artillery and air strikes, the Marines took the hill. Two days later, to the west and northwest, units of the same enemy 304th hit two rifle platoons and one mortar platoon of Company E (2/4). In these two battles, nineteen Marines were killed and seventy-five were wounded. In all three battles, eighty-two enemy dead were counted.

After those battles, all north and northwest of the Rockpile, 3rd MarDiv policies were modified again, and the downsized division required that within five kilometers of the DMZ: (1) nothing less than platoon-size patrols would be allowed, (2) nighttime defensive positions would be moved into after dark, and (3) it was mandatory for all companies to move at least 1,000 meters a day. The merits of the klick-a-day order were hotly debated by units in the field.

During this same time, infantry operations were also being conducted west of the Rockpile and northwest of Vandegrift. Rocket attacks had been hitting the bases, and the operations were designed to push the enemy back. The 3rd Marine Division had to leave Vietnam before the end of the year, and these were the last of the major operations aimed at keeping the NVA at some distance from the soon-to-be-vacated bases.

In July, Operation Arlington Canyon began when the 3rd Battalion, 4th Marines, was helilifted onto the Nui Tia Pong ridgeline approximately ten kilometers west of the Rockpile. The battalion discovered enemy bunker complexes and ammunition caches but could find only small enemy patrols and reconnaissance teams who kept the Marines under watch. There was periodic contact as the small NVA patrols harassed the Marine infantry.

In addition, in an area immediately abutting the northern boundary of Arlington Canyon, and in the same time period, 3/9 and then 1/4 landed to seek out the NVA units who were still eluding them. Enemy activity was described by Captain Buse, at that time the S-3 officer for the battalion:

> The enemy employed small groups of recon-type forces to simply harass us in our movement. We found that whenever we left, pulled a company out of the rocket belt, which lay west of VCB [Vandegrift Combat Base], the enemy would rocket VCB, so consequently, we tried to keep a rifle company maneuvering in that area at all times. The majority of contacts that we made, the sightings that were made, were made by reconnaissance units rather than by the infantry companies working on the ground.*

*U.S. Marines in Vietnam, 1969, page 161.

Then the area west of the Rockpile to the Laotian border was designated a reconnaissance zone. In addition to the 3rd Reconnaissance Battalion, there was also a Project Delta group composed of the 5th Special Forces Group, the 81st Airborne Ranger Battalion, and other attached supporting units from the Army that started operations in the general area.

Although the infantry failed to find the large enemy units it knew were in the area of Arlington Canyon, captured documents and other intelligence showed that four enemy battalions were using the trail network in the area of observation "to move men and supplies farther south in order to support a buildup in the central portion of the province. While avoiding a massive, direct attack, screening and reconnaissance elements of these four battalions did not hesitate to protect their parent units, installations, or infiltration routes. . . ."*

The Nui Tia Pong was one of the ridgelines extending down from Tiger Mountain (itself 1,700 meters high). Nui Tia Pong was 700 to 900 meters long, but it was only 300 to 500 meters across at the top. Beyond that, steep inclines descended to river valleys on both the north and south sides. The ridge was heavily covered by tall jungle growth and pointed east toward the Rockpile, about 8,000 meters away.

From May to August, the battalion sent sixteen patrols either to or near the Nui Tia Pong. During Arlington Canyon, the 3rd Recon Battalion sent several patrols into adjacent areas or into the same location where the infantry had been after the rifle companies departed. Between July 27 and 30, one team hidden in the jungles near the high trails to Tiger Mountain spotted sixty-two enemy soldiers, in different groups at different times, moving through the jungle to higher elevations west along the ridge away from the infantry operation. The enemy soldiers were wearing green utilities and pith or steel helmets. They carried packs and AK-47s. Several were wounded, and three were carried on stretchers. This was evidence of the small enemy patrols that actively harassed the Marine infantry. Intent on keeping the Marines off balance and away from the main units who were traversing the area not far away, they were willing to take casualties.

On August 13, two Recon teams patrolling adjacent to the east and south sides of the Nui Tia Pong found enemy positions without making contact. The Recon team at the east end of the finger, in the valley, found a "Malayan whip" booby trap and a harbor site in which it observed nine NVA soldiers in a shelter made of bamboo and ponchos. A fire was burning within the shelter. Enemy movement was

---

U.S. Marines in Vietnam, 1969, page 162.

toward the east. The Recon team called in an aerial observer, who himself brought in fixed wing that strafed the area. Secondary explosions were heard. The team was extracted without incident.

At the same time, a second 3rd Recon team, approximately 3,500 meters to the southwest of the other, located an unoccupied bunker system. The first A-frame bunker the team found was four feet deep and eight feet wide with tunnels leading to other rooms. One large cooking area had a sixty-foot-long tunnel leading to a sleeping room. There were ten bunkers in the area. The Reconners found Chicom claymores, 82-mm mortar rounds, 61-mm mortar rounds, fuses, and one RPG. The next day, about 300 meters away, the team found an additional bunker complex and ammunition. The team confiscated the fuses and continued its mission without making contact with the enemy. This find was very near the location of the extraction LZ for Team Sky Merchant, for which pilot Maj. David Althoff had won his third Silver Star.

One day later, on August 15, another Recon team, only 1,500 meters northwest of the one that had spotted the nine enemy in the shelter, observed two groups of enemy—one group consisting of three soldiers and the other of four. The Marines continued to patrol carefully, watch the area, and avoid contact.

On August 17, the tempo increased. Two Recon patrols made contact. The first attempted to land about 5,000 meters south of the Nui Tia Pong ridgeline, but as the choppers approached the LZ, they were taken under fire from a bunker complex. Gunships and fixed-wing had to be called in, and the mission was aborted. The second was on a mission to the top of the ridge. The team spotted three NVA foraging for food from a Marine position that had been used during the Arlington Canyon operation. The Reconners chased the enemy with artillery and were extracted the next day with no further contact.

Still another contact was made by a team in an OP position on the northeast side of the ridge, near where the team on the fifteenth had seen the two small groups of NVA. This time the team observed the enemy coming from the higher portion of the ridge down toward the OP. The Reconners engaged the enemy with small arms fire, killing two. However, additional enemy soldiers were on the high ground. The Recon team called in an AO, who brought in fixed-wing to strafe the enemy. The Recon team was extracted shortly after without taking a casualty.

The North Vietnamese referred to the 1,700-meter-high mountain simply as Tiger Mountain; the Marines sometimes referred to it as the Tiger Tooth. The slopes and ridgelines extending down from it were being well used by enemy forces, and Recon teams continued to be sent into the area to keep watch. Then three Recon missions—on August 20, 21, and 23—were made by two teams, one from Echo Company, the second from Bravo Company, and then the Echo team again. They were landed on opposing ridgelines, or in the valley between, just 3,000 meters apart. All were on or adjacent to the Nui Tia Pong.

Cpl. Steve "S.K." White led his team from Echo Company on a patrol into the valley just north of the ridge on August 20. From the team's position in the valley, it heard and reported four mortar rounds being fired from 400 meters higher on the ridge. It was shortly informed that the Vandegrift Combat Base had just received four rounds of incoming. White then called in an artillery fire mission on the coordinates from which he believed the mortars had been fired. Nine artillery shells impacted, and the team heard one secondary explosion. The enemy mortar fire was not heard again. However, the NVA had become very adept at determining that a Marine Recon team was in the area, and would immediately send out its own recon-killer teams to find it. In less than two hours, the NVA teams had begun a sweep toward the Marines' position from both the northwest and the southwest. White had on-call fires ready, and these were fired on movement they heard to their western side. The enemy units then commenced automatic weapons fire on the team from positions in the jungle. The Marines returned the fire and moved to evade the enemy. They were later extracted without taking a casualty.

On August 21, Sergeant Quinn's team from Bravo Company landed 3,000 meters from where White's next patrol was scheduled to be inserted on August 23. Quinn's team was composed partly of the same men who had landed on the Co Ka Leuye ridge in May. Sergeant Quinn was the patrol leader; Hollis Stabler was APL and carried the radio. Cox and Nagler were along, both veterans of the Co Ka Leuye patrol. The new members of the team were Richard Bryant and "Doc" Gary Ratliff.

The team's LZ was a "blown" landing zone on Hill 1123, which was down the ridgeline southeast from the 1,700-meter-high top of the Tiger Tooth. It was a rise in the very narrow ridge that proceeded on down to the plateau overlooking the Vandegrift Combat Base. The toe of the ridge was the area where the August 17 Recon team had discovered bunker complexes, and was near the Sky Merchant LZ. The ridge was covered by thick canopy, but the undergrowth was sparse and visibility was good underneath. The team was sent out to be trail watchers. The top of the steeply descending ridge was only about 30 meters wide, and the slopes to the northeast and southwest dropped abruptly, at about a 40 percent grade.

The Marines of Sergeant Quinn's team told an amazing story about a moment while they were waiting for the choppers to take them to their recon zone. As they sat in the LZ Stud, tormented by the midday heat and humidity, an NVA soldier suddenly and boldly stepped into the clearing. He wasn't far from the Marines, and he raised his AK-47 and fired a magazine into the air while watching the Reconners. Almost in unison the six Marines rose and stared at this incredible act. Then one started, then another, and finally all six had put their hands together and gave the enemy soldier a standing ovation for what Floyd Nagler said was "having the balls to do something like that." When asked if they were sure that the man had been an NVA, Hollis Stabler said, "Hell, yes. I know an NVA uniform and pith helmet when I see one—besides, no Marine or South Vietnamese would be crazy enough to dress up like the enemy and do something like that. Anyway, the guy just turned around and walked back into the jungle."

That experience set the tone for things to come.

The team was flown high into the mountains, but the heat didn't seem to dissipate even in the upper elevations on that late August day. The Reconners landed and proceeded down the ridgeline about 500 meters until they found a good trail-watching location at a point where the trail curved off the top of the ridge about 20 meters and cut across a lower contour. The visibility was good. Sergeant Quinn, Cox, and Bryant moved to the top of the ridge while Stabler, Nagler, and Ratliff set mines out to within about twenty feet of the trail.

Nagler said:

It was immediately apparent that the ridgeline was well used. From the moment we landed, we found NVA gear and other garbage here and there. Normally, they keep the place clean, and you don't find evidence of them. However, the grass was all beaten down and worn away. The trail was very traveled, and it looked like they had become sloppy. When we got down to the spot where we were going to watch the trail, I set out three claymores and had just sat down to look around at what else we should be doing when Hollis [Stabler] grabbed my leg. I looked up and two NVA were passing by about fifteen feet away. While the area we were in had heavy jungle canopy, there wasn't any underbrush. The visibility between us was perfect. Hollis and I were close together and Doc [Ratliff] was nearby also. We were just sitting there, our rifles were at the ready in our laps, but there wasn't much concealment, just trees that blocked some of the view. Then the next three NVA in their column were passing.

Stabler said, "Doc and I had just sat down to give Floyd cover while he set the claymores out, and Floyd hadn't finished. We didn't hear 'em coming; they just were there in front of us." The team of three by the trail had just paused in their setting of mines and warning devices, which were to protect their position up higher, where the other three were. They were caught sitting by the silent appearance of twenty-three enemy soldiers. The Americans froze—afraid to breathe. Twenty-three NVA soldiers with AK-47s at the ready walked quietly down a trail within fifteen feet of three Americans sitting in the open with only a few trees around and no concealment. The camouflage of the Marines was good, but it wasn't intended to make them look like tree stumps. The biggest concern for the next few seconds was that the whites of their widening eyes, or some sound from the unknowing threesome above them, would jerk the enemy soldiers into reality.

The NVA wore light-brown uniforms, bush covers or pith helmets, and most carried AK-47 rifles, except for two who held light assault machine guns, one of which had a red stock. The officer carried a pistol. It seemed to the Marines that the point and rear men were old hands, while the twenty-one in between were new, with fresher uniforms and haircuts.

Stabler said, "The third and fourth guys in the column were an officer and his radioman. The rest kept coming pretty close together. Doc Ratliff was the first one to see them, and when I looked at him, he was absolutely white, and his eyeballs were saucer-wide. These guys were only fifteen to twenty feet away."

"Why they never saw us," Floyd said, "I'll never know."

"It was a study in silent breathing—and prayer. We prayed that the rest of our team, who were above us and not visible, wouldn't make a sound because we didn't have a chance to warn them," Hollis added.

The twenty-three walked past. The point definitely was experienced and on the alert, but he had passed by without seeing the three Reconners only fifteen feet to his left. Then the others, one by one, went by. The last was an older soldier who was running rear point, and again the Reconners were in seriously deep trouble: this guy was paying attention to his job. He was probably a sergeant in the NVA and, by his bearing, obviously experienced.

Then a Zippo lighter was struck thirty feet above the Marines—one of the guys above was lighting a cigarette. Floyd said, "I know that in a normal situation that sound is hardly noticed, but this was anything but normal. It sounded like an alarm going off. We held our breath."

Stabler continued, "The last guy wore a khaki-colored uniform.

Then, with the sound, he turned around and stared silently at Floyd and me." It wasn't exactly a Mexican standoff, but chili peppers were doing a hat dance in the bowels of all four men. The universe suddenly collapsed to a fifteen-foot space. There was nothing else happening in all of life, and life indeed hung in the balance.

Stabler continued:

There was a growing distance between him and the rest of his column. Floyd and I were side by side and Doc was up a little farther. This sergeant carried the rifle at his waist with a jungle sling over his shoulder, and it was ready—he was ready. The rifle was pointed directly at Floyd, but his eyes were locked onto mine. Floyd and I were both sitting with our legs out in front. I had my rifle locked and loaded, pointed at his eyes, but his was pointed at Floyd. What went through my mind was, "If he shoots Floyd, I'm going to kill the son of a bitch. But then the other twenty-two will come back and kill us. Then again, this guy isn't just going to walk away."

Normally the experienced soldiers would have fired in a heartbeat, and none of them really understood why they didn't. The whole scene couldn't have lasted more than five seconds, but you just don't pull up a bargaining table to talk turkey in a moment like that.

But Stabler knew nut-cutting time when it was staring him in the face; he put his chips in his smile. He said:

So then I smiled, just as big as I could and shook my head no. I hoped he'd understand that this was a once-in-a-lifetime peace offering that he had only a second to think about. His eyes opened wide for just a flash of a second, and then he turned to the west and walked down the steep slope away from the trail. You could hear him sliding, maybe falling, knocking banana trees down as he went down the side away from us and his team. The rest of his team was on the trail to the southeast and out of sight now. I think we were all in a state of semishock, and I whispered to Floyd, "I hope he doesn't fire his weapon." I now was worried that he would warn the other guys, but he never did.

The three Americans scrambled up to the others above them—Quinn, Bryant, and Cox—who were starting to cook hot chocolate and had been totally oblivious to what had transpired just below them. Stabler and Nagler were tugging on the others, loudly whispering they had to get the hell out of there. They said Ratliff was still trying to recover from his shock.

If nothing else, the patrol leader had to believe the look in their eyes. Then all quickly packed and moved up the ridge a few hundred meters, cutting to the right and off to one small finger that stuck out the side. They called in artillery and air strikes, then laid low and tried to figure out what happened. That NVA sergeant had never fired warning shots for the rest of his team. The Recon team reported that he was older than the others, and maybe age and experience brought with them enough wisdom to enable him to stay alive for another day. The team spent the rest of the night lying low, harboring on that little finger. During the night, the Marines heard three more groups of enemy moving down the trail, to the southeast.

The next morning, the team continued to move down the ridge to the southeast to try to find another location on the trail to watch. This time the Marines were much more cautious.

Finally, they located a position that they felt was a safe distance from the trail, and Nagler set out the claymores. The Marines very seriously did not want to make contact in this area. It was far too difficult to get to an LZ for extraction, there was no room to maneuver, and there were just too many NVA around. Nagler had come back toward the team a short distance. He sat down to watch that pathway. He should have known better!

"All of a sudden," Nagler said, "this NVA walks quietly up to me. He had come off the trail for what reason I don't know. Whether he noticed something he wanted to check out or he wanted to relieve himself, I don't know. But very quietly and quickly we were staring face-to-face about fifteen feet apart."

It was flashback time. Nagler had sat down in an outhouse, looked up, and saw a nest of buzzing yellowjackets. This guy wasn't of the wise-age category. He carried his rifle in a jungle sling like the other. And in that same second of time, he flipped the selector switch on his AK-47 to automatic. In the same split second, Nagler did the same, then the two froze with their eyes locked for another second.

Nagler said:

> Then he glanced up behind me, and I think he saw the others up there and knew he was in deep trouble. I think that the adrenaline almost had me in a state that I was too pumped to do anything except wait for the next move from him, and I sensed that he saw he had a big problem. In that instant I knew he was not going to shoot. Then he turned and loped away back down the ridge. I often wondered why I didn't fire. I just don't really know. Maybe the same is true for him.

Later that evening, the team patrolled down the ridge to the southeast and then turned off and went to the south, to the valley below. The six Marines hoped that down in the lower hills there wouldn't be any more walk-ins. They did not know that they were in the same vicinity as the Sky Merchant patrol and near the bunkers it had recently found.

They harbored in the lowland jungle that night. But their problems continued. At about 0400, the men on alert awakened the rest of the team because of an increasing volume of noise moving in their direction. There were no noises other than brush being crushed, but the sounds were definitely moving in the direction of the team's harbor site. The Marines locked and loaded and nervously waited.

Then, rising above the top of their little knoll was the large hairy head of some kind of monkey in the moonlight. It sniffed around for a second to ascertain if it needed to do anything about the intruders. Then someone broke the silent standoff and said "Boo." The large monkey snorted and lumbered off.

Nagler said, "If there is one patrol that brings back more nightmares for me than any other, it's this one. I still can see those NVA walking past just fifteen feet away. I still wake up with those rifles pointed at me. But at least I wake up."

Stabler added, "In my Omaha Indian tribe, we are allowed to change our names if we do something in war. And I have seriously thought about changing mine to Smiles at the Enemy."

Nagler said, "It was very unique for us to find enemy gear left lying around. You know you just didn't find enemy cartridge belts beside the trail because they always were careful not to leave gear lying around. Yet we did. It was a well-traveled area. The NVA were using this as a transit route to and from other areas. There was some evidence of hospital complexes in the vicinity."

However, with four enemy battalions, accompanied by "screening and reconnaissance elements," operating in the vicinity, it was inevitable that a small team of Reconners would run into trouble with deadly results. That lethal contact was to begin on the day that Sergeant Quinn's patrol was extracted and only three klicks away from where his team had been. It happened to Corporal White's team on its next mission, August 23 to 24.

The team's call sign was Dixie Diner. While Quinn's team was out experiencing spontaneous peace with the enemy, White was brought in for a briefing. When shown his recon zone and LZ on top of the Nui Tia Pong ridge, White said:

I argued with them. They knew what was out there. There was just a lot of NVA, and they were building up. We had been running patrols in the area and making contact. To land on top of the ridge in a recent infantry landing zone, I thought, was almost suicide. We had just lucked out in the past. The only other person in the Command Operations Center at that briefing who had been out there and knew something about the area was my assistant patrol leader, Tex Anderson, and he was going out on the patrol with me. The rest of them just didn't understand about the degree of danger, particularly when we already knew basically what was out there. I almost refused to take the patrol out. Both Tex and I had made it through ten months of patrols, and in November, less than two months off, we were due to rotate to the States. I still wonder if I did the right thing, and I still ask myself, "Could I have done something different that would've saved Tex's life?"

There were eight men on this patrol. White placed himself in the second position, behind the point. Tex Anderson was with the second team of the patrol and in charge of it. Phil Symon had just joined the squad from another team and was secondary radio operator for the patrol and positioned in the latter half of the unit.

The team went down to the helicopter pad early in the morning of August 23 but had to wait in line for the choppers. Quinn's team was to be extracted later that day. If it had been left up to White, Dixie Diner would have been inserted at first light, but it was 0930 before the team was finally on board and in the air. There were no fake insertions, there had been no preinsertion helo recon the previous day, and there was no corpsman. Corporal White said, "When I first got incountry, the patrols all had a corpsman with them, but that didn't last long. For the most part, we went out without any 'Doc.'"

White continued: "I made about thirty or so patrols up to that time, and I had been given the opportunity of having a previous-day overflight only three or four times. I don't know why. Maybe they just didn't have enough helicopters."

As the Reconners were in the air and approaching their target, White said he could hear the pilots of the gunships flying over the LZ. They were reporting that they had taken no enemy fire. Then White's CH-46 pointed its nose toward the LZ and was dropping down. All men were in the one bird. As normal, they would jump out the back tailgate and run to quickly set up a 360-degree perimeter and then move out as fast as they could to clear the landing zone and reach cover. In this case, the landing zone was a small opening in the jungle on top of Hill 844. It had been blown by the infantry not too long before.

Phil Symon stated, "The LZ area was an old Marine grunt position. The cleared area would accommodate only one chopper. There were fighting positions dug in around the area. After we landed, we quickly moved out of the LZ into the jungle a few hundred meters. Our nerves were on edge, and someone said they heard something. Then two of the team went a short distance in that direction to check out the noise."

The weather was hot and humid, and the undergrowth was heavy. The ground wasn't as open as that on the parallel ridge where Quinn's team had been. Then the two-man team returned and reported seeing two NVA in uniform only about 200 meters up the ridge to the west of the patrol's position. That was quickly followed by another sighting of two NVA at about the same distance to the northeast, down the ridge. White and Anderson had been near the area on more than one occasion and knew that the NVA aggressively tracked trespassers. They decided that they had to stay close to the insertion LZ because there were no others on that portion of the ridge. The Reconners sensed that they were going to have contact with the enemy.

They were in thick brush about 400 meters from the LZ when they had the two sightings, and it had taken two hours of very careful movement to get that far. White called for an artillery mission on the appropriate enemy position to their west and the artillery threw out a few rounds. But now the main body of the team had visual contact with the NVA. The command at the battalion requested that they check the area to confirm possible casualties. White advised them that it would not be possible to do so.

They continued to carefully move to the east along the ridge, trying to avoid the enemy. It was very slow going. Finally, they found a position from which they had good observation, and the Reconners remained there for a time and watched. White also sent two men farther down the ridge to observe. Five hours had passed since the first sightings. Only a short time later, the two who'd been sent downridge returned to report that they had noted more NVA on Hill 792, directly down the ridgeline from them in the direction they had been moving. The two Marines were positive that the NVA knew the location of the team.

Phil Symon stated, "They swore that the NVA had seen them because the enemy had shot the finger at them."

White believed that the NVA knew their patrol had landed in the LZ and was now moving in from three directions since it was NVA standard operating procedure to move from different directions to find and attempt to destroy the Americans. The terrain was very difficult, and there was only the one LZ.

White felt that he couldn't accomplish the assigned mission. Counterrecon teams close by were looking for them up- and downridge from the team. They had apparently been sighted by the NVA, and he didn't have space to maneuver. White requested an extraction, but, he said, "they denied the request, and told me that if we made contact, they would reevaluate the situation."

Careful not to follow the same path, the Marines looped back to the west. Their new direction of movement would return them to the LZ. They changed their location carefully, moving through the undergrowth. The team had landed in the morning, and the slow and cautious patrolling had taken most of the rest of the day. It was now late in the afternoon.

They faked a harbor site at dusk, and after dark, the eight Marines moved to a permanent site. Their final harbor site was their one and only LZ. White said, "I knew we were going to get hit that night. We were running out of places to go, and I didn't want to be cut off from the only place where help could reach us. We set up about three or four hundred meters from the LZ at first. Then after dark we moved into the landing zone."

They were back where they had started. It was the old infantry position. Here and there were empty C-rat cans and discarded paperback books. Old fighting holes were all around. The sky was lit by a bright moon, but within the jungle the moonlight simply produced dark shadows. The eight Marines kept within touching distance of each other, and they all were nervous.

The hours began to creep by without incident. Phil Symon was one of two on watch between 0300 and 0400, but others were reluctant to sleep. They knew the enemy was near but hoped that their move after dark might have thrown the NVA off. Maybe it did, but it was only for a time. Both White and Symon said that the jungle noises spooked them. Symon noted, "At one point there was a sound like someone or something had kicked one of those old C-rat cans. We just kept quiet and kept trying to see into the dark, but there was still no certainty if the NVA were closing in."

"I was awake," said White. "I knew they were there but couldn't hear 'em until everything broke loose."

When the NVA hit, they were very close. The team members wondered whether they were sappers, because they had moved in so close so silently and used satchel charges along with small arms fire and grenades to batter the Reconners. But the Marines had not been caught sleeping, and they instantly fought back, which saved many lives. However, in that first minute, six of the Marines were wounded and the primary radio was knocked out.

Symon stated, "I saw one NVA go down and not get back up after being hit by an M-79 round. And I believe it was John Hayes who took a round in the shoulder from enemy return fire. Alan Rouse was badly wounded but stayed on the one remaining radio. Dennis Plopper stayed at his position, returning fire even though he also was hit. Plopper's wound obliterated a tattoo of a panther he had." The team was in serious trouble and had fought back in the dark against the NVA with great courage, but if it hadn't had a backup radio, the Reconners' chances for survival would have been much less.

White received shrapnel in the back but kept trying to coordinate the team's fight for survival. He had to get his Marines organized in the middle of the battle raging among the shadows. He said, "Tex [Anderson] and I were talking back and forth and then all of a sudden, bang, he wasn't there anymore. It was a grenade that killed him."

Symon stated, "We were in a tight perimeter. Tex had already been wounded, but when that grenade landed in the middle of us, he must've known that a bunch of us would die, if not everybody. He threw his body on top of it and gave his life to save ours."

Richard "Tex" Anderson was posthumously awarded the Medal of Honor. There is no doubt that if the team had taken more serious casualties it would not have been able to fight off the NVA and get to the rescue birds a short time later.

The vicious little war in the woods battled on intermittently for an hour. After the NVA were stung by the return fire from the Marines, they backed off a short distance, then made periodic sorties at the Reconners, each time being driven back.

Then gunships came overhead at 0532 and began to make strafing runs on the NVA positions. The team used strobe lights to mark its position. Then, thirty minutes later, as the early gray of the morning began to evaporate and the sun rose to show the way, a CH-46 descended through the small opening in the canopy to extract the team. Patrol Leader White said, "The guys did a heck of a job, given the shape they were in, to hold off the NVA and to help those who needed it more, including carrying Tex's body on board that chopper. We could still hear the small arms fire, and the bullets pinging off the chopper as we were running on board and going up through the trees."

Symon said, "The chopper gunners were going crazy firing their machine guns, and the gunships were still strafing the NVA. Then the chopper took us back to Bravo Med at Quang Tri."

Except for White, who was flown back to the battalion for a debriefing, the whole team got off there at Bravo Med. The patrol leader walked in an angry man and left the same. The anger and adrenaline masked his pain. After the debriefing, when his pack was off, blood was noticed on the back of his utilities, and he was taken to the medical unit, where shrapnel was found in both his back and stomach.

Symon also discovered shrapnel in his wrist and arm that he hadn't realized was there. In fact, it was two days later when the first piece worked its way out. (A few years later, after finishing embassy duty in Beirut, Lebanon, and Karachi, Pakistan, the second piece worked its way out in a Tel Aviv bar.)

After the August 23–24 Dixie Diner patrol, there was just one more month of heavy patrolling for the battalion, and three weeks after the mission, the last Reconner from 3rd Recon Battalion was killed in action not quite four miles from where Tex Anderson gave his life for his friends. However, after the battalion departed Vietnam, five Reconners lost their lives in combat while assigned to other units.

September was the first full month without Charlie Company, and Alpha would be gone by October 7. On October 23, 3rd Force would come under the operational control of III MAF. The number of patrols the battalion would be able to send out decreased. All radio relay stations were closed by November 5. On November 21, 90 percent of the battalion was boarding the U.S.S. *Ogden* to embark for Okinawa. The remaining 10 percent had to wait out a tropical storm at the Cua Viet.

Out of country and significantly reduced in strength, the battalion would immediately begin training exercises in Okinawa, where Charlie Company was awaiting its arrival at its old home base. Alpha had shipped out earlier for Camp Pendleton with RLT-3.

Over the next two-plus decades the battalion would honorably serve Corps and country, and in 1991, during the Iraq-Kuwait War, Reconners from Charlie Company would be the first Marines to raise the flag over the retaken American embassy in Kuwait. However, the U.S. Marine Corps has now decommissioned the reconnaissance battalions, and the mission of the old Recon battalions has been assigned to new Scout companies attached to the infantry regiments. Actually, that situation may mark a return to the days of George Neville, Sr., and the Scout companies of World War II.

APPENDIX A

Generals Cushman and Davis

After the departure of Gen. Lewis Walt, Lt. Gen. Robert E. Cushman, Jr., commanded the III Marine Amphibious Force from June 1967 to March 1969. During the last year of Cushman's command of the III MAF, from May 1968 to April 1969, Maj. Gen. Raymond G. Davis commanded the 3rd Marine Division. Each of the men placed into writing his philosophy regarding the employment of Recon. General Cushman did so on December 3, 1967, in a report to General Westmoreland, and General Davis's philosophy was printed in an article published in the *Marine Corps Gazette*. Each is worthy of note. General Cushman prepared his report to Westmoreland prior to the addition of a third squad to each platoon and Company E to the battalion.

General Cushman's report stated:

One of the most important facets of intelligence in Vietnam today is the requirement to conduct effective surveillance of the geography about us which we do not occupy ... With the reduction of aerial reconnaissance brought about by the monsoons, ground reconnaissance becomes more important than ever.

Each of the Marine Divisions has a reconnaissance organization consisting of a division reconnaissance battalion (consisting of a headquarters and service company and four reconnaissance companies) of approximately 32 officers and 438 enlisted men, to which I have attached a force reconnaissance company. The force reconnaissance company (headquarters, a support element, and 6 reconnaissance platoons) has 12 officers and 146 enlisted men ...

In order to give these patrols the greatest possible chance of success, their instruction concentrates on such skills as calling artillery and naval gunfire and controlling air strikes . . Additionally many of our reconnaissance men have undergone specialized training as parachutists, scuba divers and inflatable boat handlers, as well as intensive training as surface swimmers. Some have even trained with scout dogs.

Of all variations of reconnaissance patrolling available to us, we have found that the small, lightly-armed 8–12 man patrol with adequate communications, is by far the most effective. These patrols are tasked for deep or long-range reconnaissance with the primary mission of locating the enemy and collecting as much intelligence information as possible . . . Additionally, when one of these patrols sight [sic] a lucrative target, it has the capability of calling in artillery and air to destroy the enemy. Because of its capability and mission, we have called these patrols, "Sting-Ray."

The Sting-Ray can be inserted in a number of ways: By drop off from a larger sweeping element, by walking in, by vehicle drop off, by helicopter insert or parachute drop. A typical patrol is transported in 2 helicopters, accompanied by 2 UH-1E gunships and at least one flight of fixed wing aircraft standing by on station. By this arrangement, the patrol is supported by fire power which can be brought to bear immediately on the enemy in the landing zone during the critical periods of insertion and extraction. The duration of the Sting-Ray patrol is from 4–6 days. We are particularly careful to insure that the Sting-Ray is never out of range of communications. We habitually maintain radio relay sites on high inaccessible and easily defensible terrain in order to enhance our range and patrolling capabilities.

An insertion technique which we have found to be successful in the canopied areas where there are no landing zones is what we call "Blowing" Landing Zones. We drop 2000-pound Daisy Cutter Bombs into the canopy at a number of points reasonably inaccessible to the enemy but suitable for landings and then lower reconnaissance teams with engineer support into the sites, so that the clearing can be completed. After this has been done, reconnaissance patrols can be inserted at any one of a number of sites in the target area . . .

Since the results of our Sting-Ray patrols have proven so successful, we are currently augmenting each of our reconnaissance battalions with one additional company. We are also expanding each reconnaissance platoon by adding an additional squad . . .

In closing, I want to say that I know of no environment that has offered a greater challenge to our ground reconnaissance elements than has Vietnam. We don't have all of the answers to the problems confronting us but we have certainly confirmed the fact that our survival on the ground in this climate is tenuous at best without adequate knowledge of what is taking place on the ground about us.*

*Copy obtained from the LBJ Library, Austin, Texas.

Under the command of Major General Davis, the 3rd Marine Division's Reconnaissance element, the 3rd Recon Battalion, adjusted with variations to the old practices (which had always conformed to the different philosophies of each new commander). In April 1968, the month prior to General Davis's assumption of command of the division, the average number of men per patrol had been 8.65, and that was typical for the preceding year. During the tenure of General Davis, that average was reduced to 6.63 men. Most of that reduction occurred in the 3rd Force Company, which went from approximately 8 men per patrol to a yearly average of 5.04. However, all companies saw a trend to fewer men per patrol. Part of this might have resulted from cross training with the Army LRRPs at Recondo School and the assimilation of some of their philosophy. As General Cushman stated, "In order to develop optimum doctrine, our reconnaissance elements have worked closely with the long-range reconnaissance patrols of the Americal Division . . . We are also working closely with the ARVN by integrating graduates from their long range reconnaissance patrol school at Duc My into both our Army and Marine reconnaissance patrols. Our experience in the past with cross training of reconnaissance unit members has been rewarding."

Another result of rubbing shoulders with the Army might have been evidenced in the fact that fewer platoon commanders and platoon sergeants served as patrol leaders—and, when they did accompany a patrol, it was often as a patrol adviser, not as the patrol leader. The Army Recondo School at Nha Trang, in central Vietnam, emphasized a basic six-man team and, generally, it was Army SOP that officers were only involved in mission planning and coordination but not in the field. However, the reasons for the change in roles for officers were more complex.

Capt. Jim Petty served as company commander of Alpha Company from February 25, 1968, to August 24, 1968. He says that one of the circumstances that helped to remove officers from a leadership position on the teams was the addition of a third squad to each platoon. Due to the increased number of patrols possible for each platoon, the few lieutenants had to rotate among their teams and might not have been the patrol leader with any one of them. At any one time, three to six patrols might be mounted by one platoon, although normally it was three. Some Marines said that they rarely saw an officer on a patrol, and never as patrol leader, during the latter years of the 3rd Recon Battalion's stay in Vietnam. This was a significant change from the earlier years, when platoon commanders routinely served as patrol leaders, and sometimes company commanders commanded patrols in the field when two or more platoons were involved.

David Sipperly was a platoon leader in Delta Company during the first half of 1969. He said:

> I would not try to take command of the team away from the patrol leader. Rotating around among my three teams from the platoon gave me the opportunity to observe, assist, and help train everyone. The patrol leader and I would be briefed on the patrol mission by the S-3, and I would help him prepare the team for the patrol. In the bush, we would work together and confer about various situations, but he was the patrol leader, and normally he was an E-4 or E-5. However, I did go out on as many patrols as I could.

Major General Davis condensed his analysis and philosophy on the use of Recon in the 3rd Marine Division for an article published in the *Marine Corps Gazette*. In it he says:

> On a typical day, approximately 30 patrols are used [in support of his one division], including 20 in the field. The remainder are preparing for insertion or are in the process of extraction and debriefing. Of the 20 in the field, four are usually in contact with the enemy, and three of these will result in emergency exploitation by the insertion of additional forces or will require emergency extraction.
>
> Exploitation operations are undertaken when it is apparent that the patrol is in contact with a sizable force, usually 100 or more enemy troops. Emergency extraction is normal in remote areas beyond the range of friendly artillery fire.

But this philosophy was never explained to the Reconnaissance teams. When in contact, it was often very difficult for the team members to accurately determine the extent of the enemy force. As a small team miles distant from any friendly forces, its primary focus after contact with the enemy was to get out of the area as quickly as possible. In the vast majority of cases, that meant extraction by helicopter. The NVA had learned to expect Marine Reconnaissance teams, and had developed counterrecon units and immediate action techniques of their own. It was imperative for the Reconners to be extracted as quickly as possible after a contact, or to be able to move a great distance away from the first encounter. If the enemy force was maintaining contact with the Marines it would be virtually impossible for the Marines to break off contact.

General Davis went on to describe the types of Recon patrols employed under his command:

> There are two general concepts to patrol operations. Within range of friendly artillery—the artillery fan normally covers 70 percent of the entire area—a patrol concept called Sting Ray is employed. In the outer reaches, beyond friendly artillery range, a different concept called Key Hole is used.
>
> These two types of reconnaissance patrols accommodate the variety of missions given to the total effort in the 3rd Marine Division. Regardless of the breakdown into Sting Ray and Key Hole categories, the 3rd Marine Division's reconnaissance effort is considered as one cohesive effort.
>
> Though they differ in several ways, the essential difference is that the mission of the Sting Ray patrol is to strike at the enemy, while the mission of the Key Hole is to observe him.
>
> The basic concept of this form of patrolling [Sting Ray] is carried over from the earlier days of reconnaissance. Though today's tactics may differ somewhat, the mission remains essentially the same: to find, fix, and engage the enemy with all available supporting and small arms.

The general's use of the term "engage the enemy with . . . small arms" is of interest. That is a key departure from the original Stingray concept, according to which a small Recon team struck at the enemy using artillery, air, or naval gunfire, and still remained unseen. To engage the enemy with small arms meant that the patrol was intended, if the opportunity presented, to attack with its rifles in direct combat. While that concept was used in the first part of the war, those early patrols were more sizable, often a platoon carrying the M-60 machine gun.

General Davis continued:

> The size of Sting Ray patrols depends on expected enemy contact. This patrol consists of a team leader, assistant team leader, one or two medical corpsmen (depending on the size of the patrol), and special personnel necessary to accomplish the mission (e.g., demolition experts), and the patrol members themselves . . . The Sting Ray patrol is heavily armed, and organic arms are supplemented with weapons capable of sustaining heavy enemy contact. Members also carry quantities of hand grenades, claymore mines, etc.
>
> This patrol operates under the cover of the artillery fan. Artillery is continuously on call and gives the patrol constant protection even in

adverse situations when air or reinforcements are not available, particularly in poor visibility.

The Key Hole concept is based on secrecy and stealth; its function is pure reconnaissance. This type of patrol is engaged by the enemy more often than its Sting Ray counterpart, because the Key Hole patrol operates in more remote areas. It is smaller, and armed only with essential weapons and ammunition.

Of late, the division's effort to totally annihilate enemy activity has resulted in extensive use of the Sting Ray patrol, coupled with rapid reinforcement and exploitation . . .

It is interesting to note that General Davis spoke of a situation where Stingray teams could be sizable in composition and had been extensively used to "annihilate enemy activity." However, the average number of men per patrol during his tenure dropped by about 25 percent. He also mentioned that two corpsmen could be taken on patrols, when it was often the case that none were. It's obvious that the 3rd Marine Division had set out on a course that would use the Recon patrol in a manner similar to the combat patrol, as evidenced by General Davis's reference to "expected enemy contact" and his statement that the mission of the Recon patrol was "to find, fix, and engage the enemy with all available supporting and small arms . . . coupled with rapid reinforcement and exploitation."

While team members and patrol leaders indicated that they often felt they had been used in that manner, they did not see any doctrinal description of that type of mission for their teams. With the reduction of the number of men on each patrol, the use of the smaller teams in combat missions was contrary to the general's own statements.

The general went on to further describe the Recon mission:

In undertaking a mission, all support elements must respond effectively and timely to ensure early and complete coordination. The support package for a reconnaissance team is a successful combination of both air and artillery. It includes delivery aircraft (usually CH-34 [*sic*] or CH-46), armed rotary cover aircraft (UH-1E), aerial observation aircraft (OV-10A), fixed wing cover aircraft (F-4, A-4, etc.), a responsive reaction force, and finally, direct support of all available artillery when the teams are operating within range.

David Sipperly stated that during the first half of 1969, his patrols only once used the Marine Corps CH-46 for an attempted insertion. "All other patrols," he said, "involved the use of Army slicks for troop transports and Marine Corps Huey gunships for support." He added that he liked the Army birds better.

General Davis went on to outline the overflight of a proposed Reconnaissance zone by pilot and Recon team leader to identify landing zones prior to the actual insertion date, and added, "It cannot be overemphasized that the pilot who makes the reconnaissance flight is the same pilot who flies the delivery helicopter."

While these basic rules of pilot-Recon coordination are good, it must also be noted that the Marine Corps was so short on helicopter support, particularly when compared to Army airmobile units, that teams sometimes had to wait in line for insertion choppers. Several patrol leaders described being trucked to the helipad and sitting along with other teams waiting for the choppers to come back and take them out. They rarely knew whether their team had the same pilot who had taken it for the preinsertion reconnaissance overflight. It also must be stated that it was not necessarily the case that patrols would be given preinsertion reconnaissance overflights. Much of that depended on the availability of helicopters, and quite often there were just not enough to go around and the overflight did not happen.

The patrol leader would take his map to the pilot and note the LZ. If it was a UH-34, he would climb up the outside of the chopper with his plastic-wrapped map in one hand, yelling over the noise of the rotor blades a few feet above him and pointing out the proposed LZ on the map to the pilot. Many times teams were inserted during or near midday, when the enemy could obtain a better visual bearing on the insert point. Because of lack of sufficient chopper support, teams often had to be inserted by truck along Route 9 between Dong Ha, Cam Lo, the Rockpile, and Khe Sanh; or along Route 561 between Cam Lo, C-2, and Con Thien; or into the Backyard.

Since trucks were not to be on the roads after dark, they would leave and travel in daylight. Teams were often dropped by trucks between 0900 and 1600 hours along roadways, where the enemy would normally be more watchful. However, the practice was common. Earlier, it was reported that General Walt had emphasized to Capt. Tim Huff, "This Marine Corps is too dependent on the helicopter." However, regardless of the availability of USMC choppers, it was Army birds that often filled in, and those Army warrant officers gained a great deal of respect from Recon Marines for saving their hides somewhere in Boondocks, Vietnam. If it hadn't been for the reaction of Army birds and their fearless pilots, the names of more Reconners would be on the Wall.

General Davis went on to describe how the division would state the requirements for a specific mission to the battalion, which would then issue a warning order and assign the mission to a Recon company. The company would then select a team: "From this order the reconnaissance team leader can determine where his team is going, how it will get there, and the method of insertion and extraction. Meanwhile, the reconnaissance battalion staff prepares a more detailed operations order for both the company and the team . . . the Aircraft Wing has been alerted on requirements of the mission, and the pilots concerned come to the reconnaissance battalion COC to be briefed."

It did not work this way for the most part. After the first year and a half of the war, the patrol leader had little to say about the preparation of the operations order. Rarely did pilots go to the battalion COC for a briefing. It was previously the case that in order to coordinate, the patrol leader would go to the Air Wing, or the Recon rep stationed there would be the go-between. It didn't really matter where the coordination occurred, as long as the wing, the artillery, and the infantry were all prepared for the Recon team's mission and recon zone. All had to have the locations of Recon patrols noted and kept up-to-date on their COC maps, and that was the reason for the assignment of permanent Recon reps to those units. And as Colonel Kent stated, sometimes those reps were E-5 sergeants.

General Davis further states:

> When a patrol leader is assigned a mission in a specific area, he receives the latest enemy intelligence available and the most current friendly situation (including weather forecast), all of the debriefs by patrols into that area, the latest aerial observation reports and information available from the civilian population and POW interrogation. Thus he has at his disposal a vast amount of information. A careful study of this information gives the patrol leader a sound basis for his order . . .

Colonel Kent had described a "black hole" in the intelligence field, primarily as it pertained to receiving intelligence data from the higher commands. Generally, Recon teams knew only a little more than what they themselves and other battalion teams had gathered.

The idea that the Recon team would be quickly converted from a mission of reconnaissance to one of combat can be seen in the general's description of the potential extraction or relief of a Recon team in contact with enemy forces:

> Concurrently with the planning and preparation for extraction, a unit is readied to reinforce the team. Normally the team will be reinforced and the force built for combat if more than small patrol or screening enemy

forces are present and if the patrol is within effective range of friendly artillery. As soon as enemy presence is discovered, the reaction force is alerted, and plans for its insertion are completed along with plans for emergency extraction. As more information becomes available, the decision is made as to which course will be followed. In any event, supporting air strikes and artillery fires are employed while a decision is being reached . . .

Reconnaissance patrols have made a significant contribution in the overwhelming defeat of large North Vietnamese Army forces in the 3rd Marine Division area in recent months. Regardless of this success, efforts are underway to refine and improve their operations primarily in terms of responsiveness. One major improvement needed which is beyond present capacity is in helicopter lift. The Bell UH-1H is a far superior helicopter for reconnaissance insertion and extraction. It has more power, requires smaller zones, provides easy loading and off-loading and carries two side gunners.

In any event review of overall helicopter requirements, the support of an active, aggressive reconnaissance patrol effort should be seriously considered. The payoff can be high.

Two of the major difficulties faced by the Recon team in the field were (1) lack of clear understanding of the Reconnaissance mission all the way from the battalion operations officer to the commanding generals, and (2) lack of Recon experience on the part of officers assigning the missions. The type of mission given the Recon team was dependent on the ideas of the ever-changing command personalities. It seemed that few paid attention to the pre-Vietnam statements of the Task Organization concerning the mission of the Reconnaissance Battalion. Missions were assigned on the basis of what the individual commanders desired. The lack of Recon experience on the part of that officer, who could be the division's commanding general, meant that decisions made miles in the rear often had no relation to the on-the-ground situation of the team. Many Recon patrol leaders have expressed bitter sentiments toward the sources of the order "Break contact and continue the mission." It might have been difficult for the officers giving that command to understand that "break contact" and "continue the mission" were often mutually exclusive terms. Doing both just wasn't possible in most cases.

APPENDIX B

Pride Goeth Before . . . the End

In his tragedies, playwright William Shakespeare found ways to insert comic relief. Without it the audience or the reader would find it difficult to absorb the powerful passions and emotions of intense drama. With that thought in mind, recall that there have been only a few light moments—"light" at least in retrospect—scattered here and there within these accounts. However, the absurd, the laughable, and the just plain crazy were very often facts of life for the Marine in Vietnam. In these last pages, a little humility, the result of mortifying or foolhardy events, is required. It is often necessary to grab a handhold on the ankle of all that prideful tradition as it marches past and trip it up just a little.

The accounts in this book up to this point have attempted to portray the history of the 3rd Recon Battalion and its men in Vietnam in a historical, factual, and personal way. Throughout these pages, the call to duty and courage despite fears and frustrations is bound together with the pride and tradition of the brotherhood of the Recon Marine. However, there is one strong attribute of those Marines that is yet to be discussed: the ability to laugh at themselves. Over beers back in camp, stories that some would rather not have told at all were told and re-told—to the unending back-slapping laughter of these brothers of the painted faces and bush hats who won four Medals of Honor, thirteen Navy Crosses, and seventy-two Silver Stars in four and a half years.

The stories that follow, then, are quick little accounts lacking names and dates. In part, this is to hide the identity of those who don't really want the world to know, but it is also to allow all who had similar experiences (and there were many) to say, "By God, that was me!" However, it must be remembered that these stories have been told in more bars and around so many fireplace sessions that it is quite possible that embellishment has slipped in here and there. Which reminds me that this chapter is dedicated to the greatest teller of tales I have ever met—Conrad Giacalone—who served in both Alpha and Charlie companies in the early months of the war

Several tiger encounters occurred during the Vietnam conflict, but one in particular deserves a place in our memories. It involved a Recon patrol that landed at the foot of a ridgeline of grave concern. The Vietcong were known to have observation posts in the hills above. Several months earlier a major operation had taken place in those mountains and had discovered significant enemy emplacements: at least a battalion of enemy was known to exist in those hills—and they dominated, towering over the patrol. The mission began with an early-morning insertion by helicopter in hopes of avoiding enemy detection. Then, for five hours, the men of the patrol low-crawled using pig trails and did not break one blade of the six-foot-tall elephant grass or the small clumps of bush through which they carefully inched. Despite the severe discomfort caused by the miserable heat, high humidity, ever-present dust, and lack of a breeze (absolutely none), the patrol bravely and stoically pushed on. Close to noon, in the worst of the heat, the progress of the patrol came to a halt. After a few moments, the leader of the small team wormed his way to the point and whispered a question: "What the hell is wrong?" The point man whispered back that something was in front of them; he could hear the noise. The leader, mumbling about mice or men, moved forward on his own. Only a few yards in front of the point, the patrol leader parted the last of the elephant grass barrier between him and beheld the source of the noise.

Now, you must picture a person lying on his stomach, carefully parting the heavy grass with his hands in front of his painted, dusty face, and looking eyeball to eyeball at a mother tiger and her cubs. Before the Marine had time for his mouth to drop to the dirt, Momma let out a horrific roar.

Like giant mice, the small patrol leaped to its feet and trampled down a path a VC battalion could waltz through as the Reconners ran for their lives back down the hillside. Momma, apparently equally shook by the encounter, grabbed her cubs and headed in the opposite direction. No one really knows what the VC thought. However, a new path of major consequence was now in existence. Later aerial observers might have noted the same to division intelligence, initiating a storm of concern regarding a new possible enemy advance toward division headquarters, while back at camp, at the bottom of the same hill on which the high-level deliberations were occurring, a certain Recon unit was laughing hysterically on its third case of beer.

The syllabus of basic warrior training does not teach people how to relieve themselves in the midst of the enemy. Therefore, compromising positions are quite often entered. There is one true story (all of these are true) of a patrol leader's quietly moving a discreet distance from his team in order to drop his trousers. (It must be remembered that these Marines were ten to twenty miles away from friendly lines; one might say they were working the backyard of the enemy.) He selected an appropriate-looking bush in which to position his derriere. As he squatted, a mumbling Vietcong leaped up out of the bush and took one shot at the Marine as both headed in different directions. The wound to the Marine's pride was worse than the slight nick he received from the enemy's rifle. It is presumed that the VC was also panicked at the thought of the wound to his pride that was getting ready to drop on him.

The reverse sometimes happened also. One Recon team of four men set up a harbor site for the night deep in enemy country. It was dusk, and the team found what appeared to be a good position in which to avoid detection during the night. Each man was close to the others and well tucked into bushes. What the patrol had not found was the nearby trail. And, to the Marines' anger, disgust, and petrifying fear, a VC company moved in after dark and established a temporary camp around them. But worse, they now lay in that enemy company's head (latrine). All night long, the men of the other side relieved themselves in the bushes under which the four Marines silently cursed and feared for their lives. Fortunately, after a final pit stop at its favorite bushes, the enemy unit moved out before dawn.

There is also the story of a squatting miracle. One Marine was attempting to find an appropriate location a short distance from his team. He was in a rush. As he squatted, for a brief moment he thought about backing up to a tree, as he wasn't very good at the flat-foot squat. However, his need was too urgent, and he remained where he was, finished, and left. Later, another member of the team came for the same purpose to the same spot. He, however, was not in as great a rush. His inspection of the grounds noted a trip wire attached to a 155-mm howitzer shell nearby. The bootprints of the first Marine were only inches away from the wire, while what he had left behind was on the other side. The team did not want to leave the booby trap in place, even though it wasn't sure that it would really explode. Carefully, the Reconners attached a hook and rope to the wire, moved off about 150 yards, and pulled on the rope. It worked, and the first Marine trembled more than the others at the explosion.

Another thing that is not taught to warriors is the power of Marine Corps–issue insect repellent. No one is sure of the ingredients, but some have learned of its potency. One Marine woke one morning on the last day of his patrol. That day, on its way out of the hills, the team was to walk back to its base through a somewhat "friendly" village. Prior to packing up, the Marine checked himself for leeches and found several on his genitals. In utter disgust, he quickly grabbed the insect repellent and rubbed it into the leech-filled area. Well, it did the job. However, the Marine quickly learned that the fiery liquid had also done a job on him. On the march out of the hills, that Marine was conspicuous for the grimace on his face—and the tiny sling and the bandaged appendage protruding from his utilities.

Another animal story involved a patrol operating on a Stingray mission in the dry, hot summer. On top of hills, in the ceaseless summer heat, the team soon ran out of water. The men had to keep their positions and watch for enemy units. So the team leader sent a couple of the Marines with the team's canteens to find water. Figuring that water was to be found in one lower draw, the two maneuvered their way through thick brush and low trees. It was real thick. How thick? So much so that the men found that they had left the old terra firma and were walking on top of the matted tree and brush growth, which explained why they were continuously slipping through to their knees. Carefully they retraced their "steps" and found solid ground before continuing their search for water.

At last they could hear the gurgle of a small stream, and the sweet odor of fresh water urged them on. Finally, the point man, rifle in hand and fourteen canteens hanging off his body, broke through into a clearing—about eight feet over the water. With a noisy splash, the Marine, his rifle, and the canteens landed in a chest-deep pool of spring-fed H_2O. Oh, how sweet it was! But when his head came up from his first gulp of the heaven-sent, cooling liquid, he found himself eye-to-eye with a crocodile. There was no way the Marine was going to give up what God had supplied to him. Like a lion over its kill, he stared down the croc, not backing up an inch. This was his water! After five seconds or so, the leftover dinosaur turned tail and shot off downstream. Who could blame him?

* * *

There is the one short story of a team approaching a patrol checkpoint, where it was to check in with the battalion, and reporting that it had reached the appointed location. As the site was approached, the team noticed that the coordinates were located almost exactly where a tree of good size had positioned itself. Thinking that they would take a break at the tree, the Reconners moved on up the hill. But suddenly a bear broke out of the jungle bush and rushed, frightened by the patrol, straight toward them and then up their tree. It remained there, making an ungodly noise and growling deadly epithets at the Marines. Quickly, the team moved away, not so much worried about the bear as about the possible audience that might be coming to watch this circus. The Marines asked the bear to report an alpha sierra ("all secure") for them to the battalion, since he had taken over their checkpoint.

One story had the Command Operation Center of the Recon Battalion rolling in laughter in the middle of the night at the expense of some poor Recon Marine twenty miles or so out in the boonies. At about 0300 hours, in the morning moonlight, a Recon team reported via radio that it might need a medevac and stated more specifically, "Man sat on snake—in shock." When asked to explain, the message coming back over the airwaves was that this poor Marine *had* to take a squat (he had a bad case), and in the pale light of the moon filtering through the trees, he had spotted what he thought was a good log over which to position his backside. The team leader stated that when the log moved, the Marine rose five feet in an instant. Of course, as an experienced Recon Marine, he maintained total silence. The large python was at first somewhat lethargic in the cool mist, so the only noise it made was when it, now thoroughly awakened to its plight, crashed through the jungle. When asked which was in shock, the team leader replied, "Both of 'em!"

Some guys still laugh about what happened at the fight at the bamboo wall on Charlie Ridge. It was really a dangerous situation, and it could have been very tragic, with Marines fighting uphill at the wall, trying to get through it to do battle with the enemy on the other side. Some holes had already been hacked into the wall. Suddenly several members of the patrol saw one Marine about to hurl a grenade uphill. As the others were yelling, "Don't!" he unleashed the grenade, which promptly struck a tree and bounced back down. Marines dove in all directions—except for the man who had thrown it, who was standing with his face against the wall as the grenade bounced past him downhill. The grenade exploded far enough away to not kill anyone. Five men were wounded that day, but one of them had sixty small signs of embarrassment stitched into his backside by his own hand.

One nine-man patrol was searching heavy brush—tall elephant grass and just-a-minute vines—in an area dotted by clumps of trees. Finally the Reconners stumbled across what appeared to be a large VC harbor site. Carefully, they maneuvered through a trampled "doorway" into the clearing they felt could contain a storage of supplies or weapons. Of course, no one had yet seen any VC, but these were well-trained Recon Marines, so to be safe, the point group left the three-man rear team to guard its backside as it entered. Suddenly, there was a blare of trumpets and the team came running out of the harbor site for their lives with several *Elephas maximus* in hot pursuit. Never say a Marine carrying a heavy pack cannot possibly leave Carl Lewis in his wake!

APPENDIX C

Observations and Conclusions

After my own experiences, years of study, and work on recording the thoughts of the men who served in various capacities with the 3rd Recon Battalion in Vietnam, it is inevitable that I would form conclusions. Even though former members of the battalion have elaborated on and agree with many of these points, as I have reported in the book, they are expressed here from my personal viewpoint.

The following recommendations directly affect the Marine in the Recon team, and I hope they apply to the Reconner or Scout of today:

1. Train in the basics of patrol techniques. Regardless of the method used to insert the team, if the basics of patrolling are not fundamental to each Marine's way of thinking, then the mission will not be successful and disaster may occur. These fundamentals vary depending on the situation and the terrain, but there are certain common denominators.

   a. Map and compass reading. Each Reconner must know his map and compass as well as he knows his weapon. Each should know where the team is located while on patrol, and each should be prepared to take command of the team if enemy action takes the lives of the leadership.

   b. Radio and communication skills. The radio is the lifeline. Without it, the team is truly lost to friendly assistance when needed, and cannot report evidence of the enemy. The radio will not be of much use if the team leader and radioman are lost to the team and no one else knows their skills. In addition, it was not unusual to find the enemy monitoring radio frequencies. Be careful about broadcasting in the clear, and realize that the foe might have radio direction finders.

c. Practice use of all supporting arms—artillery, air, and naval gunfire. Given skills in map reading and radio work, each member of the team must know how to call in supporting arms, either to accomplish the mission or to save the team.

The combination of these first three basics must be practiced again and again to allow all Reconners to become skilled in their application. Of the supporting arms listed, the most critically important is artillery.

In Vietnam, as a general rule, the artillery was on target within five to ten minutes of the call from the Recon team. However, it seemed that it took roughly one hour for aircraft (fixed-wing or helicopter) to direct fire onto the enemy. That interval varied depending on availability of the supporting airpower at any particular time, but approximately one hour seemed to be a universal experience unless the helicopter was nearby and diverted from its intended mission to assist the Recon team.

That one hour was critical. In that time the target seen by the team could be gone or, if the team was in contact, casualties and deaths could occur to the Marines. Assuming that the team was given a Recon zone within adequate range of the proper artillery unit, the situation changed dramatically, and a small team could become a deadly adversary to any enemy force.

Regardless of the skill of the members of the team in calling on the big guns, the commander assigning the mission must also understand the capabilities of the artillery. If the team is given a mission on the lower slopes of a mountain, ridge, etc., and the guns are miles distant on the other side, then it is possible that the weapons will not be able to land on target. They will not be able to support the team if their trajectory is too flat. The 155-mm and 175-mm guns often had difficulty with accuracy in mountainous terrain. In contrast, the 8-inchers were able to launch their rounds on a very high arc and therefore could land almost on a pinpoint despite intervening elevations. However, the range of the 8-inchers was about 7,000 meters less than that of the 155-mm gun.

Insufficient helicopters was also a supporting arms problem. The Marine Corps did not have sufficient numbers of the birds, and many that were available were less than satisfactory. The large, slow-moving CH-46 could take a lot of hits, but it was very noisy and not as quick as the Hueys. Marine pilots often made the difference between life and death for the teams, but their helicopters were not up to U.S. Army standards. In fact, Recon teams had to rely on Army choppers and their pilots quite often.

The situation and the terrain in Vietnam demanded the use of the helicopter as both transport and gunship. Mechanized ground vehicles were very limited in their ability. They were best suited for movement of goods or men in "secure" areas; when used in a battlefield situation, they were easily channelized, their movement predictable by the enemy, with disastrous results.

Naval gunfire had limited use and effect. I participated in one amphibious assault from a Special Landing Force, and the Navy's 5-inch guns did not penetrate the sand bunkers of the enemy. During my two years of duty in Vietnam, there was not one other time that naval gunfire was used.

d. Practice the use of individual and crew-served weapons. There should be one basic weapon so that ammunition can be interchanged among members of the patrol as needed. However, some exceptions should be made—grenades and grenade launchers were invaluable lifesavers in many situations where rifles were not appropriate or had limited effect. If an M-60 machine gun is taken on patrol, a question immediately arises: Is it a reconnaissance or a combat mission? The M-60, for a reconnaissance mission, should not have been a normal patrol weapon. However, for the stingray mission, or where past experience dictates, take it. Remember always when given new weapons to check them out thoroughly before placing lives at their mercy. The tragic fiasco of the M-16 in Vietnam is proof that personnel dictating the design of new weapons do not always know what they are doing.

e. Practice patrol techniques and immediate action drills. Unless there is no choice, do not use trails. What is each man to do in an emergency? If contact is made, stay together and do not split up to attempt to escape and evade. Do not stay in one place for more than a short time unless in an observation post. Do not lock in to one patrol composition—the patrol could vary from as few as four or five men to nine or more. To use five men or less would mean that one serious casualty would likely cause the team severe problems, but the method of insertion and the mission might dictate numbers. Two-man patrols were tried and were not considered viable. Part of rehearsal should include what to do in case of casualties.

The rear section of the team must know how to carry out its responsibility to the patrol's back side without losing contact with the rest. Expect that the enemy will find your trail and be following.

As a general rule, the team is meant for reconnaissance, not combat; therefore, initiating contact by small arms is a risky proposition. The mission may be compromised, and once located, regardless of the available firepower of the supporting arms, a team can be overrun by a competent and determined enemy. In Vietnam it also happened on more than one occasion that a Recon team ambushed a small enemy team only to find that those three or four were the point for a much larger unit. These Marines quickly found themselves in serious trouble. Be sure of what is happening before giving away the team's position, unless there is no choice.

Think about the ambush position if one is set. Should it be placed within easy grenade-throwing distance? Enemy grenades can quickly disrupt an ambush. If possible, make them throw the grenades uphill, and be very careful about throwing uphill yourself. It is easy for a grenade to hit a tree, rock, or other obstacle and roll back down to your own feet.

The harbor site is critical. Move into a fake position if possible, and then relocate when the diminishing light makes it more difficult for the enemy to see you. However, this tactic also has its drawbacks. The team needs to know that it isn't setting a night position near a trail or other potential enemy contact point. This may not always be possible if it moves into a strange position after dark.

Plan artillery on-call missions around the harbor site for the nighttime hours, but be careful about flashlights—they can be seen after dark. To mask the brightness of the light, crawl under a poncho and use a red-lensed flashlight or similar device. There was some thought that the harbor site should be located in a horribly uncomfortable and difficult-to-get-at position. That thought held to the theory that if the enemy had to break a leg in the dark trying to find the team, he just might not do it during the night, and the team had a better chance during daylight. For choppers to try to rescue a team in contact with the enemy at night is the worst of all possible worlds. However, if it happens, strobe lights are invaluable for identifying the team's position to low-flying gunships as they strafe enemy positions around the team.

Depending on the personnel of the patrol, it might be a good idea to rotate the point position on occasion; that assignment is a tremendous strain. The team leader has to make that call.

However, just as it is important for the team members to be practiced in the Recon techniques, the command back in the combat operations center must understand them and also be practiced. There are numerous accounts from teams that called in artillery or airpower on enemy forces in low ground a few klicks from them and were then ordered to go down into that valley and count bodies. Those types of orders lack rationality in most cases. Recon teams operate in enemy territory, and they may be annihilated if they are ordered down into such a situation. An artillery barrage is not going to take out all—and probably only a minority—of the enemy. According to team members and team leaders, ill-considered orders of this sort occasionally resulted in faked reports from the team to the S-3 office.

f. The battalion S-3 officer should be Recon-patrol-experienced. The radio watch in the command bunker should also be experienced in patrolling. If not, the teams may find that the people on the other end of the communication link do not understand what's happening on the ground.

g. Rehearse prior to the patrol. The team leader should check in with the supporting arms and try to personally establish contact with the artillery and air wing. One thing that generally was not done in Vietnam, but should be considered wherever possible, is for the team leaders to visit the nearby infantry battalions and discuss their missions with their S-2s and S-3s. In Vietnam there was normally a Recon representative with the infantry regiment, but not with the battalions. However, that infantry battalion was the critical cog in the wheel, and it often had no communication with the Reconnaissance units.

Before the patrol leader shoves off for this coordination, he should go over the patrol op order and intelligence briefing, in detail, with the assistant patrol leader (both should be in the original briefing). They should agree on the tactics to be employed and prepare the patrol order, which should outline the enemy and friendly situations, the mission, the concept of operation, the coordinating instructions, administrative and logistical matters, and command and communication plans.

A map analysis should be prepared in order to instruct the patrol as best as possible regarding the terrain. This is to be done to lay out the patrol route and indicate the type of terrain to expect. The terrain then points to potential problems with artillery support and communication dead spaces. The patrol leader should then go about establishing coordination with the supporting units while his assistant briefs the patrol members. After the patrol leader returns, he should go through a second patrol briefing. The commanding officer of the platoon or the company should be present and should review the patrol before the time of departure. It is important for the officers to be integrated as much as possible into the team's preparedness (more on this later).

h. Always assume that the enemy has some indication that the team is in the area. Operate carefully.

i. Know that the odor from heating food or smoking cigarettes can carry a long distance and reveal the team's position to the enemy.

j. After the patrol, discuss both the good and bad that happened while on patrol.

k. Take a break and relax for a couple of days between patrols. Commanders should consider talking with each man individually to keep in touch with what's happening in each person's mind. Understand that a steady mental strain builds in Reconners and that various young minds will react differently. Teams should have a mixed group of older and younger together. The older Marines will have to become counselors to the younger.

2. Practice insertion and extraction techniques. The use of rubber boats, swimming, or jump inserts in Vietnam was a rarity, and such techniques will in future likely be used only in the unique situation, such as beach reconnaissance. Helicopter inserts were the usual method, with motor vehicle inserts, walk-outs, and rappelling the next most used. However, as was previously stated, the Marine Corps faced difficult logistical problems in Vietnam. The Corps never had sufficient helicopter strength and did not have nearly as many of the choppers that were so well suited for their missions as the Army had.

In addition, during portions of the war, there seemed to be a Marine Corps attitude that use of the helicopter was not critical, that the job could be done just as well otherwise. Whether using choppers or trucks, the standard operating procedure seemed to be that the time of departure for the Recon team had to be when the birds or trucks were available. Consequently, team inserts were often made during midday hours, which was not the first choice of the patrol leaders. When operating in a totally hostile terrain, as in Vietnam, truck inserts or walk-outs are very difficult and dangerous; they should be made only in areas that can give the team immediate cover and concealment. It was often the case in

Vietnam that teams were dropped into areas that were fairly open and in which it was easier for the enemy to locate the Marines. In addition, in some cases the patrol route was so close to the infantry that the mission would better be considered one of infantry reconnaissance or even infantry combat. The mission should be clearly understood by all involved.

There are other factors that should be mentioned regarding inserts. In my opinion, the landing zone should never be strafed prior to inserting the team. Even if the intent is to strafe two additional LZs to confuse the enemy, don't do it. I would recommend that the patrol leader have as standard operating instructions that, should supporting or troop ships strafe the LZ, he abort the mission. Then the battalion S-3 should support that decision and get down to the air wing immediately to find out why the strafing was done. The only valid reason to rip an LZ with gunfire is if enemy troops or emplacements are sighted. And, if that's the case, the mission should be aborted, period.

The argument that strafing may help the team fails on its own demerits. If no enemy are sighted, the likelihood of hitting anything other than earth and bush is slim to none. All that will occur is that the team's location will be surmised by an astute enemy—which the VC and NVA were. Even if other locations are strafed, the enemy is not stupid, and he has other means, including radio direction finders and dogs, of locating the teams. Expect that the enemy has seen the helicopters—so the idea of making passes at other potential LZs in distant locations is good, but don't shake heaven and earth with gunfire to help the enemy locate the team. Give the enemy the credit he deserves. The idea of a Recon patrol is to be clandestine: swift, silent, and deadly. Underline the middle word.

Never pick an LZ on the skyline. It was done in some cases, and those teams were often found by the enemy, with tragic consequences.

If rappelling in or using other rope-ladder drops, seek to find lower canopy surrounded by higher. The process takes time, and if the chopper can "hide" lower than the surrounding trees, but still hover while the Marines descend, it could save lives.

Expect emergency extractions. Plan for them. Carry extra signaling devices to be used with or without the radio. Air panels were used frequently, but other devices also came in handy: pen flares, strobe lights, mirrors. Always carry tools that can be used to cut an LZ if the vegetation isn't too stout. That might mean the use of plastic explosives, but more typically involves machetes and survival saws. Just try to figure on the worst scenario, be ready for it, then work like hell to keep it from happening.

Remember that insertion and extraction are very vulnerable situations; however, if the patrol is not well practiced in proper patrolling techniques, the extraction will likely be the worst-case situation.

3. Platoon commanders and platoon sergeants are to be patrol leaders. There were times in Vietnam when this did not occur, and it is simply not good. The right officers and staff NCOs are an extraordinary source of talent and ability. They should be schooled in patrolling techniques, and they need to lead from the bush, not manage from the rear. It might be that the officer should rotate among the patrols in his platoon and serve as an adviser to patrol leaders, but he should function as patrol leader on occasion—if not all the time.

It is possible that some of the Army Recondo School training was absorbed into Marine tradition—and that training, from all reports, was very good. However, on the point of who were patrol leaders (which was not officers), it was not. Patrols should be designed for their mission, and sometimes the officer must stay by the side of the infantry battalion commander to whom he is attached, but that cannot become a routine that prevents officers patrolling with their men.

There are other reasons for the patrol leader to be an officer or staff NCO. One is that, unfortunately, at times in Vietnam the command operation center just did understand the patrol's situation and gave wrong instructions. It might have been because too many people in command positions didn't have experience. An experienced officer–patrol leader has a better chance of convincing the COC of an alternative plan that might get the job done and save lives. In addition, the company commander could find himself in the role of field patrol leader when the battalion functioned as it did in Vietnam.

Still another reason is that it is the tradition of the Marine Corps that officers lead. It would be good if the Basic School taught the mission of the Reconnaissance unit and put those young second lieutenants on a three-day Recon patrol inserted by choppers. It should include calling artillery and handling a serious casualty. It should not be a rule that only infantry types can make good Reconners—a motivated Marine engineer can also do it.

4. Recon patrolling, although it is a tremendous physical challenge, is more a mental test than a physical one. Marines who are Reconners should be capable of meeting the psychological demand that is placed both on the intellect and on the emotions. Being a Reconner can be a hellish weight for an eighteen- or nineteen-year-old to carry on his shoulders, and a man at the age of twenty-three or more should be invaluable to the Recon team. (The average age in Vietnam was nineteen or less.)

The best Recon men may not be those most qualified physically to run standard obstacle courses. The physical challenges to the Marine on a Recon team are best prepared for by putting a seventy-pound pack on the individual's back and requiring him to hump the hills, mountains, or swamps in rain, heat, and other natural miseries, and to carry or help carry a buddy. Officers and staff NCOs should be leading in all of it.

Obstacle courses are good, but to successfully complete them requires a significant amount of physical agility and specialized strength. More important in the field are physical endurance, determination, mental agility, toughness, common sense, and "smarts" in the face of extreme danger and physical misery.

5. If the battalion trains its people and sends them on patrols into difficult and hostile situations, then those in command should believe the team leaders and work with them when assigning missions and giving instructions. In Vietnam it was sometimes the case that commanding officers from the general staff on down simply pointed their fingers at the map and asked, "What's out there? Send in Recon to find out." Reconners usually know much more about the situation on the ground than the command staffs understand.

The design of the patrol should come from meetings between the command preparing the patrol's mission and the team leader and others who have had experience in the area. Previous reports, if any, should also be reread. It is important for Recon team leaders to be conferred with when missions are being developed. If the team leader knows a part of the plan is wrong, he must state so, and the command must expect and want him to do so.

When reporting from the field, the Recon team must be believed. No one knows better how to deal with the situation than the Reconner on the ground. I heard one General Staff officer state that he did not give much credibility to Recon reports unless there was a hot LZ. It was a terrible shame that Recon reports outside the city of Hue prior to the 1968 Tet Offensive were not more closely examined.

6. In Vietnam a better plan for keeping the Reconners up-to-date on the enemy and friendly situation was sorely needed. The Vietnam experience was a great intelligence FUBAR. One problem area was the command staff's not placing sufficient trust in Recon reports, but another was in its not keeping the Recon Battalion and its Reconners informed from above. There was a great tendency to hoard intelligence data at the higher staff levels. Quite often it seemed that the intelligence data became classified information, and therefore could not be released to the Recon team. Another aspect of this same problem was the lack of instruction given to Reconners regarding what to look for, i.e., weapons and weapon capabilities, uniforms, numbers of people expected per enemy unit, enemy traits and characteristics, and other types of information that the intelligence analysts needed. Too often, despite the fact that the Reconners were one of the most vital sources of immediate intelligence available to the infantry battalion not far behind them, the Recon unit was dealt with at arm's length by the higher-level commands.

7. In Vietnam there was never a universally accepted or understood mission for the Recon unit. It might be better said that the Recon mission was modified with each new commanding officer or general. The Recon team is not structured to be a combat unit. As the standard rule, its mission should be one of reconnaissance. Going out to the bush to "find, fix, and engage" the enemy is an infantry function. The only time it should be standard for a Recon team to have that mission is when the team observes enemy forces and can utilize supporting arms to destroy them from a distance. It should not be expected that the team will use its rifles and grenades to engage the enemy.

   However, it often happens that there is no choice, and so Reconners must be practiced in how a small team can engage a superior enemy force and then quickly disengage while deep in the heart of enemy-held terrain. It should be underscored that a clearly understood mission statement for Recon must be known and understood by all involved, including the infantry battalions. This was too often not the case in Vietnam.

8. The Vietnam situation found the Recon Battalion operating independently, except for platoons attached to infantry battalions operating as Special Landing Forces or in other unique situations. However, the normal situation was that the infantry battalion had no real contact with, or information from, the Recon teams

operating in its area. A better system was needed to insure coordination and communication between the basic maneuver element of the Marine Corps—the infantry battalion—and the Reconnaissance teams operating nearby.

In 1969, I commanded an infantry company and knew that Recon teams operated not far away, but there was absolutely no coordination or communication between us. On one occasion, I went to the Reconnaissance unit (1st Recon Battalion) and asked to try a joint insert of two teams. One would be a Recon team, and one of my infantry platoons would be the other. Upon insertion by CH-46 helicopters, my platoon would run a combat patrol back the three miles toward our company CP. The Recon team would lay low in the bush until the "dust settled" and then slip away in the opposite direction and disappear into the jungle. In effect, each served as a rear guard for the other for a time. However, my company was pulled out to serve with a Battalion Landing Team aboard ship, and that was the end of that type of coordination.

Colonel Kent stated that for some of the infantry battalions, Recon was just a pain in the ass, because the only contact they ever had with Recon was when a team was in trouble and an infantry reaction force had to go out to rescue it. That system was wrong and needed to be changed. A direct and immediate line of communication was needed between the Recon teams and the infantry battalion. There has to be better respect between the two. The infantry front line should have known where the teams were, what they were doing, and what they were finding.

Lee Klein was an infantry battalion S-2 near the location of Jerry Siler's patrol during the New Year's 1966–67 time period, when the Reconners sighted enemy numbering well over a thousand. Although within only a few miles, and although he was the battalion intelligence officer, Klein was never informed of the sightings being made by the team.

9. The position of company commander needs to be reviewed. In the first stages of the Vietnam War, his role was very actively a part of the patrolling process. As has been mentioned, there were occasions when the Recon company, or a majority of it, went on patrol. It might establish a company patrol base from which smaller patrols were sent. In part, that occurred because of the limited forces available to support Recon teams if they made contact with the enemy. So the Reconners became their own support in such situations. During much of 1965 and 1966, the Recon Battalion company commander functioned alongside the battalion S-3 as

the man who prepared the missions for the teams and maintained contact via the radio with Recon teams in the field. Gradually, the battalion command assumed more of that role, and the company commander functioned as more of an administrative head. The company commander needs to be patrol-experienced, as do the S-3 and S-2 officers. He must be involved in patrol preparation and debriefing. Back at the battalion base, he must be an advocate for the team in the field. He must be prepared to take the company to the field in case the situation warrants, and the "company patrol" is an alternative that should be practiced—a need for it could arise at any time.

Capt. Don Gardner, commander of Charlie Company in the latter half of 1966, earned a Silver Star for leading a twenty-man reaction force in an attempt to support a four-man team that had made contact with the enemy and suffered one Marine KIA and one corpsman wounded. The team's radio had been destroyed in the battle, and no contact was possible. The company commander cannot be solely an administrative chief and rear manager.

10. Something needs to be said about the effects of war on the mind, particularly on young minds, and what is termed Posttraumatic Stress Disorder (PTSD). In Vietnam there was no counseling program to help individuals adjust to the myriad stressful situations. There is a tendency to feel that the Marine is superman and counseling is not needed—in fact, is something only wimps need. However, the experience of Vietnam has proved otherwise, particularly for those who were so very young, eighteen and nineteen years old. Many were not yet equipped to deal with the extremes of war. Any mind would be affected and changed by such a situation, but the younger were hit even harder. Series of encounters with enemy forces, where success in the jungle meant total focus on basic survival attitudes, left indelible impressions on young minds. Stupid, sometimes tragic, decisions by commanders also impacted the mind with never-to-be-forgotten, nightmarish memories.

On one occasion during the Tet Offensive, orders were issued from one infantry battalion to an attached Recon team to patrol to a ridgeline called Valentines Ridge (so named because of a battle that had occurred there on February 14). Marines had been killed there and the bodies had not yet been recovered. Three weeks later, the Recon team was ordered to locate the bodies and determine if NVA forces were present in the area or whether the bodies could be recovered. The Recon Marines accomplished their mission, but after they reached the site their orders were modified. Because of the state of decomposition of the bodies, the infantry battalion S-3 apparently decided it would be easier to only have the heads of the remains returned. The Recon team was told to sever the heads from the bodies of the dead Marines and bring them back for identification. The Reconners were taken aback by the orders but, trained to obey, they started to carry out their instructions. Quickly, however, they stopped and refused to continue the gruesome and stupid task. Abhorrence at the orders, not to mention the horror and stench of the situation, revolted the Reconners. They backed off from their orders, but have forever had that occurrence etched into their minds and emotions. At least two of the Marines on that Recon team still seek Veterans Administration help today for PTSD.

Fred Baker, who in April 1967 was a lance corporal in Alpha Company, told of the experiences his team "Hawk" and others had in that month outside the Khe Sanh. He stated that Hawk was sent into what was soon to become the bloody hills surrounding the Khe Sanh and was hit hard by the NVA massing in those mountains. The eight Marines were outmanned and despite waging a terrific battle were lucky to escape with only their wounds, although some were severe. However, while recovering onboard the U.S.S. *Sanctuary,* a navy hospital ship, Fred received a letter from a friend still running patrols from Khe Sanh. The young letter writer had been a gung ho Marine bent on extending his tour with Recon in Vietnam, but his correspondence with Fred illustrated his changing attitude and the effect of the war on his young mind. Fred's friend stated that dead and wounded Marines were arriving in Khe Sanh daily from the hill fights, and bodies were lying around rotting. He told of the NVA's overrunning his Recon friends in Team Breaker, but most poignantly, his friend told Fred not to go back to the fighting—that he had done his duty and he should go home.

Then one month after the Marine's final heart-wrenching "get well," the young man was killed on Team Striker patrol. He died in the inferno of the CH-46 as it came crashing to the earth, and his body was never recovered. (Appreciation is expressed to Kelly West for her efforts in tracking the fate of these Marines.)

Another Marine joined the battalion in May 1966, and extended twice. Then, in December 1967, he experienced his first episode of psychologically induced physical trauma. After more than sixty patrols and three Purple Hearts (he finished with five), he was standing radio watch in the battalion S-3 one evening and suddenly felt his esophagus constrict. He choked, gasping for air. He stated, "I'm reading *Time* magazine on Vietnam, and then all of a sudden I can't breathe. I stood up, and thought, 'What the fuck is this?' It scared the hell out of me, but it passed. I sat back down, but then it happened again, and I knew something was wrong. It was like somebody had his hands around my throat and was choking me." After a few more episodes that evening, he was sent to the medical company to be checked. Nothing could be found wrong with him, and after two days he returned to his job.

Very quickly, he was asked to take another patrol out along the DMZ. Immediately, the throat constriction occurred again, and this time he passed out. Again, nothing could be found physically wrong, although the physician found redness in his throat, indicating that the throat had swollen. He was then sent to see a psychiatrist. After the examination, he was told that it was possible that the episodes could be caused by stress or anxiety. He responded, "Oh, Christ, are you kidding me! Now I'm going to be nuts. What can I do for it?"

He was returned to duty, and again the choking happened. Finally, he was told that he would be sent back to the States. This gung ho young Marine, who had planned to make a career out of the Corps, thought to himself that his future was finished if he ended up in a "nut ward." He was sent back, and he did find himself in a naval hospital, in the section that dealt with psychological problems.

After three days in the hospital, he was visited by a stranger. The man was from the government and he told the young Marine that having Recon experience made him the type of person they needed. The man said that he had talked to the doctor and that his problem was simply related to stress, lack of sleep, and "other shit." Part of the "other shit" was the use of amphetamines (which were distributed unofficially to the Reconners to keep them awake at night when on patrol). The Marine said, "The corpsmen were giving us bennies to keep us from falling asleep at night, and being young and stupid, we had no goddamn idea what their impact on us really could be."

This "government" man said that he knew the Marine didn't

want all this on his record, and said he could put him back to work and clear his records of this psychological problem. The young man was gung ho to get out of the place, and he agreed. He was discharged from the hospital in three days, and he states that there is no record of his having been there. Then, after some training, and still on the rolls as a Marine, he served in various capacities, assisting his government in classified work that was not related to Vietnam. In 1969, still working with the same organization, he was reassigned to Vietnam. Officially, his orders stated that he was assigned to the 5th Marines, based out of An Hoa. From there, his team ran specialized patrols until April 7, 1970, when he received his two last wounds.

He was returned home and traveled between New York and Pennsylvania undergoing treatment for the wounds. During that time, he was told that he couldn't wear his uniform off the base. That stunned the young Marine, and he asked why. He was told that there were too many people in the country who would cause him problems if they saw a uniform. "This was crazy," he said. "I was proud to have served my country, and I didn't understand."

One and a half years after he was medevacked from Vietnam, he quit the Marine Corps because his wounds would not allow him to be the type of Marine he wanted to be. The Corps was going to change his MOS from airborne-Recon to an "office puke." That was too much.

For the next ten years, he battled the same throat-choking trauma. He also experienced the need to find some of the same excitement that had been a part of his life for four continuous years. As he said, "I would go alone into bars used mostly by bikers, and I'd try to stimulate some 'excitement.' "

Still alive in his mind, the Vietnam experience compounded his condition. He stated that different situations would trigger a flashback to Vietnam.

His doctor put him on tranquilizers, which masked the symptoms but cured nothing. Except for when he was sedated, it became less possible for him to control the symptoms. But when he *was* sedated, as his wife states, "He was in La-La Land." Finally, he sought help from a psychiatrist. Through hypnosis, and being taken off the prescription drugs, he was able to confront the situation. He said that, the treatment "saved my life." He gradually took command of his own life and knows how to control within himself these sensations when they occur again.

Jeff Savelkoul married his sweetheart just one year after suffering horrendous burn wounds while on the last Team Striker patrol in 1967. He endured the horror of countless operations to repair the damage done to his body in the chopper fire, but possibly the worst pain was in his mind. His wife tells of one occasion when they were walking in a shopping mall and they heard a small child ask his mother, "What happened to that man?" Because of his obvious burn wounds, Jeff had already learned to handle that question when directly put to him by a child. However, this time the child's mother quickly answered, saying, "Don't pay any attention to that man. He got what he deserved, because he was killing babies."

Jeff has matured and gained wisdom and success through his sufferings; one hopes that the mother has grown half as much as Jeff.

Many Vietnam veterans are still suffering. It has been estimated that 7 percent of the 3rd Recon vets have checked into the VA hospital system to be treated for PTSD. It is also estimated that the 7 percent is far less than the total number who actually suffer from some form of the disease but have not asked for help. However, it may be that if serious, stigma-free counseling had been available back when it was needed, there might be far fewer PTSD cases today.

Before I close my conclusions, I would like to mention a few points on a more strategic level of thinking. I recommend that all military planners, whether their positions be political or military, read, discuss, debate, and be trained in the differences between the Western form of war (which has absorbed so much from the teachings of Carl von Clausewitz's exposition *On War*) and the teachings found in the ancient Chinese Sun-tzu's *The Art of Warfare*. Ho Chi Minh, Vo Nguyen Giap, and others in the Vietnamese leadership who fought against the French and then the United States understood and used the principles as expressed in that ancient and yet valuable work by Sun-tzu. It is my opinion that their application of Sun-tzu's principles of war was superior to that being used by either the French or the United States for the situation in Vietnam.

Samuel B. Griffith retired from the Corps as a brigadier general after having spent years in China learning the military tactics and strategies of Mao Tse-tung that resulted in the Communist victory in that country. To quote Griffith's preface to his translation of Sun-tzu's work:

> Sun Tzu's essays do not merit our attentive interest simply as an antique curiosity. *The Art of War* is much more than that. It is a thoughtful and comprehensive work, distinguished by qualities of perception and imagination which have for centuries assured it a preeminent position in the canon of Chinese military literature . . .
>
> Unlike most Greek and Roman writers, Sun Tzu was not primarily interested in the elaborations of involved stratagems or in superficial and transitory techniques. His purpose was to develop a systematic treatise to guide rulers and generals in the intelligent prosecution of successful war. He believed that the skillful strategists should be able to subdue the enemy's army without engaging it, to take his cities without laying siege to them, and to overthrow his State without bloodying swords . . .
>
> In Sun Tzu's view, the army was the instrument which delivered the coup de grace to an enemy previously made vulnerable . . .

B. H. Liddell Hart, in the foreword to Griffith's translation, stated:

> Sun Tzu's essays on *The Art of War* form the earliest of known treatises on the subject, but have never been surpassed in comprehensiveness and depth of understanding. They might well be termed the concentrated essence of wisdom on the conduct of war. Among all the military thinkers of the past, only Clausewitz is comparable, and even he is more "dated" than Sun Tzu . . . Sun Tzu has clearer vision, more profound insight, and eternal freshness.
>
> Civilization might have been spared much of the damage suffered in the world wars of this century if the influence of Clausewitz's monumental tomes *On War*, which molded European military thought in the era preceding the First World War, had been blended with and balanced by the knowledge of Sun Tzu's exposition on *The Art of War*. . . .
>
> . . . in the middle of the Second World War, I had several visits from the Chinese Military Attaché, a pupil of Chiang Kai-shek. He told me that my books and General Fuller's were principal textbooks in the Chinese military academies—whereupon I asked: "What about Sun Tzu?" He replied that while Sun Tzu's book was venerated as a classic, it was considered out of date by most of the younger officers, and thus hardly worth study in the era of mechanized weapons. At this I remarked that it was time they went back to Sun Tzu, since in one short book was embodied almost as much about the fundamentals of strategy and tactics as I had covered in more than twenty books. In brief, Sun Tzu was the best short introduction to the study of warfare,

and no less valuable for constant reference in extending study of the subject.

In summary, I believe that our military planners attempted to do battle with military methods that were suited for the battlefields of Europe, but not for warfare against a skilled Oriental foe in his own homeland and utilizing methods foreign to our experience and thinking.

Semper Fi

APPENDIX D

Battalion Muster and Roll Call

There is no official list of all Reconners who served in the 3rd Recon Battalion in Vietnam. There is no official list of Reconners killed in action or medal winners. However, the muster of men below is the result of an emotion-filled search by men such as George Neville, Floyd Nagler, Pat Collins, Ray Strohl, and others. It was a search that led them into the old battalion unit diaries, command chronologies, and any documents they could find in order to locate those who served and sacrificed. There are approximately 2,300 names on this list of the located and living; however, it is known that some names are missing. It is hoped that those individuals who know them will contact the 3rd Recon Battalion Association. Following the muster of these names is the roll call of 362 Reconners killed in action and those who have died since leaving Vietnam. Now, here are the names of those who have been located and who so proudly sacrificed a part of their lives for their duty to Corps and Country.

Muster

Abelson, Thomas E.
Abernathy, Brian
Abner, Bruce M.
Acevedo, Carlos M.
Achberger,
   Charles W.
Ackerman, Jerry A.
Acosta, William G.
Adams, Gary S.
Adams, Maynard E.
Adermann, Robert W.
Aguirre, Francis W.

Ahrns, Robert B.
Albach, Robert J.
Alber, Michel C.
Alderman, James C.
Aldermann, Robert
Alejandro, Jose, Jr.
Alexander, John R.
Alexander, Johnny C.
Alexander, Thomas C.
Alexander, William S.
Alfred, Lamont Q.
Algiers, Ray R., Sr.

Alioth, Timothy C.
Allen, Bernie
Allen, Bruce D.
Allen, Harold L., Jr.
Allen, Lee Roy
   "Doc," Jr.
Allen, Michael L.
Allen, Robert J.
Allen, Thomas H.
Allen, Wayne W.
Alley, Larry "Doc"
Alsip, Robert S.

Altizer, Charles R.
Amancio, Pete
Ambrose, Harry D.
Amiotte, George D.
Amos, Richard L.
Anderson, Donald L.
Anderson, Eugene R.
Anderson, Frederick J.
Anderson, Gerald H.
Anderson, Harold J.
Anderson, James E.
Anderson, Terry C.
Anderson, Terry L.
Anderson, Thomas S.
Anderson, Wallace C.
Anderson, Wayne L.
Andress, William H.
Andrews, Warren "Doc" H.
Andrus, Glenn R.
Anshutz, Charles R.
Ansley, Roe L.
Anthony, John F.
Antico, Thomas W.
Archer, Edward K.
Ard, Robert G.
Arguijo, Charles D.
Ariola, Carl R.
Arkoos, John "Doc"
Armer, William
Armet, Ronald D.
Armstrong, James "Doc" M.
Arney, Robert T.
Arnolie, Ronald
Asencio, Charles F.
Ashley, Robert B.
Atcheson, Clifford W.
Atchison, James T.
Augsburger, Russell J.
Austin, Gary
Austin, Maceo C.
Austin, Osmond N., Jr.
Avillan, Anibal
Ayala, Daniel
Aycock, R. Mike
Babb, Clay
Babb, Tonye G.

Bach, Albert W.
Bachta, Thomas E.
Badolato, Edward V.
Bagrosky, John "Doc" L.
Bailey, Dwight
Bailey, Garner
Bailey, Paul "Doc"
Bailey, Thomas B.
Bailey, William C.
Bajewski, James P.
Baker, Dennis
Baker, Fred J.
Baker, James
Baker, Joshua B.
Baker, Wheeler L.
Baker, William L.
Ball, Kenneth D.
Ballard, Ronald L.
Ballenger, Thomas T.
Ballentine, Roger
Banek, Robert F.
Bankston, James D.
Bannister, Donald R.
Banta, Jim H.
Barham, Robert L.
Barker, Lloyd E.
Barkley, Stanley R.
Barnard, Robert E.
Barnerd, Mike J.
Barnes, James M.
Barnes, Robert C.
Barnett, Wendell H., Jr.
Barnhart, Ron "Doc"
Bartlett, Bobby E.
Bartlett, Donald L.
Bartlett, John S.
Basonic, Edward L.
Bass, Wayne A.
Bates, Lyle G.
Baumes, Peter E.
Baxley, Herman G.
Bazydlo, Thomas J.
Bean, Barry R.
Bean, Richard G.
Beard, Joseph F.
Beasock, Kenneth U.
Beavers, Rev. George R.
Beavers, Richard D.

Becker, Jerry W.
Beckman, Willie L.
Begay, Curtis L.
Behrman, Robert J.
Bell, Alfred D.
Bell, Earl W.
Bell, Maynard P.
Benick, John C.
Bennett, David L.
Bennett, Larry D.
Benyard, Raymond E.
Berg, Marvin D.
Berge, Gerald R.
Bergen, James "Doc" T.
Berghold, Gerald
Berry, James W.
Berry, Phillip W.
Berry, Sam W.
Beson, Rick L.
Best, Eugene
Best, George V., Jr.
Bettis, Ronnie J.
Bevins, Frank D.
Beymer, Gerrill C.
Bickal, Michael L.
Bickhart, Donald P.
Bieber, William
Bieganski, James
Biggs, Daniel J.
Bilodeau, David P.
Bishko, Orest
Bishop, Donald J.
Bissent, L. S.
Biszko, Ted W.
Bittercuffer, Chester, Jr.
Bittorf, D. T.
Blacklidge, Glenn R.
Blake, Bertrand E.
Blake, Clark L.
Blakewood, Steven
Blanchard, D. H.
Blankenship, Dennis R.
Blankenship, Keith R.
Blanton, Charles
Blaszczyk, Christopher M.

Blaylock, Frank
Blaylock, Marvin F.
Blocker, James C.
Blount, Warren R.
Blue Thunder,
James D.
Boaden, Timothy G.
Boatman, Johnny R.
Bockbrader, Calvin E.
Bodine, Bruce A.
Boersma, Andre M.
Bohn, John A.
Bohn, Marlin G.
Bohnert, Larry
"Doc" R.
Bohr, Harper
Boks, George T.
Boland, Thomas B.
Boll, Gerard A.
Bolling, John D.
Bonilla, E. "Eliot"
Bonnes, Douglas M.
Bonow, Charles J., Jr.
Bookout, Lee T.
Booth, David C.
Borage, Ray C.
Borecky, Michiel L.
Borger, Joseph P.
Borgheiinck,
Victor M.
Borman, David
"Doc" J.
Borowick, Paul J.
Borst, J. L.
Boudreau, David A.
Bounds, William L.
Boutwell, George N.
Bowen, Eugene
Bowen, John W., III
Boyd, Jeffery
Boyd, William D., Jr.
Boyda, Robert J.
Boykin, Burley W.
Bradford, Richard
"Doc"
Bradley, Wayne E.
Bradshaw, Gary
"Doc" R.
Bradshaw, Virgil L.
Bragdon, Ronald E.
Brami, Jeffery B.

Brand, Gregory K.
Brandenburg,
Stuart M.
Brantley, Jack
Bratcher, Ralph
"Doc"
Bratton, Gerald J.
Brause, Bernard
Bredeson, Arthur H.
Brenkus, Albin C.
Brennan, Kenneth
Brennemen, Jack
Bridges, R. Eddie
Bright, Morgan H., Jr.
Bright, Robert
Brine, David W.
Brock, Sam B.
Brocksieker,
William H.
Broll, Richard L.
Brooks, Carl D.
Brooks, Gary G.
Brooks, Layson B.
Brooks, Michael C.
Brouthamel, Michael
Brown, Arthur A.
Brown, Bryan P.
Brown, Cary L.
Brown, Charles
"Doc" F.
Brown, Doug
Brown, John W., Jr.
Brown, Randall J.
Brown, Roger H.
Brown, Roger W.
Brown, Ronald L.
Brown, Terry
Brown, Terry M.
Brown, Wayne H.
Browning,
Michael W.
Bruce, Gordon V.
Bruce, Guy R.
Bruder, Robert
Bruder, Ronald J.
Bruffy, Steven C.
Brumfield, Lyle E.
Bruner, Jack H.
Bruno, Raymond W.
Brunson, Clarence E.

Brunt, F. James
"Doc"
Bryan, Darrell G.
Bryant, Alan J.
Bryant, Richard H.
Buatte, Donald L.
Bubb, Richard H.
Bubert, Charles F.
Buchli, James F.
Buck, Stephen D.
Buesch, Rick
Buhl, William J.
Bujan, William H.
Bunner, Kenneth R.
Burden, Terrie L.
Burdett, Albert
Burgess, George B.
Burgess, Jim B.
Burk, Leroy N.
Burkhardt, David
Burnett, Dewayne G.
Burnett, F. Larry
Burnett, Kenneth A.
Burns, Roy T.
Burnside, Grant G., Jr.
Burnworth, Thomas
Burritt, Richard R.
Burwell, Lowell
"Doc" E.
Bush, Joseph P.
Busonic, Edward L.
Butcher, David F.
Butcher, Franklin J.
Butler, Douglas N.
Butler, Phillip W.
Butterworth, Barry J.
Byars, Donald R.
Byrd, Marvin R.
Cady, Monty
Calder, John T.
Calhoun, Arthur J.
Calhoun, Gregory
Camastra, John C.
Cambell, Charles R.
Camden, Donald R.
Cameron, Cecil R.
Cameron, Donald R.
Campbell, David H.
Campbell, Jerry L.
Campbell, Ralph J.
Canfield, Fredrick G.

Cannon, Glenn W.
Cannon, James E.
Cannon, Willie T.
Canterberry, James E.
Canulette, Patrick J.
Capers, James
Caplinger, Richard E.
Cappa, Michael D.
Carden, William H.
Cardenas, Anthony
Carli, Gary L.
Carlson, Clarence R.
Carlson, Stephen M.
Carraher, Joseph E.
Carrigan, James E.
Carroll, Adron
Carter, James M.
Carter, James R.
Caruso, David A.
Case, David P.
Case, Wilbur E.
Cases, William E.
Casey, Glen
Casner, F. C.
Cassidy, John J.
Cassidy, William
  "Doc" R.
Castel Franco,
  Michael J.
Castillo, Miguel R.
Castle, Richard
Causey, James E.
Cavanaugh, John A.
Caviness, Gary Q.
Cejka, Donald R.
Centurione, Dan J.
Cernich, Thomas G.
Chalfant, Terry L.
Chambers, John G.
Champion, Lester
  "Doc" W.
Chandler, John L.
Chang, Lance C.
Chapin, Peter R.
Chapman, Edward J.
Chapman, Glenn A.
Chapman, Harold T.
Chapman, Harry C.
Chard, Phillip L.
Charles, Robert M.
Chase, W. Stanley

Chastain, John B.
Cheek, Ronald G.
Cheff, Stanley W.
Chersonsky, Ralph
Chilton, Edwin L.
Chorney, Peter, Jr.
Christensen, Larry D.
Christie, Clark E.
Church, John S.
Churchill, James E.
Cimino, Peter S.
Cirino, Harold M.
Clapp, David P.
Clark, Charles E.
Clark, Frank
Clark, Richard H., Jr.
Clark, Ronald L.
Clarke, Thomas G.
Clayton, Dennis L.
Clayton, Michael V.
Claytor, Ralph O.
Cleary, John S.
Clem, Carl W.
Clendenin,
  Kenneth V.
Coates, Cameron B.
Coburn, John E.
Cochrane, Robert A.
Cody, Moses
Coffee, Steven
  "Gary" G.
Coffman, Buck
Colassard, Barry S.
Colborn, Charles P.
Colby, Dwain A.
Cole, Charles F.
Cole, Frederick A.
Cole, James R.
Cole, Robert A., Jr.
Coleman, David L.
Coleman, Ronald D.
Collet, L. Gordon, Jr.
Collins, Bryant C.
Collins, Gene
Collins, Patrick G.
Collins, Ralph C.
Collins, William R.
Colon, Rene
Combs, Travis
Conboy, Robert T.
Cone, Thomas, Jr.

Connelly, Kevin
Conte, Robert
Coogle, Ralph E.
Cook, James F., Sr.
Cook, Joseph A.
Cook, Roy E.
Cooke, Ernest R., III
Cope, Kenneth G.
Copeland, Rudolph
  V., II
Copson, Dennis
Corbett, Wayne T.
Corbin, David R.
Cordova, Roberto L.
Corey, Robert S.
Cornwell, James E.
Corsi, Curt P.
Corvin, Charles E.
Cosegrove, John
Cosgro, Anthony
Costello, Charles
Costello, James M.
Cota, Robert
Cothran, Terry E.
Cothron, James M.
Cotrell, Charles F.
Cotroneo, Joseph F.
Cotton, Glyn F.
Coughlin, Gerald A.
Courter, Harold W.
Covell, William C.
Coviello, Anthony
Covington, Albert O.
Cox, Chris C.
Cox, Kevin M.
Cox, Ronnie C.
Cox, Warren J.
Coyle, Michael P.
Crabb, Robert E.
Craig, Harrison
Crain, Elmer
Crain, James R.
Crain, Richard W.
Crane, William C.
Crapser, William
Crawford, Anpier
Crawford, John T.
Craycraft, Robert L.
Crepeau, Richard C.
Cromwell,
  Lawrence R.

Cronce, Ronald A.
Crosby, Albert B.
Crouthamel, Michael
Crowe, Michael
Crumley, M.
Cruz, Raymond A.
Cummings,
   Charles H.
Cummings,
   Woodrow W., Jr.
Cunningham, Leon J.
Curlee, Toby E.
Currier, Robert J.
Curtiss, Keith A., Sr.
Custer, Dana M.
Cuzzort, Charles W.
Dahlin, Lambert R.
Daigle, Rufus
Daily, Jimmie E.
Dallas, Wayne L.
Daly, Joseph P.
Daniels, Thomas
Dansdill, Larry A.
Dargan, Paul
Darquenne, Robert A.
Darsow, Richard E.
Dauth, John K., Jr.
Davey, Jim T.
Davey, John P.
Davidson, William O.
Daview, George R.
Davis, Frank A.
Davis, James T.
Davis, James W.
Davis, Lawrence
Davis, Ted D.
Davy, James
Dawson, Raymond K.
Dawson, Ronald A.
Day, Bob J.
Dean, Stewart
Debellis, Anthony P.
De Carlo, John T.
Decker, Dennis R.
Decker, J. B.
Dedekian, Malcolm J.
Deegan, Michael J.
Deen, Donnie H.
Deer, Joe S.
Deese, Casey C.
Deetz, Dennis L.

DeHaemers,
   Daniel S.
Dehart, Earl R.
Delaney, Francis J.
DeLaughter,
   Michael D.
Delezen, John E.
Delgrosso, Carmine
Delk, Robert H.
Dellorfano,
   Raymond F.
Delordo, Don
Delorm, Richard R.
Delossantos, Albert B.
Deluca, Joe
Deluca, Robert J.
Dement, Robert D.
Demeo, Joseph
Demoss, Francis J.
Dennis, Phillip V.
Depalo, James J.
Desjardine, Thomas
Devenney, William J.
Deyoung, Bruce
Diak, Edward S.
Diamond, Luther C.
Diaz, Rev. Manuel A.,
   Jr.
Dickerson, Michael R.
Dickson, Arden
   "Doc" C.
Didonna, Antonio R.
Dietrich, Paul
Dietz, Charles A.
Dillard, Norman G.
Dillon, Chester N., Jr.
Dillon, George T.
Dilorenzo, Albert A.
Dinho, Joseph M.
Dipboye, Richard L.
Dirr, Michael
Dismore, Michael W.
Distenfeld, Sidney
Ditterline, William
   "Doc" R.
Dlugacz, Jerry
Dobbs, John W.
Dodge, Steven
   "Doc" G.
Doehrman, David
Dohse, Gunther

Dolen, Edward
   "Doc" L.
Donaldson, Billy D.
Doner, James S.
Donnelly, Joseph G.
Donnelly, William G.
Donoho, Robert C.
Dorn, Gary F.
Dornetta, Ronald J.
Doroski, Walter J.
Doss, Kenneth W.
Dotson, Con R.
Dowling, Dan W.
Downs, Stephen M.
Doyle, Christopher J.
Doyle, Richard B.
Dreux, Robert C.
Droesbeke, James L.
Droog, Daniel L.
Dudley, Doyle D.
Dudtro, John B.
Duenskie, Patrick J.
Dunn, John E.
Durall, Ronald
Durham, Douglas
Durning, William C.
Duron, Benny
Dusenbury, James P.
Dutcher, David P.
Duvall, Ronald L.
Dye, Randall L.
Dysart, Dennis E.
Eames, Gary G.
Earle, "Doc"
Easterling, John W.
Eaton, Robert F., Jr.
Ebner, John E., Jr.
Eckhardt, David R
Edwards, Larry M.
Effinger, William E.
Ekstrom, Calvin E.
Elbert, Terrence J.
Elder, Ronald E.
Elkins, Roy
Elliott, David W.
Elliott, Norman C.
Elliott, Randy B.
Elliott, Robert T.
Ellis, Bobby
Ellis, Donald R.
Ellison, George E.

Henderson,
  Melvin D., Jr.
Henderson,
  William T.
Henderson, Willie O.
Hendricks, Edwin V.
Henning, Thomas L.
Henry, Charles R.
Henry, John O.
Hensely, Robert J.
Hepner, Robert C.
Hepp, Joseph H.
Herb, Dennis
Herber, Carl F.
Herdon, Lonnie B., III
Heriford, David
  "Doc" S.
Herkshan, Enos I., Jr.
Hermann, Walter G.
Hermanson, Rodney
Hernandez, Miguel
Hernandez, Victor
Herrin, Joseph J.
Hessing, David F.
Hickenlopper,
  Charles
Hicker, Robert
  "Doc" D.
Hicks, Philip E.
Higgins, Timothy E.
Hill, Donald W.
Hilling, Haydn H., Jr.
Hime, Shaun D.
Hines, Frank J.
Hinkle, Lawrence E.
Hinterlong, David C.
Hintz, Marvin L.
Hisle, William J., III
Hlavac, John M.
Hobbs, Curtis E.
Hodge, Joe A.
Hodge, T. S.
Hodges, Royal J., Jr.
Hoffman, James F.
Hoffman, Ronald W.
Holden, James
Holland, Calvin R.
Hollis, Charles W.
Holloway, Bobby G.
Holloway, Gerald W.

Holloway,
  Thaddies R.
Holm, R. W.
Holmes, Charles N.
Holmes, Daniel R.
Holmes, Harmon G.
Holt, Michael R.
Holt, Robert N.
Hood, Johnny L.
Hoover, Gary E.
Hoover, John
Hoover, Robert J.
Hoover,
  Ronald E., Sr.
Hopkins, G. B.
Hopkins, John M.
Horan, Dennis P.
Horan, J. Michael
Horn, David E.
Horsman, Charles D.
Houghton, Donald R.
House, Ronald E.
Householder,
  Kenneth W.
Howard, Michael C.
Howell, Maurice M.
Howes, Roger A.
Huber, Michael L.
Huddleston, Gene K.
Hudson, Melvin R.
Hudson, Walter
Hudson, William E.
Huerter, Maurice J.
Huff, Ronald A.
Huff, Ronald K.
Huff, Timothy A.
Huffer, Scott C.
Huffine, Duane W.
Huffman, Anthony P.
Hughes,
  Charles E., Sr.
Hughes, Curtis D.
Hughes, Harold G.
Hughes, Mark
Hughins, Gary E.
Hull, Gary L.
Humphreys, David K.
Humphreys,
  Johnny A.
Hunt, Homer S.
Hunt, Howard A.

Hunter, Alan M.
Hunter, Bobby G.
Hunter (Cinque-
  mani), Eugene
Hunton, Herbert R.
Hurdle, George E.
Husted, Ernest C., Jr.
Husted, William C., Jr.
Hutchins, Jack, Jr.
Hutchison, Gary W.
Hutson, Charles E.
Hutton, Frank L.
Hutton, James L.
Hylton, Leland
  "Doc" C., Jr.
Hymer, Albert C.
Ike, Louis W.
Imperiale, Carmen R.
Ingram, Mervyn M.
Innes, Ken
Irizarry, Hector R.
Irwin, Mark S.
Isacson, Gerald L.
Isitt, Jack N.
Issac, Larry D.
Jablonicky,
  Thomas R.
Jackson, Eura T.
Jackson, Jerome J.
Jackson, John "Doc"
Jackson, John T.
Jackson, Joseph H.
Jackson, Oliver, Jr.
Jackson, Steven R.
Jacobs, Andrew E.
Jacobs, Thomas M.
Jacques, Maurice J.
Jakobiak,
  Donald A., Sr.
James, Bobby
  "Doc" W.
James, Michael
James, Ottaway, Jr.
James, William T.
Jamieson, James W.
Jansen, Laurens J.
Jaramillo, Richard L.
Jatho, Norwood
Jeffrey, Wayne A.
Jenkins, George H., Jr.
Jennings, Fred V.

Lake, Robert
Lakin, Derek S.
Lamb, Gregory L.
Lamm, Phillip J.
Lammers, J. K.
Lancaster,
   Alson E., Jr.
Lancaster, Robert H.
Landreth, Michael J.
Landrum, Thomas M.
Lane, Daniel R.
Lane, Larry J.
Lane, Michael
   "Doc" A.
Lang, Jerome
Lange, John R.
Langford, James A.
Lanphear, John C.
Lansing, Robert D.
Laplaca, George F.
Laplace, Joseph A.
Large, Bennie J.
Larsen, James R.
Larsen, Thomas J.
Larson, Bruce
   "Doc" L.
Lasher, Jerry A.
Laterra, Joseph
Lathum, Bobby
Laughman, Steven R.
Lauzon, Ronald
Lawson, Dennis A.
Lay, Jerry M.
Leach, Theodore
Leal, Joseph H.
Leary, Daniel
Leathers, Roger
   "Doc" D.
Leavitt, Michael L.
Lee, A.
Lee, Herman H.
Lee, John R.
Lee, Patrick M.
Leedy, Keith A.
LeFever, Michael J.
Lehmann, Randy L.
Lehner, James C.
Leigh, William D.
Leinhos, David A.
Lemieux, Joseph R.
Lemley, Claude J.

Lentz, John R.
Leon, Lawrence R.
Leonard, Cliff R.
Lerry, Daniel L.
Lesley, James R.
Lester, Kenneth D.
Leveille, Charles E.
Lewis, Doward W.
Lewis, Jimmie A.
Lewis, William A.
Liggett, Jerry M.
Lindsay, George C.
Lindsay, James L.
Lindsay, Lawrence M.
Lindsey, Charles D.
Lippe, Myron A.
Littlefield, David
   "Doc" O.
Locke, Wallace L.
Lockett, Ellison R.
Lodahl, A. "Doc" J.
Loder, Arthur W., Jr.
Loftis, Cecil L.
Lohman, Lawrence G.
Long, Charles E.
Long, Lanny
   "Doc" L.
Long, Laurice R., Jr.
Longmire,
   Michael Q.
Lopez, Jose G.
Lopez, Josemaria I.
Lopez, Roman
Lopez, Steven D.
Lopez, Umberto
Lorfink, John W.
Lotti, Mauro
Lotto, Daniel M.
Loughlin, John J.
Love, Castel, Jr.
Lovett, Michael R.
Lovingood, Howard
Lowder, Charles L.
Lowe, Dennis E.
Lowery, John E.
Lowery, John E., Jr.
Lowery, Rev.
   Robert E.
Lowery, Steven M.
Lowry, William
Lozano, George A.

Lubarsky, Arthur L.
Lucas, Leroy
Luke, Gilbert
Lumpkin, Albert
Lunger, Brett
Lutz, Charles A.
Lyerla, Albert R.
Lynar, Donald A.
Lynch, Steven L.
Lynch, Thomas J.
Lynch, Thomas J., Jr.
Lynn, John
Lyth, Kjeld E.
Lytle, George R.
Lytle, William A.
Maasch, William
Macaulay, Kevin
Maccaskill,
   Douglas C.
Macdonald,
   Duncan P.
Macias, Felipe J.
Mackey, Richard P.
Madden, William B.
Maddock,
   Raymond D.
Maddox, John
Madincea, John D.
Magnuson, Joel E.
Mahlman, David E.
Maile, Richard
   "Doc" A.
Majoy, Ernest C.
Makela, Kent R.
Makuch, Stanislaus
Malbert, Rodney
Maldonado, Vidal
Malfara, Ronald A.
Malland, William A.
Mamazza, Robert
Manary, Gregory
Mandeville, Normand
Mangrum, Telpher C.
Mangum, Edward R.
Manieri, Clifton S.
Manley, Dale
Mann, Robert F.
Manz, Joseph L.
Manzanares,
   William N.

Montes, Juan V.
Montgomery,
    Thomas E.
Monty, George P.
Moody, Ronald K.
Moon, Steven R.
Mooney, Clifford D.
Mooney, Jeffrey
    "Doc" B.
Mooney, Walter R.
Mooney, William D.
Moore, Aaron L.
Moore, John M.
Moore, Ronald L.
Moragne,
    David C., Jr.
Morales, Roger D.
Morales, Santos
Moran, Gary G.
Moreno, Richard E.
Morgan, Jack C.
Morgan, James
    "Doc" J., III
Morici, Peter
Morley, Robert S.
Morris, Bobby Joe
Morris, Craig S.
Morris, Michael
    "Doc" H.
Morris, Richard W.
Morrissey, John F.
Morrissey, John T.
Morrow, Danny
    "Doc" E.
Morrow, Dennis L.
Morrow, Jimmie W.
Morrow, Robert E.
Morton, William L.
Moser, William J.
Mosley, Tracy M.
Moss, Dale L.
Motes, Robvyn
Mott, James
Mott, John "Doc" S.
Mueller, Lornie K.
Muelling, Roger E.
Muhlitner, Robert V.
Muldowney, James A.
Mulhall, Walter L.
Mulhern, John M.
Mulholland, John J.

Mulkey, Billy N.
Mullane, Lawrence F.
Mullaney, Robert K.
Mullin, Michael J.
Munn, Edward J.
Muns, Karel J.
Munson, Douglas A.
Mure, Joseph J.
Murkerson, Oscar T.
Murphy, John A.
Murray, David J.
Murray, Freddie L.
Murray, John M.
Murray, Robert
Murray, Thomas M.
Musselwhite, James J.
Muszalski, George J.
Myers, Edrell
Nagler, Floyd A.
Nash, Edwin W., Jr.
Nathan, Lawrence E.
Navarrete,
    Roberto J., Sr.
Navarro, Larry R.
Navarro, Victor A.
Naylor, John W.
Naylor, Richard A.
Naylor, Robert J.
Neal, Clayton E.
Neal, Fredy
Neal, Larry D.
Neddeau, Charles P.
Neel, Larry D.
Neeley, James W.
Neese, Freddy L.
Nehila, Randy
    "Doc" S.
Nelson, Gary H.
Nelson,
    Lawrence E., Jr.
Nelson, Leonard E.
Nelson, Ronald G.
Nelson, Ronald J.
Nelson, Thomas E.
Nesta, Richard M.
Nettles, Clifton W.
Neville, George G., Jr.
Newlan, Dennis E.
Newman, Ronald S.
Nichols, Carl
    "Doc" E.

Nichols, Jimmy P.
Nicholson, James M.
Nicholson, Tom
Nicolaou, Harry
Niemeyer, Donald
Niles, James C.
Nobles, Jack D.
Norris, Charles R.
Nosal, Alphanso W.
Nothhaft, Henry R.
Nottingham, Ralph
Noyes, Richard C.
Nunez, Jorge E.
Nunez, Rafael, M.
O'Brian, John J.
O'Canas,
    Maximiliano V.
O'Dell, George
    "Digger"
O'Flaherty, John J.
O'Flynn, James F.
O'Toole, Lawrence P.
Oaks, Fred L.
Ochoa, Peter L.
Oertel, George R.
Oestman, David
Ofre, James R.
Ogle, Ronald E.
Olayvar, Herbert
Oleksiak, Robert S.
Olivares, Agedo
Olivarria, Eddie M.
Olive, Gary B.
Olive, Ronald J.
Oliver, Edward J.
Oliver, Joseph H.
Olsen, Charles L.
Olsen, Gary
Olson, Michael C.
Oniszczuk, Ted
Oppenheimer,
    Robert L.
Orfe, James R.
Orris, John
Ortiz, Armando
Ortiz, Ronald D.
Ortuno, David
Osborn, Danny G.
Osborne, Edward V.
Osborne, Richard G.
Ostiguy, Nelson N.

Ostrom, Fred D.
Ottaway, James
Otto, David J.
Overholser, Gene F.
Owen, Dale E.
Owen, Michael R.
Owens, Loren F.
Owens, Thomas P., Jr.
Owings, Donn E.
Ownes, Jerry G.
Pabst, Michael P.
Pabst, Steven C.
Pace, Lawrence J.
Pagano, Robert
Painter, Rev. Ralph
Painter, Robert C.
Palemro,
   Bartholomew
Palmer, Daniel C.
Pannell, Thorace L.
Papendieck,
   Steven M.
Parker, Brian G.
Parker, Clifford L.
Parnell, Ronald C.
Parr, Michael L.
Parris, Roy L.
Parrott, Don E.
Parsons, Ed G.
Partch, James C.
Pasquale, Richard P.
Patterson, Bobby G.
Patterson, Glenn E.
Paull, Jerome T.
Paulson, Wayne H.
Payne, Benjamin G.
Payne, Jim
Paynter, Stanley
Peacock, David A.
Peake, Dale "Doc" F.
Peake, Luther
Pearce, Robert J.
Peavler, Donald R.
Peck, Robert G.
Pelletier, Michael
   "Doc" J.
Penny, George F.
Perez, Gustavo I.
Perez, Hector F.
Perez, Manuel N.
Perkins, Danny L.

Perkins, Jerry
   "Doc" D.
Perkles, Daniel
Perry, Aydlette H., Jr.
Perry, Butch
Perry, Curtis A.
Perry, William T.
Person, Peter W.
Pete, Guy A., Jr.
Petek, Allen A.
Petersen, Ronald G.
Peterson, Jerold
   "Doc" G.
Petrie, Lawrence R.
Petrovich, Joseph A.
Pettit, Kent D.
Petty, David L.
Petty, James R.
Pewton, James A.
Pfeltz, Albert R.
Phelps, Douglas R.
Phillips, Michael R.
Phillips, Ronnie B.
Philon, Robert H.
Pickens, Elwin R., II
Pickett, William
   "Doc" D.
Pieplow, Richard A.
Pierz, Gerald P.
Pilkinton, Charles R.
Pipes, Jerry E.
Pitchell, Frank G.
Pittman, Joe L.
Pitts, Carroll D.
Pizzuti, Peter A.
Plain, Gordon J.
Plattner, Robert F.
Plopper, Dennis R.
Plume, Lefay
Plybon, Wayne F.
Pokorski, Joseph A.
Polacke, Henry C.
Pooley, Edward C.
Pope, Michael F.
Popson, Kenneth J.
Porter, Sanford
Portlock, Ronald D.
Posey, Michael F.
Posey, Norman D.
Powell, Clarence A.
Powell, Thomas M.

Powers, Timothy M.
Poynor, Roy
   "Doc" E.
Prange, Steven R.
Presley, Harry
Price, Charles E.
Pritchard,
   Alexander J.
Pritchett, Danny R.
Pudetti, Patrick D.
Puida, Terrance T.
Pulcini, Don E.
Purefoy, Noland
Putnal, Herman
   "Gene" E.
Pynenberg, James J.
Qualkinbush,
   Harold A.
Quinn, John
Quinn, Patrick A.
Quinn, Ronald
   "Scott"
Quirk, James E.
Quirk, Thomas K., Jr.
Radock, Robert J.
Rager, Roy F., Jr.
Raines, Clyde D.
Rainey, William
   "Doc" F.
Rains, Charles G.
Ralesano, Gus J.
Ralston, Parker E.
Randall, Gary L.
Rankin, Clyde F.
Ratliff, Gary "Doc"
Rau, Manfred
Ray, James S.
Rayburn,
   William E., Jr.
Raymond, Ray P.
Reaver, Gerald T.
Redd, Robert B.
Redondo, Frank
   "Doc" P.
Reed, Michael R.
Reed, Ward P.
Regalot, Rene P.
Rehm, J. Mike
Reid, Gilbert E.
Reid, Sandy R.
Reid, Victor L.

Reifinger, James W.
Renard, Thomas R.
Renn, Timothy
Reskof, Johnathan
Rethlake, David W.
Revell, Joseph E.
Reyes, Raul G.
Reyes, Thomas A.
Reynolds, John D.
Reynolds, Phillip F.
Rhoads, Randall R.
Rhodes, James F.
Rhodes, John R.
Rice, Bennie
  "Doc" R.
Rich, Donald L.
Richard, Raphael M.
Richards, James
Richards, Lawrence
  D.
Richardson, Lovett T.
Richardson, Scott
Riggan, W. Pat
  "Doc"
Rigsbee, Ronald W.
Rinaldo, Paul R.
Ringler, Thomas
Ringwood, Paul
Riojas, Albert V.
Ritter, Rex L.
Ritz, Richard J.
Ritzic, James E.
Rivas, Ruben
Rivera, Richard
  "Doc" N.
Rivera, Ruben, Jr.
Rivera, Vincent, Jr.
Rivezzo, Michael F.
Roach, James L.
Robbins, Bruce E.
Robbins, Steven
Robers, T.
Roberts, Albert S.
Roberts, Gerald W.
Robertson, Colvin E.
Robertson, Robert R.
Robey, Forest A.
Robinette, William A.
Robinson, Eugene
Robinson, Jimmie L.
Robinson, Oscar L.

Roby, George D.
Rodreguez, Mario
Rodrigues, Hector M.
Rodrigues, Ramon
Rodriguez, Edward
Rodriguez, Jesus M.
Rodriguez, Ramon
Roessel, Henry F.
Rogers, Harry W.
Rogers, Henry A., Jr.
Rogers, Robert S., Jr.
Rogers, Roy G.
Rollins, Fred S.
Rollins, James
  "Doc" M.
Rollins, Stephen K.
Romero, Ramon P.
Romero, Willfred, Jr.
Rooney, Alan T.
Rooney, Robert T.
Rose, Carlton O.
Rose, Louis "Doc" W.
Rose, Roy D., Jr.
Rosenberg, David R.
Rosencrans, Gary
Rosenholm, Erick J.
Ross, Bertrand D.
Ross, Ronald "Doc"
Ross, Thomas L.
Rossi, Raymond R.
Rotchstein, Steve L.
Roth, Jack E.
Rothfus, Merle E., Jr.
Rottman, Clifford R.
Rowe, James H., II
Rowell, George R.
Rowland, Orin L.
Roybal, Aurelio
Rubinol, Jesus
Rudd, Charles D.
Ruddick,
  Morris E., Jr.
Rudolf, Thomas R.
Rueckert, John G., Jr.
Rufra, Joseph E.
Rule, Edward L.
Rupert, Bernard E.
Russell, Richard F.
Russo, Ralph F.
Ruston, Ronald
Ryan, Joseph J.

Ryan (Fenstermaker),
  Edward F
Rydel, Gregory C
Ryharduk, Ihor
Sabins, James M.
Safley, Charles E.
Salow, Terry L.
Salvi, James J
Salyerds, Allan R.
Samalonis, Richard A.
Samuelson, Guy E.
Sanchez, Ray V
Sandoval, John, Jr.
Sansbury, John L.
Sarber, Daniel J.
Sare, Dale L.
Sargent, Jerry
Sarnoski, Henry D.
Sarti, Lawrence E.
Saucier, Ritchie
Savelkoul, Jeff
Sawicki, Peter S.
Sawyer, Kenneth
  "Doc" J.
Saxton, George L.
Scallon, Hallard J.
Scanlan, Patrick D.
Scarfano, Charles
Schatz, Michael D.
Scheerer, Michael W.
Schlack, Carl
Schleman, Donald
Schlender, Walter A.
Schlicher, William G.
Schloerb, Charles
Schmidt, Jeffrey A.
Schneider,
  Lawrence E.
Schoening, Warren L.
Schokman, Darrell P.
Schomer, James M.
Schoolfield,
  Charles M.
Schrand, Robert W.
Schroeder, Joseph
Schuey, Allen "Doc"
  E., Jr.
Schultz, Fred W.
Schultz, Henry E.
Schultz,
  Raymond R., Jr.

Stokey, Paul "Doc" D.
Stone, John H.
Stout, Charles J.
Stout, Richard S.
Stoutenger, Donald P.
Stovall, Crowder, Jr.
Stover, Paul A.
Stowe, Michael
Stranko, Michael J.
Strausbaugh, Sidney R.
Strehle, Heinz H.
Striegel, Randell
Stringer, William D.
Strohl, Raymond E.
Stuart, Thomas R.
Stuber, George E.
Studds, John A.
Stugis, Anthony J.
Stussie, William A.
Sugg, Robert B.
Suquette, Oscar G.
Sustaita, Manuel
Sutherland, Bob "Doc"
Sutherland, Mitchell J.
Sutter, Harvey
Suttle, W. Gary
Swanson, Craig J.
Swearingen, Richard J.
Sweeney, Michael J.
Swenson, Charles W.
Swyers, John A.
Sykes, Roy J.
Symon, Phillip K.
Symoski, Franklin
Szajko, Theodore A.
Taber, Ronald D.
Tabor, Edwin E.
Tafoya, William "Doc"
Taft, Robert W.
Taggart, Bill B.
Talabisco, Paul E.
Tambunga, Martin, Jr.
Tanguay, Ronald D.
Tardiff, M. R.
Tardy, James S.
Tarney, Frank

Tatanish, Frank L.
Tate, Dillion
Tatro, Steven R.
Tatum, Ira L.
Taylor, Dale A.
Taylor, Douglas R.
Taylor, George G.
Taylor, James B.
Teague, Patrick
Teague, Thomas D.
Tendick, Paul "Doc" B.
Terry, Charlie B.
Tharp, Robert P.
Thibodeaux, Morris
Thoma, Jerome J.
Thomas, Alfred M.
Thomas, Gary A.
Thomas, Harry L.
Thomas, James E.
Thomas, Melvin
Thomas, Peter L.
Thomas, Robert D.
Thomas, Robert T.
Thomasson, Jay D.
Thomison, Stanley D.
Thompson, Charles H., Jr.
Thompson, David
Thompson, Don H.
Thompson, George E.
Thompson, J. Wayne
Thompson, Ranky J.
Thompson, Robert C.
Thompson, Robert E.
Thompson, Ronald R.
Thompson, William
Thornton, Carroll L.
Thorsen, Arthur S., Jr.
Threw, Steven D.
Tiffany, Ross
Tippery, Rex B.
Toffry, William "Doc" C., III
Togtman, Robert C.
Tollefson, David "Doc" L.
Tollison, Daniel W.
Tomazic, Richard
Tomlinson, Gregory

Tompkins, Roger L.
Toohey, Brennan
Toomer, Robert H.
Toomey, Robert H.
Tootsie, Will L.
Toronto, Wesley F.
Torres, Danny M.
Tote, John S.
Toves, Eugene P.
Traceski, Richard B.
Tracy, John F.
Trehy, Richard M.
Trent, Jerome
Trevino, Cruz D.
Trinidad, Juan, Jr.
Triplett, John
Trowbridge, Gary D.
Troy, Robert M.
Trujillo, Paul "Doc"
Tucci, Alan J.
Tucke, John C.
Tucker, Charles W.
Tucker, Harold
Turay, Robert W.
Turley, Alan
Turley, Jerry W.
Turner, Dennis
Turner, Ellis "Doc" D.
Turner, Larry
Turner, Robert L., Sr.
Turrentine, Harold L., Jr.
Tuthill, Bruce U.
Tyler, James "Doc" W.
Typrowicz, Thomas G.
Tyree, Roger G.
Ubert, Michael "Doc" J.
Uphold, George
Upshaw, Leland S.
Urdesich, Daniel J.
Valentine, Richard W.
Valerio, Lawrence R.
Vallotton, Horace R.
Vanaman, John
Vanassell, Stephen C.
Vance, Richard G.
Vancil, John L.

Woodall, James A., Jr.
Woodcock,
    George, Jr.
Woods, James J.
Woods, Levi W.
Woodward, D. W.
Woodward, James
Worley, Carl, Jr.
Wrench, Brian T.
Wright, Charles A.
Wright, Charlie L.
Wright, Ernie R.
Wright, J. C.
Wright, James S.
Wright, Willie
Wrigley, Joseph F.

Wyatt, Donald P.
Wycoff, Robert
Wynn, John E.
Wynn, Willis W.
Yankanich,
    Terrance J.
Yannelli, Emil
Yarber, Henry C.
Yee, Jeff R.
Yerman,
    Ronald R.
York, John R.
Young, Glenn
Young, H. E.
Young, Howard

Young, James L.
Young, Robert
Young, Robert E.
Youngs, William H.
Youngstrom,
    Nels C., Jr.
Yurek, Michael F.
Zapata, Ruben
Zawistowsky, Walter
Zeinstra, Steven A.
Zeppeda, Jose A.
Zink, Robert
    "Doc" A.
Zuger, Gary C.

Roll Call

There is a proud and old tradition at Texas A & M University, originating from the ranks of the Corps of Cadets at that tradition-filled institution, that calls Aggies together every year to read the roll call of those who have died during the past twelve months. When a name is called, a friend calls out "Here." While physically that person is gone, in spirit, he or she is still present and an anonymous voice speaks out loudly and clearly for the person who has gone on to serve elsewhere.

Taking from that tradition, I would ask that this roll of all Reconners who were killed in action in Vietnam or who since have died before their time be called. I believe that all across America, voices will be heard answering "Here" for a name that is known. Here is the roll of names to be honored.

Killed in Action

Alhmeyer, Heinz, Jr.
Allen, Anthony
Allen, Charles R.
Allen, Merlin R.
Anderson, John M.
Anderson, Richard
    A.
Andrews, Fred E.
Armitage, Robert L.
Barmmer,
    Timothy M.
Barnitz, Douglas W.
Barrera, Tomas A.

Bates, Ronald J.
Beddoe, Paul M., Jr.
Bell, Steven A.
Biber, Joseph F.
Bishop, Ted J.
Bisonett, Lawrence E.
Blankenship,
    Jackie L.
Bowlin, Paul M.
Boyer, David E.
Bradley, Dale
Bradley, Richard A.

Bridges, Robert
    "Doc" J., Jr.
Brown, John C.
Brown, Robert L.
Bryan, Charles W.
Buck, William A., Jr.
Cabrini, John R.
Campbell, Randall
    K.
Carper, Loring
    "Doc" W., Jr.
Carson, Richard J.
Castaneda, Eugene

Chaves, Allan F.
Chavez, Freddie P.
Chomel, Charles D.
Christie, Dennis R.
Conner, Idus J.
Conner, Thomas E.
Coon, Keith D.
Davis, Nevitt D.
Dean, Howard H.
Dewilde, Peter F.
Dicke, Dennis M.
Dominguez, Carlos
Dowling, Jean P.
Dray, Donald B.
Eakin, Shelton L.
Ebbs, Ralph
Egan, James T., Jr.
Eicher, Merle C., Jr.
Emrick, Steven E.
Ensign, Walter L., Jr.
Farris, Blake W., Jr.
Ferguson, David C.
Flowers, Daniel T.
Foley, John, III
Ford, Victor J.
Foy, John C.
Fryman, Roy A.
Fuhman, James M.
Gauthier, Gerald P.
Gayer, Kenneth E.
Gerdom, Richard L.
Giejc, Alexander
   "Doc"
Graves, Terrence C.
Grissett, Edwin R.
Grunewald, Bruce W.
Hall, Kenneth R.
Hall, Lindy R.
Hames, Henry M., Jr.
Harris, Bruce R.
Harris, Jack, Jr.
Havtanek,
   Michael W.
Healy, Richard J.
Henling, Richard R.
Hicks, Michael E.
Hodges, Carl F.
Hollis, Thomas W.
Honeycutt, James E.
Hopkins, Michael E.

Houdashelt,
   Francis G.
Huddleson, Rodney L.
Hunt, Eugene
Hurlock, Curtis W.
Ibanez, Di R.
Jarvis, David
   "Doc" L.
Jenkins, Robert H., Jr.
Jensen, Alan T.
Johnson, Charles H.
Jones, Terry A.
Joy, Raymond S., Jr.
Judd, Michael
   "Doc" B.
Killen, John D., III
Kirchoff, Wilburn G.
Kooi, James W.
Landi, George F.
Latimer, Richard E.
Lint, Darrell "Doc" C.
Littlesun, Thomas M.
Longenecker,
   Ronald L.
Lopez, Adrian S.
Lowry, Ronald R.
Lyons, Carl
Martinez, George V.
Matocha, Donald J.
McCann, James K.
McDermott,
   Bernard A., III
McElroy, Theodore
   R., Jr.
McGinley, Gerald G.
McGrath, James
   "Doc" P.
McLean, Ronald W.
Meggs, Marion L.
Merrell, Lowell H.
Mickelson, Dennis E.
Miller, Allen P.
Miller, Charles
   "Doc" W.
Miller, James W.
Miller, Malcom
   "Doc" T.
Minks, Raymond
   "Doc" C.
Moe, Charles M.
Mollett, Chester A.

Moody, Thomas J.
Moore, Robert
   "Doc" V.
Moore, William R.
Moshier, Jim E.
Myers, Gary F.
Myllymaki, Carl W.
Nahan, John B., III
Naimo, Joseph P., Jr.
Nasworthy, Malvin L.
Natske, Nicholas L.
Nicholas, Paul R.
Oakley, William L.
O'Conner,
   Michael M.
O'Donnell,
   Douglas W.
Olenzuk, Kenneth F.
Padilla, David E.
Pearcy, Robert L.
Perry, Dennis M.
Phipps, Gene R.
Piatt, Richard W.
Pitts, Terry D.
Polchow, William A.
Popowitz, Gregory F.
Rathmell, Henry P.
Reasoner, Frank S.
Reather,
   Wallace L., Jr.
Reich, Donald G.
Retschulte,
   Thomas H.
Rhen, Dennis
   "Doc" H.
Roach, Richard
   "Doc" F.
Rocha, Feliciano
Rohweller, Robert L.
Rosa, Juan A.
Rosas, Jose A.
Runnels, Glyn L.
Rykosky, Edward J.
Scanlon, Michael J.
Scheidel, Robert L.
Schuster, Joseph W.
Scribner, Gary D.
Shafer, Robert L.
Sharp,
   Samuel A., Jr.
Sherrell, David F.

Shinault, John M.
Siron, James L.
Sisson, Ronald P.
Skaggs, Harold A.
Smith, Richard
  "Doc" J.
Spainhour,
  Walter J., Jr.
Speir, Dale L.
Starbuck, Robert F.
Stickel, Gary S.
Stockman, John F.
Sullivan, Neil B.
Tallant, Gary G.

Thomas, Gary J.
Thompson, James
Thomson, Robert B.
Tingley, Thomas J.
Tirado, Daniel
Totten, Randy G.
Turk, John G.
Tycz, James N.
Vale, Tony
Vaughn, Howard G.
Ward, Alexander K.
Wark,
  William E., III

Wellman,
  William M., Jr.
Wenzel, Carl R.
Widener, James E.
Wilson, Gary
  "Doc" R.
Withey, Howard H.
Wolpe, Jack
Wood, Raymond C.
Wynn, Joseph R.
Yeary, Randall D.
Young, James R.
Zalewski, Stanley, Jr.
Zichek, Richard L.

Deceased

Adams, Robert D.
Akins, Leon D.
Alexander, Daniel A.
Amos, O. D.
Apodaca, Ronald R.
Ashley, Anthony
Ball, Lawrence J.
Bankson, Earl R.
Beck, Donald W.
Beekman,
  Clarence M.
Bell, Alton L.
Bevill, Ernest L.
Blumka, William E.
Boehler, Carl G.
Borkman, Donald
  "Doc" R.
Boswell, Donald H.
Brown, Edward D.
Buechler, Kenneth F.
Burleson, Ephraim
Burns, Edward
Burra, Bruce S.
Cain, Thomas O.
Carnicle, Dennis M.
Carty, John J.
Castania, Donald W.
Clark, Richard L.
Cline, James W.
Clouse, Larry D.
Cogbill, Dennis W.

Compton, James B.
Consaul, James
Constantine,
  Richard H.
Corley, Harry R.
Corsetti, Harry J.
Coyle, Maynard L.
Crouch, George M.
Cuomo, Sabino
Davidson, William
  A.
Davis, Nevitt D.
Diaz, Mel A.
Dixon, Robert W.
Donivan, Michael C.
Douglas, Joseph E.
Dunbar, Charles L.
Dunson, Fred
  "Doc" E.
Duperroir, James
Eaton, Michael D.
Ende, David L.
Flanders, Robert W.
Foster, John "Doc"
  S.
Fox, Joseph W.
Fuller, Robert C.
Garcia, Arthur M.,
  Jr.
Garner, Alfred F.

Gasper, William R.
Gatlin, Thomas
Geller, Brian E.
Goode, Michael R.
Gorski, John P.
Gribben, Michael L.
Grimes, Charles
Gsell, George L.
Hall, Arthur P., II
Hanley, Patrick J.
Harrod, Lawrence W.
Hatfield, Floyd M.
Hatfield, Lloyd M.
Herman, Charles W.
Hernandez, Gilbert S.
Herpel, Joseph
Hietala, Dalbert A.
Hill, Dan
Hill, Reuben
Hisler, Norman R.
Hughes, Robert L.
Hunter, William, Jr.
Jackson, Lawrence T.
Jacobson, Carl A.
Jennings, Orval V., Jr.
John, Raymond
Johnson, James S.
Keeler, Lawrence C.
Kerridge, John B., Jr.
Klein, Richard L.
Klupp, Gerald J.

Kostroun, Ronald L.
Kuenzer, Larry J.
Kujawa, Sylvester H.
Langdon, James D., Jr.
Laporte, Michael "Doc" L.
Lybrand, William A.
Lynch, Dennis R.
Mahr, Thomas A.
Mandre, Ernest C.
Maris, Merrick
Martin, Don H.
McLain, Ronald R.
McSparin, Warren
Merrill, Henry M.
Mertens, Edward L.
Micke, Nicholas F.
Miller, Wallace M.
Montoya, Ernest J.
Morgan, Douglas W.
Morgan, Richard F.
Morgan, Van S.
Morici, Peter
Murray, Ulis
Muter, Clyde W.
Nagle, Earl L.
Neal, William R.
Nicklow, Jonas H.

Noe, James E.
O'Brien, Tim J.
O'Connell, Henry F.
Parker, Varnell
Parr, Ronald L.
Patton, Donald R.
Payne, Harold J.
Pollard, Herman
Powless, William N.
Price, James W.
Priebe, Terry C.
Reilly, Walter S.
Robinson, Scott R.
Rosas, Elazor
Rosser, Sid "Doc"
Rouse, Alan D.
Shaul, John F.
Shields, Richard D.
Sieber, Roy E.
Sisemore, Jack L.
Sitton, Edward "Doc" D.
Sivak, David M.
Slater, Robert M.
Smith, Randall J.
Spath, Robert W.
Stevens, Edward L.
Stufflebeam, David "Doc" A.

Sutherland, Paul F.
Swalboski, Michael J.
Swift, Tommie L.
Teeter, Stephen L.
Terrebonne, Theard J.
Thompson, Robert C.
Thornton, Brian L.
Trudeau, Peter
Uphold, George H.
Vaserberg, Ralph "Doc"
Vasquez, Norberto
Wade, Robin J.
Wall, Joseph W., Jr.
Warden, Robert J.
Watson, Talbot E.
Weller, Ernest A.
Whittington, William M.
Whittmore, William D.
Wilkins, Albert J.
Williams, Marcus C.
Willis, Richard N.
Wood, James L.

Medals Awarded

Below is a list of Reconners who have been awarded Medals of Honor, Navy Crosses, or Silver Stars. Again, it was difficult to come by; and it is hoped that it is complete. This author would like to remind all of Bill Buhl's words that there is no greater award than the sincere and humble respect given to one by his peers, with or without a medal to go with it.

Medal of Honor
Anderson, Richard A.
Graves, Terrence C.
Jenkins, Robert H., Jr.
Reasoner, Frank S.

Navy Cross
Barnes, Robert C.
Bryan, Charles W.
Collins, Bryant C.
Corsetti, Harry J.
Donaldson, Billy D.
Estrada, Manuel A.
Honeycutt, James E.
Lopez, Jose G.
Lopez, Steven D.
Lowery, Steven M.
See, Roger D.
Tycz, James N.
Vancor, Norman W.

Silver Star

Bach, Albert W.
Bachta, Thomas E.
Bailey, Thomas B.
Barham, Robert L.
Barnes, Robert C.
Bell, Earl W.
Biber, Joseph F.
Blankenship,
　Dennis R.
Blanton, Charles G.
Bradford, Richard
　"Doc"
Bright, Robert
Burns, Roy T.
Carlson, Clarence R.
Cassidy, John J.
Castania,
　Donald W.
Chaves, Allan F.
Cheff, Stanley W.
Collins, Patrick G.
Compton, James B.

Corbett, Wayne T.
Cothran, Terry E.
Cummings,
　Charles H.
Dennis, Phillip V.
Dewilde, Peter F.
Dirr, Michael
Dobbs, John W.
Eaton, Robert F., Jr.
Eriksen, Darrell G.
Gardner, Donald R.
Gatlin, Thomas
Gayer, Kenneth E.
Gruerman, Gary R.
Grunewald, Bruce W.
Hanley, Patrick J.
Hart, Michael K.
Henderson,
　William T.
Henning, Thomas L.
Herman, Charles W.
Johnson, Charles H.

Johnson, James R.
Jordan, Kenny
Keller, D. W.
Lopez, Adrian S.
Lowder, Charles L.
Mathis, Jack D.
McCuster,
　Thomas M.
McGinley, Gerald G.
McLean, Ronald W.
Melson, Wilton E., Jr.
Mickelson, Dennis E.
Miller, Allen P.
Mooney, Clifford D.
Moore, William R.
Morrissey, John T.
Murray, Freddie L.
Neville, George G., Jr.
Pfletz, Albert R.
Reid, Sandy R.
Rogers, Harry W.

Ruddick,	Skinner, Robert E.	Stokes, Alvin
Morris E., Jr.	Slocum, Danny	Taylor, James B.
Scanlon, Michael J.	Soldner, Dennis M.	Thompson, David
Shainline, Thomas E.	Spainhour,	Thomson, Robert B.
Sisson, Ronald P.	Walter J., Jr.	Willson, Gordon R.

To add or correct this list, a person may contact the 3rd Recon Association at the address listed in the acknowledgments of this book.

Semper Fi

INDEX

363